AF505875

NINA CORNYETZ

Dangerous Women, Deadly Words

Phallic Fantasy and Modernity in Three Japanese Writers

Stanford University Press
STANFORD, CALIFORNIA

STANFORD UNIVERSITY PRESS

Stanford, California

© 1999 by the Board of Trustees of the

Leland Stanford Junior University

Printed in the United States of America

CIP data appear at the end of the book

■   TO THE MEMORY OF NAKAGAMI KENJI

I would like to thank the Japan Foundation for their support of this study in the form of a twelve-month postdoctoral grant spanning 1995–96. I am also grateful to Rutgers University for liberating me from teaching duties during that time and to all the members of the East Asian Studies Program, especially Peter Li, Don Roden, and Paul Schalow, for their enthusiastic support of my work and for their friendship.

Special gratitude is also extended to Paul Anderer, Brett de Bary, Edward Fowler, Carol Gluck, Victor Koschmann, Barbara Ruch, Naoki Sakai, and Edward Seidensticker for their wise counsel over the years, their generosity with their time and knowledge, their varied mentorships, and their kindness.

And finally, I thank those friends and colleagues who took time out of their very busy schedules to read and comment on portions of this book in its various manifestations and stages. I am most grateful to Asada Akira, Azuma Hiroki, Mark Driscoll, Karatani Kōjin, Margherita Long, Mizuta Noriko, Nagahara Yutaka, Louisa Schein, J. Keith Vincent, Janet Walker, Yomota Inuhiko, and Xudong Zhang, each of whom offered edifying commentary on, as well as general support for, this study. I am equally indebted to Hosea Hirata and the other, anonymous reviewer at Stanford, who not only were timely in their responses but also guided my hand toward necessary revisions. Hosea Hirata also took extra time to check some of my Kyōka translations against the original and to offer his advice on some particularly confusing passages, for which I am truly grateful. Likewise I thank Kōno Shion for his help in deciphering some of Nakagami's convoluted early writings. In the end, of course, whatever faults remain are all mine. I also thank my partner, Toshiaki Ozawa, for his love, immeasurably helpful intellectual insights, and patient tolerance of my obsessive-compulsive involvement with the manuscript during the past two-and-a-half years.

■   CONTENTS

Introduction

I begin this introduction with a reminiscence: this book has its origins in my attempt to come to terms with a representation of femaleness that I came across repeatedly in texts of modern Japanese literature, in the form of a trope that I will be calling "the dangerous woman." In the late 1980s, I began my dissertation on Izumi Kyōka (1873–1939), the first of the three writers that I focus on in this book.[1] At around the same time, I belatedly read the "ovarian" French feminist critical text of 1975, *The Newly Born Woman*, by Hélène Cixous and Catherine Clément,[2] a feminist manifesto of sorts that traces a continuum through literary and cultural representations of women from archaic myth to modern psychoanalytic discourse. The text valorizes the plurality that marks women's sexuality against male centralization of sexuality in the penis (or masculinized fixation) and the replications of this centralized paradigm in the cultural realm, or, as Jacques Derrida has phrased it, "phallogocentrism." Femaleness, argued Cixous and Clément, functions as the repressed constitutive "dark side" of a set of binaries that produce the male subject as the norm and woman as nonexistent. One site of resistance, or leakage, inherent in this system, they argued, is "feminine" writing, which they held could be produced by either male or female authors and so is not sex-specific; rather, it is a writing that encompasses the traces of unconscious drive in the Symbolic realm and is related to the maternal body (and thus closely resembles psychoanalytic theorist Julia Kristeva's notion of "poetic language").[3]

Much to my surprise, Cixous and Clément's descriptions of the archetypes of the Western mythic and literary past, such as the Medusa, the sorceress, and other "dangerous women," could practically have been borrowed verbatim as descriptions of the women that I had encountered in Kyōka's narratives. Again and again, there she was, resembling her Western counterparts, foregrounded in remote and liminal territories, enticing and destroying, entrapping and amorphous, polluting, terrifyingly maternal, alternately deadly and breathtakingly erotic. She was, for a certain generation of Kyōka's readers, simultaneously "every man's" nightmare and "every man's" wet dream. The similarities between the French feminists' litany of Western female archetypes and Kyōka's "women" are so striking that in my undergraduate literary survey course I now assign a Kyōka text alongside a chapter from *The Newly Born Woman* and watch the students facilely make the same connections.

Even more surprising was the assonance in how the French feminists wrote theory and in how Kyōka wrote fiction. *The Newly Born Woman* does not merely privilege "poetic language"; it is theory written as poetry. Incomplete sentences, illogical leaps, and associative syntax interrupt the critical flow; as I read, I felt as though I were hearing sighs, cries, whispers, threats, laments, gasps, and songs. What a wonderful alternative, I thought, to the more conventional dry theoretical treatments. Kyōka's prose similarly meanders, at times deflecting the reader's attention away from the plot, with "inconsequential" descriptions, provincial dialects, embedded narrations, associations, snippets of sentences, poems, authorial asides, and associative linkages. The texts shared a style that strongly inclined toward the elliptical, contradictory, associative, and most of all, "poetic." It became apparent to me that for Cixous, Clément, and Kyōka, an aesthetic operated that was antithetical to Western, malecentric valorization of the primacy of narrative and linguistic transparency (the notion that language and text can be made to signify without obscurity or that there can be a one-to-one correlation between sign and reality, and between the signifier and the signified). Moreover, it seemed that this "poetics" was somehow linked to shared notions of what constituted a sort of "essence" of femaleness. While Kyōka's texts were certainly not feminist tracts, they were graced by central, dominant, empowered female enchantresses; the content appeared to affect the form of the prose.

I have begun with this anecdote, rather than with an explication of the contents of the book proper, for a number of reasons. First, because it addresses a question that I know some readers might have: Is a psychoanalytic-based materialist-feminist analysis appropriate for reading a set of modern Japanese narratives? My answer is an unequivocal yes. First, clearly such a contention is not based solely on the personal encounter I have had with the texts I describe above; rather, it is the result of a careful consideration that has spanned nearly ten years, culminating in this study. Second, because both the style—a refusal of thematic univocality and a corollary attempt to allow language to signify plurally—as well as the strong feminist and psychoanalytic foundations that undergirded Cixous and Clément's critical interventions have influenced how I think of and engage in critical writing.

Some Western Asianists hesitate to have any recourse to contemporary theory in their study of Japan. This hesitation, I am afraid, reflects what must be identified as a basically Orientalist insistence that Japan is not subject to similar terms and convolutions of modernity that inform the West. Those who maintain this attitude imagine Japan to be a sort of "virgin" site so exotic that it cannot be described by what is erroneously assumed to be theory specific to Western inquiry. It ignores the information network that operates in the contemporary global marketplace and the role of mass media and reveals a shocking ignorance of the terms of modern, and subsequently contemporary, critical discourse that began to circulate within Japan from the Meiji period (1868–1912) forward. There are many contemporary critical studies of literature and culture penned in Japanese by scholars who regularly engage, for example, Jungian, Freudian, and Lacanian psychoanalysis; Kristeva's notions of poetics; French feminists' valorization of maternity; the philosophic works of Félix Guattari and Gilles Deleuze; Derridean deconstruction; and, more recently, queer theory. Moreover, a percentage of critics based and educated in Japan have far greater familiarity than do their Asianist counterparts educated and based in the United States with Heideggerian, Hegelian, Kantian, Marxist, and other so-called Western philosophies.[4]

Yet critiquing the use of Western theory may be conversely supported by the unfortunate theoretical treatments of Japanese literature or the arts that employ Western theory in a pristine format—as it has been conceived and applied in Western contexts—with little attention paid to how the Japanese context may require that theory to "warp." Such readings reflect the other side of an Orientalist gaze, one that simply reinstates the Western norm as universal, obscuring its object of inquiry in the process of rediscovering itself. Like many Japanese critics (based either in the West or in Japan) and American and European Japanologists who engage theory, I have tried to be rigorous in ensuring that the theory that I use, wherever it might "originate," is grounded in, and thus nuanced by, the temporal contexts and the immediate sociocultural circumstances specific to the texts that I analyze.[5] I intend to allow the narrative text to lead the theory, rather than the other way around.

To return to my anecdote, since the pleasurable shock I received when I first read *The Newly Born Woman*, I endeavored to broaden my understanding of the increasingly difficult feminist, psychoanalytic, historicist, Marxist, and philosophic critical texts that I subsequently came across one after another (for example, those by Homi Bhabha, Judith Butler, Jacques Derrida, Elizabeth Grosz, Luce Irigaray, Julia Kristeva, Fredric Jameson, Lisa Lowe, and Slavoj Žižek, to name a few) as well as the foundational studies that provided the modern epistemic springboards for many of those treatments, by intellectual giants such as Michel Foucault, Sigmund Freud, Jacques Lacan, and Karl Marx. At the same time, along with Japanese literature, I was reading Japanese-authored criticism and theory mostly regarding literature, culture, modernity, and postmodernity (by, for example, Asada Akira, Etō Jun, Karatani Kōjin, Kobayashi Hideo, Maruyama Masao, Mizuta Noriko, Noguchi Takehiko, Oda Makoto, Sakaguchi Ango, Ueno Chizuko, and Yoshimoto Takaaki). Many critically sophisticated treatments of Japanese literature, culture, and history written in English have influenced me, some deeply. (These include, but of course are not limited to, studies by Edward Fowler, James Fujii, Carol Gluck, Harry Harootunian, Marilyn Ivy, Victor Koschmann, Masao Miyoshi, and Naoki Sakai.) It is thus from a broad study of both Western and Japanese contemporary thought that this book emerges, following no one existing theoretical model but using, and adapting from, disparate sources. Therefore, although in Chapter 5 I borrow Lacan's term *the Real* to describe Edo-period (1600–1868, also known as the Tokugawa period) notions of something akin to Lacan's twentieth-century notion of "the Real" (a realm foreclosed to the Symbolic order),[6] I note that my use of the term references the structure of a foreclosure (that which is radically and constitutively excluded) and not the content of that foreclosure. Not just in the application of Lacanian terms but also overwhelmingly throughout this study, I have made Western theory pliant to Japanese (temporal and cultural) specificities. For example, it follows faciley that if, as many Asian scholars and Western Asianists have argued, in modern Japan there is no subject fully commensurate with the modern Western individual, interiorized one (while there is undoubtedly a modern, interiorized subject nonetheless), then psychoanalytic theory based on Western psychosexual developmental models must be made to accommodate those differences in subjectivity formation.[7] My ethic of using and reshaping existing theory and terminologies has followed the Derridean adaptation of Claude Lévi-Strauss's *bricolage*, or making use of the "means at hand." This methodology is at the same time "mythopoetic" in Derrida's sense of the word; that is, similar to the ethnographic analysis of myth, the interpretation of literature must employ the same structural terms or system as the object of analysis itself (the literary text). Furthermore, the object of literary analysis is an imaginary about which the analysis must establish (invent) a significatory cohesion in spite of the incessant play of signifiers.[8]

It is in this spirit that I have offered (sometimes extended) explications, in both the notes and text, of what I mean when I employ standard theoretical terms in cases where my definitions may differ in nuance from the classical ones. I have endeavored to quote frequently from the texts that have most shaped my understanding of those terminologies (some might call them jargon), or, conversely, to identify those texts and definitions against which I am building an argument. It is also in this spirit that I have offered notes giving explicit reference to texts that have led me to my understanding of the epistemologies behind that jargon that the intellectually curious but still-uninitiated reader may access. Although I certainly do not want to alienate my readers, I am also anxious to maintain a degree of critical rigor in the psychoanalytic elaboration of my theses. As a case in point, here is one more short anecdote. One well-intentioned reader of a conference paper based on Chapter 15 suggested that I delete references to "the phallus as a signifier of lack" and perhaps replace the phrase "function as a phallus" with a phrase such as "play the female role" or "function as a vagina." Her suggestions were not appropriate because, although I share her desire to relativize the dominance of male connotations, it is the phallocentric perception of difference that marks lack, and not the presence of a vagina.[9] In this case, as in others, I use the so-called jargon because an entire corpus of literature exists that has defined and shaped the usages of these terms, and for the sophisticated reader, those terminologies carry that body of extended argument and explication with them. The concept of "the phallus as lack" is, alongside his assertion that the unconscious is structured like a language, the most fundamental aspect of Lacan's interpretation of Freud. For both Freud and Lacan, the perception of lack emerges from (incest) prohibition and the resultant castration anxiety (that is not specific to biological men) and not from women's physical absence of a body part, the penis. Juliet Mitchell writes, "For Freud, the absence of the penis in woman is significant only in that it makes meaningful the father's prohibition on incestuous desires. In and of itself, the female body neither indicates nor initiates anything."[10] The phallus is a symbolic category that stands in for the missing object of desire and is integral to the formation of subjectivity. The concept of the phallus as lack in turn provides a foundational structure integral to the intellectual inquiries of not only French feminists but to the majority of contemporary Anglo-American and other feminist theory, whatever stance particular feminists may take toward the concept itself. Moreover, as I will further elaborate in the second half of this introduction, because I seek to describe the social coming-into-being of the modern Japanese (male) subject through a process of othering and abjecting (of the dangerous woman), the concept is crucial to this study as well.

As a feminist, I seek to relativize the convention of regarding the phallus as the culturally and historically transcendental signifier of lack, linked to the absence, or presence, of the male sexual organ.[11] In a critique of Žižek, Judith Butler states that even if one accepts that subjectivity is dependent on foreclosure or repudiation, the insistence that what is refused must inevitably be a lack indicated by the feminine (the already absent phallus) denies that "there may be several mechanisms of foreclosure that work to produce the unsymbolizable in any given discursive regime, and . . . the mechanisms of the production are—however inevitable—still and always the historical workings of specific modalities of discourse and power."[12]

Although self-apprehension may be dependent on both psychic mechanisms of abjection and othering, the assumption that the patterns within phallocentric nations are transcendental of other historical and social discourses is actually a means of protecting phallocentrism itself.

My analysis of the dangerous woman trope identifies her as embodying and occupying a site that is socially and psychically abjected. In psychoanalytic discourse, the "abject" relates to a distinction first made between the *developing* subject and the not-self (or preobject objects); it differs from the "Other," because the subject does not yet exist. Paradigmatically, the objects of expulsion, such as excrement, and the amorphous state of not-being-self, or the homeostasis that is the aim of the death drive, are the substance of the abject.[13] For Julia Kristeva, the maternal body is also abjected in the process of becoming-self. The logic underlying this axiom is that in order for the infant to identify itself as "being-self," it must *abject* (radically jettison or exclude) the (until-then) nondifferentiated maternal body. Although I follow Butler in imagining that this processing of the maternal body need not be naturalized as transcendental of cultural influence (as Kristeva has it), in this book I will argue in detail that in modern Japan an aspect of the maternal body is repeatedly naturalized as abject, as the other side of the reification of maternity as female vocation.[14] Meiji Japan was (and Japan today remains) an androcentric nation, and therefore its exclusions follow a phallocentric pattern. My objective here is to analyze this foreclosure as firmly within, and fiercely protective of, phallic power. The notions of maternity developing in Meiji played a part in the production of Japan's modern phallocentric epistemology.

The psychoanalytic term *abjection* may also be used to describe the expulsion of elements that run counter to the fabrication of a unified, modern, masculine subject of the nation state. I do not mean that it may be used metaphorically, but rather that culture (including its arts), composed by human subjects (although those subjects are in turn produced by a multitude of discourses not only psychoanalytic and including those on power), is intrinsically bound to psychological processes. (The interrelation of literature and psychoanalysis is abundantly clear in the terms *narcissism* and the *Oedipus conflict*, coined by Freud, and which are, of course, culled from literary representations.) Thus, in place of the notion of applying the terms of a particular discursive field (psychoanalytic) within another one (culture/literature), I prefer to adapt Shoshana Felman's notion of reciprocal "implication" between psychoanalysis and literature to describe the interdependent systems of psychic and social subjectivity.[15] Following a similar logic, according to Butler, the abject may also designate

precisely those "unlivable" and "uninhabitable" zones of social life which are nevertheless densely populated by those who do not enjoy the status of the subject, but whose living under the sign of the "unlivable" is required to circumscribe the domain of the subject . . . the subject is constituted through the force of exclusion and abjection, one which produces a constitutive outside to the subject, an abjected outside, which is, after all, "inside" the subject as its own founding repudiation.[16]

As anthropologist Marilyn Ivy has pointed out, the marshaling of psychoanalytic theory to interpret Japanese modernity has further resonance, because despite the differences between the Japanese and European-American models of modernization, Freud's work speaks from modernity's and industrial capitalism's moment of production.[17] And I would add that Freud also spoke from the moment of the emergence of modern phallic subjectivity as the subject of modernity. However, the appropriateness of a psychoanalytic interpretation will, I hope, become most apparent in the examples of the mutual implications of the discourses (literary, cultural, and psychoanalytic) that I uncover throughout this study.

The psychoanalytic character of my reading stresses the importance of desire in the production of literature, and literature in relation to cultural imaginaries.[18] According to the female protagonist, Mieko, of *Onnamen* (*Masks*, 1958), written by the second author in my study, Enchi Fumiko, the dangerous woman represents both a construct of male desire and "an archetype of her [woman] as the object of his [man's] eternal fear."[19] My study seeks to recuperate a pluralism intrinsic to the dangerous woman trope beyond the duality, or contradiction, explicit in Mieko's statement. That the dangerous woman is both feared and desired—and the contradictions, confusions, and ambiguities that characterize how she is written—suggests that she is a symbol for the locus of "originary" desire and the domain of the psychosexual, and therefore simultaneously culturally, abject.

By "desire" I do not mean "pleasure"; rather, I am referring to the psychoanalytic term. While desire is inseparable from drive, it can only be articulated within language, that is, within the Symbolic order. In the process, its "originary object(s)" (the desired objects of drive before the subject itself has been formulated through misapprehensions of the self/other) that is linked to the death drive, or the cessation of activity—homeostasis—is repressed, and a process of symbolic substitutions has begun.[20] Although the origins of desire are formulated before the acquisition of language, the retrieval of desire is only possible through language. For the subject to feel desire, the (non)object of desire must be substituted by a symbol in language, that is, in the Symbolic order. A process of ceaseless slippage of desire along a linking chain of changing signifiers ensues, because the original nonobject is not retrievable; this process is in fact the source of all human "animation." For modern Japan, as it has dominated Western psychoanalytic thought from Freud to Lacan, the privileged signifier for loss is naturalized as the phallus. The phallus references not only the missing object but also the process of the subject's coming-into-being through language, as instigated by prohibition.[21]

According to Kristeva, among others, the production and consumption of literature in particular has a special intimacy with desire; it is from the intimacy between articulation and desire that "poetic" literature is born.[22] As I will articulate, the dangerous woman trope, as conceived by the three writers in my study, is also about language itself, about the impossibility of capturing reality in word and the production of subjectivity in the medium of language—constitutively inaccurate and marked by lack and desire. The reading/writing subjects of poetic literature tread closely to the foreclosed and forbidden realm of (unattainable-by-definition) originary desire. This is the substance of *jouissance*. This book will show the literary productions of a coming-into-being of a phallic, national subject through the intrinsically polysemic establishment of woman as Other and the repository of literary nativism and the conterminous establishment and naturalization of idealized maternity as female vocation. The domain of the maternal, however, is split to accommodate woman's idealized aspects and the maternal body as abject. For Kristeva, this foreclosure, which predates othering and self-identification (although it is only known through the veil of, and takes its shape from, the Symbolic) and which forms the basis for abjection, is naturalized as the maternal body. As Butler has masterfully argued, this naturalization produces the maternal body as transcendental of cultural determinism and as such is an essentialism that denies the possibility of another basis for foreclosure.[23] But Kristeva's primacy of the maternal body as the Real has assonance with modern Japanese imaginaries. The maternal-abject, determined by cultural abhorrence that gives shape to the earliest psychic processes of separating self from not-self, thus becomes a locus for *jouissance*. Woman is Other in the phallic order, and within that Otherness, both her putative capacity for a *jouissance* beyond that available to men and her (actualized or not) putative constitutive inseparability from motherhood link her surreptitiously to the Real and also to the abject. The dangerous woman is a trope whose connection with the Real and the abject is made dominant and manifest.

The desire that leads toward *jouissance*—the experience of a type of pleasure that threatens the stability of the experiential subject, the one having the pleasure, because it is fueled by the death drive or the desire for homeostasis (the return to a state where stimulus ceases)—also fueled the writings of Izumi Kyōka (1873–1939), Enchi Fumiko (1905–86), and Nakagami Kenji (1946–92). One of this book's aims is to chart the transformations in the imaginary of the dangerous woman as the symbolic locus for potential *jouissance*. As it is for Kristeva, in Kyōka the site of *jouissance* is naturalized as the abject-maternal body, accessed by men through the dangerous woman's body. For Enchi, the naturalization of the object of desire (the originary object and its symbolic replacement by the phallus-as-lack) as the dangerous woman led her protagonists to seek

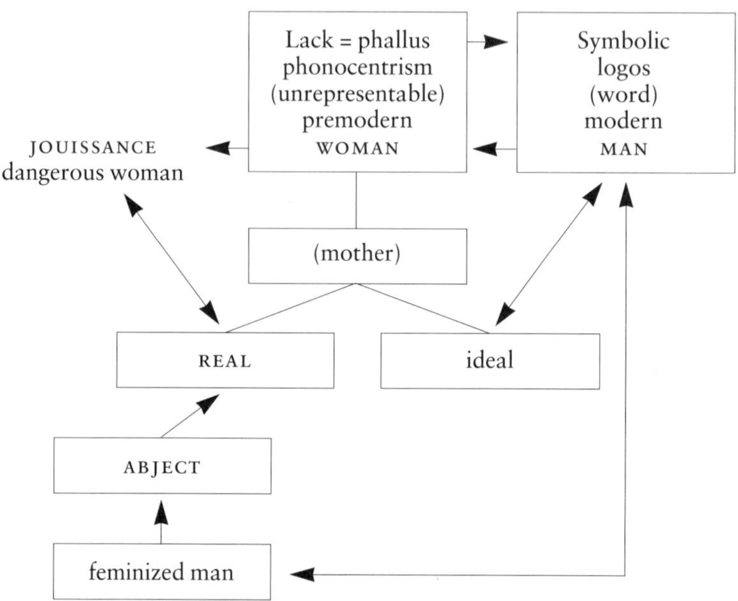

Figure 1. Matrix of Desire (Imaginary) in Kyōka, Enchi, and Nakagami

jouissance through an intimate encounter with the dangerous woman's imagined body as well, but this coming together involved *introjection* and disturbed the dangerous woman's apparent status as Other. Moreover, the desire of Enchi's protagonists is attended by a shame of recognition, and subsequently, disavowal. For Nakagami, the dangerous woman as the site for *jouissance* is relativized by the copresence of a maled, penised, alternate repository for the abject (I do not mean here the Kleinian maternal phallus).[24]

The psychoanalytic nature of my reading is thus by definition an inquiry that aims to elucidate conflict rather than resolution. It takes as its subjects of discussion the structures, images, and language (rhetoric, style, lexicon, syntax, and so on—the linguistic mechanisms that echo and also obscure the workings of the unconscious) of the texts. It is less interested in the personal, or individual, fixations or psychic singularities (or peculiarities) of either the characters or authors—as if they were real people presenting themselves for a therapy session—and more in the implication of the literary texts in the production of imaginaries bound with conterminous discourses on gender, culture, and power.

Dangerous Women is first and foremost about the processing of an imaginary, about a *literary* construct. But literary imaginaries, even when they offer fantasies aberrant to dominant notions of sociocultural norm, cannot transcend their geographical space and time. Literature is a complex site where social epistemologies may confront (repressed/suppressed) fears and desires; fantasy may highlight the fissures in putatively stable sociocultural and political, national and individual structures, institutions, and ideations. Judith Newton and Deborah Rosenfelt wrote in *Feminist Criticism and Social Change* that "Since we live within myths and narratives about history . . . literature . . . draws upon various ideological productions of history or discourses about history to make its own production."[25] I intend to analyze gender identity as produced through perceptual structures specific to a moment and a location in time and as a constitutive component in the construction of subjectivity itself.[26] Thus, this study situates literature less as an aesthetic object bracketed off from epistemological discourses on modernity and gender politics and more in terms of its constitutive inseparability from them. I also intend to describe the interplay of discourses of power on the textual surface of the trope and to historicize and contextualize the dangerous woman as rooted in (changing) historically specific androcentrism and homosociality.[27]

In early-twentieth-century Japan the grossly misogynist, Neo-Confucian–rooted homosociality that dominated the Edo period was reshaped by the startling inclusion of women in the category of "people" (akin to men). "Woman" was no longer socially abjected simply because she was woman. "Mother" was split into two components, the reified mother/ educator who accrued social value and (varied tropes encompassing) her abjected attributes (one of which is the dangerous woman). Modern Japanese homosociality fabricated and naturalized gendered divisions of public and private to facilitate the needs of economic and symbolic capital. In the process, in Meiji, homophobia accompanied the shift in women's status; social abjection was broadened and reconceived to accommodate homosexual activities alongside occupational pollution and female dirtiness—now split from the maternal mission. The dangerous woman in fact represents the foreclosure by which the modern, homosocial, phallic subject and his counterpart, the reified mother, are made possible. The maternal myth that developed in Meiji/Taisho (Taisho, 1912–26) and was thoroughly naturalized by Showa (1926–89) needed the dangerous woman as the (constitutive other) site to encompass all the elements surplus to, and those abjected from, both the maternal ideal and the "inviolate" phallic subject. She thus symbolizes, inaccurately by definition, the Real.

Rather than perceiving that any monolithic system of phallocentrism or patriarchy produces the dangerous woman for its own economic and productive needs, I view her as produced by an overdetermination of economic, psychological, cultural, political, and gendered discourses and thus as marked with internal inconsistencies and pluralities.[28] As Butler has argued, "any attempt to circumscribe an identity in terms of relations of production, and solely within those terms, performs an exclusion and, hence, produces a constitutive outside, understood on the model of the Derridean 'supplément,' that denies the claim to positivity and comprehensiveness implied by that prior objectivation."[29] Although I would not argue against the assertion that the needs of capital itself produce cultural practices and literary imaginaries, this book reflects my belief that power operates more in the manner described by Michel Foucault, dispersed between institutions and discourses and always in relation to plural, constitutively copresent resistances.[30] Foucault's schema has particular relevance to a study of modern Japan, since, lacking a clear "center" of authority, Japan offers a paradigmatic example of such decentralized power.[31] Moreover, as the collective authors of *Changing the Subject: Psychology, Social Regulation and Subjectivity* put it, "discursive practices produce, maintain, or play out power relations. But power is not one-sided or monolithic, even when we can and do speak of dominance, subjugation, or oppression. Power is always exercised in relation to a resistance."[32] Further, it is my belief that even imaginaries antinonical to dominant epistemologies are bound to those epistemologies' very laws and paradigms, discernible in the form and substance of their resistances. (This is not to deny the possibility of radical opposition, but to recognize the interrelations between social environments and individuals or groups of individuals. Nor do I mean to suggest that texts reiterating dominant ideologies with discernible fissures be regarded on a political par with texts setting out to oppose those ideologies.) And finally, to add to the dangerous woman's polyvocal nature, as I trace the trope through the twentieth century, she undergoes radical transformations that are shaped by changing historical circumstances.

That I also have a political agenda is obvious. Stated bluntly, I hope to denaturalize a set of modern truisms surrounding the trope that comprise a component of phallic fantasy about women. The psychoanalytic methodology guarantees, however, that my reading be pliant. The trope is neither purely subversive, nor conversely, (re)productive of dominant sex/

gender politics. It is a site implicated in the process of modern subjectivity and is constituted through conflict and contradiction, both cultural and psychic. I therefore apologize in advance to the reader hoping to find some sort of univocal statement of judgment on the trope. To do so would be to force closure on, and deny the complications of, the fictional texts for the sake of an imposed theory or political agenda and would thus be oppositional to the ethic of pliancy described above. I can only hope that I have succeeded in my attempts to use theory as contextually demanded.

The dangerous woman hovers at the borders of colliding and reforming ideologies of Japanese modernity. She emerges from a tangle of inter-linked and plural epistemological upheavals: the development and trans-formations throughout the twentieth century of modern phallic subjectiv-ity and the modernization of a homosocial economy; the radically changed status of women, and the reification (and later the questioning of this reifi-cation) of maternity as a naturalized female vocation; constructs of sexu-ality that established a compulsory heterosexuality (and resistances to this); and the question of narrative itself in modern Japan, centered around phonocentrism, the "discovery" of subjective and textual interior-ity; and an ambivalence regarding the narrative subject in language. This study reads the intersections of these twentieth-century epistemologies with the (imagined) body of the dangerous woman. I do not mean to total-ize the specific imaginary embodied by the dangerous woman but rather to identify the body of the dangerous woman (as it is written in narrative text) as one site upon which a plurality of ideologies and imaginings about gender and modernity are produced, inscribed, and contradicted.

Employing contemporary feminist and psychoanalytic theory, in the somewhat idiosyncratic manner described above, in this book I map out the intersections of these major, gendered epistemological logics specific to Japan's twentieth century with the dangerous woman. The study traces her trajectory through the works of three twentieth-century writers of *monogatari* (tale fiction):[33] Kyōka, Enchi, and Nakagami. The book is separated into three parts by author; each part is, more accurately, about the transformations of one imaginary (out of many) that was characteris-tic of three particular moments in Japan's modernity.[34] The first chapters of each of the three parts function as introductions to the authors, to the dominant sociocultural and political issues of their respective time peri-ods that I link to their configurations of the dangerous woman and to the aspects of their narratives that figure most prominently in my discussions.

Part I identifies the dangerous woman as she appears in Kyōka's texts, as emerging from the Meiji/Taisho–period sociocultural establishment of a set of distinctions between the modern and the premodern and the concurrent shift in gender constructs. Kyōka was famous as a quirky, anti-mainstream writer, described as a romantic-idealist, impressionistic stylist, whose narrative aesthetics ran counter to the prevailing naturalism of his time. He frequently wrote supernatural "gothic" tales haunted by a dark, perverse eroticism, and countless stories made protagonists, or antagonists, of people inhabiting the newly defined domains of the social abject, or the uncanny, such as geisha, outcastes, or ghosts and demons.[35] His realm of the uncanny was dominated by what I have since come to call the dangerous woman.

As I made my way through much of the impressive body of secondary works on Kyōka written in Japanese, I came upon the frequent assertion that his dangerous woman embodied the quintessential essence of femaleness, providing readers and critics alike with somewhat perverse, and delightful, erotic daydreams. Furthermore, the majority read this troping as inseparable from what they understood to be Kyōka's resolute resistance to modernity. She, they insisted, was convention evoked against modern realism. This standardized interpretation reappeared in the secondary literature on both Enchi and Nakagami. The dangerous woman's eroticized and deadly body is associated with an ancient animism of specific Japanese origin and is regarded as a repository for a "unique" Japanese cultural essence: she thus functions as a channel to an (imagined) "womb" of Japanese folklore. I recall feeling an intellectual discomfort, something like the sensation of a stalled engine, when I read such commentaries. She only superficially reminded me of premodern precursors. From my first encounter with her, then, my reading went against the grain of the standard interpretations.

Mountain witches, female shamans, snake-women, and other spiritually empowered women have been represented throughout the Japanese canon in virtually all genres (high and low), authored and disseminated by both men and women. Powerful women can be found isolated in the mountains devouring or bewitching the hapless men and children who wander into their magical domains, communicating with the deities, or spiritually possessing other women. These women stand as a testament to a tenacious, yet peripheral, presence in Japanese literature of powerful women who confront the dictates of male dominance and familial need.

However, modern renditions of the dangerous woman stand aloof from the archaic and medieval portrayals that preceded her. Although she is presented in the guise of, or is overtly referential to, a plurality of antecedent female literary archetypes long linked to eroticism and though she is empowered by her link to the uncanny realms of the spirits, the dead, and the supernatural, there is an unmistakable series of transformations. Once-distinct categories of female archetypes are collapsed into a general "woman of supernatural powers" in modern renditions. This process of condensation produces a thoroughly modern version of her premodern counterparts. My term *dangerous woman* is thus meant to include the variable modern representations of powerful women that are culled from, and commingle with, certain archetypes of the premodern canon. Rather than reiterating premodern archetypes, to me she appeared, though not quite parodic, hyperbolic; she "performed" herself. She reminded me of the contemporary kabuki *onnagata*, or a biological man performing a woman through recourse to a ritualized imitation of culturally sanctioned gestures, postures, and utterances meant to evoke "the female."[36]

Moreover, I sensed from the beginning that my discomfort with the standard readings concerned the dangerous woman's presence in the tangle of a language that structurally mirrored her "femaleness." The polysemic "poetics" of Kyōka's prose evoked premodern literature even while it unequivocally differed from it. In this book I consider the interdependent relationship between the trope as a repository for a feminized, othered premodernity—which also encompasses the abject—and the struggle to produce a modern subject in language and narrative. I begin a discussion in Part I that recurs throughout the book of the complicated metaphoric intertwining of so-called women's writing (*onnade*),[37] women's "voice," a polysemic style, phonocentrism, linguistic origins, and archaic Shinto. My argument seeks to denaturalize a set of axioms that are commonly reiterated in critical treatments that, by virtue of stylistic and thematic attributes, feminize certain Japanese premodern discursive traditions and, by extension, modern *monogatari*. The dangerous woman is one cultural mechanism that reproduces this set of axioms. But in fact, the dangerous woman and writing styles evocative of premodern *monogatari* and *setsuwa* (legend)[38] are thoroughly modern means to elicit the premodern—by collapsing once distinctly separated rhetorical and generic devices and a host of once-discrete archetypes into condensed plural forms. This notion of the premodern can only be formulated from a nostalgic position that is already modern (or simultaneous, as its constitutive other, with the establishment of modernity). In early-twentieth-century Japan, the dangerous woman became a fertile and abiding literary topos, appearing frequently in works by male authors, who depicted the yearning and dread of a male protagonist encountering her as "object," as a mechanism by which his subjectivity, and its modernity, is made possible.[39] It was not until the postwar that she began haunting a voluminous body of writings authored by women.[40]

Losing the Pacific War and national self-determination stimulated anew shifting anxieties about Japanese identity, language, and origins. The American occupation brought with it new laws and expectations for a rise in women's status and further upheavals in gender politics and national identity.[41] Against the prewar narrative convention whereby male narrators/characters approached the dangerous woman as a radically othered "exteriority," as an object of erotic fascination, and as a potential conduit to *jouissance* (the Real, naturalized as the maternal-body), the postwar women-authored *monogatari* inhabit her previously ciphered interior (by "ciphered" I refer to the symbol for zero in mathematics but intend for secondary meanings, of coded through substitution and "nonentity" to pluralize the meaning)[42] and modernize her as a thinking and narrating subject. The dangerous woman's interiorized female voice destabilized her confinement within a codified repository of male erotic imagination. She, originated as a modern phallic fantasy, appeared to now offer possibilities for women's resistance to that fantasy, as a site for rethinking female identity, empowerment, and erotic agency. Kyōka's dangerous women were central to his narratives, but they inhabited social peripheries, found off the beaten track, folded into mountain interiors, by bridges demarcating nature and settlement. In Enchi's texts, the dangerous woman is not only spatially shifted from periphery to center, she is imagined to reside in latent form inside all women.

The postwar Showa decades saw a revitalization of a mythic, ambivalent valorization of a feminized nativism bound to nostalgic and nationalist notions about originary language (reminiscent of the Edo-period *kokugaku* [national studies] movement).[43] Enchi sought to reclaim a "female voice" and "female empowerment" that modern Japan imagined had once informed female-authored *monogatari* and archaic Japan but had been lost within the male inhabitation of this putatively feminized origin. Enchi not only incorporated quotations from Heian-period (794–1185) literature into the body of her fictional narratives but she also went so far as to invent, and to reproduce in classical syntax and vocabulary, antecedent Heian-period narratives. Metaphoric, now-classic presentations of women thus alternate with modern explorations of their innermost voices, a structure that splits the female narrative subjects along the axis of past/present. For Enchi, as for Kyōka, the dangerous woman is a locus for the coming-into-being *in language* of the subject.

Part III describes how, in contrast to both Kyōka and Enchi, who situate dangerous women at the center of their texts, respectively as object and subject, Nakagami shifted her back to the periphery and destabilized her position of supernatural dominance and power through the postulation of a "dangerous man" as an alternative conduit to origin, voice, animism, and the abject (and through the abject, the Real). In Nakagami's narratives, the body that functions as a medium for interactions with an "other" world or the realms of the uncanny and the dead does not have to be female. Nakagami's protagonists are predominantly present-day male outcastes, or *hijiri* (ascetics of the medieval period who were both sacred and taboo), whom Nakagami troped as metaphoric ancestors of modern outcastes.[44] That these protagonists are also often bisexual or engage in unorthodox sexual activities further signals their deviance from the putative norm. Their relations to Japanese dominant culture are inevitably marked by an irony born of the doubleness inherent in being both Japanese and outcastes, or in a more complex formulation, being Japanese, bisexual, and outcaste. This ironic positioning turns nostalgia into brutality and sets the framework for a battery of assaults on Japanese truisms. The *roji* (literally, alleys; in Nakagami's narratives a euphemism for the outcaste ghettos)—a central setting for his realistic fiction—are one metaphoric site that allows Nakagami to negotiate the tensions between Japan as seen through the eyes of his protagonists and Japanese dominant culture and its aesthetics, histories, ideologies. Nakagami's so-called *monogatari* (which were mythical tales with themes and settings culled from premodern *setsuwa* and *monogatari* and set in an indeterminate medieval past) became another site for exploring the violences of "difference" and discrimination. In these stories, through a phallic retroping of archaisms, Nakagami's narratives attack the modern feminization of origin, originary language, and archaic animism and the maternalization of the abject—conceits reiterated in both Kyōka's and Enchi's narratives.

Nakagami began writing in the 1960s, after moving to Tokyo from his birthplace, an outcaste ghetto in rural Shingū on the Kinki peninsula. In Tokyo he encountered jazz and the student riots; this was also a time when Japan observed and debated the turmoil of the American civil rights movement. In the rush of consumerism, massing of information, and a jaded literary world, Nakagami's narratives, permeated with class rage, sexual differences, and oblique and ironic relation to dominant Japanese ethics, the canon and renderings of history exploded onto the literary market. Nakagami's marketability and his disclosure of his outcaste heritage—indeed, his ideological mobilization of an identity as outcaste as a position for social and political opposition—were unthinkable in either Kyōka or Enchi's generation. Following the political unrest of the 1960s, an ethnic boom and consumption of multiculturalism enjoyed by middle-class Japanese in the late 1970s and 1980s and the search for original nativities and the exotic within the Japanese heartland became the cultural backdrop for Nakagami's violent narrative attacks on the myths of Japanese homogeneity.

Nakagami's bisexed dangerous woman / dangerous man emerges, as did Kyōka and Enchi's purely female counterparts, from the production of subjectivity in language; but for Nakagami, she/he was born of and in the violence that attends naming and the difference/discrimination of all significatory utterances.[45] His assault on Japanese convention took both linguistic and thematic forms; laboring to deconstruct the binaries that form the basis of modern "difference," Nakagami unsettled the feminization of narrative origin and foreclosure that Kyōka's generation helped to fabricate and Enchi's to reproduce. Through their shared social abjection and political/economic subordination, the protagonists of Nakagami's narratives relativize the naturalized, sexed (feminized/maternalized) configuration of foreclosure.

I conclude with a last few details. I have steadfastly avoided the use of the word *novel* in my discussion of Japanese prose narratives, because, as many have pointed out, the word carries certain connotations and expectations that are irrelevant to Japanese literary texts. Japanese names are written in the Japanese order, that is, surnames first, except for those writing in English who use the Western order. Some Japanese writers and critics are always referred to by their second (given, not family) names (usually pen names), and this is the case with Izumi Kyōka. I have followed Japanese precedent and referred to him as Kyōka even in the notes, but the bibliography lists his texts under Izumi.

Izumi Kyōka

Speculum

[Izumi Kyōka's] world is, simply, Japanese. . . . His work is a
pure Japanese product.　　　— T A N I Z A K I   J U N ' I C H I R Ō
　　　　　　　"Junsui ni 'Nihonteki' na Kyōka sekai"

Even when [Kyōka is] depicting a single woman, she is all
women. This generic woman is nothing more than a vessel
encompassing archetypes (like vessels into which water is
poured!). Therefore they do not possess faces with raw contours as individuals. Women are, first and foremost, an odor
that envelopes him, a sentiment, a fleeting tactility, a "white
face."　　　　　　　　　　　　— T A N E M U R A   S U E H I R O
　　　　　　　　　　　"Suichūka hengen"

Izumi Kyōka's prolific writing career began in Meiji, continued
through Taisho, and ended with his death in Showa, culminating in more
than three hundred narratives. Known for his opaque prose (literary critic
Ikuta Chōkō called him Japan's "supreme impressionist")[1] and for his ghost
tales, he was also celebrated for how he "wrote women." And Kyōka indeed wrote women. Literary historian Nakamura Mitsuo described Kyōka
as an author of "sweet romance novels . . . [which display] a sort of feminism."[2] Kyōka scholar Muramatsu Sadataka likewise used the word *feminism* when discussing Kyōka's portrayals of women: "Even in the case
of the sorceress in *Kōya hijiri*, Kyōka's feminism is revealed as embodying
the ideal of a super being transcendental of the real—whether through a

search for an eternal woman by depicting a visionary metamorphosis or by employing the figure of a beautiful enchantress to express his longing for his dead mother."[3] Kyōka's more realistic narratives, such as his famous *Onna keizu* (Women's genealogy, 1908), were often exposés of the inequitable lot dealt to women of his time, written with obvious sympathy for their plight and a critical harshness toward the social mores that so oppressed them. These sympathies were explicitly expressed in essays such as "Ai to kon'in" (Love and marriage, 1895). In his fictional narratives, Kyōka repeatedly foregrounded idealized and romanticized female characters. This is what Nakamura and Muramatsu meant when they used the loan word *feminism* (*feminisumu*). For them feminism meant a thetic elevation of biologically female characters—commonly in the form of sexually alluring and mysteriously powerful enchantresses. Yet Kyōka's "beautiful enchantresses" are inextricably linked with death. As literary critic Noguchi Takehiko wrote, "Who can say whether the power of [Kyōka's] heroines who pull men to their deaths is that of [the Buddhist goddess] Kannon or that of a demon?"[4] According to the American Kyōka translator Charles Inouye, Kyōka's brother reported that "Kyōka's favorite image as a young boy was of a woman stripped, tied, and beaten."[5] The following chapters will show that, when one gives more than a cursory glance at his narratives, it is clear that Kyōka's rendering of women is inseparable from a Meiji/Taisho construct of a masculine subject as the norm and the concurrent crafting of the female as Other with naturalized access to a domain at once maternalized and abjected.

Kyōka's corpus may be divided into narratives depicting the mundane world (often that of geishas and the demimonde, or practitioners of the varied arts) and those venturing into topographies in which ghosts and the supernatural transgress the mundane, most frequently heralded by the appearance of a female apparition. The female ghosts embody absence and presence simultaneously and function as mediums, or conduits, to other (imagined, past) worlds. These tales of a specific transgression, where ephemeral female bodies become thresholds for passage, are the concern of this study. Although the same epistemologies inform Kyōka's more realistic fiction, in the tales of the supernatural there is a process of condensation by which the contradictions of early-twentieth-century gender imaginations and constructs are collapsed into a dense, intriguing confusion.

Kyōka's shamanic women embody and reenact—or "perform"—a particular set of gendered notions. Although Kyōka's depictions of the female shaman were not commensurate with the prevailing, developing female ideal, and so were not transparently normative (or performative), they emerge from, as I will argue, a web of ideological notions about gender that were being teleologized (or naturalized as possessing inherent purpose and design) during his writing career. The femaleness performed by Kyōka's women consisted of culturally sanctioned gender performances that composed an other side to normative gender performances.[6]

Among the myriad issues attended to in Meiji was one called "the woman problem" (*fujin mondai*). Kyōka's early works were conterminous with popular, governmental, and feminist recraftings of a "maternal-feminine ideal" in the production of a modern, industrialized, and patriarchal system of labor to support the state and to complement the construction of a heterosexual and specifically gendered modern subjectivity. The following two chapters argue that the deep eroticization that binds femaleness to deathliness and thus to the abject in Kyōka's texts is the corollary, the product, and the reiteration of the developing Meiji/Taisho maternal myth.

Most critics of Kyōka's narratives agree that his sorceress/demoness figures are symbolic of the past. But they differ in what exactly they mean by "the past." For literary scholar Maeda Ai, the past was a primordial world ruled by chaos and unfixed form.[7] Inouye has documented the attributes reminiscent of Edo-period *kusazōshi* (illustrated popular fiction) in Kyōka's texts.[8] The modern writers Akutagawa Ryūnosuke and Mishima Yukio likened Kyōka's textual structures to *nō*, a performative art frozen in its fifteenth-century form, as did critic Kawamura Jirō.[9] Overall, commentators have found affinity between Kyōka's characterizations and prose style and practically every premodern and early modern genre, including kabuki, poetry, legend, and storytelling. I argue that it is precisely this mixture of references, in terms of style as well as characterizations, to a long, heterogeneous premodern and early modern corpus of artistic productions that signals modernity. It is only by their shared "otherness" in relation to the modern that Kyōka's admixture becomes evocative of an imaginary, homogeneous premodernity. My overall goal in this first part of *Dangerous Women* is thus to counter the dominant critical insistence that Kyōka was a staunch "conventionalist," (both thematically and stylistically), by resituating Kyōka within the greater epistemological fabrics of Meiji/Taisho/early Showa–gendered reformulations that produced modern subjectivity and statehood (the process whereby in Japan the norm became the unitary masculine subject within a heterosexual libidinal economy).

Meiji-period transformations in subjectivity were, of course, multiple. The centralized yet semifeudal Edo period, which directly preceded Meiji, was characterized by a putatively rigid, hierarchical class structure: one's position as a subject was determined by tautological notions of class and gender. With the abolishment of the classes in early Meiji, individuals had to "discover" subjectivity and their personal significance through recourse to other, to some extent volitional, positionings within the developing context of Japan as a nation state.[10] As a number of mostly relatively recent studies have uncovered, the Edo-period libidinal economy was not heterosexual. (This, of course, does not mean that relations between people of different sexes did not exist, but that culturally normative love and sexual practices did not exclude same-sex partnerings.)[11] Male-male erotic love, most commonly a privilege of the samurai and merchant (educated, moneyed) classes, was celebrated in narrative text, in "how-to" booklets, and in poetry.[12] At the same time, the dense misogyny of the period (which viewed women as constitutionally inferior to men) meant that the most esteemed expressions of sexual love were to be found between men.

As part of the national modernization project, the grossly androcentric and misogynist Tokugawa legal and ideological debasement of women underwent massive reforms. As feminist historian Sharon Sievers has noted, one of the early Meiji slogans was *onna mo hito nari* ("women are people too").[13] In their dedication to turning Japan into a modern nation, Meiji educators, politicians, and intelligentsia identified male-male sexual practices as homosexuality, and a system of compulsory *public* heterosexuality, along with the newly elevated status of woman-as-wife-and-mother, was instituted.[14] There was a government-sponsored campaign to educate women under the slogan "good wife, wise mother" (*ryōsai kenbo*). Maternity as a reified institution was produced in Japan as part of the libidinal and subjective economies that came to support Japan as a modern nation state. In Meiji/Taisho Japan, within the debates on motherhood that conspired to remold and to naturalize the separation of women (from men) into mutually exclusive realms of labor supporting industrialized capitalism, the complementariness of the abject, the Other, and the subject, and their reciprocal constructivity are made transparent.[15] In the process, for Kyōka and for others, femaleness became the handy disposal bin for all that exceeded, muddied, and stained the unity of the (now-heterosexual) male subject.

By projecting the irrational, the nonmodern, the uncanny, and the "feminine" (plural, viscous, unruly) onto select "others," the modern phallic subject comes into existence. (The phallic subject is the imaginary male who comes into being only by his not-being the imaginary female; the uncanny is the returning, vaguely familiar, premodern "Other" against which, and thus constitutively by which, the modern takes its shape.) The eroticized sorceresses/demons/goddesses of Kyōka's narratives make possible the realm of masculine "normalcy," for the protagonist/reader/writer, by their distance from it. This distance is secured, in part, through a process that links femaleness with maternity and simultaneously with an imagined, premodern past.

Commentators on Kyōka's texts have generally agreed that his women, evocative of a vague past era, are frequently maternalized. This maternalization is commonly attributed to the fact that Kyōka lost his own mother when he was a child. Kasahara wrote "I think that although the special essence of Kyōka's writings can be made clear by the two extremes, beauty and eroticism, that comprise the foundational structures for theoretical treatments of Kyōka, most likely the deep passion connecting the two [extremes] can only be described using the phrase [*ichigo ni tsukiru*] 'mother-love.' "[16] My reading adds the dimension of cultural loss to personal loss (as many other commentaries also have done); because the mother represents "the past," she embodies a nostalgic configuration of an imagined bygone age. As I noted in the introduction, within one Meiji-period imaginary, the maternal dimension is split between its ideal as female vocation (modernity) and its naturalized realm of abjection (premodernity), structurally paralleling the psychosexual demarcations between the (gendered) subject and the presubject. Unlike the imaginary male subject-body, the imaginary female (Other-) body also always encompasses sticky webs connecting to the abjected realms of the presubject and the past. In the national quest for modernization, the various institutional and other transformations were accompanied by themes of nostalgia, loss, and the desire to (re)capture an (imagined) past—in both the realms of the subject and of the sociocultural. These prevailing logics underpinning the Meiji social, economic, political, linguistic, and literary reforms are inseparable from how Kyōka wrote "women." Although Kyōka's female demons appear to invert the Meiji maternal myth, more correctly, they embody the necessary, corollary abjection or othering that simultaneously creates the myth.

Japanese scholars of Kyōka's texts have frequently read his texts by subjecting them, and Kyōka himself, to various psychological methodologies, generally focusing on his purported mother complex or his infamous phobias. By dismissing Kyōka's perversions of tradition as individual pathology, critics conveniently explained away the fact that Kyōka was also markedly different from his Edo predecessors. (By "perversions" here I refer to the transformation of convention that troped the dangerous woman as the abject, and thus constitutionally as an erotically perverse vehicle for desire.)[17] Other critics, by analyzing the modernity in his pathology, saw Kyōka as possessing a pathological abhorrence for the modern. Both approaches ensure that historicity did not intrude on their insistence that Kyōka's works reiterated an historically transcendent "Japanese" aesthetics, prose style, or (mostly female) characterizations.[18] My reading attempts to situate Kyōka's "pathologies" within his historical environment, as symptomatic of a cultural, and not purely personal, imaginary.

The dominant body of secondary literature on Kyōka makes a confusion of Kyōka's writing style, the presence of the dangerous woman, a putative "female" discursive style, an ahistorical Japanese "essence," and the premodern literary canon. My final chapters on Kyōka focus on his discursive style in an attempt to further historicize Kyōka's "atmosphere" of premodernity. Like the configuration of the dangerous woman, Kyōka's writing style evokes the premodern by collapsing once distinctly separated rhetorical and generic devices into condensed plural forms. I attempt to historicize Kyōka's linguistic "peculiarities" as constituting a Meiji/Taisho phonocentric trajectory, which both echoes and differs from the naturalists' phonocentrism, rather than as a reiteration of Edo-period polysemic play (as has often been critically asserted). These chapters also historicize as a developing cultural imaginary Kyōka's naturalization of *jouissance* as located in a verbalized, feminized, maternalized, eroticized juncture of word and body, represented by the dangerous woman. For Kyōka, it was the dangerous woman who might somehow permit the protagonist/reader/writer to overcome the terms of the Symbolic (and modernity) and reunite the (now-dissolving) subject and the foreclosed (the Real) in a recapture of origin.

Although my analysis is thus attentive to the social, political, and economic conditions from which the modern shamaness—the dangerous woman—emerged, it is nonetheless about literature: I seek to engage the processing of an imaginary. For though Meiji/Taisho men and women alike hotly debated the meaning of "mothering," for Kyōka, mothering had become a teleology that fused femaleness and the abject; modernity was posed as the other to an archaism rendered female/maternal. Within her province as archaic demon/goddess/mother, the sorceress figure of Kyōka's narratives forces confrontation with an abjected plural subjectivity and the uncanny trace of the past in the present. The process of modern (social and psychosexual) individuation partakes of the necessary expulsion of the pluralities of the pre-Symbolic/premodern. For Kyōka, as well as for Meiji modernity, the exclusion that forms subjectivity is teleologized as the abjected aspects of a reified maternal body. The dangerous women of Kyōka's imagination threaten to break apart male selfsameness, returning the male protagonists to presubject formlessness;[19] this process parallels the social process of modernization and the threatening, enticing, erotic return of the irrational or premodern.

Leaky Archetypes

Kōya hijiri (The Kōya ascetic, 1900; sometimes translated as *The Saint of Kōya*) is the story of a young Buddhist ascetic on pilgrimage who detours from the customary path and winds up on an abandoned mountain trail in an attempt to follow and assist a peddler. Barely surviving a terrifying path, which is overrun with fearsome serpents, and an almost-fatal attack by multitudes of leeches inhabiting a deep forest, he emerges from the forest, crosses a little bridge, and discovers a ramshackle home tucked in the mountains inhabited by a mysterious, alluring woman, her infantilized "idiot" (*baka*) husband, alternately referred to as "the youth" (*shōnen*), and a manservant about to take a horse to market. The following quote is from the middle of the story, narrated by the ascetic, and describes how the woman marshals her powers to coax the reticent horse into following the old man to the market:

The woman adjusted her kimono, holding it closed under her breasts . . . and minced out toward the horse.

Dumbfounded, I watched her stretch up on tiptoes, extending a graceful hand skyward to stroke the horse's mane.

Erect, facing the horse's large head, she looked suddenly taller. She fixed her eyes on it, mouth shut and eyebrows lifted as though in a trance. Her ease and charm and coquetry, all signs of conventionality, vanished in a flash. Was she a goddess? Or a demon? I found myself wondering. . . .

White flashed between the horse's front legs as she deftly uncovered its eyes, gliding beneath its belly through its legs, and emerged at its side.[1]

After spending the night at the woman's cottage, the ascetic reluctantly resumes his pilgrimage in the morning. Feeling torn by his sexual desire and his resistance to that desire, he pauses by a waterfall to ponder his commitment to the priesthood. The manservant, returning from his errand, happens upon the confused ascetic and reveals that the woman is a "demon/goddess" who turns lusty men into beasts and that the errant peddler (whom the ascetic was tracking) has already been transformed into the horse just sold. Enlightened, the ascetic escapes and lives to tell the story later to a young man (the primary narrator).

Inouye has discussed *Kōya hijiri* and "Kechō" (Transfigured bird, 1898) in his "Water Imagery in the Works of Izumi Kyōka" as prototype manuscripts that yielded a "privileged narrative (or metastory) in which a young male encounters an older, sexually alluring woman in a watery (and therefore threatening) environment."[2] This part of my study will aim to redescribe the demon/goddess/mother figures of Kyōka's "metastory," primarily in these two prototype texts as well as a later narrative, *Yōken kibun* (The tale of the enchanted sword, 1920), as markers of an historical nostalgia in relation to a *gendered* imaginary. (Nostalgia differs from tradition in that it begins only where tradition is perceived to be lost. Whereas tradition is imagined as revitalizable, preservable, and reenactable, and thus marks its object with presence, nostalgia marks its object with loss. Nostalgia represents the quest for and the fear of an imaginary past in the present—as a discursive production of the past clearly subordinated to the political and sociocultural agenda of the present. By using the word *nostalgia* I hope to highlight the constructivity of purported origin.) The texts evidence a modern production of an imaginary origin, which has been summarily maternalized, alternately abjected and othered—pluralized, partialized, eroticized, polluted, and spiritualized.

This chapter focuses on how the dangerous woman signifies in Kyōka's narratives as a perpetually slipping signifier, ciphered and displaced and composed of condensed *fragments* of premodern literary archetypes. Moreover, her "alterity" is most evident in her lack of self-containment, or unboundedness, that overflows the borders of her as individual to "contaminate" or otherwise affect the natural and human environments around her. Brief synopses of the other two tales follow.

Yōken kibun essentially consists of two parallel tales. The narrative present is 1793. Seisaburō, the young page of a samurai who is visiting Koishikawa (one of the 35 prefectures of Edo, located in present-day Bunkyō-ku in Tokyo) encounters, and is instantly smitten by, an outcaste woman (a *torioi*) named Omachi.[3] Her gift to him, an iris flower, pollutes him:

With faintly trembling fingertips, she placed the iris into Seisaburō's outstretched hand. That she had not cut short the stalk and trimmed the leaves revealed her gentle, compassionate, and merciful nature. The thin blade swiftly shaving the water's surface was like the shimmer of a young silvery fish, and a vermilion flash, quick as a pinky-finger pledge was her sleeve lining fluttering like boiling blood.[4]

Although Seisaburō, urged by his companions, discards the blossom, he has been irrevocably "enchanted" as well as "polluted," and he searches to find her again. The parallel tale focuses on the mystery of two underwater caves near a waterfall bordering a temple in the same province, which have long been the site of repeated drownings. Suddenly the number of fatalities rises precipitously. A local temple caretaker challenges the demon spirit assumed to be lodged within the underwater caves and responsible for the drownings. The caretaker dives into the caves, discovering and removing a strange sword. Mysteriously, the sword appears to repeatedly return on its own to the cave where it was found. Eventually the two tales are interwoven, as it is revealed that Omachi has been stealing the sword and returning it to one of the caves to stab herself, thereby purifying her own polluted blood.[5] Seisaburō pulls her from the cave and drinks her blood as she dies, receiving both her pollution and a mysterious knowledge of swordsmithing.

"Kechō" is more impressionistic than emplotted: the little boy protagonist, Ren, slips effortlessly between a world of fantasy and the everyday world, guided by his ever-present, idealized mother: "Returning home, we'd have dinner. Afterward, in bed, I would look at Mother's thin, beautiful, noble face, gentle and reliable. Her hair would be loosely gathered back, and when I tried to talk, she would shush me. Fully intending to stay awake, I would drift off into sleep" (413–14).[6] Mother is the toll taker and proprietress of a bridge that separates the town from the provinces. The boy and his mother inhabit geographical liminality—neither urban nor rural, bordering both. The bridge, of course, is an index of passage; here it entices diffusions. The narration is split between the deeply reflective adult writer-narrator, who attempts to reinhabit the consciousness of his younger self, and that younger self, the barely reflexive, more purely experiential child for whom the distinction between reality and fantasy is still porous and uncertain. Meandering through various associative details from Ren's childhood, the last several pages describe his search for a mythical winged sister who, according to Mother, has saved him from death by drowning.

All three narratives are structured around enigmas. There are three interlinked mysteries in *Yōken kibun* that are never solved: Who and what is

Omachi, where did the sword come from and is it magically empowered, and what is the relationship of Omachi and the sword to the demon caves? These three enigmas, continually displaced onto one another, propel the narrative. Moreover, the material sword is repeatedly displaced, as is the polluting iris handed from Omachi to Seisaburō. The sword can neither be confined/held nor explained. After Omachi stabs herself in the cave, the sword imparts a mysterious mastery of swordsmithing to Seisaburō, who is thereby simultaneously sainted and defiled: he becomes the supreme grand master of swordsmithing and yet remains *hinin*. The three mysteries merge in connection to Omachi when Seisaburō dives into the water to save her. Omachi's confession that she stole the sword, "If you actually touched me, I can never apologize enough—it was I who borrowed the sword Sakuden took from underwater—twice, three times—as many as three times" (674), does nothing to solve the original enigmas: What is her connection to the demon caves, and how did the sword get there in the first place? Instead of solving these mysteries, she dies. Seizure of the searched-for signifier (Omachi) splits and disintegrates meaning, rather than yielding significatory certainty, by once more displacing significance. The mystery of the caves remains as it was before her appearance:

Under the big waterfall was a rock platform called Large Mortar, and every year several people were dragged off it and drowned. So, since antiquity, it had been called the Sekiguchi demon dwelling. Everyone knew this, and feared and avoided the spot, but with summer came swimmers, and people chasing fireflies, and four or five men or women alike would undoubtedly lose their lives. However, beginning two years ago and last year as well, there had been a sudden increase in fatalities, up to eight or nine people per year. This year, horridly, six lives had already been claimed just since the water had turned warm. And, because it was said that you did not even have to go into the water, but that simply walking along the river bank would make a person weak-kneed and dizzy, they suspected that early summer daylight might be mistaken for some illusory darkness and turn the scattered, churning waves into white mountain roses and sunflowers from the countryside, and suddenly, at the outskirts of town, the Koishi tributary of the wide Edo River would resemble a trail through deep mountains. (636–37)

Jacques Lacan has written that the desire for a never-graspable object (in Lacan's episteme, naturalized as the nonexistent phallus, which stands in for the missing object of originary desire) is the primary law of motivation and that this desire is enacted through a series of displacements.[7] All attempts in *Yōken kibun* to explain "origin" and to seize the signifiers of a disappeared past—Omachi (who, as I will elaborate, could thus be described as the phallus or the ciphered signifier for the originary object)—

end in further displacement. Omachi dies but continues to appear as a
ghost; her presence within the narrative is essentially unchanged. As she
was before her "death," she is ephemeral and unseizable.

In *Kōya hijiri*, the ascetic sets out after the offensive herbal medicine
peddler into the woman's realm, but his motivation to help the herbalist
soon yields to his battle against his own sexual desire for the woman. As
in *Yōken kibun*, there is also an explanation of sorts about the mountain
sorceress, given to the ascetic by the old man. However, it amounts to little more than an account of her life and her gradual control over and use
of her powers. She remains ciphered, as does Omachi. Most intriguingly,
why is the ascetic spared, when it is written that at the stream, which is
somehow connected to her and which endows her with additional powers, "she has spared no one"? (436). Likewise, Ren's search for Sister in
"Kechō" never truly solves the question of who Sister is. Does she exist?
Or is she merely an aspect of Mother? In these narratives, the woman embodies mystery and is the motivating and desired forbidden object; she is
both lack and a symbol for loss. All three stories are internally motivated
by the desire to represence loss (to find, hold, or have the woman). Loss is
entangled with female bodies as partial objects and as floating, cipher-sig-
nifiers. The woman defies seizure and demystification; she is tantalizing
yet always beyond the grasp of the men (or boy) who seek her.

Premodernity in Kyōka's texts is most frequently embodied by the dangerous, enchanting women—symbols of loss—who also function as mediums to past and imagined worlds, as in this passage from *Yōken kibun*:

In the haze from the incense smoke that hung like a scented black gauze, her hips
partly obscured by the collection box, was the mysterious white nude figure of a
seated woman, her bare, translucent back turned, sloping shoulders gleaming like
reflecting snow, upswept, fancy hair shining. Blankly, at the unexpected noise, the
loose hair framing her face flouncing, she jumped up. . . . In the line of her nose and
her long eyebrows, touched with a faint blush, was something that recalled a previous world.

Seisaburō retreated, retreated, and retreated and stood there trembling.

And then, inside the door, there was not even the faintest breath of anything
at all.

Surely it could not be—was it a phantom? A dream? Seisaburō suddenly felt as
though he were returning to his senses. The woman's figure faded as the day darkened slightly all around him and he saw that dusk was at hand. (666)

Kyōka's exteriorized female characterizations were reminiscent of earlier genres, in marked contrast to others of his generation that reproduced

popular discourses valorizing "civilization and enlightenment" (Western rationalism) and narrative interiority modeled on the Western novel.[8] In this Kyōka's project can be compared to that of Yanagita Kunio (1875–1962), who led Meiji *minzokugaku* (folk studies), which historian Harry Harootunian has described as having been culled from the remnants of Edo nativism to form one ideological trajectory within the larger realm of Meiji cultural discourses.[9] Harootunian argued that for folklorists like Yanagita, the "critique [of the modern state] . . . turned toward constituting a culture from the dispersed fragments of the past, as an alternative to modern civilization [*bunmei*] and the bureaucratic state that had evolved since the beginning of the Meiji period."[10] In Kyōka's work, it is precisely gathered fragments that appear to constitute a premodern whole. Although for both Yanagita and Kyōka women were certainly not the only vessel for the premodern, Kyōka differed from Yanagita in his fetishization of femaleness as the predominant vessel for the nostalgic uncanny.[11] Although this gendered imaginary also appears in Yanagita's writing, Kyōka obsessively, and, one might say compulsively, portrayed women as the supreme repository for premodern "fragments," thereby linking women, exteriority, and supplement.[12] "Woman" in Kyōka's narratives is the site that enables the circulation of male desire — the desire for the othered, premodern, and the not-self; as such she is fully subordinated to the phallic (and homosocial) libidinal economy. Indeed, she has no presence except as the discursive location for a homosocial imaginary, nostalgia, and eroticism. As Seisaburō and his companions happen upon the outcaste quarters, they call out requesting permission to pass through. Omachi's answer constitutes *Yōken kibun*'s first encounter with her:

A voice answered from inside the dim earthen-floored hut, a purple shadow with a faint white face. . . . She glided out toward the eaves beside the little stream, her fancy, upswept hair so glossy it looked wet—spillable. The minstrel girl was so captivating that she was more eye-openingly lovely than the irises, her bare legs snowy against the scarlet silk crepe of her skirt.
    "Welcome."
    "Thank you. Shall we?"
    Gennoshin said reflexively.
    "Let's go."
    "Quietly, please—"
    Only her red-rimmed shadow touched the water, her pale, blue-spotted sash bending as she courteously bowed slightly as though seeing them off. (643)

The narrator compares gazing at her to "peering at a blurred shadow of some far-off place, in a past more than one hundred years ago that separated the boundaries of the world of men and that of enchantment" (645). In *Kōya hijiri*, the ascetic finds the dangerous woman (sorceress/demon) far off an ordinary path by following an ancient, disused footpath, folded deep within the mountain interior beyond a deserted town. He must traverse a forest so deep that he hears leaves falling and wonders "for how many decades had these leaves been delayed in their descent before finally touching the ground for the first time?" (392). The woman is unable to offer him hot water for tea or a bath; her house, harkening back to precivilization, stands open, exposed to the elements. "There was nothing suggesting a gateway" (396). He ponders, "Where was the rest of the world?" (403).

Meiji folklorists rejected the Western (ethnically) racialized Other to modernity (which would have included Asians) and instead posited as Other, as Harootunian stated, "the repressed alterity of a more authentic life that had existed prior to the imperative of Western rationality, which had to be recalled before Japanese were altogether assimilated to the imperial requirements of Western epistemology."[13] For Kyōka (and constituting one Meiji propensity), this authentic nativism works best when feminized in the trope of the dangerous woman. She may then be consumed, as the site of alterity that allows for the circulation of male desire and imagination. She embodies the delicious (im)possibility of nostalgic return.

Her alterity repeatedly takes forms that are antithetical to "boundedness"; she embodies spillages and excess, liquidities and viscosities. Femaleness as enigma or cipher yields only to representations of the dangerous woman leaking through the boundaries of her own containment and making heterogeneous the purported internal homogeneity of the masculine subjects who struggle to find and possess her but who cannot hold (define) her. Abetting the quest to "refind" loss, tying together the three apparently disparate female figures from *Kōya hijiri*, *Yōken kibun*, and "Kechō," is their bodily seepage into uncanny topographies (*ikai*) reminiscent of either a premodern past or an amorphous primordial or other, supernatural worlds. As has been amply argued in many commentaries on Kyōka's works, the dangerous woman is materially indistinguishable from the fluidity of water. Tanemura wrote, "Precisely because . . . a yearned-for woman glides through and emerges from water, it is also a flow that brings relief and ties present-day agony to bygone days."[14] Tanemura identifies femaleness (through water as her abode and symbol) with nostalgic comfort and modern desire as the marker for a romanticized past.

As the *Kōya hijiri* ascetic takes his leave in the morning, the woman laments,

We will not likely meet again, and I will grow old and withered in the mountains, but if you ever see white peach blossoms floating anywhere, even in the tiniest trickle of a stream, think of them as me, sunken deep beneath the waters of the valley stream, torn to tatters. (428)

Later, seized with desire for the woman, the ascetic pauses indecisively at a stream bank. Staring into the flowing water, he envisions her body tossed among the waves:

I saw her visage float up and sink in the . . . waterfall, vivid as a picture. It sank only to resurface, her skin pulverized to powder as the water fragmented into a thousand threads, like petals scattered upon the stream. Repeatedly her face, breasts, arms, and legs formed a floating, sinking figure, dissolving in a flash and reforming just as quickly. (429)

Water is one medium by which a putative female uncontainability may transcend the borders of individuated subjectivity and leak out into the narrative topographies, transforming and merging with the landscape from which she emerges. In each of the three narratives, and throughout Kyōka's works, not only is woman inseparable from and dissolved in water, but in her environs water overflows its boundaries to establish new, porous ones, viscously demarcating the premodern, abjected female realm from the modern, rational, phallic world. Strangely flooded paths reroute both *Yōken kibun*'s Seisaburō and *Kōya hijiri*'s ascetic from their intended pathways into the women's domains. In *Kōya hijiri*, a magic, healing stream that rejuvenates the woman also serves as the location where she transforms seduced men into beasts. In "Kechō," Sister only appears in the river at the moment when Ren is in between life and death.

In *Kōya hijiri*, femaleness seeps out of the woman and taints the landscape in myriad manners, rendering it amorphous. Thus, rain and leeches become a merged, plural phenomenon:

I screamed out my terror. What next? A long, black, sinuous rain poured down over me. I watched as it piled up over my sandal tops, and more amassed over that, and more, clinging alongside my feet until I could no longer see my toes—was it my imagination?—one by one the black strips swelled and thickened, attaching themselves to my veins, living, sucking blood. (394)

Or trees turn to leeches. The ascetic imagines that the leeches, "greedy, primitive creatures . . . camped here since creation" (394) will suck the blood of all passersby only to vomit all the blood they had sucked—a vomit that would dissolve the earth and turn the entire mountainside into a single grand swamp of blood and mud. One after another the huge trees blocking out the sun and darkening the forest even in daytime would break apart into fragments that turned into leeches. . . .[15]

Dazedly I envisioned that the destruction of the human race would not come from some rupture in the earth's thin crust, or from fire raining from the heavens, or because great oceans flooded the earth. This transformation of Hida Forest into leeches was the beginning of the end as thin, black worms swam in muddied blood and gave birth to a new age. (394)

Pathways become snakes. "The path forked. One side soared steeply, thick with grass to the pathsides. It snaked around behind a single cypress tree some four or five armspreads thick" (385). And later, "Up the twisting, serpentine incline I went, for some five more miles, right into the heart of the mountain" (391). Along this snaky path lurk snakes "like wriggling bridges, heads and tails buried in the grass on opposite sides of the trail. . . . Six hundred or so yards beyond, another, sunning its body, head and tail concealed, just like the first one, squirming" (389). Pine trees resemble serpents, with "bark like the scales of a snake. Pine trees have often been aptly likened to vipers. There was one robust pine on the cliff in particular that was twisted just like an awful snake; incredulous, I envisioned it as a lengthy, enormous snake, head and tail buried in the grass" (412). Water commingles with snakes to become eels:

I glanced at the cypress tree that intersected the narrow trail, jutting upward like a rainbow toward the sky, extending above the endless rice fields. The earth at the grand base of the trunk was gnarled with innumerable exposed roots like a swarm of large eels. Water gushed in a single stream from those roots, to flow straight down my intended route. Strangely, rather than pooling in the rice field, the water cascaded along the path like a rushing river for some two or three hundred yards, as far as a patch of trees. (385)

Female seepage into the landscape begins to transform the ascetic, long before the woman's actual appearance, into something snakelike: "Seeing no alternative, I stepped over it [the snake]. Just then the snake stretched. The hair on my body prickled in horror, my pores grew clammy, and all the blood drained rapidly from my face, turning me pale as the snake" (390). Phallic self-containment, or modern subjectivity, is profoundly unsettled by the women who inhabit Kyōka's estranged, phantasmatic topographies.

Actual encounters trace female figures with a mixture of partialized descriptions and allude to a variety of tropes from the earliest writings and the medieval canon. *Nanchi shinjū* (Southern love suicides, 1912) is modeled on the *nō* play *Dōjōji* and on the serpent-demoness who has enjoyed a long reign of terror in virtually every classical Japanese genre and who appears in many of Kyōka's other texts, such as "Ehon no haru" (Picture-book spring, 1926).[16] (The popular Western assumption that the snake must be symbolic of the penis notwithstanding, in the Japanese canon, as in Chinese and Indian tales, the snake-deity or demon is consistently gendered female and thus represents "the phallus" more than the penis.) Yet, as Muramatsu notes, *Nanchi shinjū* is also modeled on a tale from Yanagita Kunio's *Tōno monogatari* (Tales of Tōno, 1910) as well as on a tale from the *Konjaku monogatari shū* (*Tales of Times Now Past*, ca. 1108).[17]

In apparent resistance to modernity and interiority, Kyōka molded the dangerous woman by revitalizing a synergistic and thickly eroticized version of female figures of the medieval tradition. She is thus *not* the archetypes of Heian, or medieval, or Edo fiction. For example, the woman living isolated deep in the mountains in *Kōya hijiri* evokes the medieval archetype of the *yamamba* or mountain hag, a witch who pounced on and devoured those hapless male travelers who strayed into her domain. The *yamamba* proper, however, was a fixed medieval trope.[18] In Kyōka's narratives, she is displaced from her fixity and set afloat in a plurality that eroticizes her and mixes her up with Shinto shamanesses, archaic serpent-demons, and the bird-woman deities of folklore and fairy tales. The winged sister of *Yōken kibun* takes her form from the bird-women of Japan's earliest texts, such as the *Kojiki* (712), medieval collections of legends such as the *Konjaku monogatari shū*, and from a variety of regional fairy tales and folklore.[19] *Kōya hijiri*'s woman is also reminiscent of the *miko* shamans who acted as mediums for Shinto deities. The snake-woman, as discussed above, an archetype of archaic and medieval written, performative, and orally transmitted narratives, makes a veiled appearance in the ascetic's first encounter with *Kōya hijiri*'s demon/goddess. Announcing himself at the cottage, the ascetic hears "a woman's voice answer . . . from the direction of the storehouse. I retreated . . . expecting a strange creature, white neck scaled like a reptile, to crawl forth, tail dragging" (398). Later, the ascetic likens her to the infamous lover of the Chinese Tang emperor Xuan Zong, Yang Guifei, foreshadowing the potentially disastrous consequences of an erotic liaison with her: "The truth is, I was thinking that she surely would not have been out of place on Li Mountain, were she adorned with hammered-gold, carved, and jeweled hairpins, draped in a butterfly-light kimono, wearing jewel-studded slippers" (423–24).[20]

Many critics have noted the Meiji "flavors" that nuance Kyōka's work even as they insist that Kyōka represents a "premodern Japanese aesthetic" transcending specific time frames to "fragrance" all Japanese art forms throughout history. The premodern, which is also held to be distinctly Japanese, so often heralded by eroticized women, is present, argued many critics, in the structures, themes, and literary style that mark Kyōka's writings. For example, on the topic of how Kyōka's dramas "enticingly string the spectator along in suspense [*hippate iku*]" in a 1991 dialogue with the actor Bandō Tamasaburō, Gunji Masakatsu proclaims, "To speak broadly, that [stringing along] is a special characteristic of Japanese plays, such as kabuki. That Japanese feature [*Nihonteki na tokoro*] takes on an intense emotionality in Kyōka."[21] Although Tamasaburō seems to want to nuance Gunji's reading of Kyōka as "purely Japanese," Gunji insists that Kyōka is "extremely Japanese-ee" (*sugoku Nihonteki*). Gunji compares Kyōka's writing with Edo *ukiyo-e* (paintings) as well as with kabuki and notes the Meiji "odor" (*nioi*) in his narratives, shifting easily from any of the modern markers of a premodern "aesthetic."[22] Even those critics who have argued for an historicized reading of Kyōka, such as Tanemura Suehiro, who wrote "Kyōka was new. He was so new that he was too new to be thought of as new"[23] have accepted his rendering of dangerous women as the "essence" of femaleness and thus as a temporally and socioculturally transcendental configuration. I seek to problematize, through a shift in perspective, the predominant critical insistence that Kyōka somehow transcended his time as a signifier of an ahistorical "Japanese aesthetic." Indeed, Kyōka's perceived transcendentalism (whether rendered in terms of gender constructs or his discursive project as a whole) is itself part of the phallic agenda (an agenda dedicated to the maintenance of the hegemony of a masculinist, phallocentric system that is in part consolidated through discourse) that is reiterated through such insistence. The dominant critical framing of Kyōka as a "traditionalist" protects both "Japaneseness" and phallic integrity by disguising their constructivity. The "policing" of Kyōka as "the Japanese Thing" serves to protect the borders of the construct against the slippage of the "Japanese Thing" itself.[24] For Kyōka, "mother's" abjected borderless slippages (her abjected aspects and the positing of her as the locus for originary desire, troped as the dangerous woman) provide the site for the safe, and mediated, circulations of his protagonists'/readers' desire. Male distance from the borders of the abject is secured through *her* inextricability from bodily and discursive pluralities.

At the same time as it differs from (even as it evokes) premodern archetypes, the description of the woman coaxing the herbalist-turned-into-horse also departs radically from the standards of early-twentieth-century Japanese realism and naturalism:

In a wave the mountains behind, the ridge opposite, the peaks to left and right, front and back, one by one turned their beaks, raising their heads to peer down upon this group gathered in another world, a beautiful woman beneath the moon, motionless, facing a horse, an old man await behind her. The deep mountain air darkened and closed in upon us.

Was that a breeze? It was tepid. Just then the woman bared first her left shoulder, then slipped her right arm free and brought it around in front. She was holding her summer kimono crumpled at her full breasts, her nakedness not even veiled by mist.

The skin on the horse's stomach and back sagged, soaked now with sweat, and the braced legs grew supple; atremble, it lowered its head, blowing out a handful of white bubbles, and bowed down on its front legs. Placing her hand beneath its jaw she draped her kimono lightly over its eyes. Just then.

The rabbit danced lithely, face upturned to the hazy moonlight, suffused with a ghostliness. White flashed between the horse's front legs as she deftly uncovered its eyes, gliding beneath its belly through its legs, and emerged at its side. (417–18)

Most writers from Meiji through Taisho eagerly adopted characterizations of the new, modern woman. One example is Tayama Katai's "Futon" ("The Quilt," 1907), a text commonly heralded as the prototype *shishōsetsu* (personal, confessional narrative), the genre that dominated the literary scene for most of the twentieth century. In contrast to Kyōka's prose, a description from Tayama's "Futon" adheres to the principles of Japanese naturalism. The narrator/protagonist, Tokio, describes his female student's room as follows:

The large bookcase that had dwarfed the Western-style one in Tokio's study was to the side of a lacquered papier-mâché desk. On top of the desk lay a mirror, a tin of rouge and one of white powder, and a large flask filled with potassium bromide. This last item was to relieve her otherwise severe, occasional nervous headaches. A brand new set of the complete works of Turgenev stood out prominently from among the collected works of Kōyō, some puppet plays by Chikamatsu, and the English textbooks on the bookshelf.[25]

Much of the commentary on "Futon," the story of a middle-aged male writer's erotic infatuation with his young female student, has focused on the tormented, confessional interiority of the protagonist. Interiorized characterizations, as the critic Karatani Kōjin has shown, were inseparable from the linguistic movement through which modern subjectivity was configured by an inversion that reshaped language to produce a "thinking subject" in text who reflected on the exterior world of objects.[26] About Kunikida Doppo, an early proponent of linguistic standardization and realism in literature, Karatani wrote,

[For Kunikida] the illusion that there is something like a "true self" has taken deep root. It is an illusion that is established when writing has come to be seen as derivative and that voice that is most immediate to the self, and that constitutes self-consciousness, is privileged. The psychological person, who begins and ends in interiority, has come into existence.[27]

Just as a shift in perspective produced modern subjectivity, the intrinsic phallicism and maleness of that subject was dependent on a perspectival change predicated on femaleness as the repository of a literary nativism (as I will elaborate) and as the arena of exclusion or the supplement to the subject. Tokio, unlike Kyōka's protagonists, desires the symbol of the modern, here epitomized by the young girl, and regards his old-fashioned wife, the mother of his children, with erotic distaste. The student functions purely as an object of exchange among her father, her boyfriend, and Tokio and is devalued when her virginity is questioned. The wife-mother has been severed from erotic value. In spite of the thematic conflicts over modernity and tradition, what "Futon" actually chronicles is an already functioning, self-justifying, modern homosocial libidinal economy. (To borrow Karatani's phrasing, its "origins" are already suppressed.)[28] In Kyōka's texts, it is the struggles over establishing modernity that are chronicled—the Meiji/Taisho ambivalence toward its own modernity, co-present with Tayama and other naturalists' postures. Unlike the naturalists' female characterizations and writing styles, Kyōka's dangerous woman is not an attempt to produce a sign of narrative transparency.

Transparency not only assumes a one-to-one correlation between signifier and signified but it also presupposes an individual who has a distinct, modern interiority from which a "true" voice may emerge. Kyōka's female narrative "abject," as the supplement to the subject, possesses contours rather than an interior. She defines man's parameters by her aberration from him. The texts rarely speak from her internal subject position to report her thoughts (although her *enunciations* are reported as if verbatim, but as with other speaking subjects, they are actually embedded within a web of deferred narrations).[29] She is an overfilled signifier. Surplus to any one-to-one correlation between herself and a significance, she epitomizes slippage and plurality.

Seizing on the overt difference between Kyōka's "archetypal" (exteriorized) female figures and the realism of the women depicted by his contemporaries (by writers such as Tayama), critics have (re)inscribed Kyōka's work with a thick veneer of exteriority. Tanemura, as quoted at the beginning of this chapter, called Kyōka's women "archetypes filled with water." Takahashi Yoshitaka wrote: "One special characteristic of Kyōka's narratives is his character types. That is, they are the stereotypical characters who appear in the scenes of *setsuwa, rakugo, kōshaku* [legend, comic monologue, storytelling], and the *monogatari* [tale fiction] of antiquity."[30]

Yet the supposedly stereotypical or archetypal figures are precisely no more than fragments of an imagined past. Kyōka's female figures are defixed pluralities circulating a modern idea of tradition. Far from the realistic descriptions that accompanied the naturalists' discovery and expression of inner voice, Kyōka's narratives searched for literary origin: the poeticized location inhabited by legend, the inscription on an oralized landscape of the uncanny. This quest is again reminiscent of that of Yanagita Kunio, who likewise sought to locate a Japaneseness in many of the same previously marginalized voices: children, people of the mountains, old oral tales. (In a commentary on Yanagita included in a volume of Yanagita's collected works, Nagaike Kenji mentions Kyōka several times, for example.)[31] Unlike Yanagita, who wanted to locate a people and a culture (even if his project turned out in the end to be purely discursive), Kyōka *looked* for an inscription, a writing, a discursive production. Kyōka's "metastory" functioned as did Yanagita's "folklore" to produce the dangerous woman as the nameless surplus within, yet as always exceeding the symbolic or discursive.

Harootunian's following comment on Yanagita has resonance for a reading of Kyōka: "Yanagita's countryside was an imaginary, constructed from a discourse aimed at conserving and preserving traces of a lost presence . . . to constitute a timeless rural Japan that was 'always already there.'"[32] The sorceress is a modern *discursive* construct—she is enveloped within always once-more deferred narration. Harootunian holds that Edo nativists' foregrounding of the body as the site for becoming commensurate with the Real through revitalizing an (imaginary) past is transformed into *discourse* for Yanagita in Meiji.[33] Yanagita, says Harootunian, sought fulfillment through "the *description* of the figure of folk life. . . . in the formulation of *minzokugaku*, discourse itself became place—that is to say, the former discourse on place was inverted into the place of discourse. . . . Daily life as the lived experience of the folk . . . existed in ethnology only as an effect of a constructed discourse called folklore" (Harootunian's emphasis).[34] Kyōka's women *inhabit* topographies that are, as noted above, *already* no more than language (the material landscapes are subordinated to their poetic inscriptions).[35] These linguistic topoi usher protagonist and reader alike toward ever-increasing *lack*, as they, like the dangerous woman, signal the intersection of death and language in the very body of "maternalized-femaleness." It is from this supplement that the protagonists, and the readers, may approach the abject but then retreat to (re)discover their own materiality, existence, modernity.

As Marilyn Ivy has written, as a pretext to the Meiji-period folklorist Yanagita's nostalgic gesture toward recuperating something unmistakably "Japanese" in the face of encroaching Westernization and modernization, was the a priori disappearance of the object of study. She notes a collusion between ethnography and certain literature of the period in their movement toward uncanniness or their "ghostly complicity."[36] Yanagita undertook studies of old Japanese oral tales as they were told in Meiji Japan. Many of the tales that he recorded were of ghosts and mysterious, unexplainable happenings. To gender Ivy's discussion within the context of my study, it would be well to take into account Yanagita's description, in his *Yama no jinsei*, of the *yamamba*, a description that vacillates between "rationalism" and "inexplicability" (she is partly reconfigured as an hysteric and her madness is attributed precisely to her maternity), and she is even likened to the Virgin Mary. An indulgently long, but I think rewarding, sample follows:

Even in late Meiji, rumors abound about the sightings of female mountain deities [*yamahime*] mostly around the Hiroto waterfall by Nippokōge in the foothills of Nakinosen in Sakushū. These *yamahime* are naked but for rags wrapped about their hips and have glittering blue eyes and reddish hair. They have been killed by loggers when, on occasion, they wandered too close to where people live and were caught peeping into the huts of those loggers. However, a careful investigation of such rumors reveals that these *yamahime* were once [ordinary] women of adjoining towns who had gone mad long before and abandoned their homes.

It was not discontent and weariness for life that had sent these women off to hide in the mountains. It is clear to anyone who saw what they did that they had gone mad. Kanō Kōkichi told me a story about a young woman who tried to flee into the mountains from the foothills of Tashirodake, which borders Ugo and Tsugaru. A large group of her neighbors ran after her, but when they caught her and tried to bring her back with them, she shook them off with an amazing show of strength and disappeared into the mountains.

. . .

That many of the village women who fled to the mountains did so after giving birth may well be an important clue to the problem. Since antiquity Japan has abounded in stories of how women who served at shrines received summons from the gods and bore the children of deities. That is to say, *miko* [virgins serving shrines] who served as the holy mothers of the sons of deities were revered as possessing a special, holy spirit, quite similar to practices such as the Christian belief in virgin birth [The Virgin Mary].[37]

Yanagita's web of confusions creates more mystery than explanation: from a mixture of reified maternity and unfathomable hysteria emerges the modern *yamamba*. There are indeed underlying structural complicities (even in their confusion) between Yanagita's discursive productions of the past, Meiji discourses on maternity and "Western rationalism," and Kyōka's clearly demarcated fictional ones. As Slavoj Žižek has written, "The end of classical subjectivity, of course, is the very point of the emergence of the modern hysterical subject."[38] In *Yama no jinsei*, moreover, Yanagita employs a pseudoscientific causality with rationalized roots to tame the uncanny through the medium of writing side by side with his transformation of the *yamamba* into the hysteric; at the same time, he refuses his own "rationalism" so he may vicariously enjoy the thrill of the delightfully terrifying and disappeared past. Yanagita's discussion of the mountain women shuttles between the two alternatives described by Hélène Cixous and Catherine Clément:

As long as the sorceress is still free, at the sabbat, in the forest, she is a sensitivity that is completely exposed—all open skin, natural animal, odorous, and deliciously dirty. When she is caught, when the scene of inquisition is formed around her, in the same way that the medical scene later forms around the hysteric, she withdraws into herself, she cries, she has numb spots, she vomits. She has become hysterical.[39]

Kyōka's narratives sought, perversely, to reiterate the experience of approaching the uncanny, yet just as in Yanagita's tale, it is an experience distanced by writing.

The process of seeking a hidden premodern is thus also a drive toward the annihilation of the object, since its very *difference* is erased in the possession/production by the modern. To recapture "origin" in the body of the Other, if the Other has been configured as the abjected self (the culturally repulsive aspects of the premodern and the undifferentiated maternal body), either its radical difference must be reconceptualized within a web of homogeneity and deep familiarity (thus effectively destroying it as abject) or abjection must be differently affirmed to maintain the integrity of the subject. Although, as Harootunian argued, through Yanagita's folkloric studies, the *jōmin* (common people, previously not seen as homogeneous to the elite urban population) are subsumed within a discourse of the same, and, as I have argued, mothers become people too, for Kyōka and Yanagita the maternalized femaleness that is always surplus to the phallic (her erotic, leaking, boundless, and, moreover, penisless otherness) is simultaneously radically excluded as the locus for abjected alterity. From this perspective, both Yanagita and Kyōka, as well as other Meiji/ Taisho writers, can be described as "socioculturally" borderline or as straddling that confusion between subjectivity and diffusion, if one extends the psychoanalytic terminology. Modern renditions of archaic female archetypes thus become one vessel for an attempt to work through the schisms inherent in modernity.

Perverse Maternity:
Blood from the Breast

Umbilicated with death in his aggressive thrust towards the
desired object, warding off death through symbolic fecundity,
which creates objects of wisdom, man goes round the feminine, which is his abyss and his night. Respectful and re-
spectable love for an idealized (maternal) object spares the delights and the pangs of sadomasochism—the divine is finally
a goddess, priestess of archaic power, which allows less to re-
press than to separate raving desire from its refinement, from
its dialectic and academic education on behalf of the city-
state.   — J U L I A   K R I S T E V A
Tales of Love

The deep passion connecting the two [extremes of beauty and
eroticism in Kyōka's texts] can only be described using the
phrase "mother-love."   — K A S A H A R A   N O B U O
"Kyōka ni okeru 'haha naru mono' "

"Kechō" is a tale overtly about maternity and its relation to borders, boundaries, and transgressions. Ren describes the episode in which
his mythical sister has saved him from death by drowning:

A flash of light, a pure red ray, illuminated the area, my body wrapped within it; I
was gasping for breath, and it felt as though my body were separated from the
earth, carried in the arms of something cold, up to a place taller than the summit

on the tip of the mountain, which I could see far in the distance. I remember big, beautiful eyes, wet hair cascading over a shoulder and sticking to my cheek as I clung steadily, eyes shut. It was not a dream. (430)

Determined to locate the beautiful winged woman who Mother claims saved him, Ren begins his fruitless search at a bird store. Redirected by Mother, he continues to seek Sister in the vast open expanse of fields and sky. The topographical marginality in which characters and readers are placed facilitates thematic transgression of realism and the narrative ascent into other realms. Ren's description of the wilderness where he goes in search of Sister is eerie, mysterious, and awesome:

Because it seemed as though I were distanced from the world, separated from people, I felt loneliness, I felt sadness, uncertainty, and apprehension. A bad feeling. A bad feeling.

The blurry plum branch seemed to be standing with outstretched hand. Looking over the area, it was pitch-black—what was that far in the distance calling "Ho, ho"? As though pushing open the fields' edges with its clear call, "ton, ton, ton, ton," echoing like the beating of a drum, the birdcall coming from far away was that of an owl. (434)

The enigma of where Sister dwells is never resolved: Ren wonders, as the narrative ends, is Sister perhaps really Mother?

For Kyōka, though maternalized femaleness is the locus for alterity, not surprisingly even the "maternal" turns out to be, on closer examination, a dubious construct. Multiple reaffirmations of Kyōka's "mother complex" in the critical writings about Kyōka discover maternity in nonmothers.[1] For Kyōka only occasionally (in texts such as "Kechō," for example) wrote about actual mothers. More commonly, the figures that have been rendered maternal in critical commentaries are women who are more mature than the male protagonists but who are not their biological, or even provisional, mothers. In *Kōya hijiri*, the woman's idiot husband generates her maternity. Helpless and crippled, he is described thus:

[He] had a childlike aura, his expressionless, heavily lidded eyes were clouded. . . . He sat as though half dead, in a skimpy kimono. . . . A padded vest was fastened over his chest, but as though he were dressed in baby clothes, the fat flesh of his sleek, curved belly swelled out, resembling a taut drum. His strangely shaped navel protruded like a squash stem. He was fingering this with one hand while dangling the other in midair like a ghost. (397)

This unusual navel (which is, of course, a remnant of the umbilical cord, the ever-present trace of presubjectivity and of the maternal-infant symbiotic dyad) is the object of repeated (masturbatory) fondling by the idiot youth-husband, an act subjected to reiterated notation by the observing protagonist. The passage above, since it is meant to be humorous, moves the text toward primary-process discharge of excitement (developmentally the earliest means by which the ego handles the discharge of drive energy), both easing the rupture of separation and soothing the textual retrogression toward the abyss of self-diffusion.[2] The idiot's bizarre navel links him to a maternalized, idealized, and yet othered pre-Symbolic realm (also to death); barely able to talk, the youth sings beautifully. The ascetic marvels that it is "as though a voice from a previous life were channeled through his swollen belly from the spirit realm" (423). Severed from signification (the expression of interiority through words with meaning), the young man has access to music, rhythm, or vocalizations that suggest, in Kristevian terms, the semiotic, or poetic language.[3] The transformation of nonmothers into mothers reiterates the postulation of the eroticized maternal-body as the site for the circulation of desire and the erasure of the subject. As Other, the woman offers the possibility of *jouissance*. Maternalized, she also threatens the dissolution of the self.

As Ren's confusion indicates, even "real" mothers are produced in verbalized reconstructions of a romanticized past imaginary, as the split between the child and the adult narration relegates the tale to the untrustworthy realm of "narrations of the past." (The text has a doubled narrative structure, with the adult serving as conduit to the child's "voice" in a posture of an erasure of mediation and the simultaneous exposure of that mediation.) Mother straddles this world and that world; Sister is explicated within mother's narrative and significantly appears to Ren only at the moment of his imminent death, as he is losing consciousness in the river. The condition for Sister's textual presence is its own absence and erasure; she is unlocatable and inhabits the boundary between life and death. Ren's search, like the *Kōya hijiri* ascetic's penetration of the mountain interior, moves the text into a retrogression, toward a place where immersion in the maternal promises (threatens) to dissolve subjectivity (death).

Like Sister in "Kechō," Omachi, in *Yōken kibun*, transgresses the boundaries of absence and presence. "In a glimpse there was the white figure of a beautiful woman, which should not be passed by unnoticed, indistinguishable from an illusion" (671). Omachi stands silent at the narrative's opening, "a purple shadow with a white face" (643) hiding in the shadow of her cottage, an illusory decoration associated with the iris flower, bending and waving in the wind, fragile and transient. She is a beautiful "grounding flower, a flower to offset the other" (644).

Again and again, the male protagonists of Kyōka's narratives experience psychic diffusion and temporal and spatial confusion as they infiltrate woman's textual space. The *Kōya hijiri* ascetic grows dizzy as he approaches the mountain woman's domain: "I was fated to die in that forest. In a flash, I felt that the confused fantasies floating in my mind were what happens when a person is aware of his impending death" (494–95). In *Yōken kibun*, before Seisaburō dives into the river to save Omachi, he wanders in search of her as though enchanted:

Each step he took along the path was quiet, buoyant, and light in his leather-soled sandals, eyes riveted on something to one side, clothes fluttering even through still reeds. He walked as if to hide himself, but if he concealed the discreet fragrance of his clothing, their color brightened; if he hid the color, the fragrance was enhanced—like, for example, the unnoticed scattering of full-bloom peach or cherry blossoms when there is no wind—how sad and moving! It made one suspect his was the roving of a manipulated sacrificial victim straight toward the demon-sword's target.—-And yet, he did not seem to find it unpleasant [*Yoshi sore tote mo itofumaji*].

All those mesmerized appear so. Takamatsu Seisaburō seemed to have found his way in a daze, drawn there by some enchantment. (665)

The protagonist of *Nanchi shinjū*, Hatsuzaka, also descends into confusion within the serpent-woman's domain. The first lines are his description:

"It was the weather that made vapor rise up in heat waves from the surface of Yodo River toward the castle turret; vapors that flared to tint the famous castle in a gorgeous mirage [*shiro no na o tenka ni irodotte iru*]. But inside the flare of color was something wavering like a waterfall, undulating stealthily; something with long, pitch-black hair." As he spoke Hatsuzaka was as though intoxicated by the colors tinting the castle he described. (364)

The women appear, distract, and vanish, leaving behind only traces. Along with their tenuous materiality, they signal the evaporation of significance and rationality, enticing the male protagonists toward a collapse of interiority/subjectivity. Repeatedly, the dangerous woman is, to borrow the Derridean term, "under-erasure." She is both the inaccurate, yet necessary, signifier and its simultaneous deletion; she is the origin that has been constructed and erased; she is "trace."[4] In the insistence of Kyōka's prose on discursive and thetic surplus, the phallic subject, formed in the embrace of the Symbolic and the radical exclusion of the abject, seeks the *jouissance* of reuniting with that which would obliterate its own unity through the vehicle of the dangerous woman.[5] She fulfills the phallic agenda, as Žižek would have it, as the Lacanian "symptom of man,"

as a particular signifying formation which confers on the subject its very ontological consistency, enabling it to structure its basic, constitutive relationship toward
jouissance . . . if the symptom is dissolved, the subject loses the ground under his
feet, he disintegrates. . . . In other words, man literally *ex-sists*: his entire being lies
"out there," in woman. Woman, on the other hand, does *not* exist, she *insists*,
which is why she does not come to be only through man. Something in her escapes
the relation to Man, the reference to the phallic enjoyment; and, as is well known,
Lacan endeavored to capture this excess by the notion of a *"non-all" feminine
jouissance*.[6] (Žižek's emphasis)

In Kyōka's works it is *in women* that significance evaporates, and it is in
proximity to women that male dizziness, desire, loss of self-control, and
loss of rationality come together in a knot of eroticized, masochistic, violent pleasure. The dangerous woman is nothing but "language" in its infi-
nite separation from the Real, because she signifies that which she is not.
Nonetheless, she is linked to the Real—as the site of potential *jouissance*—
and she is always, of course, its scripted (mis)representation. As the vessel
of necessary abjection, she becomes the discursive device that makes possible the phallic subject, whether he is to be found in the transcendental
prose of the modern writer Natsume Sōseki or in the tortured subjectivites
of Tayama Katai.[7]

It is toward *jouissance* that Kyōka's protagonists are compelled, toward
something that, if embraced, would dissolve the subject. Their pleasure is
not about pleasure; rather, it is "beyond" pleasure, for the seizure of the
abject is synchronous with the dissolution of the experiential subject. It is
a retrogression toward self-annihilation (presubjectivity) and inseparable
from the compulsion to repeat. For Žižek, it also must be related to the
formation of national sentiment, since it is "enjoyment" or "*jouissance*"
that leads one toward group identifications or the "national Thing."

The national Thing exists as long as members of the community believe in it; it is
literally an effect of this belief in itself.

. . .

A nation *exists* only as long as its specific *enjoyment* continues to be materialized
in a set of social practices and transmitted through national myths that structure
these practices. . . .

The national Cause is ultimately nothing but the way subjects of a given ethnic
community organize their enjoyment through national myths.[8] (Žižek's emphasis)

What makes others "Other," claims Žižek, is the way in which they organize their (different) enjoyments and pleasures: odors, tastes, and sounds
that are *unfamiliar*. According to Freud, since the Other is, nonetheless,

nothing other than "the other in the perceiver's interior," when gendered it is also the same process informing the perverse fascination with those viscosities that have been bound to the female Other's maternal aspect and abjected in the construction of the phallic, bounded self.

Kristeva has described abjection as a process whereby the infant, as a still-preindividuated subject, expels from the developing self those partial objects that must be differentiated for the completion of normative subjectivity. "If the object . . . through its opposition, settles me within the fragile texture of a desire for meaning, which, as a matter of fact, makes me ceaselessly and infinitely homologous to it, what is *abject*, on the contrary, the jettisoned object, is radically excluded and draws me toward the place where meaning collapses."[9] The abjected threaten the unity of the body; they are nonobject objects, or drive, prior to the constitution of object and subject, that is, coming before the process by which the self is clearly delineated through separated apprehension of the other is completed. Maternal primacy, for Kristeva, is a teleological reality. Thus, the formation of subjectivity following this logic unavoidably—given the putative naturalness of the *psychic primacy and significance* of the maternal-infant dyad as an unalterable biological truism—requires, as part of the process of self-formation, the expulsion of the mother and unleashes the terror of losing bodily and psychic integrity through a merging back into and within the female-as-preselfhood.

Judith Butler has queried this formation:

Kristeva describes the maternal body as bearing a set of meanings that are prior to culture itself. She thereby safeguards the notion of culture as a paternal structure and delimits maternity as an essentially precultural reality. Her naturalistic descriptions of the maternal body effectively reify motherhood and preclude an analysis of its cultural construction and variability.[10]

Precisely because the maternal is for Kyōka (as it is for Kristeva, Žižek, and others) teleologized, mirroring the tightening Meiji/Taisho maternalized epistemology, femaleness is bound with both the process of othering and the earlier process of abjection. For Kyōka, the female sorceress became the locus for his ambivalence toward nostalgia: she—a partial object of the premodern, the erotic, yearned-for, not-yet-formed object of incestuous desire, seeping through the tenuous borders of the absent, the other, and the abject—returns. And the abjection that encompasses the sorceress of Meiji absolutely ensures the function of the Meiji modern rationalistic system. The myth of the mother is inescapably ghosted by the myth of the *yamamba*.

The consolidation of the phallic subject, through the projection of the abjected premodern from the body of the modern subject onto that of the dangerous woman, is accompanied by a fierce desire for the projected abjections, or what is thereby lost to that subject. Time and again, Kyōka's male protagonists seek the *jouissance* of self-diffusion in the body of the dangerous woman; sometimes they succeed so well that they die. Whether the protagonists die or not, the chronicling of the encounters in text enables the reading/writing subject(s) to repeat (in fantasy) and to experience a sense of both self-abandon and mastery over his or her desire, while remaining "phallic." Because the dangerous woman is encompassed in text, she is subordinated to a process of rationalization and taming (writing); yet this incorporation permits the reader/writer/imaginary protagonist to flirt with the threat and the pleasure of the abject, always relegated to the realm of language, and thus he or she is simultaneously protected from self-disintegration. This and other similar cultural imaginaries were necessary for Meiji modernity in general; they comprise the required aberrance that produces the norm.

However archetypal they might appear, Kyōka's female figures are simultaneously conduits to a type of textual verticality and thus also bear intimate relation to the modern. The condensation of Kyōka's sorceress figures described in Chapter 2, whereby once separated, specific archetypes of the premodern tradition lose their medieval specificities and are collapsed into a composite, empowered and eroticized plurality, is actually a locus for a particular sort of depth that is a product of modernity.[11]

Kōya hijiri is basically a confession by the ascetic to his young acquaintance, replete with shame and thus omissions. Comments such as the ones following are introjected throughout the ascetic's narration:

How shameful. Talking so specifically about a woman's body. . . . Quite inappropriate for me, a priest who has served his temple many years. But a story is a story. Please forgive me. (384)

. . .

How shall I put this—I have not told you everything. That night the woman had returned to my side by the hearth after putting her husband to bed. (427)

. . .

I did not care if I died on the spot, if only I could be enveloped in her warm, fragrant petals.

That is what tormented me by the waterfall. How ashamed I am. Even now I'm clammy with sweat. (428)

The compulsion toward shameful confessions of a sexual/erotic nature is further evidence of how Kyōka's texts are (ambivalently) clasped within the grasp of modernity (and *resemble* the narratives of the *shishōsetsu* naturalists).[12] What Karatani has called the "compulsion to confess that produces an 'interior' which must be hidden," a corollary of the *genbun'itchi* movement, is part of the overall system or paradigm of modern verticality.[13]

Kyōka's project, by *differing* from the simple reiteration of a fixed signification to a fixed (imaginary) referent, moves to muddy the signifier with overdeterminations, multiplicities, and contradictions: in short, depth, but absolutely not transparency. Inviting one to search for her meaning, which is floating *beneath* the surface, the dangerous woman yields meaninglessness. Standing by the stream where she transforms men, the sorceress of *Kōya hijiri* is described thus: "She had finished washing the rice and rose, her collar in disarray, just revealing the upper curves of her full bosom, her sculpted nose, closed mouth, face, and entranced eyes turned up towards the summit" (406). The hint of *void* (the loss of subjecthood in trance: *me o uttori to*) in her eyes is complemented by her *depth*: she begs the ascetic to promise not to speak of the capital to her, and he muses, "She seemed to have a special reason. But what the reason was—I assumed it stemmed from her isolated life, for her words were as unfathomable as the height of a mountain or a valley's depth" (399).

Karatani has argued that a major perspectival shift that marked modernity was the foregrounding of "depth." Comparing the deepening interiority of modern literature with the discovery and subsequent dominance of the "vanishing point" (or linear perspective) in modern Western painting, Karatani holds that:

When we read so-called premodern literature we often have the feeling that it is lacking in depth.

. . .

The depth we sense in modern literature is not something found in reality, perception, or consciousness, but in a single type of perspectival configuration prevalent in this literature. We see it as a result of the deepening of "life" or "interiority" in modern times because we are not aware that modern literature represents a mutation of this configuration. When we say premodern literature lacks depth, then, we are not so much saying that people of the time had no conception of depth as that they lacked the configuration that makes us feel "depth."[14]

The very process of seeking a hidden premodern within the modern establishes depth, since it entails looking for something beneath or beyond the surface. It supposes "layers" and contradictions. As discursive devices, Kyōka's mystified, narrativized female bodies (while they also paradoxically signify premodernity) thus bring concealment and confession to the text. The textual duplicity is modernity in process. Depth surrounds femaleness (this occurs topographically as well, often in the form of watery depths, underwater caves, or mountain and forest depths) and asserts itself in the contradictory, alternating descriptions of the women's maternal gentleness, wondrous sexiness, and terrifying power to encompass, pluralize, and transform. In the following selections from *Kōya hijiri*, the narrator of the first line is the ascetic. Then it is the embedded enunciation of the old man talking to the ascetic:

The gentle kindness and intimacy accorded the young man by this woman of rich flesh and mysterious charm gladdened my heart. (424)

"She takes her pick of men, and after she's tired of them, turns them into animals with a puff of breath. Ever since the flood, that miraculous, magical stream, threading its way through the mountains and entrancing men, has spared no one.

"She burns with an innate lust, most passionately for young men. Oh, sure she spoke seductively to you, but dare you take her at her word! Before she's through with you, once she's sated, you'll grow a tail, your ears will wiggle, and your legs will elongate, suddenly, you'll be transformed. Truly, you should see that demon seated cross-legged feasting on this carp." (436)

Depth lurks in the maternal dimension and hinges on the corollary doubled process of recuperation and abjection. The cruelty of Kyōka's sorceress, which alternates with her gentleness, is an inseparable component of idealized maternity: she remains "unperturbed" when the old man strikes the idiot with his fist; she "callously" brushes aside the idiot when he refuses to return her sash (402–3; 416).[15] Here "Mother" is radically split, paralleling the split between Meiji maternal ideals (the mother of "Kechō") and the demonesses, goddesses, and other irrational, empowered, or eroticized females who also appear in Kyōka's narratives. She is never commensurate with herself.

Maternity as depth and as shameful eroticism that must be confessed *in text* are abiding features of Kyōka's narratives. At the same time, unlike the *shishōsetsu* writers, whose confessions emerged from a conflated author-narrator-protagonist paradigm, in *Kōya hijiri*, a separated narrator (the young man who hears the ascetic's tale) becomes the scribe, and thus the confession is deferred, or transferred, locked within its own defiance of interiority, ultimately confessing "nothing." For though the ascetic only *desires* the woman (he never "has" her, which mirrors many of the tortured confessions of the *shishōsetsu* such as in "Futon"), removing the enunciation from the primary narrator *defers* and *puts into question* even the confession. Moreover, it is not the *woman* who confesses; she lacks the interior to do so and she is not a subject. But it is through the male's need to confess his fantasies of her as partial object that *his* modernity/subjectivity is performed.

Just as maternal depth, for Kyōka, cannot be equated with transparency, it also does not signal (modern) unified subjectivity. It signifies that which is irretrievably lost, since the deeper the exploration and the more fervent the quest to signify the mother, the more elusive she becomes. Maternity functions as a trope that provides (hidden/modern) depth and marks the presence of loss in his narratives. Maternity has been ferreted out of its hiding places in the textual folds, and it produces (and in turn is produced by) the ambivalent, alternating presence/absence/abjection/eroticization that is affixed to the mother. Maternity is only partly vitalizable in language, because the Symbolic order cannot express the Real aspects of a reified mother. She is doubled, as an idealized configuration of the Other, embodying modernity (by mirroring phallic unity) and yet containing deep within herself the abjected, the returning uncanny, or the unknowable, unvocalized, the suggested, the viscous and the revolting; she is not what she appears to be, and so she must be deciphered. Kyōka's texts invite the gaze to penetrate beneath its surfaces through the mystery of the maternalized feminine.

Kyōka's eroticization of the female outcaste in *Yōken kibun* most transparently hovers between the articulation of desire and the aghast: she is a composite figure that compels as it repels.[16] Critic Yomota Inuhiko wrote,

According to Kyōka, the other world represented by the *hisabetsu burakumin* [outcaste] is distanced from the public, outside world and at the same time is a space that supersedes the natural. The protagonist, invited into this space by a mysterious, beautiful woman who is made sacred, undergoes a *motherly* feast [*boseiteki na kyōō*] in which dream and reality become indistinguishable.[17] (emphasis added)

Omachi also has a *dangerous* depth, most overtly in her contagious, entrapping pollution. As Seisaburō wanders in search of her, he is depicted as her bewitched victim, and she is linked to the demon-sword: "Dancing through the air, the arrow had chosen its mark and was already in mid-flight having left the bowstring. . . . It made one suspect his [Seisaburō's] was the roving of a manipulated sacrificial victim straight towards the demon-sword's target" (665). In his obsessive quest to relocate Omachi, a literalization of the enactment of a drive *other* than that toward life, of one toward the obliteration of subjectivity, Seisaburō finally sights her through a peephole in a shrine gate (see the passage quoted in

Chapter 2). Omachi is a beautiful, partialized body caught in his gaze, fading even as he, enthralled, desires her. Once his attention has been engaged by her-as-lack (her illusory presence) and by her sticky, defiling touch (the pollution imparted by the blossom she has given Seisaburō and his resultant trancelike obsession), the narrative progresses, as do "Kechō" and *Kōya hijiri*, toward the peripheries of Meiji civilization and the boundaries of selfsameness into a mysterious depth, a deathly, maternalized female world abounding in profound threat, great erotic delights, and (mis)apprehensions.

Just as Seisaburō knelt on one knee, shoulder aslant against the dais, facing the door, which resembled a *nō* stage side door, there, moving chillingly through the reeds beneath him, was a woman, her skin pure white like a white goose.

By the time he exclaimed in response, it was already too late, and like the vanishing trace of an amorous glance, or barely glimpsed azaleas, her colored, layered skirts seemed to disappear as they scattered hem first to the water and sank quickly beneath the Big Mortar platform. (672)

In swift pursuit, Seisaburō plunges into the river and descends into the depths of the underwater cave, where he finds the wounded Omachi. The repercussions of his irrevocable pollution through contact with her pulses toward its climax. Kasahara has noted that repeatedly in Kyōka's tales, "in the taboo forest [*mori*] the beautiful woman reveals her spectacular figure, exhibiting her 'pure-white breasts' while she must simultaneously be 'sacred.' "[18] At this climactic moment in *Yōken kibun*, from Omachi's beautiful breast, the maternal vessel for pure, life-giving, healthful milk, the source of "all good things," instead flows tainted, deathly blood.[19] Omachi is the embedded narrator for her own confession:

"Thinking that if I slashed my breast, yearning and aching with desire, I could cleanse my dirty blood, I sneaked into the main temple. . . . I hugged the sword to me with my sleeve, opened my bodice, and pressed the blade to my breast. . . . (675)

"Your words are so merciful and sensitive, I feel so warm, so relaxed, as though my body were dissolving, gushing—spilling—my blood is flowing—step back! Oh! You'll be defiled, tainted, defiled, tainted with filthy *eta* blood, *hinin* blood."

The cloth, folded down and back—there, beneath her breast, jewel-pure crimson liquid.

She had flung herself into the abyss beneath the platform of Big Mortar, where the light of the full moon on the translucent, sparkling water was phantasmagoric, glittering on the silver-white platform, staining her sash a coral, faint peach hue against the deep jade green of the cave. She had collapsed on the demon-chair, hugging the sword to her chest. When Seisaburō drew close, the thickening, coagulated, bluish blood on her gemlike nipple was a single purple iris blossom in Seisaburō's eyes.

"Tainted? What? Your blood—"

As Omachi clung, his hand in hers, her body convulsed, and Seisaburō gathered her tightly in his arms, her lips still rosy with life, and drank the blood pouring from her breast, swallowing in huge gulps. (678)

Kyōka's fascination with the abject suggests collusion with modernity through its "perverse" nature—most transparently, in this eroticized mix of the maternal breast and its polluted flow. Foucault has argued that in the West, through the translation of sexual practices into the discursive, modern society becomes perverse. The type of power regulating sexuality

did not set boundaries for sexuality; it extended the various forms of sexuality, pursuing them according to lines of indefinite penetration. It did not exclude sexuality, but included it in the body as a mode of specification of individuals. It did not seek to avoid it; it attracted its varieties by means of spirals in which pleasure and power reinforced one another. It did not set up a barrier; it provided places of maximum saturation. It produced and determined the sexual mosaic. Modern society is perverse, not in spite of its puritanism or as if from a backlash provoked by its hypocrisy; it is in actual fact, and directly, perverse.[20]

Although premodern Japanese sexual mores differed radically from those of the West, the Meiji-period establishment and Taisho/early Showa refinements of compulsory heterosexuality, the ascension of medical treatises on hygiene and sexuality and of naturalist, confessional literature and modern *monogatari* chronicling sexual "perversion" in the wake of linguistic and social reforms suggest that something similar occurred in Japan.[21] The turning into text of delightfully erotic horrors or in Noguchi's words, "eroticism . . . heightened by the concealed fragrance of death," which nuances the discursive presentation of so many of Kyōka's eroticized female figures, is testament to what Foucault called the modern "pornography of the morbid."[22] Blatant in Kyōka's "Gekashitsu" (The surgery room, 1895), where a chance glance exchanged between a medical student and a countess culminates in a bloody double suicide nine years later as she lies before him, now a surgeon, on his operating table, perverse eroticization of the morbid is also evident in *Yōken kibun*. Tanemura wrote that

a taste for bloodshed and an awe of women (Beardsley's Salome), which are distinguishing characteristics of Kyōka's work, while expressing a longing for sexual union with women distanced by death, are the result of an imaginary murder of the object—the only ritual of "love that preserves distance," rooted in circumstances in which actual sexual union is not achieved because of the impossibility of direct contact and moral taboo.[23]

According to Kristeva,

These body fluids, this defilement, this shit are what life withstands, hardly and with difficulty, on the part of death. There I am, at the border of my condition as a living being. My body extricates itself, as being alive, from that border.

. . .

Devotees of the abject . . . do not cease looking, within what flows from the other's "innermost being," for the desirable and terrifying, nourishing and murderous, fascinating and abject inside of the maternal body. . . .

The eroticization of abjection, and perhaps any abjection to the extent that it is already eroticized, is an attempt at stopping the hemorrhage: a threshold before death, a halt, or a respite?[24]

The abject transgresses bodily and psychic boundaries and hovers at the distinction between meaning and void, life and death. Precisely, when Kyōka's protagonists do not die, it is female slippage that ensures their survival and the progression of the texts themselves. The ascetic of *Kōya hijiri* emerges enlightened from his encounter with the woman, while Seisaburō is mysteriously changed:

Omachi dropped limply to her knees, and Seisaburō took the blade of the sword, the surface of which shone like snow, like ice, vertically into his mouth and sucked the dried blood from its tip.

As he held the sword in his mouth, Seisaburō learned with his lips and tongue the secrets of all its parts—the shinning reflector, the ornamentation, the fine tempering and metallic color—the entire artistry of the sword.—

In other words, the deep-water cave was a workshop, the greenhouse a bellows, and the chair a workbench, where the heat of the water refracted the purple gems and the fire of her gushing blood came together to make him a master, both hue and heart of the lover—was it the teachings of a god?—or a demon's artistry?— he became the very finest swordsmith of his time.

This youth became that grand master, the one who himself chose the name, Hinin Kiyomitsu [Nonhuman Purelight], which he embossed on all his swords. (678)

Approaching death, tasting death, clasping death in an erotic embrace, these male protagonists emerge transformed, tainted, yet somehow alive. Seisaburō is turned into a master swordsmith and the Kōya ascetic into a "realized" mystic (*hijiri*; sometimes translated as "saint"). Omachi dies, but not only has her presence always already been informed by absence but she also lives on, as a phantom, reappearing to close the narrative, forever linked with the now-aged Seisaburō/Kiyomitsu:

A beautiful minstrel girl with erect posture slipped between elderberry trees, a graceful hand held to her hat. She lifted her lovely, charming face, breathtakingly white against her pale yellow hat strings . . . smiling, almond eyes staring straight at Kiyomitsu. The old man smiled too.

As the drumbeat boomed, peach flowers scattered, and his plain coat fluttered in the mountain wind, Kiyomitsu began to weep and the minstrel girl suddenly vanished. Mingled in the faint echo of the little mountain stream were the strains, not of a koto, or a biwa, but a samisen's ongoing melody. (682)

Kyōka's male protagonists flirt with the diffusions of the abject, reiterating time and again the desire to return to presubjectivity through the maternal link to the Real. Kyōka's narratives are compelled toward a quest for "origin," but because they tease the borders of phallocentric unity, they reinstate the conceit of female seepage.

Focused on the sociocultural implications, rather than on the psychosexual individualized (and, not paradoxically, universalization) of a modern binding of femaleness with the abject, Elizabeth Grosz has argued that

the female body has been constructed not only as a lack or absence but with more complexity, as a leaking, uncontrollable, seeping liquid; as formless flow; as viscosity, entrapping, secreting; as lacking not so much or simply the phallus but self-containment . . . a formlessness that engulfs all form, a disorder that threatens all order? I am not suggesting that this is how women *are*, that it is their ontological status. . . . These may well be a function of the projection outward of their corporealities, the liquidities that men seem to want to cast out of their own self-representations.[25] (Grosz's emphasis)

I would reframe Grosz's statement to dispense with the binaristic, sexed distinction of a male agentive casting out of their own formlessness and instead regard this particularly gendered abjection, and the ambivalence toward the uncanny, as *requirements*, subtexts if you will, of the formation of phallic modernity and the positing of maternity in its modern teleologized configuration. Whereas the uncanny, according to Freud, is eerily familiar, since it is of the repressed self, the abject, holds Kristeva, is *unfamiliar* because it is prior to subjectivity. As the national subject is construed within modernity as fully contained, rational, and phallic, the premodern is repressed, and the antiphallic, now bound to the maternal, is abjected. Tracing its trajectory in a collusive embrace of capitalist, industrialized labor reformations, the maternal teleology seeks to domesticate women within the home and to sever them from public function. In the phallic construct of norm, the female is that which never was, while the premodern is a repressed memory. Maternalized femaleness is made to accommodate both, as the porous, boundless vessel for all that modern man is not.

Borrowing arenas of abjection from the medieval canon, sites of literary mystery and taboo, intersections of the mundane and the magical and of life and death, Kyōka's textual topography is turned tenuous. This feminized, boundless land holds the threat of diffusion—and the enticing promise of taboo sexual union. They and/or we imagine that they and/or we have returned to the moments just before (through abjection) and those accompanying (othering) the grasp of subjectivity, indelibly inscribed with the political discourses framing Meiji-period maternity and nostalgia. The relentless teasing of the borders of modernity and subjectivity, for Kyōka's protagonists, is predicated on absence (lack), which creates the desire. They retrace the romantic task of recuperating a mythic past through the erotic yet polluted, leaking and absent female body, seeking women who exist only as a by-product of modern phallic subjectivity-production, as other to, or dispelled from, their (tenuous) phallic unity and self-containment. The dangerous woman of Kyōka's phallic fantasy thus comes to constitute the vessel for the abjected elements of a maternalized femaleness that operates as a primary site for the circulation of homosocial desire in a heterosexual libidinal economy.

Michiyuki Toward *Jouissance*

Critical response to Kyōka's work (both during and after his life-time) in Japan, and reproduced in the limited English-language sources, often took the form of two reciprocal metatopics: "tradition" and "style," regardless of whether the focus has been on the thetic or the formalist aspects of the texts.[1] Critics debated how and to what degree Kyōka was a traditionalist, or antimodernist, in opposition to the then-dominant literary trend toward realism and interiority. This approach often parallels what I argue was Kyōka's "imaginary" of the premodern and functions to erase historicity in complicity with Meiji nostalgic recraftings of tradition. It is this process by which Kyōka becomes a repository for an ahistorical Japanese aesthetic. Commentators have also focused on the specifics of Kyōka's distinctive prose, paying particular attention to rhythms and structures. Many studies of Kyōka's style were employed as foundational structures to support the contention that Kyōka was a conventionalist. Kyōka's prose is read as interlocked with premodern discursive traditions, as against the dominant literary trend of his contemporaries toward a more "Western-style" narrative.

I have argued that for Kyōka, the maternalized and/or feminized sorceress trope supplies the locus for a struggle between modernity and its abjected and othered aspects. This chapter and the following will move the argument deeper into the discursive realm, to question how Kyōka's putatively "antiquated" prose similarly grapples with and veils a partial collusion with modern subjectivity, the changing systems of representation, and their underlying logics of phonocentrism and phallocentrism.

In the opening passages of *Yōken kibun*, the narrator sketches a brief description of Omachi, the *buraku* (outcaste quarters) where she lives, where the irises are blooming by a little stream and addresses the reader directly: "Visions of damp purple blossoms entice us to begin there, but first we must follow the path along a short journey into a tale of doomed love" (631). What I have translated as "journey into a tale of doomed love" is the Japanese word *michiyuki.* Nakanishi Susumu has defined the *michiyuki* as a travel passage that functions as:

a literary technique for capturing the process of death and rebirth in the imagery of space, [that] has its roots in myth. . . .

[The *michiyuki* is] a technique used to depict characters' movements, typically their approach toward imminent death, by stringing together a series of place names. The most widely known examples of this kind are the michiyuki in the jō-ruri [puppet play] narratives by the Edo-period writer, Chikamatsu Monzaemon.[2]

Typically, the *michiyuki* of the early modern (mid- to late-Edo) period hastened the tempo of the narratives toward their culminations in the lovers' double suicide. Frequently, the doomed lovers were a geisha and a married man or a poor man unable to purchase her contract for himself or two lovers unsuited because of class. Through their intended togetherness in death, they defied the socially impossible terms of their love affair. Kyōka's Omachi is doubly unavailable to Seisaburō: she is a *hinin* (not human) and not of this world. By using the word *michiyuki,* Kyōka fore-warns of a tragic, deathly resolution to a socioculturally defiant love affair.

Nakanishi also noted that there are reversed *michiyuki* in which the narrative travels toward a type of rebirth achieved by means of a purifica-tion ritual that classically took place in a river. The rivers in these *michi-yuki* were symbolic, permeable borders between the world of the living and the world of the dead. According to Nakanishi, the reversed *michi-yuki* was bound to

a particular type of party called ozume . . . a gathering for an exchange of poems, [that] always took place by a bridge. It was a form of utagaki, a celebration held by a body of water to celebrate revival through the pleasure of marriage or sexual union. A revival was possible only in a place where the world of the living bor-dered the realm of the dead. . . . [Names of bridges suggest] the tragic death, as well as the eventual rebirth, of the protagonist and his lover.[3]

If there is a *michiyuki* in Kyōka's *Yōken kibun,* it is not a *michiyuki* proper. Rather, it floats between the alternatives; it is an erotic story, en-gaging death, purification, and transformation in and by a river, while sexual consummation is held in abeyance. Seisaburō is transformed. Although Omachi dies in her pursuit of purification, before her death she was already not-subject, othered, and abjected. The transformations freeze time rather than place it into motion: Seisaburō and Omachi remain bounded, their connection predicated at least partially on the logic of Omachi-as-lack. After her death, Omachi continues to appear just as she did when she was ostensibly alive, in partial, fleeting odors, sounds, and visions. Kyōka appears to have taken from convention that which aesthetically appealed to his personal narrative project and to have simply left, or twisted to his own ends, the rest. As idiosyncratic as his narratives may appear, it is also important to recognize that his personal project emerged within his negotiation of a modern narrative subjectivity. That it appears so individualized signals the extent to which Kyōka was *already* modern, that is, able to shape the text differently from what tradition or trend dictated into a personalized imaginary (although this imaginary, of course, was not independent of its own historicity).

Michiyuki, reversed or otherwise, are inextricable from literary impulse. The relation of *michiyuki* to landscape is *premodern* in that *michiyuki* replicate, to borrow Karatani's description, "a weave of language" given signification by poetry.[4] The *ozume* described by Nakanishi above is a gathering for poetic composition and exchange. Place-naming in the *michiyuki* shares little with the appreciation of landscape found in modern description. Rather, it should be epistemologically classified alongside such classical rhetorical devices as the *makurakotoba*, or a word, frequently a place-name used to modify another and assigned an additional significance through poetic convention.[5] On its purely discursive level, the naming of place in the *michiyuki* is evidence of "landscape as poetics" and of word inseparable from enunciation. Opening the final chapter of *Yōken kibun* is a litany of place-names, as if to fulfill the early narrative pronouncement: "Mount Wilderness, Mid-mount Wilderness, Mount Timber, Slope Plain. Mount Return. Devil's Peak, Mackerel Inlet, Mackerel Wave, Cedar Harbor, Animal Field. Hot Spring Lower Pass, Leaf-Bud Pass. Layers of mountain ridges, peaks on peaks, valleys on valleys, huge trees pillared to the heavens, cliffs of scarred boulders" (679). But it is not doomed lovers who travel the mountains in this final troping of the *michiyuki* in *Yōken kibun*, but two peripheral characters, a traveling comic duo. As noted above, the transformations of the lovers do not follow tradition either.

Kyōka's iteration of Edo or earlier convention was, as in the use of the *michiyuki*, regularly accompanied by an *individual* quirk, a very modern noncompliance with the expectation. When the ascetic of *Kōya hijiri* and the primary narrator first meet on the train, they have the following encounter. The opening comment is from the narrator.

(It's snowing.)

(So it is,) he responded laconically, without directing even a cursory glance towards the sky. It was not just snow he was indifferent to; he merely nodded when I pointed out Shizugatake and the old war site, and scenic Lake Biwa. (380; Kyōka's punctuation)

The ascetic is markedly indifferent to the celebrated views of narrativized landscapes, sites that would have elicited poetic response in Heian and later medieval classics. The snowflakes (perhaps likened to the ephemeral qualities of white blossoms) would commonly have provided an occasion for conventional poetic affective expression for Murasaki Shikibu in Heian, for Zeami in Muromachi, and for Matsuo Bashō in Edo.[6] (Although of course what constituted convention was for each of them also historically specific.) Even though Kyōka's work is replete with poetic aspects or references to sites of literary history, he often dissolves this associative lyric sensibility. But in doing so, he does not replicate Edo parodic *gesaku* (light, or vulgar writings), in which the poetic landscape would have offered an opportunity for some vulgar, irreverent punning. Kyōka's rendering of landscape cannot be neatly ordered in keeping with Heian classical models or early modern Edo parodies or Meiji/Taisho romantic naturalism. Kyōka may invent a fictitious site within a classically celebrated one or transpose one site onto another, as in *Kōya hijiri* (in which he transports the famous Amō Pass from its actual location and deposits it in the Hida Mountains), or choose an area of Tokyo and set his tale in its past, imbued with mystery through imaginary renderings (as in *Yōken kibun*, which takes place in Koishikawa, present-day Bunkyō-ku). From the site of an existing inscripted landscape, Kyōka sheds convention to embark on a *different* (modern) engagement of the uncanny, the grotesque, and the abject. The ascetic's clear indifference to Biwa Lake, as quoted above, signals a rejection of Heian convention. Instead, *Kōya hijiri* turns toward a new site masquerading as the premodern, toward an "underside" in a shift that mirrors the one performed by Yanagida, in which the previously "nonhuman" (that is, women, people of the mountains, and children) become the supreme repository for an abjected nativism. For Kyōka, the feminization of nativized sites ensures that these sites cannot exist, either as a faithful reiteration of the poetically inscribed or as material. Rather, they are necessarily transformed into "other worlds" (*ikai*), as topographies that can only be approached through language yet are also always surplus to the Symbolic.

As with the dangerous woman trope, landscapes, poetic references, rhetorical devices, narration, and, as I will continue to illustrate, conventions of previously discrete discursive genres are capriciously sampled and willfully set afloat as a tangled mix of inscriptions sundered from their various fixities. A cursory glance might suggest that this "generic seepage" is commensurate with eighteenth-century *gesaku* polysemy. A closer analysis, however, reveals that the affect and (assumed) intention of Kyōka's generic mixtures and citations were deeply distanced from those of his Edo predecessors, whom Naoki Sakai has called "parodists." Sakai has written,

The emergence of parodist literature in the eighteenth century . . . [was] an effort to dislocate the junctures of the economy of generic discontinuity.

. . .

It was not the content of a work but rather its stylistic—or, more precisely, its graphic—arrangement that was considered to be the distinguishing mark according to which it would be classified.[7]

By transposing a quote or a slightly altered version of a Buddhist, didactic, or historical authoritarian prior text, the *gesaku* stylists "defamiliarized the space of literary conventions" and simultaneously rendered it absurd, ridiculous, and bound to the physical body and thus to immediacy and the present mundane, bawdy world. This defamiliarization is also, said Sakai, familiarization, since the canon was quoted in order to laugh at it.[8] Quite to the contrary, although Kyōka's incorporation of references to and citations from the classics reiterates in *form* the generic seepage of Edo parodic narratives, a distinct perspectival shift dramatically redefines the function: the incorporations and citations operate as a modern nostalgic refabrication of the specific intertextuality of the early medieval period. Then, according to literary scholar and historian Konishi Jin'ichi, "style consisted essentially of already extant expression. Harmonizing with already extant expression therefore yielded literature that was favorably received. Beautiful expression was possible whenever diction and concepts rested completely on literary precedent."[9]

Both *monogatari* and *waka* (Japanese verse) relied heavily on echoed poems and tales. Within Kyōka's texts references to poetic, performative, and other antecedent texts are common. Although Kyōka alternated between humorous and serious passages, most often if the antecedent text was humorous, Kyōka's reference to it reiterated humor; if it was serious, then so was Kyōka's passage. In *Kōya hijiri*, the ascetic responds to the woman's preliminary cool reception of him by musing, "She did not even ask me to sit down. From the start it seemed that Tsuneyo was away and she was not likely to let anyone spend the night" (398). The Chinese characters for *tsune* and *yo*, read independently, mean respectively "regular" and "world," but as a compound they are usually pronounced *tokoyo* and refer to the archaic land of deities who were believed to be sacred and yet taboo. But, to further complicate the ascetic's comment, when the compound is pronounced as "Tsuneyo," as the *rubi* (pronunciation guide) indicates, the characters signify the name of a character in the *nō* drama "Hachinoki." In this play, an important priest disguised as an itinerant mendicant seeks lodging at Tsuneyo's house when he is caught in the snow. As noted previously, equating the beauty of the woman in *Kōya hijiri* with that of Yang Guifei hinges on the reader's capacity to recognize and associate specifically to the mention of Li Mountain. The reader lacking a particular literary sophistication would miss this polysemic overfilling of the signifiers. Noguchi Takehiko notes (with chagrin) that this has led commentators to feel that they must "finish off [any reading of] Kyōka's work by adding on the ideology of prior-knowledge, which is premodern, as a special characteristic of Kyōka's work—exactly like *makurakotoba*."[10] Femaleness repeatedly functions as the *makurakotoba* did, as the signifier for a vague and plural premodern, emptied of its own significance, indicative of a now *differently* poeticized site (a topos increasingly exterior to language although necessarily within discourse—and thus also nothing but voided discourse—and not substance/material) and co-opted for Kyōka's discursive phallic agenda.

Neither strictly late-Edo nor early-twentieth-century prose, Kyōka's sentences are meticulously edited compounds becoming, in places, incomprehensible and troubled by a multiplicity that does not yield to a unitary reading. Japanologist Donald Keene has described Kyōka's writing thus: "The long sentences are broken up into seemingly unconnected fragments, following their own logic rather than that of normal syntax, and the expression can be as indirect as that in the later Henry James."[11] The eminent literary critic Kobayashi Hideo stated flatly, "It would not be an exaggeration to say that 'the sentence' is the only god of this writer."[12] Kyōka's earlier narratives were less complex; increasingly, into late Taisho and early Showa his texts deviated from the developing standards for punctuation and grammar.[13] Kyōka's style shifted toward a deliberate approximation of the premodern, adapted from disappearing discursive practices, as evidenced by the fact that his later texts are more polysemic (a supposed sign of a retained premodern) than his earlier ones.[14] (Again, this puts into question the description of Kyōka as "conventionalist" and suggests instead that his works were informed by a radicalism framed within a constructed "mood" of premodernity.)

Kyōka's original manuscripts are crisscrossed with corrections and deletions; Kyōka obviously labored over every sentence. Such fastidious constructions yielded a purposeful ambiguity and/or catechrises: individual words may be doubled or trebled in significations, while often a modifier in a sentence can be assigned to two or more modifieds. The moon and a monkey in the treetops become entangled in *Kōya hijiri*:

[The monkey] glided from branch to branch as it swept up the tall tree, finally reaching the treetop, rustling [*Eda kara eda o tsutau to miete, miageru yō ni takai ki no, yagate kozue made, kasakasa gasari*].

The moon, ashine through sparse leaves, had separated from the mountain ridge, there, in the treetops [*Mapara ni ha no naka o sukashite tsuki wa yama no ha o hanareta, sono kozue no atari*]. (411)

I read the "there, in the treetops" (*sono kozue no atari*) of the second sentence as both the monkey and the moon. That the Kyōka scholar Muramatsu glosses this phrase to advise the reader that it "should" be interpreted as "the moon was in the treetops" is actually indicative of its significatory slippage.[15]

On the first page of *Yōken kibun*, the narrator muses: "Merely uttering the word flower. Can I truly convey its purple color—I don't know" (kō yō hana to sae iimasu. Sono yukari no iro o, umaku utsusemasu ka, dōka wakarimasen ga) (631). The words *yukari* and *iro* both denote more than one meaning. *Yukari* refers to a "mystical connection" or bond to a person or place that stems from a former life and is related to Buddhist concepts of fate and karma, incomprehensible since it predates the individuals in their present incarnations. *Iro* means color, but in the Edo period (and before), it was commonly used to indicate eroticism or as a euphemism for sexiness. *Iroppoi*, or having the tendency to color or easily colored, today still means erotic or sexy. *Yukari no iro* (literally, the color of karmic bond) means purple, an interpretation based on precedent in the *Kokinshū*.[16] But the words still encompass their other significations. If the words *no iro* were deleted after the word *yukari*, it would mean "Can I truly convey the connection I felt?" *Iro* suggests a voluptuous foreshadowing of

Omachi's eroticism. Omachi herself is entwined with, and symbolized by, the purple iris—the *kakitsubata*—which itself happens to be a *makurakotoba* for *nioi* (odor or fragrance).

In documenting these indexes of the premodern, some critics have noted the modernity implicit in the manner by which such rhetorical devices resignify in Kyōka's works.[17] Others have reproduced Kyōka's nostalgic sculpting of the past.[18] Takahashi's comment, quoted in Chapter 2, bears repeating: "Kyōka's . . . characters types [are the types] who appear in the scenes of *setsuwa, rakugo, kōshaku* and *monogatari* of antiquity," since it collapses once-delineated genres into a homogeneity constituted only by their mutual distinction from modernity.[19] Only with the modern as a normative framework do such disparate genres become unified. Yanagita Kunio's proclamation that "led by Kyōka, one realizes what poetry still exists in the world today" poses the question, What sort of lingering poetic form was he imagining, since there was no such classical genre?[20] One could pose a similar question to Itō Sei, who recommended that "one should not read the novels of author Izumi Kyōka in order to verify their settings or ascertain their plots but rather, one should taste and enjoy their scenes, one by one, as one does kabuki [popular theater] or *bunraku* [puppet plays]."[21] Akutagawa Ryūnosuke's comment on Kyōka's tendency toward mixture concludes by linking him to the medieval giant of the literary past, Zeami: "Not only were there no other authors in the Meiji/Taisho period who, like Sensei [Kyōka], used colloquialisms, literary language, words from Chinese poetry and language, and was capable of using nouns, all in one work, but moreover, if one tries to locate similar figures we probably find only the genius of the Muromachi period who independently created *nō* chants."[22]

What should be carefully scrutinized here is that Kyōka's *invention* of an imaginary past into which he has collapsed previously distinct aspects of a long literary history into some sort of a unity that erases generic distinctions (and by which Kyōka thus also appears postmodern) has become, for these critics, the hallmark of culture and tradition. This valorization of Kyōka turns his narratives into harbingers of "things Japanese." It reaches its zenith in Tanizaki Jun'ichirō's claim that Kyōka's prose epitomizes some pure Japanese essence,[23] even though Kyōka has, in short, fabricated an individualized reorigination of a modern idea of the past that *reiterates* Meiji nostalgic reconstructions, most particularly in how subjectivity is performed through a gendered handling of the necessary abjections and otherings. Kyōka's narratives offer a distinctly Meiji notion of Japan's premodern literary history and aesthetics, linked to the project of defining Japan as a modern nation state and Japaneseness through the rubric of an "authentic" and increasingly feminized literary nativism, conjoined with maternalized femaleness, as the locus for approaching the repressed, missing, desired, feared, and abjected not-self.

The drive toward *jouissance* that, as explored above, marks so many of Kyōka's narratives amply resurrects structural and locational elements from the *michiyuki*—the abundant bridges and rivers, the transformations in water of the male protagonists, the incestuous, erotic yearning (which is halted before fulfillment), death, and loss of selfsameness— while for Kyōka, the abject, or the potential matrix for *jouissance*, is specifically gendered. It is this contemporaneity—the production of origins in keeping with modern gendered desire—that I imagine has made Kyōka so passionately revered by such a diverse group of (mostly male) Japanese writers spanning the twentieth century, making a community of the disparate Mishima Yukio, Tanizaki Jun'ichirō, and Nakagami Kenji and the kabuki *onnagata* (biological male who specializes in female roles) Bandō Tamasaburō (hereafter Tamasaburō).

Jouissance is evident in the *michiyuki*, which provides the site where language, death, and a decentered subjectivity intersect. The *michiyuki* proper reached its apex in the puppet theater, one of many medieval and early modern multimedia performative genres in which music, lyric, speech, gesture, and other signifiers combine.[24] In most of these mixed-media performances, but especially in the puppet theater (because the puppets are made of wood), as Sakai has written,

> the narrative voice is separated from the fictional locus of the speaking subject (the puppet's body). . . .
>
> It is not feasible to ascribe the voice of a character directly to the actual utterance of an actor. . . . [The puppet play text] plainly indicates an irredeemable disparity between the enunciation and the enunciated, thereby debunking any humanistic ideological "frame up" by which the subject of the enunciated might seem to coincide with the subject of enunciation, the myth of subjective interiority.[25]

The *michiyuki* serves as the vehicle for an emotionally charged, tragic crescendo to the play, while it is definitively split from the expression of an inner, individualized voice. Tragic emotion is evoked through place-naming and the formalized form of the chants rather than through a personalized utterance of an individual voice. The *michiyuki* embodies a process of narrative dispersal, indicative of a difference in Edo artistic renderings of subjectivity/identity. In this sense, the *michiyuki* runs throughout Kyōka's tale, threaded through the foregrounded words and places, so that the modern and premodern, language, landscape, subjectivity, and abjection encounter one another in a tangle of displacements and affirmations. Kyōka's *michiyuki* resembles the classical paradigm in that it foregrounds a complicity of *language* and movement toward death, or the "place where meaning collapses." Yet voices are also assigned to characters, however displaced they may be at times, most clearly in the moments of confession that punctuate so many of his narratives. Still, again and again it is a poeticized, and for Kyōka, a feminized *landscape*—words inscribed in space—that becomes the repository for nostalgia and that destabilizes through *enunciation* the phallic unity of the modern subject. In an equal variance from tradition, Kyōka's texts do not move backward toward a stasis but forward to open the *michiyuki* into an embrace with modernity (that is, into imaginary fictitious sites wherein origin is produced through a maternalized/feminized abjection).

For the actor Tamasaburō, the overlapped productions of the abjected, othered, revered, and feared female *in language meant to be performed* provide him, *as an onnagata*, with the perfect vehicle for enacting femininity. Over and over, essays about Kyōka identify the women of his narratives as embodying "the essence of femaleness." (Some essays are sophisticated enough to recognize this notion of femaleness as a male imaginary). *Onnagata* are precisely concerned with theatrical femaleness.[26]

For Tamasaburō and for Kyōka as well, there seems to be a tacit affirmation that "gendered essence" lies not in the subject, but in the discourses and words themselves that produce that subject. In 1995, Tamasaburō performed in and directed a film version of Kyōka's "Tenshu monogatari" (The tale of the castle tower, 1917) that appears not to have altered one word of the narrative script but to have faithfully supplied the supplement, in the form of the body, the visual, the gesture, the music.[27] Femaleness is inherent in a linguistic deferral, always already absent from the purported speaking subject and severed from the "sexed" body.

Similarly, in "Kechō," Ren's quest is precisely for the "narrated." Sister is the orated embodiment of the uncanny, linked as she is to tales long past. She is an origin constructed in storytelling. As origin she is repeatedly deferred and transferred, missing, sought, and reinvented. "Ehon no haru," which shares with "Kechō" the narrative split between an experiential youth and a more mature recollection of that youth, centers on a twice-told tale of a woman cruelly murdered in the Edo period who "lives on" as a ghost. The tale is embedded as an orally transmitted story and as a magic picture book that the ghost gives to the little boy. That the tale is then written down (by Kyōka) is yet another narrative layer or deferral. In *Yōken kibun* and *Kōya hijiri,* the pattern of deferral plays on the discursive surfaces as well in the layering and the transferal of tale. *Kōya hijiri*'s primary narrator's voice basically frames the story but is quickly replaced with the ascetic's and a variety of other voices that weave in and out of his tale. The primary narrator of *Yōken kibun* remains unnamed. Beginning with descriptive passages, from its outset the tale nonetheless seeks to incorporate "the verbal" through reported speech embedded within reported speech. The narrator announces that "recently I heard this story," disengaging the narrating self from the tale's origin. Subsequently, voices overlap, as the narrator quotes an old man quoting the temple caretaker, until narrative authority, or the speaking subject, has been firmly dislodged. Reproduced below, in English, is an example of this transferal of narrative:

It is this resident priest's resolution to confront the people-drowning, life-stealing Little Mortar and Big Mortar, which has not even left alone the purification spot that should lie pure and unsullied at Acala's feet.

    If you look closely you will understand.—In preparation he had painted his undershirt and loincloth black with dark lacquer and doubled and knotted his loincloth in a wrestler's style, topped by a tight sash.

    All of you must have seen and heard how this Temple of Immobility is lonely as a fox's cry in broad daylight. Because some demon, or spirit, has intentionally usurped its power and authority.—As the guardian caretaker, I am mortified. . . . Today I have resolved to dive in and carefully search the suspicious depths. (651–52)

The first lines are in the resident priest's voice, addressing those gathered before him. The second paragraph shifts to the primary narrator's voice (the implicit "I"), and the "you" is now "you the reader." In the third paragraph, the narration has shifted back. Sakuden is once again the narrativized (verbalized) "I," and the "you" is the assembled guests, although there are no quotation marks to indicate the shift. To complicate such narrative transferals, Kyōka also makes frequent use of quotation marks in the conventional manner. The passage above continues briefly in Sakuden's voice. At the next indentation, an opening quotation mark appears, but the voice is still that of Sakuden.

Unlike in Edo-period puppet plays, by 1920, when Kyōka wrote *Yōken kibun,* narrative conflation of direct and indirect speech had become less common. Edo texts used a variety of markers, generally "extratextual," such as gesture or voice, or supplemental to the text "proper" (proper names written in the margins above the individual's direct speech, for example) to delineate direct and indirect speech. These markers, however, became inappropriate in the Meiji *genbun'itchi* movement toward transparency. The loss of these conventions for differentiating enunciations, along with the "discovery" of interiorized narration and the conflation of author-narrator-protagonist, necessitated the incorporation in some form of new punctuation standards.[28] Kyōka's adamant rejection of then-developing quotation (and other punctuation) standards is inseparable from his ambivalence over positing an interiorized narrating subject, although again, the choice to reject is inevitably predicated on either its prior or its simultaneous establishment. Unlike Edo narration, in which there is no "speaking subject" per se, for Kyōka there has been a shift whereby a narrator is delineated as speaking subject and subsequently displaced by polyphonic narrative cacophony. This polyphony is specifically manufactured in pursuit of an "atmosphere" of Edo that is crafted from an ideological site mired in Meiji subjectivity and modernity. One must read Kyōka's works not only with the utmost attention to discerning multiple meanings of individual words, as Noguchi recommended, but also to the polyvocality of the sentences. As Ikuta Chōkō wrote, "[Kyōka's] sentences are styled like a whirlpool, churning confusion to its utmost, mixing together the low tone of colloquial speech and the high tone of literary language."[29] Or as Mishima claimed, part of Kyōka's appeal was that he wrote of "common" people.[30] Although Kyōka is famous for his intricate prose, many of his narratives, such as "Itoyū" (Seasonal vapors, 1882) consist of conversations strung together with descriptive interludes.[31] Kyōka is also known for his dramatic scripts and has been loudly lauded for his talent for incorporating "natural" dialogue. Kyōka's interest in reproducing utterance stems from the same perspectival twist that informed the efforts of the *genbun'itchi* naturalists, even as it took his work in a different direction. For Kyōka, the narrative voice that has already been discovered is deferred or displaced from the primary speaking subject. Commonly, Kyōka's tales are embedded narrations, and though the identity of the primary narrator may implicitly be "Kyōka" himself, layers of additional narration disperse the enunciations away from any "originary" speaking subject.

The narrative deferrals, and the decentered subjectivity they signal, have led commentators to discover *nō*, kabuki, *renga* (linked verse), *monogatari*, puppet theater, and *setsuwa* (legend)—virtually every pre-modern genre—in Kyōka's modern prose. Mishima described Kyōka as

cultivating the utmost extravagance and possibility within the Japanese language, while utilizing the parlance of the common people's storytelling and human-interest narrative, [Kyōka] created monumental texts with vocabulary rich as the ocean, and pushed his way through, practically bare-handed, into the dense forest of symbolism and the highest mysticism. His prose structure, although it was not posturing along the lines of an antihistorical high intellectualism, revived the splendor of the Japanese language, brimming with images and flights of imagination that characterized linked poetry and that modern Japanese literature has left behind.[32]

An ambivalence toward the modern subject lurks in Mishima's valorization of the manner in which Kyōka's prose recalls linked poetry. *Renga*, the linked verse to which Mishima refers, is usually composed by three poets who link lines, by either word association (*kotoba*) or conceptual connection (*kokoro*), to ones composed by a preceding poet. Earl Miner, scholar of Japanese poetry, describes the system of stanza linkage:

Stanzas have three related but distinguishable existences: as individual poetic units, as stanzas combining with predecessors to make a single poem, and as stanzas combined with successors to make another single poem. A given stanza (though possessing such close semantic connections as to make an integer with its predecessor and successor) possessing *nothing* integral with any other stanza. That is why we call it linked or chain poetry. Often an addition effects profound semantic change in a stanza.[33] (Miner's emphasis)

Linked poetry is mentioned directly by *Yōken kibun*'s narrator in the temple by the haunted river: "A frog croaked somewhere, as though it were a signal for a master poet to add his line of poetry" (*dokokade katakata to kasen ga ura ni naru aizu no yō na kawazu ga nakimasu*) (651). Kyōka's prose tends toward associative rather than linear progression, reminiscent of the changeable subject of both the enunciation and the enunciated of *renga*. Moreover, grammatical irregularities are capped with imagistic and purely associative passages. Agreeing to let the ascetic spend the night at her cottage, the sorceress of *Kōya hijiri* asks him to refrain from telling her about "the capital." She warns the ascetic that although she will labor to coerce him into breaking his promise, he must be steadfast and not yield to her queries. But the subject never recurs, and within the space of the related tale she does not ply him with questions about the capital. This "error" is glossed by editor Muramatsu in the annotated version.[34] Rather than interpreting this ellipsis as an error, it seems to me that for Kyōka the passage has already served its purpose. Although the temporal framing of the embedded story is clearly late Edo, in Heian tradition, separation from the capital (which was then Kyoto) signified unbearable exile from society. The woman's plea serves to stress her isolation through literary precedent, and whether it is further supported by plot is inconsequential.

In another comment, Mishima claimed Kyōka to be a master of an opaque prose that comprised

an overflow of dazzling colors; it faithfully pursues the senses wherever they go. *Instead of pointing bluntly at the subject*, the passages invite the reader to enjoy a pure, sustained sensual experience. Once entrapped in this style, the reader has *no time to examine the subject* through a close look or touch; he drowns in the colorfulness of the language and falls into a kind of intellectual trance.[35] (emphasis added)

Renga was deemed successful more by its overall sophistication in linking verses than by the quality of any individual verse. The subject of the utterance is interwoven with a plurality that precludes a specific assignment of voice to an interiorized speaking subject. The layering of image and displacements of voice in Kyōka's text offer a studied recreation of the affect of such narrative dispersal within a unified and narrativized individualism. The nostalgic performance of such reiteration is dependent on the sense of loss and reorigination based on an othered premodern. In Kyōka's narratives the shifting locus of subjectivity is still usually framed within an authoritarian "I" who can be identified as the primary narrator (even when the tale being related is hearsay). In general Kyōka does not equate his narrators with his protagonists or with himself and is thus unlike the naturalists, who naively believed they could write "truth" and achieve absolute narrative transparency by writing tales about themselves in which the individual author was written into the text both as the narrator and as the protagonist. However, the narrator in *Yōken kibun* frames the tale with explicit references to an existing corpus of ghost tales and thereby implicitly identifies himself as Kyōka: "Recently I heard this story. . . .—A ghost will make a brief appearance in my tale, but please, do not say, 'What, again?' " (631). This bears some resemblance to the positing of the author's life as a supposed factual repository that lent authority to the prose text, common to the *shishōsetsu* writers/readers.[36] (It differs in that it refers to Kyōka's writing corpus and not his personal life.) Later, after having introduced an actual historical figure, the famous kabuki actor Bantō Hikosaburō (1754–1828) into his tale, the narrator interrupts the narrative to confess,

If the truth be told, when I first began to write this story, I thought that my readers would be disappointed if I merely introduced this precious Yamato star, and if I invented a love story between Hikosaburō and Omachi of the outcaste quarters, mixed with the eerie Big Mortar and Little Mortar, it would delight and please the ladies, but that is not how the story goes. (654)

Reminding the reader of the narrative constructivity even as he reaffirms a commitment to "how it really went," Kyōka displaces the narrative from "origin." Who is telling the tale? And from where does the tale originate? Is there a subject of the enunciation? The text employs a variety of devices to rotate on an axis of ambivalent subjectivity. Such entanglements of ambivalence and alternation, of citation and reshaping, of reinscriptions and resituations of conventions embedded in the modern, and of the classical dissociated from its standard positionality can be identified in multiple discursive levels characterizing Kyōka's "unique" prose. The site of enunciation, the narrative origins of the enunciated, narrative transparency and opacity, individual interiority and its converse, exteriority, embrace one another in a web of internal deconstructions. As the following chapter will further elaborate, the reader is left with nothing but language, poised tantalizingly over a play of significatory presence and absence, hovering between articulations of self and not-self. Language itself travels to the fore and collapses within its own distance from the real.

Language and Bodies; or, Never Write Words on Sitting Cushions

Kyōka has been frequently labeled a conventionalist precisely because what I regard as his literary *radicalism* steered his texts away from the pattern characterizing the Western novel, in a move that illustrates his ambivalence toward the subject and its representation in prose. In general, most discussions of Meiji modernity have been plagued by the incessant positing of Western modernity as a standard, be it implicit or explicit. Even many studies that have argued for a more historically and culturally nuanced description of Japanese modernity have tended to resituate the Western norm through negative difference. If, as many others have argued, the Western "subject" has in fact never existed in Japan, then Japanese modernity must be redescribed as inseparable from its correlation to individual and state subjectivity.[1] The relentless labeling of Kyōka as a traditionalist not only obscures the insistent presence of "Meiji/Taisho" in his work but also conceals how his works were in fact gendered collusions with the productions of modern subjectivity, thus conspiring with Kyōka (intentionally or not) to serve the modern, phallic agenda that I seek to "uncover." Kyōka's quest for (linguistic) *jouissance* and foregrounded, empowered female characterizations might appear "antiphallic" when contrasted with the refusal of linguistic pluralities by naturalists and the male centrality of their characterizations and those of writers of "constructed" fictions such as Sōseki. But Kyōka located the Real in the body of the dangerous woman. This locating bound abjection to the maternal body and thus is also, although differently, productive of the modern Japanese phallic subject.

Moreover, as Karatani has written, that the naturalist project to produce an interiorized and unified "subject" akin to the Western narrative paradigm soon shifted toward a rejection of that subject (as in the ascension of Shiga Naoya [1883–1971] as the "god of modern Japanese fiction," or the consummate master of the *shishōsetsu*), suggests that Meiji/Taisho phonocentrism was somehow linked to an *ambivalence* toward narrativized interiority.[2] This ambivalence is clear in Kyōka's writing.

In this chapter I will show how Kyōka marshals *language itself* as a signifier, employing conterminous notions of the feminine and the conceit of feminized discourse in the task of recuperating an imaginary past (whereby modernity is fabricated). In this recuperation, early-twentieth-century phonocentrism inscribes itself as inseparable from Kyōka's *seemingly* antiquated prose. (By phonocentrism I refer to the putative link among sound, voice, and the Real and the produced perception of a gap between writing and the Real.)[3] In Kyōka's narratives, phonocentrism is gendered; it is *feminized* within the debated relation between word and signification. Though phonocentrism has generally been narrowly applied in Meiji only to the *genbun'itchi* (linguistic standardization) stylists' quest for narrative transparency (and thus potentially "masculinized" by extension), I contend that Kyōka's concern with the relation between enunciation and the Real constitutes another Meiji phonocentric trajectory, collusive with folkloric studies, that is summarily erased as phonocentrism in its variance from the Western narrative norm.

In his 1959 *Bunshō tokuhon*, Mishima Yukio placed all (Japanese) prose into two categories: the Dionysian, characterized by opacity and polysemy, and the Apollonian, which privileged clarity. According to Mishima, both styles originated in a Heian-period demarcation between men's and women's discursive "languages." The Apollonian style, argued Mishima, was an outgrowth of classical Chinese and was marked by masculinity, logic, clarity, and public function. The Dionysian style, to the contrary, was rooted in classical Japanese and was *feminine*. This discursive style, he claimed, was closely linked to the representation of voice (or sound) and to *kana*, used by women rather than men in the Heian period, and became the dominant style for Japanese literary production. Kyōka, held Mishima, was a master of the Dionysian (feminine) style.[4]

Clearly, "masculine" and "feminine" here are employed descriptively and are not purely bound to sexed bodies. At the same time, it should be clear that certain gendered attributes are assigned "originary" sexes in Mishima's classificatory scheme, by which narrative texts could be de-

marcated along a binary, gendered axis. Mishima was by no means original in this particular genderization; he merely reiterated what had become
a dominant structural paradigm for classifying Japanese literature in the
twentieth century.[5]

Whereas Mishima placed Kyōka in the "feminine" category, this study
has, quite to the contrary, focused on the phallic nature of Kyōka's narrative project. How does this phallic discursive production become a marker
for a feminized aestheticism? How are Meiji/Taisho *modern* phallic subjectivity and the feminization of premodern Japanese literary aesthetics related? As I have argued, for Kyōka, the dangerous woman is linked to language/discourse as a signifier for the Real and is therefore the site for an unseizable j*ouissance* (unseizable because seizure would obliterate the phallic
subject). Kyōka's female construct thus complements the modern *feminization* of traditional poetics/discursive aesthetics, as seen in Mishima's
study. In Meiji/Taisho there is a gendered constellation in which "traditional" Japan, in particular, archaic (pre-Chinese influence) Japan, and
Heian-period Japan and its literature, become "feminized" against both
paradigms of the West and modern Japan. It is in part this historical construct that "feminizes" Kyōka.

As a first step toward unknotting the construct in which Kyōka is seen
as "feminine," I would like to detach thematic femininity from feminized
discourse, or *écriture*. Here I would differ in emphasis from Ann Sherif,
who argued that it was largely thematic attention to women that led to a
writer being labeled "feminine," and I would claim instead that it is more
how Kyōka wrote than *what* he wrote that garnered him the label. Certainly that was how Mishima used the terms. Mishima contrasts Mori
Ōgai (1862–1922; hereafter Ōgai) as a paradigm of "masculine style" with
Kyōka as a master of "feminine style." On the one hand, holds Mishima,
Ōgai is masculine, or Apollonian, because his sentence structure is firmly
rooted in Chinese discursive tradition. Ōgai's prose is "terse and pure and
has no flourishes." Mishima writes that Ōgai employed words exclusively
in the service of realistic description and refrained from "dirtying images
with superfluous words, well aware that [verbosity] would only sully the
clarity of the things he described." On the other hand, Mishima described
Kyōka's style as enticing the reader toward a "drunkenness of reason" engendered by a "sorcery of word," a use of word as a "medium" for a loss
of rationalism.[6]

Though classical Chinese verse addressed itself to both politics and
love, or the public and the private, in Japan, says Mishima, discursive

realms were separated and sexually specific. Women wrote of the "private"—love and emotions, men of the "public"—politics and philosophy. Moreover, the public realm was deeply influenced by foreign (mostly Chinese) concepts, and thus men were displaced from "truly Japanese" expressions of themselves. Ever since the Heian period, maleness as written in text was overwhelmingly subordinated to descriptions of men of active deeds (*kōdōteki*). Men of the female-authored *monogatari*, argued Mishima, were a female "imaginary." He wrote, "the descriptions of men that were cultivated by the women writers of the Heian period were, so to speak, depictions of men following female sentiments and passions."[7] Yet it is not a biological *woman* who Mishima offers up as a master of his "feminine" style in post-Edo Japan; it is Kyōka. In Meiji/Taisho at least, a male-authored discourse functions in place of "the female" to produce a femaleness that is, Mishima's criticism of Heian depictions of masculinity notwithstanding, a *male* imaginary. Furthermore, it is Mishima's perception of a "split" phallic self—a masculinity formed by exclusion of the feminine—that generates his thesis. Male-authored Japanese discourse has *always* been adulterated by the dominance of the "Other" for Mishima—be it through "feminization" or "Sinification" (that is, to adapt to or bring under the influence of Chinese cultural, historical, discursive, or other practices). Mishima's ahistorical notion of the private and public realms, as well as his conflation of modern narrative self-expression with premodern literary impulse, moreover, fabricate a *modern* "individual" and "social" body where there was none.

Mizuta Noriko, literary scholar and specalist in women writers, has offered a feminist version of Mishima's gendered history of Japanese literature that helps clarify the above. She has shown how it was "gender" rather than "sex" that became affixed to specified sides of a system of developing binarisms through Japan's middle ages, rendering the "private" production of art and literature as feminine against the masculinized "public" realms of politics and scholarship.[8] Gender functioned symbolically or was turned into metaphor as a fundamental aspect of specified genres—those genres deemed to be "female" were to be narrated by women, regardless of authorial sex.[9] Ki no Tsurayuki's *Tosa nikki* (*The Tosa Diary*, ca. 935), in which the male author employs a female narrating persona, is an early example of the metaphoric use of gender. Subsequent narratives colluded in employing gender as a now conventionally established metaphoric figure:

The education of the women of Heian was completely severed from politics; theirs were intellectual skills, artistic skills, and competencies that were posited in opposition to politics. Because they were excluded from politics, women achieved artistic freedom. Within the cultural framework and social system that placed art/politics, literature/scholarship, and private/public in binary opposition, gender distinctions (maleness and femaleness) were each affixed to only one side of [the other developing] binarisms. Thus, gender distinction itself, as a determined constituent component of the system, functions to further rigidify the existing structure. . . .

Because genres incorporated the issue of gender from the moment of origination, genre relies on gender. Genres become inseparable from a standardized production of gender in text. Gender is transformed into symbol, or metaphor, which then independently generates signification. Genre is sustained and reproduced by a [predetermined] genderized narrative stance.[10]

Increasingly, says Mizuta, narratives were demarcated into separate genres by virtue of particularized "modes of expression" (*buri*) that reinvigorated the metaphoric male/female binarism:

What I mean by "mode of expression" [b*uri*] is akin to the classification of "style" [*ryū*] in the term "the school of women's style" [*joryū*], and does not simply designate literary/linguistic style [*buntai*]. Moreover, it is not a particularized female imagination, or theme [*shudai*], or female soul [*kokoro*]. It is an "engendered" stance by which one produces *waka*, *nikki* and *monogatari* as genres, it is a gender that has become metaphor.[11]

The term *onnade* (woman's hand) used to describe writing in *hiragana* (cursive phonetic syllabary), which was poised against "masculine" writing in Chinese characters, links female discursive production and "voice." Importantly, however, as Mizuta deftly showed, *onnade* does not identify a particularly sexed body as the subject of the enunciation, as some modern convolutions would have. Men, too, used *onnade* when writing poetry, private correspondences, and so forth. As countless commentators have pointed out, the female author of *The Tale of Genji*, Murasaki Shikibu, could competently read and write Chinese. (And Kyōka, the modern master of "feminine" writing, was, of course, biologically male.) *Onnade* has no intrinsic relation to female subjectivity or voice or "her" expression (or her genitalia, for that matter); rather, it is a metaphoric term that indicates the private, the light, the sexual and its yearnings, as separated from "public" and "significant" writing marked with erudition such as politics or history.[12] The coexistence of *onnade* and writings in Chinese by men is not, as Mara Miller would have it, a "copresence" but a hierarchized discursive constellation.[13]

Mishima held up *The Tale of Genji* as one example of premodern "feminine" *écriture*. Leaving aside for a moment the important issue of its female authorship, *when* does *The Tale of Genji* become a paradigm of discourse? And how is it, as *écriture*, "feminized"? At the time of its writing, *The Tale of Genji* was not considered high art—poetry was. *Monogatari* were considered mere "entertainment," primarily circulated among women of the court aristocracy. How does a genre that is seen as oppositional to the high poetic tradition (the highest of which was written in Chinese) become inverted to represent Japan's finest moment of literary achievement? It is with the Edo-period *kokugaku* (national learning / nativism) quest for texts with "originary enunciations," as I will discuss in greater detail later in this chapter, that *The Tale of Genji* is first canonized as a text with *import* other than that of pure entertainment. Its import is located in a phonocentrism, lodged in words that embody *mono no aware*, an expression of emotive harmony between "self" and "thing."

Comparing Edo Japanese valorization of phoneticism with, as an example, Dante's privileging of the vernacular over Latin, Karatani has argued that the modern nation is shaped alongside a movement toward a vernacular-based *écriture*.[14] Dante's quest was for an *écriture* separated from the "Latin cultural sphere"; Japan's quest was for an *écriture* freed of the influence of the Chinese cultural sphere. It is here, in this movement, argues Karatani, that modern nationalism makes its first appearance and that world empire begins to reform into modern nations. More important for this study, the earliest gestures toward modern nationalism are thus interwoven with an *aestheticization* of the nation-in-formation.[15]

In Japan, Motoori Norinaga's (1730–1801; hereafter Norinaga) phonocentric passion for words that elicited *mono no aware* was informed by an aestheticized nationalism that reiterated itself in literary discourse. *The Tale of Genji* was not the only classical text valorized by the Edo nativists. Others, such as the *Kojiki* (712) and the *Man'yōshū*, were thought of equally, or for some nativists, privileged above *The Tale of Genji*, as repositories of originary enunciations linked to immediacy.[16] (By immediacy I refer to the notion of absolute transparency between utterance and signification; by originary enunciation I refer to the notion that ancient pronunciations were innately linked to meaning.)[17] Both Motoori Ōhira (1756–1833) and Hirata Atsutane (1776–1843), for example, argued against what they perceived as Norinaga's excessive valorization of *The Tale of*

Genji.[18] As Sherif has also noted, it is *not* the "feminine" qualities of *The Tale of Genji* that lead to its canonization.[19] Or, more accurately, the qualities that in the twentieth century are labeled "feminine" have merely been *rediscovered* as "feminine"; in Edo they were "defeminized." Nativism was produced in Edo as an "authentic Japaneseness" against Chineseness; in the process, a once-feminized, archaic culture is *retrieved* from its Heian privatized (and thus feminized) position and reconfigured as nonfeminine. Even Norinaga, who heralded *The Tale of Genji* as the supreme vessel of *mono no aware*, sought to sever phonocentrism from its Heian feminization, and return it to the realm of the "commonly human."[20] Harootunian wrote that Norinaga "elevated the sensation and emotionalism of immediate, fleeting, 'feminine' experiences, such as kindness, affection, tenderness, and love. *Despite recent opinion associating these values with women, he wrote, such expressive emotionality belonged to the original spirit of all humans* . . . invention and artifice identified with manliness—fell short of expressing the real state of affairs" (emphasis added).[21] Norinaga was neither interested in a putative femaleness nor, it should be stressed, in a reading of Murasaki's "voice" in *The Tale of Genji*; rather, he sought descriptive detail, commonality, and *mono no aware* in its pages.

It is also important to remember that although *hiragana* was feminized, *katakana*, another phonetic syllabary, was not. *Katakana* was first employed as *rubi* (a pronunciation and grammatical supplement) alongside Chinese characters in the production of *kanbun* (Chinese read in Japanese). Both *katakana* and *hiragana* are formed from simplified versions of Chinese characters, employed for sound, not meaning. *Katakana* continued to be used in alternation with Chinese characters on documents, social science studies, and other "public" writings well into the modern prewar period. For fiction (nonfactual) writings geared toward reader entertainment, *hiragana* in combination with Chinese characters was the paradigm. "Women's writing in *hiragana*" has always been a combination of Chinese characters and cursive phonetic symbols. There was never an actual separation of the phonocentric from the nonphonocentric and Chinese from Japanese along sexed categories. Chinese characters in combination with *katakana* comprised the norm for "public" and governmental or political (factual) writings, while Chinese characters in combination with *hiragana* became the standard for literary (fictional) writings. The linkage of female "voice" with phoneticism through *hiragana* usage is little more than a (admittedly complex) modern myth, in implicit service of a phallocentric agenda.

In twentieth-century prewar Japan, as Tetsuo Najita and Harootunian have shown, culture functions as the repository of Japaneseness: "Japanese culture" is posited, and reiterated, as a static, irrational "essence" of national identity.[22] Ivy analyzed the trajectory of modern massification and consumption of Japanese culture through the construct of the *furusato* from Yanagita through the 1990s.[23] I argue that a constitutive element of the "discovery" of an exotic (erotic) Japaneseness within Japan was its discursive feminization in the works of writers such as Kyōka. In this imaginary, nativism thus shifted again in Meiji, when an(other) inversion, in which it was refeminized, was rewoven into a nostalgia collaborative with modern gender ideations (also influenced by Western gender notions): the realm of nonlogic is now (again) female. This refeminization intertwined neatly with Japan's immediate political project of creating a gendered social basis for modern industrialized capitalism.

In one trajectory of twentieth-century Japanese production of the premodern, the Heian aesthetic is simultaneously rediscovered, valorized, and (re)feminized as a complementary site of familiarized alterity (collusive with the developing maternal myth and an uncanny nativism)—all to be consumed by an ambivalent homosocial subject as part of the overall project of modernization. The industrializing, capitalist twentieth-century production of a demarcated female realm (which was also a component of the separation of sexed labor realms) had affinity with, and use for, the Heian aristocratic separated and gendered sensibility. Desire was created and circulated; separation was ensured.

To further complicate the issue, the lack of attention to the modernity, constructivity, and phallicism of the feminization of Heian-period Japanese poetics has led some critics to imagine that they have discovered the repository of a true "female voice" in its literature and/or a Kristevian sort of feminized poetic language in all Japanese premodern polysemy. Such readings are often applied to Kyōka's narratives. These readings, however, are based on two primary inversions that work in tandem with a modern phallic agenda, attended by a reconstruction of the premodern in the image of the modern. First, there is a conflation of premodern female authorship with modern narration that locates an interiorized narratorial speaking subject where there is none. Second, there is a reiteration of the Heian genderization of discourse that is here confused with a modern subjectivity, while the different sorts and functions of premodern polysemic conventions are mixed up, resembling how the premodern appears in Kyōka's texts. Premodern variances thus become fused as likenesses only by virtue of their radical differences from conventions of modern prose.

If, following the work of Fowler, Karatani, Miyoshi, Sakai, and others, there is no speaking subject akin to the modern Western model in pre-Meiji Japanese narrative, then where does the idea of "female voice of the canon" come from? *The Tale of Genji*, though authored by a woman, is characterized by deeply layered narration, much like that found in Kyōka's texts: the primary narrator addresses the reader, while other "voices" intersect and take over the enunciation from *within* the primary narration.[24] The search for "female voice" began with the twentieth-century proclamation that "women are people too."[25] That there was a female discursive tradition in premodern Japan certainly deserves analytic attention; however, this tradition should not be conflated with "voice." At least for *monogatari*, as Mizuta has shown, it should be understood as "metaphorized gender."

Polysemy itself as a term and concept must be further unpacked: Edo *gesaku* polysemy, as Sakai has shown, was subversive to the Heian polysemic tradition, while representing the most extreme form of Japanese polysemy.[26] As Karatani has argued, as Edo drew to a close, literary prose had become so divorced from content and so concentrated on textual surface that subsequent narratives needed to reinvest word with signification or disintegrate into meaninglessness.[27] Miyoshi described Edo texts as being inhospitable to characterizations and engrossed in the verbal surfaces of the texts.[28] Harootunian wrote that, "Many [Edo] writers were convinced that the very opacity of language, its inertia, now offered the occasion for reuniting the present with the intentionality of antiquity."[29] Edo polysemy, which resembles Bahktin's "carnivalesque" in its abundant vulgarities and "baseness" more than Heian "intertextuality" does, is not, however, the polysemy linked to Heian female discursive production. *Onnade*, or feminized (putative) "vernacular" writing, was marked by elegance and refinement.

Kyōka's taste for thick, opaque prose was undoubtedly stimulated by Edo traditions. Yet Kyōka's nostalgic, rather than parodic, incorporation of polysemic devices and references to canonized texts represents a different displacement of the classical than that of the Edo models; it harkens back to Heian-style elegant intertextuality and is indicative of an ambivalence toward Meiji subjectivity that arises precisely from having already become that subject. Kyōka's desire to dissolve the subject by returning it to a condition of plurality can only emerge *with* the fact: it is only as the constitutive by-product of its crafted, identified, and isolated site that a subject can yearn to unknot its own putative unity. The *yukari no iro* (purple/karmic connection) of *Yōken kibun*, discussed in the previous chapter, whispers of a decentered subjectivity—since it is a connection in surplus to the construction of any of the particular individuals involved—belonging to lives lived as *others*. Rather than sporting with the spiritualized aesthetics of the classical canon, Kyōka's polysemy asserts their authority, in a modern, generalized defixity and newly produced mythic homogeneity.

Regarding eighteenth-century Japan specifically, it is important to remember that the nativists sought to bring the human subject into harmonic accord with the Real through "feeling" accessed by the enunciation of words. As Sakai has written, this

feeling is the structural linkage between the human body as passage toward the heterogeneous and the performative situation as *topos* of what makes an utterance meaningful but is unrepresentable itself. . . .

[Feeling cannot be] limited to the identity of an individual person or thing, since it is neither a phenomenon taking place within the inner mind nor a state of things. [It is] . . . a linkage of the human body with the Other.[30] (Sakai's emphasis)

Sakai has shown how Edo parodists in particular put into question the manner in which subjectivity was represented in the canonized literary discourses of their time. The Meiji naturalists' desire to reveal (and thus the production of) an inner, alienated self through a transparency of word is both radically different and curiously similar: both seek the Real, but the concept of the Real, and the subject in relation to it, are not the same. The Edo subject was believed to be endowed with a "natural" function in accordance with (subjugation to) a divine order, the "way" of which had been passed from deity to the emperor to the people.[31] Harootunian writes that, moreover,

Since both language and work had been covered by a sedimentation that concealed their true purpose to humans, nativists believed it was possible to remove the rubble in order to initiate a praxis that would recover its lost meaning . . . an effort to supplement what many believed was missing. The object of desire inspiring this "supplement" was to overcome the separation between mental and manual labor (coded by the acknowledged separation of public and private), in which contemporary culture and its "crisis" had originated. The way to reunite mental and manual labor was to return to the identity of speech and work as activities centered in the body.[32]

The quest for immediacy, which underlay the different projects of both Edo *gesaku* stylists and nativists, is transformed by Kyōka into a differently nostalgic gesture toward (a modern desire for) an imaginary (feminized) past as the site for healing the split self or regaining the abjected viscosities of the phallicized subject. What has already changed for Kyōka are subjectivity, the body and its "gender," representational systems, and the concept of the Real. But for Kyōka, as for the nativists and the *genbun'itchi* stylists, ideally word and the Real may embrace each other (in contradistinction to the postmodern Lacanian notion that this is an impossibility).

Literary critic Shinoda Hajime praised the *musical* quality of one of Kyōka's works, a long fiction entitled *Sankai hyōbanki* (An account of the rumors of the land and sea, 1929), commonly dismissed as a lesser narrative because it lacked the sort of unity that would make it recognizable as a "novel" (*shōsetsu*). "The truth is, I too suffered as I began to read this unknown long fiction until I had read about one-third of it. The threads of myriad plots were left in a tangle, and I was unable to discern, endlessly, anything that resembled an expressed theme." However, Shinoda continues that upon the appearance of a mysterious apparition in the text, he suddenly understood Kyōka's narrative intention.

Completely put at ease over the disordered thematic threads and the obscurity of subjects, as though I held it in my palm, I was able to understand this tale of mysterious transformation as an altered form of leitmotiv within this long *shōsetsu*. The word *leitmotiv* I use not as it is used in the terminology of literary criticism; I borrow it verbatim as the musical term used by Richard Wagner. That is to say, I did not read this work as a *shōsetsu* but listened to it enraptured, like music. In other words, leitmotiv is the playing over and over of a single-theme motif that encompasses a variety of changing patterns of sound, forming and disintegrating before my eyes an ever-changing crowd of mysterious images that supersede one another, to which one listens in a semiconscious state and which makes one's heart leap. Listening to music is different from reading a *shōsetsu*; one takes in the sounds one by one, each in its own instant, and in the next instant forgets them. . . . There is simply no other Japanese author whose writing was so like music as was Kyōka's in *Sankai hyōbanki*. Questions regarding lack of plot, clarity, and the like quickly become irrelevant.[33]

Word, for Kyōka, written or not, is a carrier of (potentially archaic) sound. In his "Ehon no haru," the murdered woman is cursed because she was born on the "sixth day of the sixth month of the sixth year"; the character for "six" (*mi*) not only means "snake" but also signifies the sign and time of the snake in the archaic calendar. (An aside: *hemi* is an archaic pronunciation of *hebi*). In Kyōka's text the cursed sound repeats: "*mi mi mi mi, mi no nengetsu no sorotta wakai onna no ikigimo*" (the time of

birth of the young woman lined up the dates of six/snake six/snake six/
snake six/snake, six/snake) (142). Moreover, because "six" is followed by
"seven" (*shichi*), which contains the syllable *shi*, a homophone for the
root of the verb "to die," the young boy's interaction with the ghost is followed by repeated flooding of the nearby generally tranquil river (during
which, naturally, countless snakes are revealed). From Kyōka's text,
"*Meiji shichinen shichigatsu nanoka, taiu no furitsuzuita sono nanoka
nanabanme ni machi no mō hitotsu no taiga ga osoroshii kōzui shita*" (On
the seventh day of the seventh month of the seventh year of Meiji, on that
seventh day for the seventh time after continuous heavy rains the river
flooded dreadfully one more time)(147). Sound interlocks with symbol in
a polysemic, phonocentric, yet also discursive, knot with the abject.

For Kyōka, as for the *genbun'itchi* stylists, not only does sound travel
to the forefront of prose through enunciation (and/or through the pictor-
ial aspects of Chinese characters), word may be bound to the Real. In
"Kechō," Kyōka gives considerable narrative attention to the little boy
narrator Ren's refusal to accept his teacher's hierarchized schema of the
natural and human world, in which human beings are accorded superior-
ity because they can speak in words with signification. Ren clings instead
to a vision of the world *told him by his mother*, in which bird song and
flower blossoms are given equal importance to and are regarded on a par
with human words. Mother claims that she too can understand the enunciations of animals and plants. The thetic challenge to logos in "Kechō"
complements Kyōka's stylistic foregrounding of sound as integral to the
process of narrative. Literary critic Taneda Wakako employed "Kechō"
as a primary illustrative text when she likened Kyōka's prose to Kristevian
"poetic language," thus rendering a *challenge* to the (Lacanian) Symbolic,
through the manner in which sound and repetition, among other textual
flourishes, muddy the relationship of signifier to signified in Kyōka's narratives.[34] Kyōka's reverence for word, especially word as enunciation or
sound, resulted in thematic storylines and a prose that when subjected to
a Western critical analysis resembles the Kristevian semiotic. But akin to
his postulation of the dangerous woman as the site for *jouissance*,
Kyōka's prose was informed by a modern phallocentrism quite removed
from a putatively "feminine poetic language."

Part of the *genbun'itchi* stylists' aim was to reclaim voice from its subordination to writing, and they therefore tried to render colloquial
speech, or utterance, verbatim within the confines of their written narratives. Of course, the incorporation of colloquialism has its immediate
roots in Edo *gesaku*, in which reported colloquial speech, in its supposed

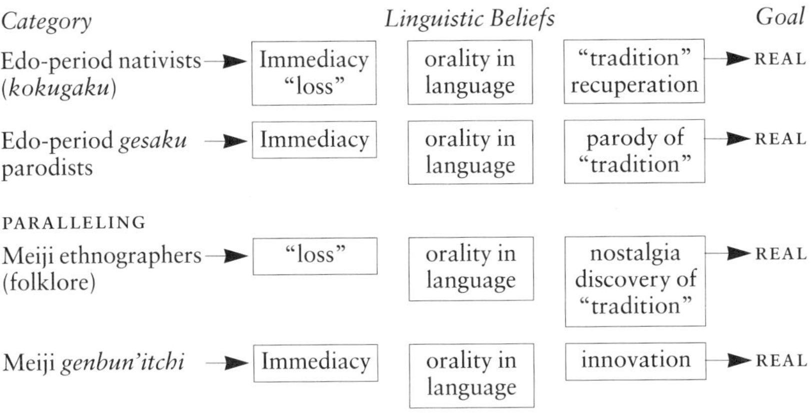

Figure 2. Language and the Real

"natural idiom," alternated alongside classical description in literary language. As discussed above, the seemingly incompatible agendas of the parodists and the nativists are structurally linked through the quest for simultaneity with the Real. In Kyōka's texts, narrative play that in form resembles *gesaku* parody also mirrors *gesaku* as it unfolds along the axis of the relationship of word to meaning and the proximity of voice to self.

I would like to temporarily place into doubled parallel structures the Edo-period movements of *gesaku* stylists and nativists alongside the Meiji *genbun'itchi* advocates and ethnographers (as spearheaded by Yanagita) (see Figure 2).

In Edo the nativists rallied to the task of recuperating an (imagined) originary language with immediate intimacy with the Real (a quest for tradition); the *gesaku* parodists were similarly concerned with how language signified in relation to immediacy.[35] In part, the Edo project was stimulated by a desire for, and in resistance to, the internalized Other epitomized by Chinese writing. Meiji ethnographers and *genbun'itchi* adherents similarly sought immediacy in language's relation to the Real (although in Meiji *nostalgia* was the province only of the ethnographers, who like the Edo "traditionalist-nativists" believed their project to be recuperative). The parodists of Edo and the *genbun'itchi* stylists of Meiji shared a rejection of such nostalgia and privileging of tradition, but they are interlinked with the nativists/ethnographers through their engagement in a phonocentric movement inseparable from an anxiety about how language signified.[36] Kyōka's narratives take plentifully from both

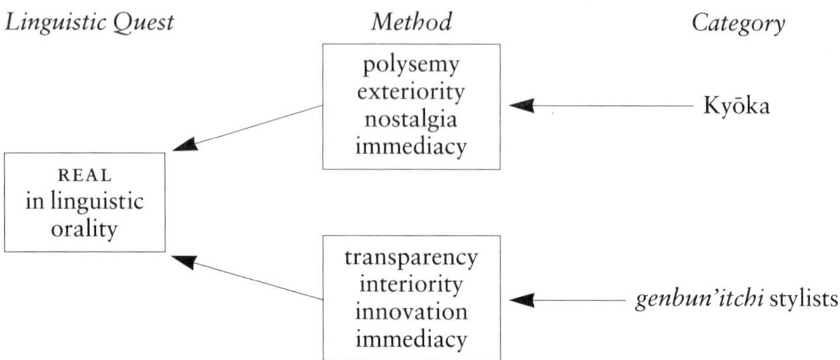

Figure 3. The Meiji Quest

Meiji positions in their *ambivalence*. But for both Kyōka and the *gen-bun'itchi* stylists, not only is their project actualized in *word* but the Real is primarily located in an orality (see Figure 3).

Undoubtedly, there is a clear rift between the prevalent Meiji discourses on realistic prose and how Kyōka set language into play through sound as well as through the polysemic and catechrestic devices discussed previously. *Genbun'itchi* followed Edo colloquialism but required a specific shift in perspective, hinging on the identification of narrative voice or the subject of enunciation and its relation to language, the Real, and the assumed reader of the text. *Genbun'itchi* stylists sought to banish multiplicity from complicating a then-privileged one-to-one correlation between word and meaning. To do so they looked to simplicity and "artlessness." In their discussions of *genbun'itchi*, Kyōka's contemporaries identified literary language as a primary site of debate.[37] Naturalists rejected the polysemy of the classical literary canon and searched to express their inner selves in a plain, apparently unmediated, prose. As Karatani has shown, this position was the postulation ("discovery") of an interiorized narrator who reflected on the world around him/her.[38] Kyōka's description of the priest's night at the woman's cottage travels far afield of such clarity and realism:

Suddenly I heard something outside.

It sounded like animals approaching, already rather close. I tried to reassure myself, reasoning that monkeys and toads lived in this wilderness. But these were something altogether different—

The sound of something by the front door; a sheep baaed.

My pillow was to the door, and I heard them right there, just beyond where my head lay. Wings flapped beneath the blooming hydrangeas to the right.

What was that squeal? Maybe it was a giant winged squirrel flying towards the roof-ridge. Something huge sounded so close that my heart pounded. A cow mooed. The sound of mincing, hurried steps coming in waves from a distance made me envision beasts wearing straw sandals, walking on two legs. The cacophony of wing flapping, panting, snorting and whispering seemed to emanate from some twenty to thirty creatures that suddenly surrounded the cottage. These bizarre moonlit beasts, just beyond the single, thin shutter, brought to life a picture of the beast realm in Hell. What were they? Mountain and river demons? All was astir with the crackle of leaves.

I held my breath and, from the back,
The woman gasped as though deep in nightmare.
(There is a guest tonight.) She shouted.
(Don't you see my guest?) The second time she spoke, soon after her first outburst, her voice was cool and clear.
In a very low tone,
(I have a guest.) I heard her toss. Again, I heard her turn.
The cottage swayed and rocked with the commotion outside.
I invoked a mystic incantation:

> *If anyone shall oppose my prayer,*
> *Disturbing this preacher*
> *His head shall be split into seven parts*
> *Like the branches of the Chinese rose tree*
> *Such a sin is akin to the sins of patricide and matricide*
> *And akin to the evil of forcing oil*
> *Like deceiving others with scales and measures,*
> *Like the sin of Devadatta.*
> *Whoever commits such a sin against this preacher*
> *shall suffer these consequences.*

I concentrated deeply. The wind rose, tossing the leaves on the trees, blew southwards and abruptly abated. Sounds from the couple's room ceased.

(426–27; Kyōka's punctuation and format)

When Seisaburō meets Omachi, the scene is both intertextual (because of the reference to the "Song of Musashi Plain") and unrealistic:

For some reason, Seisaburō suddenly went back. No sooner had he retraced his steps than he knelt low on the stream bank.

"Won't you give me that flower?"

It was the elegance celebrated in the Song of Musashi Plain: here, one stalk with a single purple blossom and there, separated from Seisaburō by the narrow single-board bridge, the minstrel girl, unexpectedly like a grounding flower, a flower to offset the other, vibrant in the water.

"Why, whatever—"

As she looked up, her eyelids were suddenly painted dazzlingly with light. At that very moment the youth wiped a single bead of sweat from his forehead. (644)

Kyōka's linguistic choices diverged in methodology and practice from the Meiji/Taisho movement toward romantic naturalism, but it is also imperative to note how they converged in a philosophic reverence for the power of words. The *genbun'itchi* movement, and the naturalist/realist/romantic texts that were produced in its immediate wake, were, it bears repeating, linked to phonocentrism. Mishima wrote that, "Since Meiji through the present, Kyōka was one of the very few Japanese writers who was a medium for the spirit of the Japanese language [*kotodama*]."[39] The word *kotodama* (language spirit) refers to an archaic Shinto belief that a spiritual power resides in word and is activated by enunciation. In ancient Japan it was widely believed that, in Konishi Jin'ichi's words, "*kotodama* would not lodge in a work simply because it used Japanese diction: language suitable for inhabitation by the *kotodama* must attempt to resemble that spoken in the past, in a period closer in time to the age of the Gods."[40] The emphasis on proper accentuation meant that *kotodama* could only be realized through human voicing. Kasahara Nobuo also used the word *kotodama* when he wrote of Kyōka's "reverence" for language.[41] *Kotodama* as a concept was crucial to the Edo nativists search for "origin" (which could supposedly be revitalized in the present) in an attempt to heal a perceived split between the real and the experiential "subject." (Although of course what constituted subjectivity was not commensurate.) Harootunian has written that for Edo naturalists "the linguistic sign, like the human body, housed a spiritual force that could be recognized by the act of speaking or doing. The living body of language was the form manifesting the *kotodama*; its forthcoming, as Husserl might have said, was realized in its coming forth."[42] People, the nativists believed, had lost a connection with "natural" things. This connection had once been present in word, and word had been inseparable from enunciation and body. Speech had originated in gesture, in antiquity, in a time when people spoke "pure sounds." Then, Edo nativists believed, there was no separation between voice, deed, and work (done by the body). And here, as in the Meiji-period response to Westernization by folklorist Yanagita (and Kyōka), it was against the perception of an Other (in Edo, the adulteration of Japanese by Chinese) that antiquity was refabricated. The Edo nativists' project was, to speak generally, to recoup the sense of connection through "resituating language (speaking) to its locus in the body."[43] Yet the site for discovering the *kotodama* was discursive, and often literary: ancient songs were thought of as the best place to look for words possessing that privileged natural oneness that linked nature and the body.

A similar quest for originary enunciation bound to the Real is again rearticulated in yet other forms in Meiji, as I see it, with a minimum of two trajectories, the one followed by Kyōka and Yanagita and the other in the naturalist, *genbun'itchi* movement toward linguistic transparency (see Figure 4). Whether the solution was nostalgic or avant-garde, the problem perceived was the same: word had become stripped of its connection to the real world, and thus the Real was lost to immediacy. The Meiji solutions lie in the shifting objects of desire (a romanticized past / a romanticized present moment). Meiji naturalists and folklorists, as well as Kyōka, shared with the Edo nativists a perceived need to heal the split self (by relinking it with the Real) and the need to identify something "Japanese" against the encroaching other (in Meiji, the West, in Edo, China). There is crossover between the *gesaku* stylists' desire to subvert the prevalent (static) romanticization of past tradition and the *genbun'itchi* proponents' goal to construct a new literary language: both were concerned with "immediacy" or the perceived slippage of the contemporary subject from contemporaneity. Conjoining the particularities of the varied solutions was an insistence that word, inextricable from enunciation, contains a power to access the Real; for Kyōka, words were magical. As Noguchi described it, "one of Kyōka's special characteristics was letter [*moji*] fetishism. Kyōka most surely possessed a sensation, a sensory tactility [*hada ni shokuchi sarete kuru yō na kankaku*] of words themselves being endowed with a kind of incantory power."[44] The sounds of words are bound to the Real—word evokes things and has the power to call forth the Real into the symbolic order. Kyōka was both nostalgic and concerned with immediacy. His words as signifiers slipped between potential signifieds, yet he also believed, as did the naturalists, that words *especially when enunciated*—the sound of word—had the dual power to draw the referent into play and even to engage the Real (see Figure 4).

Kyōka was (in)famous for possessing a reverence that was frequently bound up with a sense of taboo regarding certain words. Although Kyōka was obsessive about sound and enunciation, he was equally attentive to the pictographic power of the word-as-sign. It was not only through sound, but through visual image as well, that words (signs) might access the Real. Kyōka refused to write some words as they were usually written. The degree of defixity of certain words was limited, and some words could not be "floated" (that is, taken out of context, made to signify catechrestically or

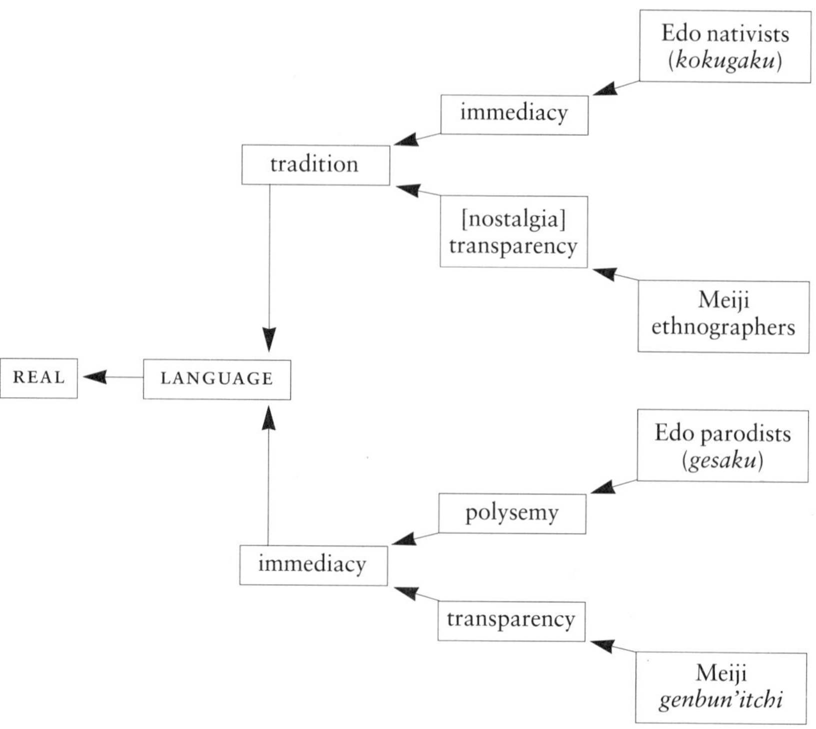

Figure 4. Language and the Real

otherwise untethered from a semantic fixity). Words that could be floated could only be made polysemic in a specific manner that was quite in contrast to the Edo scatological or otherwise vulgar play.

Kasahara relates a few often-repeated tales about Kyōka's "reverence for words" in the preface to his *Izumi Kyōka: Bi to erosu no kōzō.* Apparently Kyōka relished *yudōfu* (hot bean curd). But he refused to write "bean curd" with the customary Chinese characters, which combine the sign for bean with one for fermented (*fu*). Instead, he sometimes replaced the sign for "fermented" with a homophone *fu* signifying urban prefecture or government office. Kasahara explains:

He had a physiological abhorrence for the image of rottenness inherent in the sign *fu*. Could it be that Kyōka, like the people of the archaic period who believed in the "*kotodama*," believed that there was a moment when word joined with and embodied magic, as did incantations? Undoubtedly, he had an infatuation for word, a sense for word that one could label "belief in word." There are any number of monomaniacal episodes of Kyōka regarding words, whether it was ripping off the letters on the department store wrapping paper, or when someone tried to show him a character by writing it with their finger on top of a sitting cushion, crying out in consternation, "Never! not on something where you put your behind," and erasing the traces with his own hand.[45]

The limitations of play, for Kyōka, concerned certain vulgarities and relations to the body. Typical of Kyōka's linguistic play is his unusual manner of writing *tanomoshii* (reliable) in Ren's description of his mother: the syllable *mo*, usually written in phonetic form, appears as the Chinese character for "mother" ("Kechō," 414). Kyōka's reverent respect for words is here a clear demarcation between his version of how word was bound to the Real and that of the *gesaku* parodists, who made a genre out of *irreverence*, including tales dedicated to descriptions of farting and defecating. Instead, for Kyōka, surplus and excess are thoroughly eroticized (and turned into discourse) in the *narrated* body of the demon/sorceress, for which his protagonists yearn perversely and nostalgically—a desire that they then confess. For Kyōka, the discursive return of the abjected in any other form (words carelessly tossed about, written on a sitting cushion) is disallowed; the abject must first be channeled into word that frequently was somehow linked to the figure of eroticized, feminized, discursive nativism.

For Edo nativists, there had been a time when language was affixed, through sound, to the Real. The *genbun'itchi* stylists looked to the future, not the past, to form (they thought) a novel prose that was similarly affixed, through sound, to an immediate Real. The floating signifiers of Edo *gesaku*, conjoining the breaks within a representational system putatively bound to a rigid class fixity, are rebound in the abolishing of the Edo-period class system. The Edo loosening of fixedness in *gesaku* and the Edo nativist quest to link word and the Real are both present in Meiji naturalism and in Kyōka's "antiquated" prose. The reformation of the matrix of subjectivity and its production in discourse bind naturalism and Kyōka. Kyōka's prose replayed the struggle between the perceived Real and how it was signified—the slippage and recovery of a teleological oneness of word and things. But for Kyōka, the Real was accessed by recuperating what was abjected or othered (rendered threatening as well as desirous to modern phallic unity). The tenuous nature of the "self" (subject) for Kyōka opens the delightful abyss of possible interface with the Real. Kyōka's signifiers float to reveal an erotic danger in the healing of the split between enunciation, visual representations, and the Real. For Kyōka both word and women threaten dissolution and hold the capacity for seepage in their depth.

A transformation of what constituted "surplus" was inseparable from the historical shift in how a subject performed its own subjectivity. Žižek's description of the transformation that took place between the eighteenth and nineteenth century in Europe has some affinity with Japanese modernity, because "the objectal surplus which sticks out from the intersubjective network is no longer the elusive semblance of pure phallic sexuality but rather the embodiment of the saintly-ascetic *jouissance* beyond phallus."[46] Compared with the Edo-period *iki* (commonly called an "aesthetic" ideal; I would rephrase it as "phallic eroticism," or "a phallic economy of the feminine as erotic commodity"), Kyōka's passion is for a diffusion rather than for consolidation of phallic privilege.[47] Related to the shift in "enjoyment," the affinity of Meiji and Edo phonocentric discourses notwithstanding, there was also a radical conversion in the idea of the body and its relation to word and immediacy. In a shift from the nativist perception of the body as the material locus for connection, for Kyōka the body is already the repressed Christian body from which seeps modern sexual perversion. The seventeenth-century Christian compulsion to confess sins of the heart, argued Foucault, established an imperative in the West: "Not only will you confess to acts contravening the [Christian] law, but you will seek to transform your desire, your every desire, into discourse."[48] By the nineteenth century, Foucault maintains, this imperative had extended to the realm of literature. The technologies of sexuality were a part of the greater "deployments of power . . . directly connected to the body—to bodies, functions, physiological processes, sensation, and pleasures."[49] (In Japan, in 1909, Mori Ōgai wrote his infamous *Vita Sexualis*, a confessional text depicting the protagonist's struggle with his sexual desires and detailing his self-abhorrence, born of the modern demand that one "police" even one's thoughts of sex.) Through the need to police the body and its thoughts, repression is born, and repression gives birth to modern sexuality. Wrote Foucault, "These polymorphous conducts were actually extracted from people's bodies and from their pleasures; or rather, they were solidified in them; they were drawn out, revealed, isolated, intensified, incorporated by multifarious power devices. The growth of perversions . . . is the real product of the encroachment of a type of power on bodies and their pleasures."[50] Karatani has argued similarly that in Japan "it is through this repression . . . that the body as simply body, the 'natural body,' was discovered. No wonder, then, that the Japanese who had become Christians in the 1890s and early 1900s soon turned to naturalism. The flesh and the sexual desire that they explored had been produced by the repression of the body."[51] The perverse body is born through its translation into discourse and confession. Like many of the naturalists, as a youth Kyōka was influenced by Christianity through his English teacher. The institution of compulsory heterosexuality, the policing of women's erotic and maternal bodies, the repression of the "natural" body, and the production of the national subject were the context for the production of "perverse" modern sexual desire.

Gracing the text erotically as *burakumin*, as sorceresses, as bird-women, as snake-demons, the women of Kyōka's narratives are the bodily representations of the "othered" and "abjected" of language (and also what the *genbun'itchi* stylists abjected in their search for transparency). But as their bodies never materialize but tenuously and fragmentarily, they are never anything other than language-as-desire, words moving backward toward an imaginary, originary, forever-displaced enunciation—that which is always surplus to the sign. By this movement toward origin, the origin is repeatedly displaced; the discursive movement repeatedly rids itself of (any anchored) significance.

Harootunian asserts that Yanagita's ethnographic studies were complicit in the establishment of a "coherent and homogeneous subject," which by erasing the "heterogeneity of the other (the site of difference) . . . [left nothing] to function as the object of desire."[52] It is my contention that this shift in particular, which absorbed a previous "heterogeneity" within Japanese national identity, was abetted by the increasing abjection of, and thus desire for, feminized excess. Although the "common folk" may be translated into word, something of the "other side" of the humanized, maternalized woman escapes the Symbolic, to dangle ever more enticingly as the constitutive other and as interlinked with the Real. Kyōka's style and "metastory" increasingly reiterated a construct of the premodern in which the abjected supplement is feminized. Kyōka's famous reverence for words, enveloped in a nostalgic desire for the Real, which lodged itself in a feminized nativism, signals another phallicized trajectory, rather than a rejection, of sociocultural and linguistic ideologies of his time.

■ PART II

Enchi Fumiko

Vengeance

[The author of *The Tale of Genji*, Murasaki Shikibu] was able
to combine women's extreme ego suppression and ancient female shamanism, showing both in opposition to men. . . .
    Just as there is an archetype of woman as the object of
man's eternal love, so there must be an archetype of her as the
object of his eternal fear, representing, perhaps, the shadow of
his own evil actions. The Rokujō lady is an embodiment of
this archetype.[1]
                                        — E N C H I   F U M I K O

Enchi Fumiko first entered the literary scene as a playwright, but
she is most celebrated for the prose fiction that she wrote after the Second
World War. The next chapter will focus on how Enchi's narratives stood
against the socioculturally dominant maternal myth by exploring mother-
daughter relationships characterized by disharmony and mutual enmity.
This shared disdain is a product of female (de)valuation in modern androcentric Japan and is linked to her female characters' internalization of the
male, phallic gaze. Frequently choosing aging women as her protagonists,
Enchi's texts detail their exclusion from circuits of sexual exchange, in
spite of their vibrant sexual desire. But it is precisely this unsatisfied sexual passion that links the mature women of her narratives to the trope of
the dangerous woman.

The subsequent chapters in Part II discuss the dangerous woman in
Enchi's texts and highlight how the trope is reconfigured. Like Kyōka's,
Enchi's narratives were distinguished by a diction suggestive of premodern

texts and the intertextual incorporation of motifs, archetypes, and tales canonized and reiterated in a wide variety of narrative and performative texts. In the *Namamiko monogatari* (The tale of the false shamaness, 1965) and *Saimu* (Tinted fog, 1975) she both borrowed from the existing corpus of Heian *monogatari* and invented late Heian antecedent texts. Her *Onnamen* (*Masks*, 1958) is indebted to *nō*, and she incorporated elements of Ueda Akinari's "Nisei no en" (The bond spanning two lives, ca. 1802) to produce "Nisei no en shūi" ("Love in Two Lives: The Remnant," 1958).[2] Enchi's versions might be termed deconstructions of, or perhaps more accurately, subversive supplements to, the classics. Enchi's invented supplementary texts reveal previously undisclosed (fictive) "secrets" of female spiritual power and Heian-period Shinto rituals. The narrator of the *Namamiko monogatari* writes, "I wanted to compare the *Namamiko monogatari* to the *Eiga monogatari*, [*A Tale of Flowering Fortune*, ca. 1092], not because it quoted directly from the *Eiga monogatari*, but rather, as the subtitle to the *Namamiko monogatari*, 'Supplement to *Eiga Monogatari*' indicated, because the *Namamiko monogatari* narrated things that were not depicted in the *Eiga monogatari*."[3] Frequently, descriptions and explorations of female eroticism and sexuality comprise that which is "disclosed" by Enchi's invented classics. From the *Namamiko monogatari*,

Although it was in general customary that *miko* [female mediums] served shrines as virgins, in actuality, more frequently than one might imagine, they indulged in affairs. Although virginity was desired for religious rites, female impurity was not despised. Perhaps they took the propitious viewpoint that fancied that the deities would be pleased by the type of woman to excite [human] male desire. (297)

Enchi most commonly wrote of a female rage fanned by jealousy and born of a tangle of female political and sociocultural oppression, Buddhist doctrines on female sin and female pollution, and latent (and suppressed) female sexuality. For many of Enchi's modern female protagonists, rage spills beyond the confines of each individual female-as-subject and finds its only and ultimate outlet in shamanistic "spiritual possession."

That Enchi, like Kyōka, found likeness in once-separated tropes of the premodern canon (including the *yamamba*, *miko* shamans, and snake-women) is evidence of the tenacity of the mythic, feminized configuration of premodernity established in Meiji/Taisho and its relation to the abject. The troping of femaleness in Enchi's narratives sometimes makes use of the symbol of the serpent, at the same time as those narratives foreground the "possessed women" of the medieval canon. For example, in *Onnazaka* (*The Waiting Years*, 1957),[4] a snake makes a brief appearance in the (female) protagonist's bedroom; in *Saimu*, a female character endowed with mysteriously seductive powers is linked to a performance of the classic serpent play, *Dōjōji*. But it is in the mingling of pollution and divinity, attended by an unrelenting eroticization of the dangerous woman, that Enchi's texts most resemble Kyōka's. Enchi's narratives reiterated a gendered imaginary that functions as a repository for abjected and othered (nonphallic) aspects of the social and individual (Japanese) body. Part II shows how Enchi discovered and reproduced an ambivalent empowerment in the repetition of the defixed and pluralized dangerous woman trope: her reiterations recirculated, yet unsettled from within its interiors, the conceit of maternalized femaleness as an abjected site.

Repeatedly, and obsessively, Enchi evoked literary precedent, "perverted" by a *modern* female narrative position: her protagonists are interiorized versions of the women who functioned metaphorically, often as male imaginaries, in the classics, whether female or male authored. The shifting of the figure from narrative object to narrative subject was her boldest and most innovative literary contribution. The sorceress thus reconfigured is now interiorized. Known as a writer of psychological fiction, Enchi's narrative project more accurately combined a fiction of archetypes with vacillations between "gestalt" interiority and "individual" interiority. (I use "interiority" here to refer to the postulation of an "inner" voice and consciousness that is produced as part of modern subjectivity; and "gestalt" to describe a subjectivity comprised of component individual psyches that operate in cooperation to form a unified whole, or "system," of subjectivity.)[5] For Enchi, "psychological interiority," as written in text, was both deeply individual and personal but nonetheless inseparable from the collective, sociopolitical experience of being a woman in modern Japan. Her gestalt womanhood was indelibly scoured with the remnants of femaleness as scripted in the premodern and medieval canon, while her protagonists' frequently aging bodies are also inscribed with powerlessness as devalued commodities. In texts such as *Masks* and *Saimu*, Enchi seeks to overturn this condition of powerlessness by "discovering" a suppressed shamanic power within female figures of the canon, revived within the bodies of modern postwar Japanese women. The "gestalt" community of women penned by Enchi makes use of the conceits of pollution by blood, female unboundedness, and the sacred/erotic dualism that marked Shinto shamanesses of the literary past.

Enchi's discovery of a link between a type of collective unconscious potentially tappable by all Japanese women and their vengeful, lusty, and mysteriously empowered literary antecedents became a primary repeated conceit of modern Japanese female-authored prose narrative. A split between the maternal ideal and femaleness embittered with suppressed anger (and sometimes mother's abjected aspects) became a common theme of posterior Japanese narratives written by women. The dying protagonist of Ōba Minako's "Yamauba no bishō" ("The Smile of a Mountain Witch," 1976) is possessed of a psychic split between the maternal and the rageful components of herself: "Half her face was smiling like an affectionate mother, while the other half was seething with demonic rage. Blood would trickle down from half her mouth while it devoured and ripped the man's flesh apart. The other half of her lips was caressing the man who curled up his body in the shadow of one of her breasts, sucking it like a baby."[6]

Unlike Kyōka, Enchi transports the dangerous woman from social and geographic borders into the center of society and the city proper. Following Enchi, the Shinto shamaness and the mountain witch no longer need be found by a bridge or other liminal site. No longer do they inhabit only a mountain top or an archaic text; now they live inside (all) women, as the suppressed, enraged "other side" of the modern maternal ideal.

The collective woman of Enchi's narratives, moreover, repeatedly embodies a densely scripted femaleness, since she cannot be severed from the archaic, medieval, and modern history of how women have been written in Japanese text. The *Namamiko monogatari*, Etō Jun wrote, was "a tale of the rivalry between the female principle and the male principle."[7] I argue that Enchi did not, as many other critics have held, write as much of "female psychology" and "real women" (or femaleness as a principle, or "essence") as she did about a *literary* configuration of femaleness.[8] Hers was a quest to *rescript* femaleness.

Although Enchi, in what could be called a feminist gesture, seems to have consciously sought to rebel against Japanese dominant restrictive notions of maternalized femaleness, she nonetheless usually reproduced femaleness within the confines of an already circulating, differently restrictive, trope of vengeful otherness. Her attempt at liberation through the dangerous woman trope frequently collapsed into a modern inhabiting of a femaleness-as-site as it was already circumscribed by a phallic agenda. The political limitations of empowerment bound by the confines of inhabiting a male imaginary are obvious: the trope becomes a site for enormous ambivalences, resistances, and collusions. That Enchi won numerous literary prizes (she remains the most lauded modern female Japanese author to date), awarded by panels of primarily male judges presiding over a phallocentric literary agenda, suggests that the "essence" of femaleness that these judges feted in her narratives reproduced a femaleness collusive with or supportive of notions of the phallic subject as norm.[9] Her dangerous women ultimately bolstered, however unintentionally, the phallic agenda they were designed to undermine.

(Un)reproductivities: Maternity and Sex

The 1947 Japanese constitution, which guaranteed gender equality and was promulgated during the American occupation, was undercut by, as Sandra Buckley wrote, "gender-based discrimination . . . across all levels of society throughout the postwar period."[1] Regardless of the law, the de facto economic and sociopolitical subordination of women to men ensured that most women could neither support their own households nor ascend to the higher levels of their chosen professions. Rather, women's social participation continued to be restricted to maternal and spousal roles. Against the postwar sociocultural context of a fully naturalized restriction of women to the dual roles of wife and mother, with motherhood taking clear primacy,[2] Enchi's "Hebi no koe" (The snake's voice, 1970) conceives of a strikingly different mother-daughter relationship:

Shiga often quarreled with her daughter. The quarrels were intrinsically different from the sort that arise from the mutual indulgences mothers and daughters tend to grant each other. Shiga had assumed that human beings were born with a receptacle for love inside their hearts. She knew early on that her own receptacle housed a very meager share of such feelings. Even so, hers was like that of a two-quart flask when compared with the one that her daughter possessed—which was as tiny as a miniature doll's flask. Her daughter lacked even temporary empathy for Shiga. Though she never tired of usurping Shiga's authority, she didn't even visit her mother when Shiga was ill in the hospital.[3]

Shiga lacks the supposedly innate maternal instinct for unconditional love. The daughter, in turn, feels no deep gratitude toward or attachment to the mother. Problematizing the simplified ideal of unambivalent maternity, Enchi's mature female protagonists, such as Shiga, are often mothers (and grandmothers) separated from their function as nurturers, mothers who even on occasion view their daughters with distaste. These heroines stand in contrast to the conceit of a putatively natural and historically transcendental maternal-child harmony; their ambivalence destabilizes the myth of absolutely unconditional, undepletable motherly love. Konishi Jin'ichi wrote that "Japanese literature has been imbued from its beginnings with the primitive disposition of Japanese mental states and with the homogeneous nature of child and mother during infancy," evidence of the pervasive rewriting of Japanese history in service to this Meiji/Taisho production.[4] As Kathleen Uno wrote, in Japan, maternity regarded as female vocation was a social construct "that emerged in modern times. . . . the evidence presented concerning the division of reproductive labor in Tokugawa and early Meiji households implies that to view mothering as woman's universal and natural destiny is to deny history."[5] In her gesture against the naturalization of maternity, Enchi appears to be allied with some postwar Japanese feminists and writers, who adamantly challenged the pervasive maternal myth.

Shiga of "Hebi no koe" is a writer. Although her own relationship with her daughter is characterized by mutual disdain and disengagement, in contrast, one of the two tales that she is writing, which is embedded in the narrative present, depicts a thoroughly symbiotic mother-daughter relation. Now both elderly, mother and daughter share a small house by the seashore. The daughter, Nobu, ekes out a meager living as a seamstress and supports herself and her mother—both of whom are in ill health. An apparent stroke has left the mother unable to speak. Nobu suffers from heart disease. Refusing any sort of help from social welfare agencies (which would remove the mother from the daughter's care), Nobu engineers a double suicide by poisoning when she can no longer properly see to their mutual needs.

But what has precipitated the ongoing maternal-daughter mutual interdependencies is the daughter's gynecological disorders, discovered shortly after she has married, which have left her "inadequate for sexual intercourse and lacking a body capable of bearing children" (374). The various family members are surprised that her husband, Harumichi, remains married to Nobu even after her gynecological surgery and the subsequent disclosure that she cannot serve as either a sexual partner or a mother. Nobu insists that her mother accompany her and her husband on the many pleasure trips they take, because she suffers from "anxiety unless her mother always came along" (374). Yet Nobu guesses that the true reason for Harumichi's willingness to remain in the marriage is that he is deeply attached to her mother, not to her (375). Does Nobu use the connection between Harumichi and her mother to hold on to her husband? The question is not answered, but one can imagine that the economic and social gains must be in conflict with her narcissistic wound. Nobu, after all, lacks both qualities that might earn her social value as a woman in this phallocentric society: she is severed from value as a sexual commodity and through maternal reproduction.

Complex webs of symbiosis and sameness here vie with erotic competition. Overturning the modern Japanese logic that severs mothers from sexuality, here the childless daughter is divested of sexuality, while her mother replaces Nobu as the object of her husband's erotic desire. It is unclear whether any illicit sexual activities arose from this turn of affairs; the attachment between Harumichi and the mother is merely suggested. Yet this (albeit timid) inversion somehow enables the continuation of the mother-daughter symbiosis. Nobu can devote herself to her mother because separation is not required of her, split off as she is from all exchange value in Japan's homosocial economy. It is the mother who suffers passionately when Harumichi dies. It is the daughter who remains inextricably bound to the caretaking of the ailing mother. This tale of maternal-daughter intimacy is a tale within a tale, a "fairy tale" constructed by Shiga, who is, of course, constructed by Enchi. And her fairy tale notwithstanding, Shiga is, it bears repeating, quite at odds with her own daughter. A functional daughter, one who has a secured position within the phallic economy, as mother or as sexual commodity, would have an altogether different relationship with her own mother.

Mirroring the distaste felt by Shiga for her daughter, Sano of Enchi's *Saimu* dislikes what she sees in her daughter, Nanmi. She muses:

How unpleasant a woman she is, Sano thought suddenly. Maybe the thicker the blood, the deeper the roots of this sort of flash of abhorrence. In short, the hatred she felt for her daughter in the end came right back to herself. It seemed that in a glance Nanmi, though taking a liberal view of matters, had discerned the special nature of the nephew-aunt relationship her mother shared with Yatsuo. (61)

The distaste of Enchi's mothers for their daughters, and of daughters for their mothers, is predicated on their erotic likeness. Perhaps this distaste also arises from the inevitable displacement of the mother by the daughter in the social and erotic market. Yet it is also true that each reproductively functional daughter will in turn be displaced. Sexual value is transitory and does not transcend mothering. In either arrangement of these (split) values, maternal or sexual, women are valueless outside the phallic economy. Daughters hold within their own bodies the same fate of socially "disappearing" that matured mothers are facing, or will face. Sano sees the same body, the same "intuition," and the same positionality in her daughter and in herself. This sameness arises from the shared condition of their existence as erotic commodity and also as abjected site. (Idealized maternity disguises the abjection while producing it.) Mother's distaste for daughter is essentially a distaste for herself. In their maturity Sano and Shiga have lost their value as sexual commodities and are possessed of a (hystericized) desire that only circulates within their own bodies and that is powerless to affect the objects of that desire.

Similarly, "Fuyumomi" (Red leaves of winter, 1959) is a short story of a middle-aged, widowed actress named Eiko. Eiko meets a young man, Tachibana. She introduces him to her twenty-five-year-old daughter, hoping to marry her off. Unexpectedly, Eiko herself begins to desire Tachibana. The narrative opens as Eiko gazes at herself in the mirror:

"I am in love [*coi*] . . . ,"
Eiko intoned. She looked at her face in the mirror. The skin spanning her cheeks to the corners of her mouth was slightly, unevenly, concave. Hers was an unnatural, indecent expression. It looked as if she were holding back pain, and yet, also as if it were happiness that she was suppressing. It encompassed the struggle raging between the force of a flaming vigor that shockingly rose up within her at this inappropriate age, and the opposing force to suppress that vigor—so thought Eiko.
The flesh of her cheek, just beneath the delicate skin, undulated like a jellyfish. She touched it with her fingertip. Its soft lack of elasticity was unpleasant to the touch.[6]

The gaze that Eiko submits herself to is her own, internalized phallic one; the signs of female aging fill her with self-abhorrence and disgust. In her self-appraisal, Eiko harshly judges her own relative (lack of) value as sexual commodity. Irigaray has written that, "The commodity is . . . a dual entity as soon as its value comes to possess a phenomenal form of its own, distinct from its natural form: that of exchange value. And it never possesses this form if it is considered in isolation. A commodity has this phenomenal form added on to its nature only in relation to another commodity."[7] The value given to other women's bodies, mostly young and sometimes virginal women's bodies, marks Eiko's aging body with lost exchange value. Enchi's women gaze upon themselves, and are gazed at by others, as commodities, in Irigaray's words, *"divided into two irreconcilable 'bodies': her 'natural' body and her socially valued, exchangeable body which is a particularly mimetic expression of masculine values"* (Irigaray's emphasis).[8] (That the word *natural* is in quotes suggests that Irigaray is well aware that there is no body transcendent of discourse and culture.)

Eiko's "natural" body desires. But the phallic gaze overlooks her in pursuit of its own reproductive and erotic ends. In many of Enchi's narratives, such as *Saimu*, "Hebi no koe," "Fuyumomi," and "Yō" ("Enchantress," 1956), Enchi chooses the most devalued of all femininities—aging women—as protagonists. Chigako, the protagonist of "Yō," is an unhappily married woman. She is sexually and emotionally estranged from her husband, and her two daughters have grown up, married, and left home. Chigako is in her (probably late) forties and suffers the indignities of aging: she has lost her teeth, and her graying hair is perceptively thinning:

Soon hormone creams, dark lipsticks, and a succession of other such articles took their place on the dressing table alongside the hair tonic. Seating herself before them, Chigako would apply herself assiduously to the task of restoring her youth.

When she looked at herself closely . . . she recognized with loathing the face of middle age.[9]

As Chigako furiously endeavors to hide her advancing age beneath increasingly thicker layers of makeup, inside she has begun to burn with a sexual passion entirely novel to her. It is at this time in her life that she has also discovered a passion for her work—translating the classic early Heian narrative, the *Ise monogatari*. The only chapter of the *Ise monogatari* tales that is specifically mentioned in "Enchantress" is one about an "old woman in love" who successfully seeks and acquires a lover. Chigako notes that although the woman in the tale is purported to be old, in Heian, "old woman" most likely meant a woman of Chigako's age.

Inside these mature women smolder passions and rages; the women waver between fierce, unabated lust and self-abhorrence. Their advanced age highlights the transience of female value in modern Japan, in tales far more wrenching than the more conventional versions of unrequited love stories. Erased as erotic objects, they nonetheless survive as erotic subjects, yearning and lusting and despising themselves for it. Frequently either widowed or estranged from their husbands, loose of flesh, with faces and bodies marked with signs of age, and unable to bear more or any children, Enchi's women dream of sexual pleasure. Closed out of the exchange/circulation system, they (re)produce nothing—or else, as do so many of Enchi's protagonists, they write.

Eiko of "Fuyumomi" has a close male friend, Fujiki, who has been indulging in extramarital affairs most of his married life. Deeply infatuated with his latest lover, Tomoko, a young woman almost thirty years his junior, Fujiki confesses that he is considering leaving his wife to marry her. Eiko at first feels as though she understands his passion; she, after all, is also feeling quite passionate about Tachibana, a much younger man.

Eiko's whole body quivered with an indescribable tremor. Leaning her elbow against the surface of the dining table, she supported her head with her hand. At some point, as she had listened to Fujiki tell of his love affair with Tomoko, she had felt it somehow analogous to how her own heart had been drifting toward Tachibana. But with his latest words she realized clearly that their feelings were of totally disparate natures. In Fujiki's facial expression—a man in love with a woman nearly thirty years his junior—was none of the unsightliness that she had discovered in herself when looking in the mirror before. Eiko sensed that this signaled a difference in their circumstances.

That difference was the naturalness of Fujiki's situation, born of the fact that Fujiki still had the power to impregnate a young woman. Fujiki was likely a year older than she was. But the fact that she was a year younger made no difference; and no matter how young a man she might love, she could never birth a child, Eiko thought.

Feeling that crystal-clear difference between men and women, a sadness permeated Eiko's body. An old woman's sadness. It was like a cold mist. (393)

Although the sociocultural inappropriatenessof the aging female body in matters of love appears to render Eiko unsuited for sexual love, her epiphany marks the difference between her value as erotic object and Fujiki's continued suitability for erotic attachments, along the axis of maternity/paternity. It is the loss of the ability to provide a man with a child (focused here on the paternal need for a child, not on maternity in itself) that is the root of the inequality and the source of Eiko's undesirability.

Though elderly woman may best mark this fierce split between desire and its (lack of) circulation (or its perverted circulation in the form of spiritual possession and vengeance or its sublimated circulation as literary expression, as I discuss later), it is not necessarily bound to advanced age. The Japanese title of Enchi's most famous work, *Onnazaka* (translated as *The Waiting Years*), literally means "Woman Slope," a metaphor for the relentless, uphill battle of protagonist Tomo's difficult life. Married at the tender age of fourteen to a civil servant of moderate position, Shirakawa

Yukitomo, at fifteen Tomo is mother to a retarded son and to a daughter soon thereafter. The narrative opens as Tomo travels to Tokyo in her early twenties, having been entrusted with the cruel task of finding a mistress for her husband, for whom she has already lost her sexual value. Beneath meticulous descriptions of kimonos, flower arrangements, and household details, which imbue the work with the flavor of classical romances, is layered an exposé of Tomo's deep, repressed passions, her jealousy and desire, and her rage at and despondency over her husband's insatiably wandering eye. Beholding the innocent, virginal girl, Suga, whom she has just selected and purchased for her husband's sexual pleasure, "pity welled up at the sorry fate of the girl fluttering before her like a great butterfly, and with it a jealousy that flowed about her body in a rapid, scorching stream" (28). Yukitomo's lust for fresh, young female flesh is not satisfied by one or two mistresses, but ultimately leads him to seduce his son's wife as well. Overseer of the household finances and business transactions as well as the concubines, maids, children and eventual grandchildren, Tomo tirelessly subordinates her needs and passions to the longevity, reputation, and health of the family, indoctrinated, as she is, with a "feminine ethic that had taught her to yield to her husband's wishes in every respect, however unreasonable they might seem" (43). Betrayal follows betrayal at the hands of her despotic husband, and finding nothing for herself in her dependent and sorrowful female plight, Tomo progressively turns to Buddhism and the promise of salvation in the afterlife. In spite of her determination to outlive her husband, her life of suffering finally takes its toll, and she dies before he does. On her deathbed, she announces, "Tell him [Yukitomo] that when I die I want no funeral. Tell him that all he need do is to take my body out to sea at Shinagawa and dump it in the water" (202). Reflecting her Buddhist-inspired belief that an improper burial without funeral rites ensures that the deceased spirit will return to haunt this world, Tomo has revealed her intention to forfeit salvation so that after she has died she may return as a ghost to seek vengeance on her husband.[10]

Born in the Edo period, married just before the Meiji restoration of 1868, Tomo's value as a woman is informed by Edo axioms on female inferiority; Neo-Confucian ideology, as propounded in texts such as *Onna daigaku takarabako* (A treasure chest of greater learning for women, 1716), flatly demanded female subordination because of women's intellectual and emotional inferiority. Japanese feminist historian Niwa Akiko has argued that in Edo, mothering was not seen as women's vocation as it has been constructed in post-Meiji Japan. Quite to the contrary, the *Onna daigaku takarabako*, a handbook to educate women on their duties as women, has, Niwa points out, not a single article on mothering. Instead, it advises that "A woman's infirmities include a lack of submission, ill temper, resentfulness, jealousy, slander of others, and stupidity. Seven or eight out of ten women are afflicted with these infirmities. Thus, women are inferior to men. They are not fit to raise children since they tend to be carried away by their love."[11] Imai Yasuko concurs, writing that, "child-rearing was not the exclusive domain of mothers either, or even of women; especially in the nurturing of boys, men were involved. Child-raising guidebooks for the warrior class were reprinted. . . . in the Edo period all Japanese men, whether in the upper or lower classes, considered women incapable of raising male children."[12] Although the Confucian classics and "child-raising guidebooks" were only accessible to the literate classes, Uno has pointed out that mothering was not the primary vocation of peasant women, either.[13] Although Edo wives were needed to bear male progeny, that is, they were needed as wombs but not necessarily as caretakers of the children they bore, their other (at least equally important) duties included caring for their husband's parents; they also loomed fabrics and looked after clothing and oversaw various household matters. Peasant women worked long, arduous hours in the rice fields. Edo wives had value neither as mothers nor as sexual commodities. Rather, they had value in their capacity to do other (gendered) work.

Further complicating Edo notions of femaleness, the Edo period is infamous for its circulation of a sexual "aesthetic" (*iki*) based on an educated, moneyed male consumer of various types of sex for sale.[14] Handbooks abounded on how to choose and purchase sex, on how a prostitute should behave, and on how his or her client should comport himself.[15] Regarding Edo-period androcentric standards for reproduction and female prostitutes, Chieko Ariga wrote:

During the Edo period, sexual women such as geisha, courtesans, and whores, who sold their sexual services to more than one man, were excluded from motherhood in the family system. . . . Pregnancy and abortion meant time away from work and it always led to the devaluation of their bodies. . . .

The geisha/woman has no part or power concerning reproduction; her body is an empty vessel where male procreation takes place. The maternal womb is possessed, conquered, mapped, tamed, and appropriated in the masculine terrain.[16]

Whereas sex with one's wife (the mother of one's children) was relatively "private," sex in the pleasure quarters was relatively "public."[17] What was private about sex in the public spheres of the brothels was the secrecy shared by men in a consolidation of power; the "private" (that is, the household and the wife) were shut out of that sphere. (This, of course, can be likened on many levels to Western feminists' claim that in the West "privacy" denotes male homosocial privilege; women have no privacy.)[18] *Iki* provided an aesthetic privileged male "distance" and self-control; a man of class did not let his erotic pleasures interfere with his household's harmony. Yukitomo's greatest crime may well have been his lack of *iki*; he brings his courtesans into the home and disrupts the household harmony, most egregiously when he takes up with his son's wife. The private is therefore interwoven with the public; Yukitomo's very public position—as a prefectural official—endows him with the economic and sociocultural status of one who is permitted (expected?) to have multiple courtesans. Moreover, he has carried Edo practices (as understood from a Meiji perspective) over into Meiji, the era of the new fabrications of maternal mission and "enlightenment."

Masks and *Saimu*, like many other Enchi narratives, are, however, set in postwar Japan, during a time when maternity and female value have been firmly fused. Unlike Edo, when gross misogyny devalued women as mothers, the modern Japanese housewife has solid and important social value as the mother of a particular man's children and as the manager of his household. Yet the maternal continues to be radically split from the sexual and relegated to an entirely "private" realm from the male perspective; from a female vantage point, maternity is also very public and a source of women's identity and community within their own female social circle.[19] Yet the circuits of exchange that offer the most titillating forms of the sexual, the common insistence that they are private notwithstanding, remain (furtively) "public," that is, split off from the home and circulated within and by groups of men in public arenas such as clubs catering to any and all sexual inclinations. These sex clubs and activities fall under the rubric of the private; through secrecy the "private" protects the parameters and the frameworks of male homosocial privilege and power. Male sexual adventures (homosexual and heterosexual, normative or "perverse") are hidden from spouses and families under the cloak of "the private." Phallicism—which encompasses the privilege to penetrate however and whomever—is safeguarded through recourse to the gendered, epistemic structure that has been affixed to the ideas of public and private. Japanese homosociality encourages the sharing of sexual partners and sexual experiences by like-minded men in variously overt performances of sexual power; the notion of what constitutes male "privacy" makes possible modern and contemporary Japanese male group sex tours to Southeast Asian nations, group visits to various clubs and houses of prostitution, and even the socially self-imposed blindness to male homosexuality.[20] Prostitution, in Japan, it should be noted, was only outlawed in 1956— just two years before Enchi wrote *Masks*. Nonetheless, today sex industries in Japan are prolific. Virginity (or a theatrical performance of virginity in the form of pubescent prostitutes and an entire category of pornography featuring pubescent girls) marks a young woman's body with extra cash value. Notions of "public" and "private" interlock with the exchange values within the sex industry. In Japan, as in other phallocentric societies, old women are generally locked outside of these circuits of exchange.

The reification of maternity as a female vocation has, for so many of Enchi's female protagonists, been surprisingly empty of satisfaction. The child has not, so to speak, replaced the phallus. For these women, desire still circulates, desire for power, for sex, for self-expression. Sano of *Saimu* and Mieko of *Masks* defy the power discourses inscribed on their aged, sagging bodies. They have not accepted the "passive" position; yet the circulations of unsatisfied desire meet with no external linking outlets. Possessing neither youth nor reproductive capacity, they circulate their passions either on the written page or in the (modern) form of a revitalized erotic archetype predating both Edo and Meiji constructs of maternalized femaleness. The maternal myth of modern Japan evaporates (or is exposed as myth), and in its place another side of the myth—the side embraced by Kyōka—of a dangerous, lusty, and empowered shamaness figure comes to the fore. But for Enchi, this "other side," or the abjected aspect of maternalized femaleness, is frequently embodied in women without sexual exchange value. (Kyōka's idealized female figure may be more mature than the desiring male protagonist, but she is never "old.")

Enchi's texts highlight the constructivity of the female body and how it is inscribed with values by empowered men in a homosocial society. Women's two values, procreative and sexual (intertwined and yet rendered incompatible in one body), encounter each other—often in negated forms such as infertility and sexual frustration—on the bodies of Enchi's women in impossible contradictions. Enchi's manipulations of modern Japanese gender constructs resonate with the following suggestion by Judith Butler: "Consider gender . . . as a *corporeal style*, an 'act' as it were, which is both intentional and performative, where '*performative*' suggests a dramatic and contingent construction of meaning" (Butler's emphasis).[21] Enchi's women are bound to their bodies, as inscribed by the phallo-centric capitalism in which they live. Their bodies, as the surfaces for multiple power discourses, are nonetheless simultaneously experiential bodies or symbolic of a psychological interiority that is both produced by, and at odds with, their sociocultural encoding. The desires emanating from these bodies, as inscribed and produced by notions of femaleness, are incommensurate with their loss of youthful status as commodity with value. They are either powerless, impotent, barren, desiring women of no commercial value, or, at the apex of their sexual and social frustration, they are transformed into vengeful, dangerous women.

Scripted Women Bound by Blood: Polluted Flows, Sacred Flows

Enchi Fumiko's texts surpassed those of other women writers of her generation, on par with stories by Izumi Kyōka and Tanizaki Jun'ichirō, wrote Nakagami Kenji, because of their sense of drama. This sense of drama, Nakagami argued, was inseparable from a "spilling of blood" that also made the narratives of Kyōka and Tanizaki powerful.[1] "When writers of *monogatari* are touched by the dramatic, there is a murmur of blood-like dizziness savored; pleasure is born from this. It engenders and it destroys language."[2]

In Enchi's *Masks*, blood functions as an index of female identity and as a marker of female pollution and divinity. Blood further forms the basis upon which a community of women, exclusive of men, is constructed. Blood is presented as a structural component of female "otherness," in keeping with Japanese gendered ideations that commingle the stubborn traces of premodern pollution practices with modern representations of women as "fluid," in contrast to putative male "solidity." As Grosz has queried, following Irigaray: "Could the reduction of men's body fluids to the by-products of pleasure and the raw materials of reproduction, along with men's refusal to acknowledge the effects of flows that move through various parts of the body and from the inside out, have to do with men's attempt to distance themselves from the very kind of corporeality—uncontrollable, excessive, expansive, disruptive, irrational—they have attributed to women?"[3] Whether it is blood abstracted and symbolized by "heritage" or the actual physical substance of childbirth and menstruation, in *Masks* the manner in which female bodies are inscribed by blood articulates male empowerment and avails itself of already circulating ideations of femaleness. An essay written by the character Mieko, and embedded within the primary narrative of *Masks*, proclaims: "Sin is inseparable from a woman's being. It is a stream of blood flowing on and on, unbroken, from generation to generation" (57). Yet, as I argue in this study, blood's seepage and formlessness incorporates the capacity to defraud or contaminate the phallocentric systems that it, as a marker of female otherness, ostensibly substantiates.

A lament by Mikame of *Masks* crystallizes male anxiety over the potential for a singularly female deception: "A man may try as hard as he likes, but he'll never know what schemes a woman may be slowly and quietly carrying out behind his back. Children—think what endless trouble men have gone to over the ages to persuade themselves that the children they bore belonged to them" (133). Sperm, having left the solidity of the male body, are lost within the void of deceitful female flow. A scheme using precisely sperm as the means to female deceit is a central theme in *Masks*. The son who was to become the Toganō heir has no Toganō blood and is not the product of Toganō sperm: patrilineage is furtively contravened by matrilineage in protagonist Mieko Toganō's revenge on her dead husband. Mieko's deceased son, Akio, and his brain-damaged twin sister, Harume, were fathered by Mieko's lover, not by her Toganō husband. With her now-widowed daughter-in-law, Yasuko, Mieko successfully schemes to impregnate Harume. Harume's male child thus replaces Akio as the second fraudulent Toganō heir. The biological father of Harume's baby, Ibuki, is tricked into impregnating her, and he too is defrauded of his patrilineage by being denied his "material" and physical connection to his son. Fraud is perpetrated through the abstract blood of lineage and facilitated by a social gender imagination that projects male viscosity onto the feminine. This traveling of solid to liquid resituates abstract name within the maternal/material body and forms the nexus of Mieko's vengeance.

Locating the wellspring of discourses on self and other in the medium of blood is a familiar configuration for Japanese notions of (national) identity. In modern Japan, distinctions between Japanese (male and female) "self" and non-Japanese "other" have been persistently constructed, argues historian John Dower, through recourse to axioms on blood purity, remnants of ancient Shinto and Buddhist tenets regarding purity and pollution.[4] Perceived purity of blood lingers on as a marker, although it may shift toward a *metaphoric* sign, to identify and distinguish "Japanese" from Asians of other nationalities and from others who share the Japanese islands, such as *burakumin*, Okinawans, and Korean-Japanese. In a simple generalization, the empowerment of some and exclusion of others have frequently been validated through fictive "historical" narratives that affirm a never-violated, pure blood lineage linking the sociopolitically empowered to the ancient Yamato tribe. This pattern is repeated in myth and genealogical narratives from the earliest writings through the mid-twentieth century, symbolized on the highest level in the legitimization of the inherent bodily authority of emperors as direct descendants of the deities. The narrative of a supposed unbroken line of imperial descent was written into the first article of the new Japanese constitution drafted in the 1880s, and the Meiji emperor became, wrote Carol Gluck, "as the descendent of the sun goddess, the deified evidence of the ancestral ethnicity of the Japanese."[5]

In modern Japan, as in many other nations, women are marked by bodily and additional (assumedly natural) signs of difference from a male paradigm that constitutes the norm. The premise of blood as the medium for purity or pollution, which forms the matrix of Japanese racial distinctions between self and other, has also operated to maintain distinction between male and female: even "pure Japanese" women were once perceived as cyclically defiled through the natural bodily functions of (differently polluting) menstruation and childbirth.[6]

To map out an overview of how premodern pollution practices are perceived in postwar Japan (although the specifics of pollution prohibitions differed by region), women were frequently excluded from festivals and certain sacred locations and shrines, especially during menstruation and for varied but specified lengths of time after giving birth. In some regions women were restricted from leaving the birthing room for weeks after giving birth because their putative "pollution" was viewed as potentially contaminating. Conversely, men were denied entry into rooms inhabited by menstruating and postpartum women. In some practices, purification rituals were required, along with periods of isolation.[7] Although pollution prohibitions have since waned, the legacy of premodern pollution practices continue to nuance how women's bodies are inscribed with impurity and contagion in the modern period. In *Masks*, the mostly medieval pollution beliefs lose their religious specificities and are enfolded in general representations of female uncleanliness, stickiness, viscosity, fluidity, and boundlessness and are symbolized by female bleeding, very similar to Grosz's descriptions, as quoted above and in Chapter 3: "Ibuki recognized the viscid flow of emotion between Yasuko and Mieko as, he felt, unclean, yet he was also aware of his own paradoxical desire to enter that unclean moistness" (80).

Echoing premodern practices, in the modern narrative *Masks*, the damaged and polluted Harume is isolated from society as she bears the child who will defraud the Toganō bloodline. Her unruly menstrual periods are given unusual and explicit narrative attention, so that Harume in essence becomes her periods, "continually leaving a trail of crimson drops" behind her (74). Although menstruation may no longer literally validate exclusion of women from specified locations, the disgust, fear of contamination, and the abjection associated with feminine bleeding lingers on, at least partly bound to female putative unfathomableness. In *Masks*, not only Harume but also Mieko is associated with "filthy" menstrual blood when her lover positions her "ambiguity" as inseparable from her pollution: "You contain a curious ambiguity that enables you to get along without distinguishing between the truth and falseness of your actions in the real world. Because of that trait you seemed at once incomprehensible and unclean to me (I admit to the unreasonable fastidiousness of the Japanese male, to whom the blood of menstruation is of all blood the dirtiest)" (104–5).

Yet a doubling occurs at the site of pollution, once again evocative of the premodern. The modern Harume is both defiled as a menstruating woman and elevated as a vessel of fertility; she is a source of a flow that is at once unclean and life-giving. Ethnographer Iijima Yoshiharu has noted that in many Japanese villages "it was customary for villagers to hang sacred straw hung with cut paper [*shimenawa*] around the [child-birthing] hut," evidence of its archaic duality as a taboo and sacred site.[8] "Motherhood" and "fertility" in *Masks* are similarly fused as complex arenas in which the boundaries demarcating the sacred and the polluted are elided. Harume's death after the birth of her son makes concrete the polluting potentiality symbolized by the abjection associated with the blood of childbirth in the medieval period.

As a young wife, Mieko suffered a miscarriage from a fall that may have been deliberately caused by her husband's mistress.[9] In retribution, Mieko's modern-day scheme of vengeance (the birthing of children secretly fathered by her lover, not her husband) is enacted on the plane of birth giving, centered on the ambivalent sacrifice of her mentally dysfunctional, fertile adult daughter, Harume. Harume suffered from brain damage caused by the pressure of her twin brother Akio's feet against her head while they shared Mieko's womb. And after her birth, Harume continued to suffer male oppression at the hands of her brother: "Akio had seemed to harbor an inborn hatred for Harume . . . pulling her hair, hitting her over the head, and otherwise tormenting her" (71). Akio was to be Mieko's revenge upon her cruel and unfaithful husband, purposefully passed off by Mieko as the Toganō heir. Once Akio dies, Harume's future baby becomes the only possibility for the fulfillment of this revenge. But the scheme requires appropriation of Harume's sexual and reproductive body, and ultimately, the sacrifice of Harume's life, to carry vengeance to its ultimate fruition: Harume dies shortly after she gives birth to a son. The sacrifice, of a daughter damaged by male domination for a healthy male heir, is perhaps facilitated by the deep ambivalence made inevitable by community through taint. Female pollution through blood is passed from mother to daughter, and thus the mother must view the daughter with the same ambivalence with which she views her own impossibly defiled female body:

A vision came to her of an ancient goddess lying stretched out in the underworld, prey of death. Her flesh was putrid and swarming with maggots, her decaying form covered with all manner of festering sores that smoldered and gave off black sparks. The luridness of the sight sent the goddess's lover fleeing in horror, and the moment that he turned and ran, she arose and swept after him in fury, all the love she had borne him transformed utterly into blinding hatred. A woman's love is quick to turn into a passion for revenge—an obsession that becomes an endless river of blood, flowing from generation to generation. (127)

Mieko's vision is culled from the pages of Japan's earliest written mythologies, *The Kojiki*, in which the deity Izanagi views in horror the polluted corpse of his lover, Izanami.[10] Linked to their archaic counterparts through the flow of tainted blood and jealous passions, the modern women in *Masks* are the reincarnations of the goddesses and the *miko* shamans of ancient folklore, the mad women of *nō* drama and the jilted, jealous women of Heian *monogatari*, whose spirits escape the confines of their bodies to wreak havoc on their female rivals—with one important discrepancy. The shamanesses of *Masks* join forces against men, not female rivals. Mieko is likened to the *ryō no onna* female archetype of the *nō*, as a woman who will not sublimate her strong will to male dictates and whose only outlet for jealousy and passion is revenge through spiritual possession. *Masks* is a stinging indictment of female disempowerment, depicting a legacy of communal female insubordination born of repressed rage and enacted through supernatural empowerment.

Mieko, Yasuko, Mikame, and Ibuki, the primary characters, share a passion for the Heian arts, the *nō* theater, and most important for my inquiry, the study of spirit possession. The men approach the subject of spirit possession as scholars (through logos), while the *bodies* of Mieko and Yasuko become vessels reincarnating the spirits, earning the women the appellations of witch, medium, and spirit. Ibuki's wife asserts, "That [Toganō] house is a witches' den. Serves you right for wrapping yourselves up in a weird subject like spirit possession—you [and Mikame] . . . are both under a witch's spell" (119). Mieko's vengeance calls on the spirit of the Rokujō lady of the classic *The Tale of Genji*, the deity Izanami, and the shamanesses of archaic Shinto, becoming a tributary to the abstract and material "river of blood" flowing through generations of oppressed, polluted women. These modern women, empowered by their ties to premodern figures, invert the conventions that produce Eiko's capitulation to her erotic powerlessness in "Fuyumomi," as already discussed.

Saimu, like *Masks*, evokes the premodern canon. It is the story of Tsutsumi Sano, a female writer of seventy who is given an ancient picture scroll (*emaki*) by Kawahara Yukiko, an ailing female acquaintance, before Yukiko dies. The scroll is marked with a dire warning, written in blood, to keep the contents of the scroll secret; it further warns that men who view the scroll will be cursed. Sano carelessly (or perhaps because of the scroll's own mysterious powers) leaves part of the ancient wrapping out in plain sight, and her secretary, Yamakawa Katsuko, discovers and reads it. Because she is almost functionally blind, Sano can only fully appreciate the written script after sharing it with Katsuko. The scroll reveals in graphic (apparently nearly pornographic) illustrations, accompanied by a narrative text, a sexual ritual engaged in repeatedly by an actual historical person—one of the Saiin (Shinto priestesses) of the Kamo shrine, Senshi.[11] Shockingly, to Sano, it is an aging, and finally aged, priestess who is depicted as being sexually attended to by an (originally) virgin boy. The accompanying narrative explains that his services are essential to revive the Saiin from the near-death state to which she is repeatedly transported in her fulfillment of her official function as a medium for the deities.

There was the beautiful, naked woman with long hair (Sano guessed that she was the *Saiin*) lying as though dead on the purification spot, which was surrounded by sacred *sakaki* trees. Draped on top of her body, as though kneeling over her, was a young man wearing a Shinto priest's robe. It was unmistakably a depiction of sexual intercourse. As she unrolled and looked with trepidation at the next segment of the scroll, there was the same naked lady, now standing straight and tall like a statue of the goddess Kannon. Before her, with a countenance of joy, arms flung open in a posture of worship, was the same man in his Shinto priest's robe. (55)

In the final illustration, "the woman's face was as beautiful as before but it appeared that her long hair had turned completely white . . . and her naked body, being embraced by the same man as before, was now bone thin. Curiously, she nonetheless did not look unattractive" (63).

After acquiring the scroll, Katsuko and Sano learn, little by little, many frightening details about the promiscuous life of the scroll's previous owner, Kawahara Yukiko: man after man fell passionately in love with her only to meet with mysterious deaths. It also becomes clear that Yukiko had disregarded the warning to keep the scroll secret and had shown it to many men. One of these men is Kariya, a younger man who serves her diligently until (and after) her death, obviously mirroring the relationship between the Kamo Priestess and the young man as depicted in the scroll. As the events of the past are revealed, Sano and Katsuko inexplicably begin to undergo mysterious transformations. Yukiko's life (and the Kamo Priestess's spirit) intrudes and interlocks with their lives. Sano has the sensation that she is possessed by Yukiko, and through Yukiko, the priestess herself. And the nature of this possession is erotic.

In the beginning of *Saimu*, Sano clings to the romantic fantasies she believed in as a young girl. "Sano had always longed for love, but there was no doubt that her longing at the present was stronger than it had ever been. Like the mirage of a flowing stream seen by the traveler wandering lost in a desert, Sano searched for love just as did young girls of fourteen or fifteen. . . . Deep within this old woman of seventy that silly dream still lingered and smoldered" (8). With the narrative's progression, and the deepening possession of Sano by the mysterious scroll, Sano's desire grows less romantic and more powerfully erotic. But it is not simply that she lusts. In a more important twist, she is now desired. The possession is not purely psychic; the scroll transforms her physical body—its appearance to and effect on men (and women) who gaze upon her. In spite of her advanced age, Sano begins to appear more youthful—specifically, her skin shines with a luster and has an elasticity marking youth, and therefore, sexual value. As seen by Katsuko, "There were fine lines on Sano's neck and hands, but her back was sleek with a lustrous whiteness. One would never imagine that a woman of Sano's age could have skin like that. Katsuko felt sudden jealousy. She could imagine just how glossy Sano's stomach and thighs must also look" (185).

Because of her rejuvenated, possessed body, Sano's long-suppressed erotic desire for her nephew, Yatsuo, turns from tentative fantasy to physical reality. The narrative closes as Sano burns the "cursed" scroll after her successful seduction of Yatsuo. She thus belatedly rejects its magical, erotic power.

As in so many of Enchi narratives, historical fact entwines with invention: the scroll is Enchi's supplement to the varied Heian-period narrative precedents such as the *Eiga monogatari* and the *Ise monogatari*, which described the historical Kamo Priestess's life and times. In both the *Namamiko monogatari* and in *Saimu*, actual historical personages interact with Enchi's fictional ones, while selections from the Heian texts that are incorporated into her narratives bolster the "factual" appearance of her inventions. Quotations from the classics are frequently inverted by Enchi's versions, thereby recirculating in a different troping how femaleness was scripted in Heian and how it is scripted in modern Japan. One definition of the word *miko*—used to describe the vocations of the Kamo and Ise Priestesses—in most modern dictionaries is "a virgin girl who serves as a medium to Shinto deities at Shinto shrines."[12] Those narratives of Enchi's that make reference to the *miko* challenge the apparently modern privileging of virginity by repeatedly coupling the *miko* with promiscuity. Such reconceptualizations of the relationship between *miko* and sexual purity are not Enchi's alone; rather, they recirculate the notions of the *miko* "discovered" by Japanese ethnographers such as Yanagida and reiterated in a variety of forms and mediums.[13] In *Saimu*, Enchi goes even further. She reverses the paradigm by rendering the *boy* who serves the priestess a virgin.

Classic portrayals of female spirit possession ascribe it to the desire for vengeance (reiterated in Enchi's *Waiting Years* and her *Masks*) and female jealousy (as depicted in the portrayal of the Rokujō lady of *The Tale of Genji*) so powerful that it transcends human death and human will to produce vengeful, female ghosts capable of possessing others. In *Saimu*'s scroll the gendered assumption that also accompanies this model is reversed: the unnamed youth (Nanigashira) is possessed of a fierce jealousy over the priestess's sexual licentiousness. He serves her faithfully and adoringly until her death, and beyond it, with the portrayal and preservation of her tale in the scroll. Yukiko, descended from two families of Shinto priests and priestesses, is a modern woman with the power to entrance men to serve her, worship her, kill for her, and even die for her. Her young attendant, Kariya, and Shinoda (another young previous lover) outlive her, but like the unnamed boy of the scroll, they serve her beyond her death by setting fire to the house where she had lived, in accordance with her wishes.

In the *Namamiko monogatari*, Enchi's troping of the shamaness takes a different and unexpected turn: that which has appeared to be possession of the character Ayame (daughter of a Shinto *miko*) turns out to be a connivance with a fully logical explanation. Ayame's sister, Kureha, has been planted in the close service of the Empress Teishi by Fujiwara Michinaga to serve Fujiwara's own political interests.[14] Information passed from one sister to the other enables Ayame to perform as though she were possessed by the Empress Teishi. Female spirit possession is here revealed as a *fiction* invented by men to effect the consolidation of their own political power. There is, however, a moment in the text when Teishi's spirit *does* possess another woman—but it is to deliver a message of love, not vengeance, to her husband the emperor. Here, the more common conceit generally reiterated in Enchi's other tales, of female jealousy as the catalyst for spirit possession, is overturned.

In a similar reshaping of classic portrayals of female sorcery, through their communion with the spirits of female figures of narrative antiquity, the modern women of *Masks* and *Saimu* forge a special community. These spiritual "ancestors" are empowered female archetypes who have been consistently represented in oral folklore and written text, in legend and myth, from the earliest times to the present. Contact by modern women with the varied archetypes is through *inscription*—such as the scroll of *Saimu* and the supplementary text of the *Namamiko monogatari*—or it is accompanied by inscriptions—Mieko is the author of an essay entitled "Nonomiya" ("The Shrine in the Fields)," a reference to a chapter in *The Tale of Genji* and to the *nō* play based on that chapter.

I noted in the Introduction that Japanese literature contains a long litany of spiritually empowered female archetypes. As in Kyōka's texts, once-distinct categories of female archetypes are frequently collapsed into a general "woman of supernatural powers" in Enchi's modern renditions. *Masks* and *Saimu* reference several premodern variations simultaneously: the shamanesses and the goddesses of the archaic period and the possessed or possessing women of medieval tales. The title of Mieko's essay, "The Shrine in the Fields," is also an actual historical site related to both divinity and pollution. Mieko explains:

The Shrine in the Fields . . . was a sacred place where unmarried daughters of the emperor or of imperial princes would retire for a period of purification before leaving the capital to serve as high priestesses at the Grand Shrine in Ise. In shamanism, transmitters of the divine oracle are customarily female, and so it seems likely that the choosing of an imperial princess for such a post reflects the influence of ancient shamanistic tradition in Japan. (46–47)

The intermixing of empowered women, most frequently Shinto priestesses, from historical and fictional texts of the Japanese Heian-period canon with Enchi's own (usually modern-day) narratives is a device employed throughout Enchi's corpus. In *Saimu*, the Shinto Kamo Priestess Senshi Naishinnō becomes a primary referent, as does the Rokujō lady in *Masks*. Replicating the embedded fictional scroll, which in turn replicates the *Eiga monogatari*, Yukiko has direct "bloodline" connection to both medieval aristocracy and to Shinto shrines, even the Kamo shrine in particular, through her father's lineage (and a shrine in Kumano on her mother's side):

One of Yukiko's ancestors had tumbled from royalty in mid Edo, but succeeded as a Shinto priest to the house of Shimokobe. Since then Yukiko's family tree boasted of an enduring high-class lineage as descendants of that Shinto priest. There were no daughters born to the family for several generations, and the family heritage was passed down through their sons. Yukiko's mother, the daughter of the priest of a shrine in Kumano, married into the family as the wife of the previous generations' patriarch. Their daughter was Yukiko. (169)

Enchi's texts, written in Japan's postwar, construct an imaginary female archetype based on conterminous gender myths, images, and ideations validated through a specific (at least partially "inaccurate") historicization of the archaic period. Butler has written that "gendered bodies are so many 'styles of flesh.' These styles are never fully self-styled, for styles have a history, and those histories condition and limit the possibilities."[15] Gender in Enchi's narratives, to borrow Newton and Rosenfelt's words, serves as "a structure of perception that helps maintain a particular set of social and economic relations at a particular juncture in history."[16] Subversive to the system from which it emerges, Mieko's resistance is bounded by patrilineal limitations, and women are only empowered through *covert* action into which repressed rage against men is channeled. The "discovery" of a polluted female Shinto shaman in *Masks* and the secret erotic Shinto rituals depicted in *Saimu* are thus not simply culled from Enchi's personal myth, but are the products of other circulating contemporaneous social, political, and economic conceptualizations, which froze the representation of shamaness into a myth transcendental of history. Simultaneously, the origins of these ideations are suppressed, creating the illusion of the self-evident.

I am therefore concerned in this study with "history," not as "an assortment of acts in a linear arrangement . . . but as a process of transformation. . . . Literature and culture . . . as sites at which ideology is produced and reproduced, are also sites on which the outlines and contradictions of ideology may be made visible. Since we live within myths and narratives about history, . . . literature . . . draws upon various ideological productions of history or discourses about history to make its own production."[17] The "history," or gendered social imaginary, that produces the modern conceptualization of the premodern shamaness and informs Enchi's texts, is constructed in the time of its writing. It is therefore deeply indebted to the modern folkloric studies of Yanagita and Origuchi, who "discovered" and foregrounded women's role in archaic ritual Shinto religious practices.[18] It is also culled from antecedent versions by writers including Kyōka, Akutagawa, Tanizaki, and Edogawa, among others, who popularized these and similar tropings of dangerous women in a variety of literary forms.

As evidenced by Mieko's claim that the transmitters of the divine oracle were usually women, in postwar Japan there is a conviction, shared by scholars and laypeople alike, that women shamans performed most of the important rituals in archaic Shinto. Mieko places the high priestesses of Ise at the pinnacle of female shamanic power and empowers the female protagonists of *Masks* by summoning the spirits of, and affirming their "blood" connection to, the bodies of such divine women of the past. Sano of *Saimu* is simultaneously empowered and possessed by the Kamo Priestess, through the medium of yet another old woman's (divine/erotic) body—that of Yukiko. Although the authenticity of the assumed special link between women and Shinto has been recently called into question, early modern folklorists such as Yanagita went so far as to claim in 1948 that mediators with gods were "in principle women."[19] Shinto scholar Jean Herbert likewise noted in 1967 that many scholars of Shinto are convinced that female shamans represent "the oldest form of Shinto worship. . . . the tradition still continues among common people of having old women (also called *miko*) who go into trances and convey the words of the Gods, drive out devils, heal the sick, communicate with the dead."[20] There is substantial evidence that female shamans did enjoy considerable political power, on par with male shamans, before the influx of Buddhist and Confucian modes of governance in the sixth century.[21] Today, in some southwestern regions of Japan, only a few select men are permitted limited participation as assistants to the priestesses who perform Shinto rituals, while other men are fully excluded from the performance of rituals and denied entry into sacred places, suggesting that in modern practices this ideation persists.[22] *Masks* and *Saimu* are explorations of female empowerment within the confines of an archetype spawned by a malecentric imaginary. These texts also stand as a testament to the tenacity with which this gendered imaginary has linked women to archaic Shinto practices. From Enchi's employment of this construct emerges a deeply contradictory figure.

On the one hand, historical, fictive, and other narrative depictions of female shamans provided Enchi, as a modern woman writer, with a "position of empowerment" from which other resistances to malecentrism could be envisioned and explored. On the other hand, the empowerment sought through the medium of the myth of the female shaman was an already ambivalent discourse. According to Yoshida Teigo, "the notions of pollution and sacredness or divinity associated with women cannot be rigidly opposed, but are often blurred. . . . Whether Japanese women are regarded as polluted or as holy beings, traditionally they are seen to have certain spiritual or mystical powers."[23] By choosing for her essay's title the name of a Shinto shrine that functions as a site of purification, Mieko disinters an underlying aspect of the relationship of female pollution (blood) to a specifically female power. According to Mieko, this power has been rendered sinful by Buddhist theology: "In our own day, shamanism seems to have withered and died. Yet does it not, on second thought, offer a partial explanation of the power women still have over men? Perhaps it is true, as Buddhism teaches us, that this power constitutes women's greatest burden and delusion—and ultimately her greatest sin" (*Masks*, 57). As the next chapter will further elucidate, feminized animism is poised in rebellious relation to Buddhism and circulates anew a now-suppressed historical hegemony.

Gendered Performances: Masculinizing Buddhism, Feminizing Shinto

The syncretism of Buddhism and Shinto, in premodern and modern Japan, has been the focus of many studies. Yet the ascension of governmental systems valorizing Buddhism, and the concurrent sociopolitical upheavals, also fostered texts collusive with Shinto's growing subordination to Buddhism. According to W. Michael Kelsey, scholar of classical Japanese literature, the changing relationship is inscribed in the rewriting of old tales (such as the Dōjō tale) from the *Kojiki* (712), the *Nihon shoki* (720), and the *Nihon ryōiki* (ca. 822) in the later *Konjaku monogatari shū* (ca. 1120):[1]

In the Dōjō story we have the introduction of the power of Buddhism over the native Shinto deities. Here we have a clear example of a relatively old story being appropriated by a Buddhist preacher who changes it to make it conform to his own purposes. . . .

[In another version of the tale] there is direct conflict between the Shinto deity and the interests of Buddhism, and the Buddhists are the undisputed winners. This is not a merging of two belief systems, for there is no cooperation between them; the Buddhists have the upper hand and are able to give the orders. The hero gains control over the deity not by means of a Shinto charm such as the metal rod the farmer used in the Dōjō tale, but with a Buddhist weapon, the Lotus Sutra.[2]

Materiality is subsumed within the discursive and symbolic order, as Buddhism supplants Shinto as the primary source for the validation of political power. In her doctoral dissertation, Gerry Yokota concurs, arguing that in the medieval canonization of *nō*,

Honji-suijaku [true Buddha body/manifest trace] is clearly a hierarchical dualism: The true body of the Buddha is superior, the *kami* merely its inferior local derivative. It is a construct aimed at establishing the supremacy of the institution of Buddhism. One rarely hears of the Shinto attempt to counter with the principle of *shinpon butsujaku*, declaring the *kami* as origin, the Buddha as trace. We speak of Buddhist-Shinto syncretism, but it is well known that coexistence was not always peaceful.[3]

Masks inherits this complexity—Buddhism is partly separated from Shinto, because it is presented as having reordered sexual mores, repressed female erotic agency, and the (polluted) female body. As in Christian discourses on paganism, shamanic (Shinto) women become symbolic of sexual excess. The contention that Buddhism and Christianity suppressed female sexuality, which is metaphorically linked to Shinto rituals, is reiterated in *Saimu*. Sano muses that in the *Kojiki* tale of creation depicting physical intercourse between the male/female deity couple Izanagi and Izanami, "there is not the glimmer of a consciousness of sin." Sin as a concept, she imagines, was born of an intellectual fear of human sexual desire, as it is depicted in Buddhism and Christianity (187). A similar idea is reiterated in the *Namamiko monogatari*: "Even being possessed by deities was a sort of sexual transaction for *miko* shamans. One could therefore say that these women were, rather than cloistered by deities, released through deities. Therein lies a fundamental difference between the abstinence of Buddhist and Christian nuns, and the Japanese *miko* of archaic Shinto" (298). Ibuki in *Masks* describes the erotic agency of the Shinto high priestess of Ise as subversive, situating her "outside" dominant (androcentric) ideations on female sexual chastity: "There is an episode in the *Tales of Ise* in which Ariwara no Narihira visits his younger cousin the high priestess of Ise and exchanges a vow of love with her. The fact that of her own accord she goes into Narihira's bedchamber at night, despite her supposed chastity, is interesting because it shows that she took a shamaness's view of sex, as something intrinsically sinless" (77). In this passage, Ibuki not only posits a connection between a guiltless sexuality and shamanism but also one between shamanism and Shinto, while clearly referencing Mieko as subtext: Mieko has already been identified as a shamaness. In *Saimu*, according to Yukiko, one of her lovers, Katsurai, used the word *miko* to describe her: "When he heard that I was the daughter of the head priest of the Kamo

Shrine he nodded, saying 'you have the blood of a *miko*.' That is why when I embrace a man, I am transformed into something other than my usual self; and what's more, my partner also experiences that transformation. I was with Katsurai the first time that happened to me" (37). For Mieko of *Masks*, mystical ecstasy and sexual pleasure seem likewise entwined; Mieko in trance seems to resemble a woman in orgasm:

[Mieko] dropped to her knees on the bedclothes, face tightly pressed against the pillow, and from her lips came anguished moans like prayers or lamentations. . . .

[She rose and] her expression was calm and unflickering as always, but beneath the chill weight of her sagging breasts her heart raced in a mad elfin dance, while from hips to thighs a powerful tension enveloped her, anchoring her to the floor. (102–3)

Ibuki theorizes that the conflation of spiritual and erotic ecstasy toppled the shamaness from sociopolitical influence and power (77). But it is Mieko who overtly links female sexual aggression, the shamaness's physical body (and its polluted nature), and Shinto as mutually interconnected in suppressed opposition to Buddhism and male privilege. Buddhism teaches, claims Mieko, that female shamanic empowerment is a primary source of female sin and pollution (57), a now-familiar mythic metaphor.

This metaphoric function persists overtly in *Masks* (and less obviously in the *Namamiko monogatari*, *Saimu*, and other texts by Enchi), in spite of the fact that in actual past and present-day practices, Buddhism and Shinto alike encompass both rationalistic sects and mystical, esoteric ones. It also persists by severing ancient-shrine Shinto from state Shinto, which in the modern period was used as a discourse to validate political authority, and by reproducing a (temporary) modern disengagement of Shinto from Buddhism.[4] Mikame seems to speak for Mieko when he claims that in spite of men's efforts to subordinate women, "in the end they were unable to penetrate even one of women's secrets. Even the sadistic *misogyny of Buddha* and Christ was nothing but an attempt to gain the better of a vastly superior *opponent*" (133; emphasis added).[5]

Although historical studies affirm that female pollution myths predated Buddhism in many regions of Japan, as androcentric Buddhist governmental practices gained favor, pollution myths may have functioned to weaken powerful female shamans. In her general study on pollution practices, sociologist Mary Douglas has argued that the degree to which female pollution was historically stressed had direct relationship to the extent of male power: when men were more firmly empowered by other social institutions, pollution myths were not needed as ideological means of disempowering (threatening) women.[6] The concept of female pollution has flourished when male dominance is "contradicted by other principles such as that of female independence."[7] In sixth-century Japan, Prince Shōto-ku attempted to adapt an innovative Buddhist- and Confucian-influenced Chinese model of governance to the existing governmental system. Scholar of Japanese religion Joseph Kitagawa has described this as a shift from reliance on shamans to a "rational" system: "[Prince Shōtoku] accepted the Chinese concept of the emperor as 'Son of Heaven' who was to rule the nation with the help of his bureaucratic officials, and not on the basis of the *unpredictable divine oracles transmitted through shamanic diviners*" (emphasis added).[8]

Recent studies have shown that Shinto prohibitions against menstruating and postpartum women were largely reshaped and fortified in the medieval period, supporting the contention that as Buddhism's influence on government grew, female pollution myths proliferated.[9] If indeed in early Japan religious and political power were not exclusively male realms, the myth of Shinto as (only) female province, bolstered by the strengthened pollution myths in the medieval period, may have served to divest previously powerful women from public influence as malecentrism ascended. As shamanism is feminized and Buddhism masculinized, while employed to validate "rational governance," the metaphoric relationship deepens and may be marshaled to political ends. The result was that the developing binaries within the epistemological system, such as public/private or Chinese/Japanese, became components of a *gendered* teleology. Shamanic activity is thereby constructed as an aberrant and antisocial eruption exterior to a passive/aggressive binarism by which (nonshamanic) women are increasingly relegated to inactivity. This notion circulates in the modern period; Ibuki's complaint in *Masks* contemptuously links female voice and aggressivity to the menstrual cycle and devalues both in a single stroke: "The more outspoken and aggressive women become, the less attractive they are. . . . There's nothing in the least appealing about a young woman who tells you she's feeling excited because it's her time of the month" (87). Conversely, he is aroused by Harume's lack of vivacity; her vocalizations consist of childhood songs and formulaic statements, representative of the appropriated (and thus emptied) female narrative voice. The modern men in *Masks* continue to associate women with pollution, while divesting them of voice and erotic agency. "In her [Harume's] blank and fair-skinned face, the dark eyes brimming with melancholy shadows like those of a handsome cat, he was relieved to find a beauty so great that its lack of vivacity was all the more moving. . . . He stood there a long time, looking in reverence at the beautiful idiot whose flesh was as if steeped in uncleanness" (136). Though Ibuki finds beauty and pollution in Harume's vacancy, he cannot recall Mieko's features: "He had oddly no clear mental image of her face. . . . It was a face like a Nō mask, while the impression it gave was one of even greater obscurity and elusiveness" (91). Rendered vacant, or filled with uncontainable abjection, the women of *Masks* are starkly antithetical to male paradigmatic "selfsameness": they are primarily negative mirrors to the social construct of a solid masculine self. Mieko even overtly identifies the Rokujō lady, and thus by extension herself, as embodying this gendered imaginary: "Just as there is an archetype of woman as the object of man's eternal love, so there must be an archetype of her as the object of his eternal fear, representing, perhaps, the shadow of his own evil actions. The Rokujō lady is an embodiment of this archetype" (*Masks*, 57).

Cixous and Clément have claimed that woman stands outside of and is unrepresented by, and unrepresentable within, the dominant (Western) phallocentric system of (negative) representation. They also identify the sorceress and the Medusa as Western archetypes of male fear in terms that uncannily mirror *Masks*'s depiction of dangerous women:

The "Dark Continent" is neither dark nor unexplorable: It is still unexplained only because we have been made to believe that it was too dark to be explored. Because they want to make us believe that what interests us is the white continent, with its monuments to Lack. And we believed. We have been frozen in our place between two terrifying myths: between the Medusa and the abyss. . . . (Cixous's emphasis)

Wouldn't the worst thing be—isn't the worst thing that, really, woman is not castrated, that all one has to do is not listen to the sirens (because the sirens were men) for history to change its sense, its direction? All you have to do to see the Medusa is look her in the face: and she isn't deadly. She is beautiful and she laughs.[10]

In a passage reverberating with the depiction of feminized abjection in *Masks*, Clément has described the witch's contagion as spreading

through bits of bodily *waste* and through *odors*. . . .
Menstrual blood, excrement, a lock of hair; these scraps of the body are what will act as a charm. As partial objects detached from the body, they are especially powerful, in the same way that '*object a*,' the part where the object of desire settles . . . is powerful in its very detachment.[11] (Clément's emphasis)

In *Saimu*, the scroll passed on to Sano is the source of contamination and empowerment: an inscription in *blood* warns of its secret nature, while an illustrated narrative (script) serves as the medium for its pollution and power. Regardless of the warning, as Katsuko and Sano surmise, the scroll is actually intended to be shared; its power lies in being read. The exhortations for secrecy actually fan the desire to peer into its forbidden contents. Unread, the scroll is powerless; read, it may contaminate. As in *Masks*, the Shinto shamaness is here bound to sexual excess, but the material blood pollution that links women to one another is displaced in favor of *narration* or *inscription*. (Yet the warning written in blood also reimplicates, and entangles, material blood with its abstract, inscribed representations; in *Saimu* there is also a short rumination by Sano on menstruation, in which she normalizes her "feeling of unexpected pollution," as to be expected as a young girl in mid Taisho.) But the motif of blood is elsewhere firmly abstracted and restricted to notions of "lineage" (175). A shift in foreground and background thus occurs in this later work of Enchi's (and in the *Namamiko monogatari* as well): rather than women's bodies per se, it is how those bodies have been inscripted that functions to produce "femaleness." Woman's body becomes a surface for intersecting narratives that have produced "femaleness" in the Japanese canon.

Sano muses that ancient portrayals of women in Japanese art were quite different from those made popular in Edo; once upon a time artists had celebrated "radiant aristocratic women of authority and power, women for whom religious belief and erotic passion were intertwined, and those artists had left behind for succeeding generations their images of plump female bodies" (187). These were, Sano asserts, not women who lived austere celibate lives but women who were "loved by men, worshipped by men" (187). These were women of archaic Shinto.

In *Masks*, Mieko writes that "the Rokujō lady . . . possessed a spirit of such lively intensity that she was incapable of surrendering it fully to any man. . . . Passion transforms the Rokujō lady into a living ghost. . . . [She] turned unconsciously to spirit possession as the only available outlet for her strong will" (50–51). In her essay, Mieko locates the will, erotic agency, and voice of a suppressed shamaness within the Rokujō lady and her own body and psyche, producing an alternate, feminist reading of Murasaki Shikibu's *The Tale of Genji*. Mieko's connection to feminine literary expression is also personal: she writes *tanka* (short verse), a literary genre with its roots in *waka* (Japanese poetry), the privatized "female" mode of expression, which was poised in subordinate relation to *kanshi* (Chinese poetry) in the Heian period.

Both the *Namamiko monogatari* and *Saimu* go so far as to incorporate sections from the classics *in the original classical Japanese*, while sections of the supplementary, invented narratives are also incorporated in classical Japanese syntax—as written by Enchi. These texts are thus not just thetically, but also directly, materially bound to the premodern (feminized) conventions of letters. It is worth repeating that Enchi's protagonists are frequently writers: Mieko, Sano of *Saimu*, Shiga of "Hebi no koe," Chigako of "Yō," and Enchi herself (within the text), as the narrator of the *Namamiko monogatari*, are all writers. These women writers are further entangled in writing by name—Shiga's name references one of Japan's most famous modern writers, Shiga Naoya, while Sano's family name is Tsutsumi—an unmistakable reference to the *Tsutsumi chūnagon monogatari* (ca. 1055), a collection of short tales believed to have been written by women of the late Heian court. Female characters who are not writers are frequently given literary intertextually suggestive names: in "Fuyumomi," Eiko's daughter is named Kanako, written with the character for "phonetic syllabary" that was associated with female discursive production (*kana*). Names, personages, and motifs incorporated from previous texts overwhelmingly hail from the Heian period, the apex of female literary production in the Japanese canon (Shiga's name is an obvious exception). Women's identities are crisscrossed with writings that are made present in their names, in their writings, and in their inseparability from text. The women writers write because they cannot do otherwise; writing is transformed into a gendered vocation as though scripted women must in turn scribe. Shiga finds herself somehow merged with her own discursive productions; when seated at her desk writing, she speaks out, "her voice overlapping with that of the mother's" (357). In *Saimu*, a letter written by a male acquaintance (one of Yukiko's many lovers) to Sano muses that: "You have the invisible magic mantle of literature, and so perhaps you can live without finding it necessary to engage in actual, awesome sorcery. But, a crude [*nama no mama*] woman lacking that magic mantle may well perform acts of awesomely skillful sorcery, and deceive men" (25). The uneducated Tomo of *The Waiting Years* has no such magic cloak: "Barely able to read and write, she had no shield to defend herself other than the existing moral code" (43). (But she also has no recourse to sorcery until the very end of the tale.) In the beginning of *Saimu*, Sano herself reflects: "If I were asked why I write, my answer

would have to be none other than that I write so I can go on living" (29).
As she becomes increasingly possessed (and therefore erotically inclined
and desirable), her writing turns sloppy; her penmanship has worsened,
and she uses incorrect Chinese characters (200). By circulating their desire "harmlessly," writing may temporarily halt the frightening powers of
desiring women, yet it is also somehow implicated in spirit possession.
Yukiko's lover's comment to Sano notwithstanding, Sano is eventually
possessed, and empowered, despite her position as a writer. Women who
write are actually made vulnerable to text, especially when those texts engage premodern female sorcery. Writers are somehow drawn into and become a part of the classic troping of dangerous women. Mieko's essay
suggests her deeper spiritual entwinement with shamanesses of antiquity;
it is the scroll that entices Sano into the mysterious realm of possession;
and Chigako of "Yō" complains to her editor that "I believe their [Heian-
period women writers'] spirits have possessed me" (355).

For Enchi's women, writing is evidence of a powerful, barely suppressed,
vibrant libido: the title "Hebi no koe" (the story of another female writer)
brings the Heian conceit of the woman-turned-serpent (and all its attendant motifs of lustful women) to mind. Although it is at her husband's insistence, Chigako of "Yō" translates pornography—an endeavor that,
perhaps not surprisingly, brings her in a circuitous manner to the Heian
classics. Although Chigako surmises that she has been approached to translate the classics by an editor who must have seen her other (pornographic)
translation, there is, I believe, a less logical premise: Chigako's suddenly
blooming erotic desire. Chigako's married life has been sexually bleak,
and as a young woman she had no interest whatsoever in pornography.
Now in her forties, and perceiving herself as aging, as she embarks on the
pornographic translation, to her own surprise

the forthright descriptions of sexual intercourse that had merely disgusted her
then would now, as she did the translation, make her lay aside her pen from time
to time and sit wrapped in a kind of ecstatic daydream. In real life, she had never
known the moments of happiness that a woman could supposedly find through a
man, yet her whole being now thrilled at the suggestion that they could be found
through an intercourse of the flesh. (345)

Only after she has "erotically ripened" can she become "possessed" by her
Heian ancestors. That her erotic ripening so much postdates her moment
as erotic commodity in modern Japan only thickens the desire: having
nowhere to travel, it circulates within her, leaks onto pages of text, and is

transformed from text to sorcery in collusion with her scripted archetypal antecedents. When women write, they release a libidinal pressure—both erotic and aggressive. Far from holding sorcery in check, writing often brings it to full flower.

This incessant linking of Heian Japan, tale writing, eroticism, spiritism, and femaleness everywhere in Enchi's work is an outgrowth of modern Japanese reconstructions of the Heian female discursive tradition. According to Mizuta, Heian-period female-authored *waka* (Japanese verse), *monogatari* (tale fiction) such as *The Tale of Genji*, and *nikki* (diaries) were first vehicles for women's discursive productions and often incorporated moments and spaces critical of and resistant to female sociopolitical subordination.[12] As I described in the chapters on Kyōka, gender itself, holds Mizuta, became affixed to specified sides of a system of developing binarisms, rendering the private production of art and literature feminine against the masculinized public realms of politics and scholarship.[13] Gender took on a metaphoric function as a fundamental aspect of discrete literary genres. "Female" genres required narration by an identified woman— a specifically sexed narrator—although it did not require that the author be of the same sex as the narrator he or she invented to disseminate the narrative. Mizuta has argued that this metaphoric genderization of narrative functioned in collusion with sociopolitical restrictions that severed women from public realms such as politics. Gender distinctions were thus affixed to alternate sides of the developing binarisms that rendered literature and the arts on the side of the "feminine."

Once a particularly sexed body was moored to genre as a structural component of that genre, female narrative discursive production was placed in the service of the genre itself and was employed to bolster a phallocentric agenda.[14] In *Masks*, Enchi has recourse to this existing conceptual dualism by which Shinto, female (shamanic) power, and phonetic "voice" (*kana*) are metaphorically linked and form binarisms with, respectively, Buddhism, male power (rationalism), and writing distanced from voice (Chinese/logos).

The genderization of genre further associates women with phonocentrism through the "female" genres' use of *kana* (phonetic syllabary) and tightens the link between women and Shinto. Shinto had no written scriptures until after Buddhism, and the Chinese writing system, was adapted, an important factor in the association of Shinto and phonocentric practices. Nakagami Kenji used the concept of Shinto as preliterate to collapse certain categories of "naming" and "writing" (difference and distinction).

According to Nakagami, writing in Chinese characters added new significations, while it also began a process of freezing phonetic representations into single, set signifiers.[15] *Kotodama* (Shinto enunciations with sound-activated spiritual power) previously surplus to their semantic components were bound by symbol. Tales, which were up to that point passed down orally, were written. Nakagami asserted:

Stories were altered in the repeated retelling, but the changes were radicalized in the process that transformed them into *monogatari* as they were transcribed into a written language after Buddhism was imported. . . .

Once Buddhism was imported, something that was nameless was named, or, that which could not be subsumed within a name was suddenly compiled under a name.[16]

In the process, Buddhism, and by extension Chinese characters, became bound with logocentrism and political empowerment, and (Japanese) voice and body, symbolized by the polluted Shinto shamaness, were thrust into the margins. This shift is reminiscent of Christianity's ascension, as described by Clément: "The sorceress, who in the end is able to dream Nature and therefore conceive it, incarnates the reinscription of the traces of paganism that triumphant Christianity repressed."[17] Akin to Western paganism, Japanese premodern animism was not an exclusively female realm, but was rendered metaphorically feminine in the process of subordination to a growing (Buddhist) phallocentrism. It is worth repeating that Mikame links Buddhism and Christianity as *misogynist* attempts to subdue female empowerment (*Masks*, 133).

The fact that genderized narrative stance had been co-opted in the service of genre facilitated the later appropriation of female-authored texts in the eighteenth-century phonocentric nativist movement. Seeking an indigenous literary tradition to affirm separation from Chinese discursive conventions, which had severed voice from written symbol, the nativists imbued with value the Japanese voice they "discovered" in feminized genres.[18] By the modern period, *The Tale of Genji*, written by a woman and devalued as low art and mere entertainment at the time of its production, was canonized as Japan's highest premodern literary prose achievement, supplanting works in Chinese. The body of commentary on *The Tale of Genji* has sundered the text from its originating impulses, holds Mizuta, rewriting the tale in the service of phallocentric interests.[19] In the process of canonization, *monogatari* loses its function as "resistance," and the discursive productions by women become codified within an androcentric tradition.[20] The revitalization of the shamaness by contemporary women

writers of *monogatari* (including Enchi Fumiko) is an outgrowth of the
reinhabitation of the genre in rebellion against such codification. In this
sense, Enchi's *Namamiko monogatari*, as supplement to the *Eiga monogatari*, and her invention of the picture scroll in *Saimu* place Shinto rituals
and female shamans at the center of (supposedly Heian) narrative, rather
than at its peripheries. (Although the *Namamiko monogatari* reveals this
to be a phallocentric construct, not bound naturally, or innately, to "femaleness" itself.) Mieko's essay reclaims *The Tale of Genji* chapter "The
Shrine in the Fields" from its veil of Buddhist axioms:

Commentators generally agree that the Rokujō lady was jealous and vindictive—
traits, they say, that Genji abhorred and that drove him from her. This view is colored by Buddhist teaching. As passion transforms the Rokujō lady into a living
ghost, her spirit taking leave of her body again and again to attack and finally to
kill Genji's wife Aoi, the commentators see in her tragic obsession a classic illustration of the vile karma attached to all womanhood. (51)

The author Murasaki, says Mieko, empathized with the Rokujō lady,
who in turn had an essentially "shamanistic" influence on Genji himself
(48). Mieko's primary allegiance is to the suppressed shamaness dwelling
deep within the Rokujō lady, and by extension within all women. Just as
the Rokujō lady is forced by social circumstances into devious and mystical reprisal in order to assert herself in the context of a repressive malecentric society, so too is Mieko compelled to resurrect the female shamans
of antecedent narratives in defiance of male dominance.

Ibuki reflects upon Mieko's essay:

Ibuki was intrigued by Mieko Toganō's theory. From his readings in the *History
of Japanese Shamanesses* and elsewhere, he was familiar with the idea that the ancient Yamato tribe might have brought Ural-Altaic forms of shamanism to Japan.
And in Japanese folklore, the prominence of the sun goddess Amaterasu Ōmikami
suggested that the gods had spoken through shamanesses in prehistoric times.
Supporting evidence could be found in the *Kojiki* episode concerning Emperor
Chūai, in which a deity enters the empress Jinjū Kōgō and through her decrees the
invasion of Korea.

But the proposal of a link between the Rokujō lady and ancient shamanistic
spiritism was new to Ibuki. He sensed the amateurish dogmatism and boldness in
the leaps in Mieko's thinking. (57–58)

What Ibuki calls amateurish and bold is Mieko's infusion of Shinto shamanism into Buddhist doctrines on spirit possession, or the highlighting
of Shinto "trace."

As the Heian period itself, and the narratives affixed to it, become fem-

inized, female discursive production at its apex is simultaneously transformed into the moment of woman's metaphorization. Femaleness is cap-
tured and circulated by a phallocentric agenda. The binaries constructed
in Heian, which opposed a type of literary discourse against another, linking one type of narration to the male sex and the other to the female, thus
delimited (both) sexes to predetermined types of narrative expression
(again, this does not mean that men could not write women's genres and
ostensibly vice versa as well). That women overwhelmingly did not write
in "male" vernacular, while men had the discursive freedom to dabble in
either, suggests that this genderization functioned to solidify phallic privilege.[21] Women were thereby restricted to that which metaphorically provided the opposing spaces to whatever was deemed masculine. Simultaneously, the linkage of femaleness to shamanic powers circulates the very
phallic fear that female sexuality, once unleashed, turns uncontrollable
and insatiable.

In *Masks*, the shamaness, like the Western pagan sorceress, is temporal-
ized as predating logos, and her polluted/divine body is the cultural surface on which are inscribed the traces of archaic Shinto phonocentric incantations, words surplus to signification, which link her to actual empowerment. This gendered split is thematically supported in *Masks* as
men relate only to spirit possession through logos (scholarship), while the
women *embody* spiritual power.

This embodiment of power is, as this study has argued, tightly interwoven with (feminized) abjection, symbolized by the identificatory marking of the female body with blood. Mieko as medium for the repressed
shamaness uses her power to wrest abstracted blood (that of lineage)
from its appropriation to word and return it to a female materiality, inverting what Cixous has described as the patrilineal displacement of the
mother with the father as the originating and validating source:

A law emanates . . . with her body for its locus. . . .

What is a father? The one taken for father. The one recognized as the true one.
"Truth," the essence of fatherhood, its force as law. The "chosen" father. . . .

And one day . . . the matriarchy is done for, the sons stop being sons of mothers
and become sons of fathers. . . .

On one side there is mother, belly, milk. The bond passing through flesh, blood,
and milk, through the life debt. What is owed to her? A debate begins over sperm
and milk: does she provide food only, or does she also provide a germ? Who begins? . . .

A matricide . . . marks the end of mothers and inaugurates the sublime era.
How do you estimate the value of a mother's murder? What value does blood

have? What is the value of words? In the struggle between Blood and Words, the marriage pact—a commitment made with word and will—is stronger . . . than the blood-tie. The link to mother loosens. The link to word tightens. . . . Legality is to come to the assistance of the father's order.[22]

Mieko resituates sperm within the flow of female objects of abjection, through her appropriation of the name of the father.[23]

Conversely, maternity and procreation are severed from the province of the sorceress in *Saimu* (notably, Yukiko has no children). Instead, through the medium of spirit possession, enscription empowers, and the abjected female body itself—often that of the aging woman—is resituated within the flow of the phallocentric systems of exchange.

For both Mieko and Sano, however, the various resituations are impossible without their bodies being rescripted as sorceresses through the myth of Heian femaleness and the attendant discursive productions of female erotic power. Enchi's women turn to the dangerous woman of the past, becoming mediums for her, and thus they rewrite their own bodies and re-form themselves in her image. As the *Namamiko monogatari* makes abundantly clear, regardless of the actions of most of Enchi's protagonists, this shamaness nonetheless is modeled on (the negative mirror of) maleness. It, Enchi has asserted, here, is not an ahistorical female "essence."

Matrix and Metramorphosis

Although the shamanesses of *Masks* and *Saimu* are reinscribed with many of the modern Japanese phallocentric conceits of female lack, pollution, contagion, and spite, Enchi also fills the emptied cipher with a modern interiority. She attempts to explore the "dark continent" by narratively inhabiting the bodies and consciousnesses of the shamanesses of antecedent texts. The references to Heian *monogatari* that drift as constant motifs throughout the primary narrative are often put askew by the undertones of interiority generated by a female narrative voice emanating from the classic archetype. In this sense, Enchi's gender construction is "theatrical"; she deliberately borrows terms of a specific gender configuration that questions its own nature first, precisely by its (almost parodic) excess, and second by structurally and thematically contradicting the standard imaginary.

In the introduction to Chapter 6, I quoted Enchi as writing that the *Namamiko monogatari* intended to reveal "things that were not depicted" in the Heian-period *Eiga monogatari*. Female spirit possession is, as noted earlier, exposed as fabricated by men to further their own political agendas. However, there is an additional project—an attempt to produce a "real" female "voice," a voice that speaks from, and for, the female character(s). In other words, Enchi's renditions "interiorize" the dangerous woman trope. At the same time, it seems that Enchi endeavors to show by contrast that the Heian narratives were not, as has been commonly asserted in modern Japanese literary commentary, "true" expressions of women's thoughts and actions.

Mizuta wrote that although the Japanese canon was replete with depictions of powerful women,

nonetheless, for [posterior] women, these did not become guiding lights beaming self-awareness. Because, first of all, the *monogatari* that depicted female interiority [*naimen*] were inverted [*uramen*] *monogatari*. Those *monogatari* exiled women of ego [*jiga*] to the other world [*ikai*] as evil spirits or demons. There was no way to depict women of will [*jiga*] who lacked the resolution to become demonic or evil. Women writers have taken the offensive in the modern gothic *monogatari* by means of those inverted *monogatari*. They have sought to assert female interiority by employing *yamamba*, witches, and demonesses as protagonists.[1]

The move toward empowerment in the narratives of modern women writers makes use of the existing tropings of women yet warps those tropes in an agenda of resistance. Thus, the critic Saeki Shōichi takes Enchi to task for "over-explication" of the circumstances that led Mieko of *Masks* toward spiritual reprisals. In the rationalism that underlies Mieko's empowerment is, he writes, a "loss of charm" (which is unlike, he notes predictably, the successfully erotic portrayals by Kyōka and Tanizaki). Lamenting Enchi's preference for a heroine of determination and strong ego, or will (*jiga*), over a more romantic heroine who might languish at the borders between dream and reality, Saeki criticizes: "As a result, although the text as a whole is overfilled with an atmosphere of erotic liberation, in *Masks*, the main character [Mieko] ends up seeming strangely shallow, only weakly fragranced with eroticism, and her overly-dramatic behavior at the conclusion of the text produces [in the reader] an irrepressible dissatisfaction."[2] The demons-temptresses-enchantresses of Kyōka's narratives are simply what (or who) they are; no psychological motivations are offered. In Enchi's texts, women are turned into jealous, sexually frustrated women precisely because of the individual men and the sociocultural systems that oppress them. Their personal pasts merge with their narrative ones: they are inscripted with their antecedent textual counterparts yet they are also "psychological" characters with modern depth and motive. Mizuta argued,

Much of Enchi Fumiko's writing, though depicting the lives of women inside the framework of the *monogatari* and the [canonized] discourse on *monogatari*, skillfully manipulates the ambivalence that the *monogatari* originally connoted. Enchi endeavors to produce a women's narrative that rejects *monogatari* discourse, and conversely, to highlight the assertions of women's selfhood and will [*jiga*] that [this discourse] sought to conceal.[3]

I would argue that the manner of departure from medieval portrayals is, moreover, inseparable from a modern conceptualization of "subject": in the psychological characterizations of Mieko and Yasuko, the cipher is filled with subjecthood. In *Masks*, the court ladies of the Heian *monogatari* become three-dimensional, reflecting on self and other, conflicted with and anguished by inner turmoil and hesitation. Yasuko actively participates in the deception of Ibuki, and yet she cries out, "I have to go away from here, Mother. The longer I stay, the more I feel like a puppet in your control, the more I begin to hate myself" (67). Mieko, too, suffers the pangs of conscience:

She meditated on the deep and turbid female strength within her that had all but taken possession of Yasuko, wondering silently what power on earth might deliver her from the heavy load of karma that weighed upon her. The road down which she must blindly grope her way, helplessly laden with that unending and inescapable burden, seemed to stretch before her with a foul and terrifying blackness. (126)

In *Saimu*, one can locate a similar dualism: even as Sano is being "possessed" by the ancient scroll, she wonders if this possession is actually the repercussions of her own (repressed) sexuality and muses that "perhaps this was a problem that she [should] discuss with a psychologist" (194). Structurally, *Saimu* resembles a mystery tale, replete with unfolding enigmas that function as "hooks" to entice the reader to read on; these narrative techniques are balanced by inner-monologue ruminations, mostly Sano's, on what the women are thinking and feeling. This anguished interiority of Enchi's female subjects has led many critics to call her work "psychological novels." The translator of *Masks*, Juliet Winters Carpenter, wrote that Enchi was famous for "her brilliant probing of feminine psychology and sexuality," while critic Takemori Takao saw Enchi's empowered, shamanic female characters as a projection of her own will, actualized only on the pages of her narratives instead of in her personal life.[4]

In his *Origins of Modern Japanese Literature*, Karatani has said that the modern narrative subject is produced in modern Japanese literature through a process of defamiliarization: the individual becomes identified as perceiving subject, and the objects of perception are delineated anew as objects for (scientific or realistic) observation.[5] The linguistic standardization movement (*genbun'itchi*) liberated both landscape and "the individual" from antecedent, standardized portrayals and paved the way for the "discovery" of interiority, generating the modern subject in text.[6] Modern linguistic, psychoanalytic, and philosophic discourses have produced, and split, the "layered" narrative subject.

The lack of a specific configuration of depth in classical texts compounds the modern readers' perception of female "vacancy" in the canon.[7] Premodern texts were not subordinated to the production of interiority; and gender, like other social discourses, tended toward metaphoric function, unlike modern textual counterparts in which gender may become a source, or a teleological component, of specific, individuated identity. As Butler has written, "Discrete genders are part of what 'humanizes' individuals within contemporary culture."[8]

In Enchi's narratives, "psychological" depth of character is, however, complicated by a historical depth. What might be called a collective female "past" (history or legacy) functions side by side with each individual woman's personal past to generate her actions in the narrative present. The historical subordination of women is a "past in the present"; it is a past that produces the present. This is not to suggest that some sort of "fatalism" is at work in Enchi's narratives. To the contrary, Enchi's protagonists do battle with the terms of their historical subordination. As Etō Jun wrote, in the *Namamiko monogatari*, male political power is partly relativized by Enchi's foregrounding of how women manipulated (behind-the-scenes) political matters, while conversely exposing how women were used by men as political pawns.[9]

Different texts upset differently what Mizuta has called the ambivalence of the original *monogatari*—its encasement in a metaphorized femininity. The *Namamiko monogatari* mirrors the classics in its relative lack of interiority or supposedly unmediated reportage of a character's inner monologue; instead, character interiority is split *between* women. Etō hypothesizes that, "Kureha is a character who expresses the interior [*naiō*] of the female principle [*genri*] that is represented by Empress Teishi."[10] *Masks* alternates between vacant surface archetypes, uncontainable female seepage, and modern, interiorized, narrative subjects. Vacillations between such familiar but seemingly irreconcilable narrative subject positionings is enacted through the changing narrative voices of different characters but also *within the bodies* of each of the female protagonists. Female characterizations are compound: metaphoric, classic presentations of women are conjoined with modern explorations of their innermost voices, a narrative structure that *bodily* splits the female narrative subject along the axis of past and present, mirroring the split between pollution and divinity while also drawing on the continuities of the feminine-as-abject, plurality and uncontainability, or seepage at the boundaries of a modern, individuated identity.

The vacant and unclean Harume offers marked contrast to the deeply self-conscious narrative voices of and positions held by Mieko and Yasuko. Harume becomes the foil against which Mieko and Yasuko take on additional interiority. Unlike Mieko, who as the educated and refined poet and head of her household resembles the middle-ranking aristocratic women writers of the *monogatari*, Harume embodies the modern male imaginary of Heian femininity, lacking interiority and alternately perceived as alluringly and dirtily erotic and as a blank to be filled in by a male longing. She is persistently compared to representations of women from the past. "Against the pallor of her face, lusterless and empty as a blank white wall, her big dark eyes and heavy eyebrows stood out exactly like those of an *ukiyo-e* style beauty drawn in India ink on fine white Chinese paper" (70). Without utilitarian function as long as her brother Akio is alive, Harume is sent away to be raised elsewhere. She is brought back by Mieko only after Akio's death makes her necessary to Mieko's plan of defrauding the Toganō name. Even then, her utility lies purely in her sexual and reproductive body and in her capacity to conform to Ibuki's fantasies. Notably, it is she who is sacrificed for the defrauding of the patrilineage.

Harume is thus the perfect "bait" for the women's trap. Yasuko and Mieko place her strategically within Ibuki's gaze, allowing his erotic imagination to "fill" her. He notes that "her face might be perfectly inlaid on the *zō no onna* mask [described as cold, beautiful and cruel] . . . the interior of her mouth was dark and strangely alluring" (40). When one night his physical advances to his lover Yasuko are rebuffed, he is allowed a glimpse of Harume and feels "the desires left unsatisfied by Yasuko now gathering around Harume, whose arms and shoulders had seemed so round and firm. He longed to seize her roughly" (80). Ibuki collapses the separate women into a composite figure as "flowers of darkness": "Amid the flowers breathing their mysterious perfumes into darkness floated the face not only of Mieko but of Yasuko—yes, and of Harume as well" (92). When the pregnant Harume is "viewed in dim light, her face with its haggard eyes became startlingly like that of Mieko" (121).

The success of Mieko's scheme to replace Yasuko with Harume in bed with the (unaware) Ibuki, and thereby to impregnate her, is dependent on the generalities of the male imaginary. Enticed by a series of transitory sightings of Harume, Ibuki collapses Yasuko and Harume into an archetypal, or nonspecific, femaleness, epitomized by the facility with which the bodily replacement is actualized. On the exchange of women in phallocentric systems, Irigaray has written that

when women are exchanged, woman's body must be treated as an *abstraction*. The exchange operation cannot take place in terms of some intrinsic, immanent value of the commodity. It can only come about when two objects—two women—are in a relation of equality with a third term that is neither the one nor the other. It is thus not as "women" that they are exchanged, but as women reduced to some common feature—their current price in gold, or phalluses. . . .

Woman thus has value only in that she can be exchanged.[11] (Irigaray's emphasis)

The interchangeable nature of femaleness, as seen in the gaze of Enchi's male characters, and female exclusion from circuits of exchange as consumers seems to generate, in part, a type of ambivalent female community in many of Enchi's narratives.

Chapter 7 focused on the ambivalent relations between mothers and daughters in Enchi's narratives. But a wide variety of female-female relationships, not limited to mother-daughter dyads, are central to Enchi's corpus. The *Namamiko monogatari, Saimu, Masks, The Waiting Years*—each of these long fictions has been discussed in various published commentaries as treatments of female (hetero)sexuality, of how the repercussions of suppressed (hetero)sexual desire lead desperate and frustrated women to spiritual vengeance against the men who have been cold to them. Yet quantitatively, the narratives focus far more on details of the relations, conversations, and all manner of interactions between women.

Among the middle classes (that is, the salaried classes) in modern Japan, the institution of marriage has not ensured that a married woman's primary companion was her husband. To the contrary, with marriage, and especially with the birth of children, social spheres become increasingly sexually segregated. Housewives fraternize with housewives, husbands primarily with other men in the varied "public" work-related spheres (which may include drinking after work). Married middle-class women spend quantitatively far less time with their husbands than they do with their children and other housewives and mothers.

Thus, it is not surprising that although Enchi's most celebrated novel, *The Waiting Years*, is structurally organized around the marital relationship of Tomo and Yukitomo, the book is more accurately described as being about the relationships among the women who are bound together by varying degrees of powerlessness against the malecentric social fabric that enfolds them. The protagonist, Tomo, has no recourse but to serve her husband lest he abandon her; her husband's first "consort," Suga, has no survival skills to support a different sort of life. A fierce camaraderie develops between the women, in spite of copresent jealousies over the inevitable inequities of their rigidly hierarchized social positions of wife, concubine, or maid. The women who thus might have been bitter rivals are unified through their economic and social dependence on, and suppressed anger at, Yukitomo. Tomo, as household matriarch, becomes progressively possessed of an awesome inner strength, born of her capacity to endure repeated emotional trauma. When Yukitomo seduces his daughter-in-law, Miya, Tomo experiences "a fierce wrath that stood up to Yukitomo, the ungovernable male, and took beneath its protective wing Suga, Yumi, and even the offending Miya herself" (105). Structurally replicating the narratorial paradigm of the classical *monogatari* by tracing a family history through the years, *The Waiting Years* also overturns many of the standard elements of its source text(s), becoming a powerful inversion of the model *monogatari* in which the jealous spirits of spurned women wreak havoc on their female rivals. In *The Waiting Years*, the women (even the rivals) are bound together in subordination, and their anger is appropriately directed not at one another, but at the patriarch and the patriarchal system that is more accurately to blame for their suffering. The repressed spirits of jealous women emerge in Heian works to attack their female rivals, but Mieko of *Masks* seeks vengeance on her husband, not his mistress, and Mieko's essay reinterprets the Rokujō lady as a victim of male oppression rather than as a villainess. Two conventionally separated female roles, the helpless, pliable object of male erotic desire and the manipulative witch (who conversely becomes the active agent of her own erotic desire) are collapsed within the body of Yasuko, who is both.

Bound by body, blood, and the tropings of antecedent narrative that are the sources of their polluting and divine Otherness—liquidities that seep out of insubstantial "female" boundaries—the women of *Masks* are thereby made capable of additional resistance to the classical portrayal through a female fellowship. This fellowship is exclusive of men and cooperative in bodies, blood, intention, erotic desire, and ultimately, a newborn baby. Describing the connection between Yasuko and Mieko, Ibuki calls it "a quality of moistness, of clingingness, like that of something animal; he was reminded of a spider's web. Then, entangled in that web, soft and white as marshmallow, the image of Harume's face floated up in his mind" (90). Mieko acknowledges to Yasuko, "you are my real daughter; the woman in me that I tried, but failed, to pass on to Harume has found new life in you" (68). Polluting menstrual blood, especially Harume's, entwines the three women of the household: "Mieko insisted on laundering the soiled undergarments herself when Harume had her period. . . . Harume, totally lacking in feminine discretion, was continually leaving a trail of crimson drops . . . or arriving at the dinner table accompanied by a pungent odor" (74). Similarly, a special bond is forged between Yasuko and Harume:

There were times when she [Harume] would resent being touched, and she would attack her would-be helper like a wild animal. Such episodes came only during her monthly period. Once Yasuko had been the victim, receiving a bite on her little finger so savage it had drawn blood. Ever since that time Harume had seemed more comfortable around Yasuko, more eager, even, to draw close to her. (72)

The mutual "bleeding," of fertility and of a sympathetic wound, is a metaphor, and the medium, for a female unity, or "gestalt." Within this gestalt, what has been socially abjected is reclaimed as part of the female subject, but by virtue of this reclaiming, the subject is also made communal. Yasuko, Harume, and Mieko's sexual, spiritual, and reproductive bodies and minds merge into an intuitive knowledge of and communication with the other(s). Harume "senses" Yasuko's physical presence (70); Mieko's sense of smell enlightens her to the fact that Yasuko and Ibuki have become lovers (64); Yasuko instinctively knows that Mieko had a lover (68). Even as Yasuko complains of losing self-determination, claiming that Mieko's feelings and desires have somehow invaded her own body and mind, she thrills to the scheme to impregnate Harume as Mieko's "accomplice" (126). Mikame's uncertainty over which woman controls the other suggests that the collusion is not as clearly hierarchized as is asserted elsewhere: "Do you really think that Mieko has that much of the shamaness in her?. . . . It wouldn't surprise me if it were Yasuko who dominated *her*, behind the scenes" (13; Enchi's emphasis). The women are mutually linked to the multiplicity of the spirits of women of past narratives.

Although similar to a Western witches' coven, the female community in *Masks* stands *against* the Japanese tradition of isolating the shamaness from all positive interaction with other women. The witch in Japanese folktales is generally happened upon when her victim has strayed from civilization, most frequently on mountaintops. Unlike the Western witches, who form communities of women to prey on male victims, the Japanese witch archetype is usually a solitary figure. Yet even after Harume has given birth in fulfillment of the women's plot, Yasuko chooses to remain in the Toganō household to raise the baby, rejecting Mikame's marriage proposal.

Scrutinized by Ibuki and Mikame, both of whom are in love with Yasuko, the intense female intimacy shared by Yasuko and Mieko of *Masks* is profoundly disconcerting. The "deep and powerful" (89) bond between Yasuko and Mieko makes Ibuki feel secondary. Ibuki and Mikame repeatedly note with discomfort a dialogue transcendental of enunciation, "the passing of a private and wordless communication" (20) between Mieko and Yasuko. But the men don't leave it at that. They ponder just what goes on between the two women in private, rendering it erotic. Ibuki asks Yasuko about her intimacy with Mieko: "Are you sure you weren't in love with her?" She answers, "In love? Perhaps I was, in a way" (34). Ibuki confides to his friend Mikame, "There's something awfully suggestive to me about the relationship between those two," to which Mikame responds, "They're lovers, you mean? Lesbians? Hmm, I doubt it" (88). Later, however, Mikame muses, "Those two never left each other's sides. You know you're quite right, Ibuki, they do act as if they were lovers. Yasuko alone is enough, but with both of them hanging on to each other, it gets to be damned suggestive" (95).

In *Saimu*, Katsuko and Sano are brought together by the scroll; as I noted previously, "writing" replaces "blood" as a medium to interlink women with other women. Partners in unraveling the mystery of the scroll, Katsuko and Sano form an ambivalent community, based on enmity, compassion, attachment, and affection. As in *Masks*, the male gaze eroticizes their intimate relationship. Tsuda says to Katsuko, "It looks to me as if you are actually enamored of Ms. Tsutsumi. Mr. Katsura said so too. He said that even if you have important business to take care of there, when something comes up with Ms. Tsutsumi, you race off. He said it's as though you were lesbian lovers [*resubian no ke ga aru*]" (142).

Though it is thus clearly the men who eroticize the relationships between the women, there are, however, collusive with the scopic male gaze that seeks an erotic element in the women's intimacy, moments of voluptuous suggestion within Enchi's omniscient (supposedly "unmediated") descriptions. Awakening from a nightmare one night, Yasuko seeks solace in Mieko's bedroom: "She lay encircled in Mieko's arms, her chest heaving so that it brushed with each sharp intake of breath against the round swelling of Mieko's breasts" (62).

In discussing the nature of female bonding in Enchi's narratives, I have been tempted to borrow Eve Sedgwick's term *homosocial*, which she has used to describe male-male relations; the term, however, is inappropriate, first, because of the different power positions that inform male-male and female-female relations in patriarchal and phallocentric systems. Second, as Sedgwick has shown, "homosocial" bondings are stripped of their homoerotic components as a constitutive aspect of the positing of the term. (Her *Between Men: English Literature and Male Homosocial Desire* attempts to disinter the underlying homoeroticism that informs, yet is denied, in those homosocial bondings.) Quite to the contrary, female-female bondings of a nonsexual nature may be invested with an eroticism to serve as a spectacle to entertain a male scopic gaze. (This is not to suggest at all that lesbians are not subject to sociocultural and political suppression, but rather, to highlight the difference in dominant framings of lesbian and nonsexual female bonding and gay male/homosocial bonding.) Notably, because women are already "feminized," especially since they are naturalized as the ones who are "supposed to be" penetrated in the sexual act, when watching (or imagining) two women making love (and becoming vicariously aroused), there is little of the attendant revulsion and abjection on the part of the phallic subject that characterizes his homophobic response to two men making love.[12]

Thus, with some hesitation, I describe the relations between women in Enchi's narratives with an adaptation of Adrienne Rich's term *lesbian continuum*, understood as, in these texts, a bonding between Japanese women in like circumstances, women who are brought together because of work, family, or other causes and who find a community with one another that is at least partly resistant to the patriarchal status quo. Rich coined this term "to include a range—through each woman's life and throughout history—of woman-identified experience, not simply the fact that a woman has had or consciously desired genital sexual experience with another woman."[13] Rich intended to describe a broad range of "female-bondings" that are not necessarily lesbian or sexualized but that occur among women living with the restraints of compulsory heterosexualism. Such female bonding can be in resistance to, or simply parallel to, heterosexual relations. Although, as has been well noted by critics, Rich's concept of "lesbian continuum" may have been weakened by its original elision of classist, racialist, and other particulars that cast any generalized notions of "sisterhood" under the rubric of "woman" into question, in Enchi's narratives the suggested female community is usually composed of Japanese women who may occupy the same household, interact with one another professionally, or share intellectual or artistic activities, although they may be of somewhat differing class. (In *The Waiting Years*, for example, the women live in the same household and thus are brought together by a variety of shared experiences, most obviously, by the sexual appetite and crass cruelty of the patriarch Yukitomo.) In addition, the homoerotic *potential* suggested by the term seems appropriate to a reading of Enchi's narratives, in which female bonding is often an act of resistance that teeters at the borders of lesbian sentiments, without becoming concretely sexualized or "genitalized."

As I have argued, the dangerous woman represents the (original) object of desire and is the repository for that which has been abjected; for Enchi's protagonists, she is still "the desired," and thus, the relations between women who represent her or are "possessed" by her are by definition eroticized. This desire is also disavowed and attended by shame. When Sano burns the scroll (in a belated disavowal), she does so in response to her shame and humiliation at having seduced her nephew. This desire differs from that enjoyed or disavowed by Kyōka's male protagonists, because its object (the dangerous woman) is no longer the "Other"—but more purely the "abject"—potentially representing the "surplus" aspect of all women. Moreover, for Enchi's female protagonists, to "possess" her means to *introject* her (identify with and incorporate her as a part of the self), not couple with her. The dangerous woman *merges* with the female protagonist, making her "abjected" aspects dominant and defying the notion of a bounded female subject.

In keeping with phallocentric notions, Ibuki's assumption of masculine priority allows him only to envision the intimacy between Yasuko and Mieko as a temporary and second-rate replacement for an erotic, heterosexual affair: "Once she [Yasuko] falls in love with someone else, Mieko's influence will disappear. It stands to reason. A woman can't help being attracted more to men than she is to other women" (15). However, Ibuki is proved wrong. Yasuko confesses to Mieko, "I'm as excited as you . . . a baby with Akio's blood in its veins. That instinctive feeling underlies all the strange things I've done. You and I are accomplices, aren't we, in a dreadful crime—a crime that only women could commit. *Having a part to play in this scheme of yours, Mother, means more to me than the love of any man*" (126; emphasis added).

The blood shed in childbearing and menstruation unifies the women "in body," while abstract discourses on blood as pollution, as divine lineage, and as flow facilitate the transgression of the women's individual psychic, emotional, and even physical boundaries. In agreement with Mary Douglas, Grosz comments that "what is considered disruptive or transgressive of borders or boundaries is represented as dirt and may be experienced, in keeping with [Julia] Kristeva's terminology, as abject."[14] The transferal of the uncontrollable from the male body to the female is a doubled process that renders femaleness boundless, ciphered, and multiple and thereby potentially subversive to phallocentric self-containment. Yasuko confesses to Mieko that "time and again, your feelings seem to take hold of me. This is not just some crazy excuse; so many times I've found myself doing things that don't make a bit of sense—and every time, without fail, I feel you there in the background, manipulating me like a puppet" (67). Unlike medieval portrayals of possession, in which the possessing spirit speaks in its own voice out of the mouth of the possessed woman, who has disappeared as subject during possession, Yasuko as speaking and thinking subject is aware of Mieko's presence within her.[15] Mieko's formidable will joins Yasuko's in Yasuko's body without displacing her spirit or consciousness. As Harume is being sent off to Ibuki's bedside, Mieko whispers, "you won't be alone tonight. I'll be with you. You must carry out my plan for me—I'm relying on you. And you will, won't you?" (102). Even when Harume functions as a composite vessel for Mieko's will, her body interchangeable with Yasuko's body, she appears to retain a subjecthood. As it dawns on Ibuki that the woman to whom he has just made love is not Yasuko but Harume, he muses that her "face was the face of Masugami—the mask of the young madwoman which he had seen. . . . Despite the clear apprehension in her look, she showed no sign of fear. When Ibuki suddenly released her body, her eyes roamed his face in blank amazement, a smile of physical satiety curving her mouth" (110). In this moment, Harume is all three women of *Masks*, and more, holding within her putative vacancy the suppressed, tainted fertility and divinity of the female ghosts of the scripted Japanese past. Transcending all other alliances, the substratum of blood as a material medium bonds the women.

Likewise, in *Saimu*, Sano experiences possession as a female "multiplicity." From the dizzying and indistinct confusion of self and possessor, Sano hears a voice within herself: " 'I am here, inside you, from now on.' Sano was keenly aware that the muffled, indistinct voice was that of Kawahara Yukiko. A chill spread through her body and her teeth chattered" (189). The plurality ushers Sano into an erotically charged experiential state previously unknown to her; through Yukiko, and therefore through the priestess depicted in the mysterious scroll, she is initiated into a realm of sexual license and *jouissance*:

Her toes and fingers grew numb as she reclined in bed. A slight spasm would spread the numbness throughout her body. It didn't have any unusual effect on her stomach or her intestines, but her heart fluttered offbeat, and it seemed as if her breasts suddenly swelled. She heard a wail, like a summons, from her "venerated valley" [*mihoto*] as it was referred to in the *Kojiki*.[16] A sensation, like that of waiting, and also like that of sucking, generated that wailing voice from down there. At the same time her body writhed with a bizarre motion—it was a sensation as though her body were simultaneously her own and not her own—as though her body had become that of a starfish, or, as Kawahara Yukiko had once described it, a spider. Dragged there by her uncurbed, pliant, sucking hands and feet, came male bodies one on top of the other. A strong-smelling, hairy-chested German; an American whose eyebrows and eyes were a single line of shiny blonde down; a man tall for a Japanese, lips shut fastidiously. These bodies were as if responding to the summons of the wail emanating from her sucker.

[When Sano returned to reality] she didn't think she had been dreaming. Nor did she think that she was not herself. But it was also true that a sweet, sticky sensation, like a honey that Sano had never herself tasted, remained with her after these strange sexual couplings.

Had the Saiin [Shinto Priestess, depicted in the scroll] possessed her through Kawahara Yukiko? (192–93)

Through the introjection of the dangerous woman, Sano's orgasmic *jouissance* becomes the sort Lacan called supplemental, "a *jouissance* beyond the phallus," a "not-all" female *jouissance*.[17]

In her intriguing article "Matrix and Metramorphosis," Bracha Lictenberg Ettinger proposes a psychosexual developmental stage called the Matrix and a process called metramorphosis to "describe certain aspects of human symbolic experience and to relativize the prevailing status of the concept of the Phallus in Lacan's (and Freud's) psychoanalytic theories."[18] The Matrix does not replace either the Oedipal or symbiotic state, but it is developmentally prenatal (although, like the symbiotic stage, continues to exist in the unconscious) and as a concept would "serve to explore the feminine as an otherness beyond the Phallus"—that is, beyond negative binarism, lack, and difference.[19] Metramorphosis posits a discourse within which the female pluralism of *Masks* and *Saimu* can be positively, not negatively, described.

The Matrix involves a subject(ivity) which is either multiple/plural or partial/split/ fragmented but not schizophrenic. The elements of the subjects which meet in the Matrix recognize one another without knowing one another.

. . .

I relate the Matrix to the process I call metramorphosis dealing with *I* and *not-I(s)* in emergence and in co-existence, with neither symmetrical nor identical nor mirroring relationships. These are processes of change without domination. . . . The borderlines between them are surpassed and transformed to become thresholds. When these transformations relate to transformations in the borderlines and in the shared spaces, metramorphosis may occur, creating redistribution in the shared field and a change in the common subjectivity. . . . There is a shift aside for the Phallus, an-other symbolic filter.[20] (Ettinger's emphasis)

Julia Kristeva has identified "the semiotic" as a partly repressed pulsational pressure within the signifying process that is lodged in the "chora," the psychic repository for pre-Oedipal primary-process thought.[21] Ettinger's Matrix is not commensurate with the "chora," because it identifies an *other* subjectivity that is not oppositional to, but *copresent with, the Symbolic* (or the Oedipal identification of self through negative difference). The breakdown of boundaries between the women in *Masks* bears some resemblance to the crossing of the thresholds described by Ettinger as the traces of metramorphosis experienced in normative adulthood.[22]

The modern project of interiorization and individuation of the archetypal shamaness in *Masks* and *Saimu* is thus rendered ambivalent by a simultaneous erasure of individual boundaries in a "gestalt sisterhood" that mirrors neither the model of the isolated shaman archetype nor that of the modern subject. Mieko, merged with Yasuko and Harume, is also simultaneously herself and the Rokujō lady, who in turn has been depicted as a plurality, and who embodies traces of multiple, ancient shamanesses and deities. Sano likewise becomes a plurality, intermixed with Kawahara Yukiko, and through her, with the priestess of the Kamo shrine. These female "gestalts" are brought into being by excavating the origins of pollution and divinity suppressed within a continuous material and symbolic female blood connection and the narrative troping of dangerous women. The metaphoric, multiple, or emptied female archetypes of *Masks* and *Saimu* are deconstructed by this unexplained and inconceivable, neither undifferentiated nor individuated, state.

Female shamans cast their spells from Japan's earliest oral folklore well into and beyond Heian *monogatari*, in which they inhabit marginalized sites on the borders of society proper. It stands to reason that the shamaness has so engaged the imagination of many contemporary women writers, and that Mieko "discovers" the traces of a suppressed shamaness, both empowered and polluted, in the Rokujō lady, and that Sano finds an ambivalent eroticized empowerment in the troping of the Kamo Priestess. And the figure of the female shaman is the most vacant and ciphered and thus most ready for "filling" by the modern reader/writer who seeks to produce the "inner voices" of characters. *Masks*, *Saimu*, and the *Nakamiko monogatari*, as well as many of Enchi's shorter narratives, produce a modern resistant female voice as a supplement to female-authored medieval *monogatari*.

Simultaneously, the female bodies of Enchi's texts are the sites upon which contrasting discourses on femaleness, such as divinity, plurality, vacancy, and pollution, are inscribed. In a variety of modes, abjection is recirculated as a primary identificatory province of these female bodies. Enchi's narratives thereby collude with dominant representations of women by maintaining the binarisms of metaphoric gender, which has produced female archetypes empty of subjectivity or filled only by a male imaginary replete with the projection of body secretions (partial objects) and objects of abjection. But Enchi's narratives also marshal these markers and objects of expulsion to subversive ends through positing community and camaraderie between modern shamanesses, and, in the *Namamiko monogatari*, through revealing the troping itself to be a male construct for an androcentric agenda. *Masks* reclaims the matrilineal origins of "blood lineage" from its subordination to patrilineal ideology, while duplicating a phallocentrism whereby polluted blood circulates within all women as a "carrier" of sin. *Saimu* and the *Namamiko monogatari* shift toward a community framed by inscription. Enchi's literary metaphor of blood, or inhabitation of the extant troping of dangerous women, frames resistance within the logic of phallocentric difference.

Nakagami Kenji

Dangerous Men and All That Jazz

Short, savage sentences are one of the signatures of Nakagami Kenji's prose style; his narratives abound with abbreviated distillations of event, emotion, and thought into shortened, staccato, and stressed syllables. "The woman wept. Tears streamed from her eyes. 'Saint,' she moaned. He hit the woman again. 'I am not a saint.' " (Onna wa naita. Namida ga, me kara, izumi no yō ni deta. 'Shōnin sama-a' to umeita. Kare wa mata onna o nagutta. 'Shōnin jya nai.')[1] Such truncated yet emphatic phrases are uncharacteristic of mainstream Japanese, written or spoken. One wonders what inspired him to whittle away language to such spare forms. Nakagami has written that when he first came to Tokyo he spent hours listening to modern jazz. Perhaps one of his inspirations was modern jazz syncopation—modification through shortening—of older tunes. Here is an excerpt from his 1976 "Sakka to nikutai" (The writer and the flesh):

For a long time, I lived like a hippie, listening to jazz day after day. *That is where I must begin writing about working, and writing about writing [itself]*.

I graduated from high school, and came to Tokyo from Shingū City in Wakayama Prefecture. I was eighteen at the time. I arrived in Tokyo, rolled into a friend's cheap, rented room [*geshuku*], and the next day heard jazz at a modern jazz coffee shop in Shinjuku. It was my first experience with jazz. It was fresh. It was stimulating. More than anything else, I was taken with a sense of liberation. My arrival in the city called Tokyo meant liberation from the provincial [*fūdo*], and from the ties of my blood relationships—ties that persisted no matter how I tried to sever them, and jazz literally flowed into me, reverberating, penetrating deep into my body, to the deepest recesses of my soul.[2] (emphasis added)

His actual introduction to jazz, confessed Nakagami, coincided with a period of intense drug experimentation and abandon, accompanied by an unprecedented sense of liberation that he experienced upon moving to the urban sprawl of Tokyo. He was eighteen.[3] It was the 1960s. It was thus within a context of enormous social and political upheavals—the American civil rights movement, the student riots in Japan—that Nakagami encountered jazz. At that time in Japan jazz was ideologically linked to the struggle against discrimination by African Americans. For the young Nakagami, just out of high school, born a member of the outcaste community in the small, rural, seaside city of Shingū, jazz and Tokyo, personal liberation and political resistance, drug experimentation, his maturation into a young adult, and the beginning of his career as a writer of fiction, were all intertwined. Jazz, and the discourse by which it was presented in Japan of the 1960s, inspired some of Nakagami's earliest literary endeavors. An essay published in 1969 in the journal *Chūō kōron* discussed jazz as it related to political action and as a type of African-American political discourse that stood in resistance to the dominant white culture in America. The writer, Aikura Hisato, used a Japanese translation of Amiri Baraka's *Blues People* as a foil for his argument.[4] In *Blues People*, and in a short essay rearticulating his ideas published in 1990, Baraka had argued:

In the earliest years of black presence in the New World, black art was initially (after the conquest) a *threat*. It could fuel and communicate rebellion. The drum was banned, which should draw attention to its *political* nature. . . .

[Black] music is *about feeling*: the feeling generated by black life, which is defined by its opposition (contradiction) to the dominant culture. Its most advanced (even its healthiest) existence is in some fashion predicated on resistance.[5] (Baraka's emphasis)

The "meaning" of jazz as a socially defiant yet celebratory music written and performed by (mostly) African Americans held great significance for Nakagami. Whether Nakagami actually read the translation of *Blues People*, Baraka's assertion that jazz was an outgrowth of the blues, emerging as a mixture of African and American influences and in response and opposition to American oppression and racism, was clearly a dominant voice in the 1960s discourse on jazz in Japanese. In a 1968 special issue of the music journal *Ongaku geijutsu* on modern jazz, the Japanese commentators repeatedly rely on Baraka's analysis of jazz. They read jazz as an expression rooted in a racial community (*minzoku*) that has progressed beyond the bounds of its originating impulses to provide a forum for resistance to (all) Eurocentric musical conventions; thus, it has meaning, argue many Japanese jazz enthusiasts, for the Japanese as well.[6] Others find a correlation between their experience during the postwar occupation and growing up black in America. Though his understanding of the term *white Negro* seems questionable, poet, performance artist, and filmmaker Terayama Shūji comments that, "Just as in America, where there has been the emergence of a type called white Negroes, I feel as though we were raised very much like yellow Negroes in the upheaval of all values during the immediate postwar era in Japan. I think there is a resemblance in, so to speak, being 'under-domination.' "[7]

For Nakagami, however, engaging in such convolutions in search of assonance were unnecessary: he had, after all, been raised under the mark of difference and ethnic subordination as a *burakumin*. In 1983 Nakagami reflected on his early days as an eighteen-year-old in Shinjuku:

I have to smile sardonically at how as a young man, this was what I was most proud and boastful about, but from the perspective of leftist jazz enthusiasts, nothing gave us more pleasure than participating in a violent antiwar day, rock-throwing in Shinjuku and near Shinjuku Station, overturning cars, setting things afire, rioting.[8] What was fun about Shinjuku were those joyfully characteristic [*menboku yakujo*] street incidents; Shinjuku was like a Disneyland prepared for any eventuality. No one dissented when a lover of jazz intoned "that is free jazz."[9]

The "free jazz" of Nakagami and his companions nonetheless reconfined them as a marginal minority even within the resistance movement. The paragraph just quoted concludes by noting that the "left-wing lovers of jazz" were in discord with, and felt alienated from, the student movement. Nakagami was not in college. He was a physical laborer. And he was burdened by a huge rage, both personal and classist in origin. An essay he wrote in 1969 exploring the origins of—and celebrating—the infamous, anarchic, violent murders committed by a nineteen-year-old Japanese youth, Nagayama Norio, commingles Nagayama's imagined "inner voice" with Nakagami's own:

Kill. Shoot and kill. That's right, despicable worms, always blocking my path. When my index finger is on the trigger of the gun, that finger subjects the world to my own, indisputable judgment. Blowing up the world inside myself! Actually, I have not even one lingering connection to the world. Ah, even if I had such a connection, I would blast through it. What in the world do I have left? And at this point, what would you have me remember? I come from shit. I am piss. You cunt maggots squirming along the street. I am neither the son of a fine country squire nor raised with piles of money, listening to the tinkling of a piano played by a pretentious father. Ah. All I want is pussy. But you, taking a little bite of your spaghetti Neapolitan—that looks like pink intestinal worms—and politely declining the rest, it makes me want to puke

. . .

My filthy blood; I am dying; a languor like slumber
Rip apart!
Rip apart the ocean, rip apart the sky, rip apart the boat, rip apart the earth!

. . .

Why do I write? To fabricate a new Japanese literature? That's shit. To fabricate a new Japanese aesthetic? I would make the lot of those who say such things drink piss. I want to batter and destroy everything.[10]

From "Umi e" (To the ocean, 1967), shadowing a poetic, deeply sexual, and descriptive passage in what is basically an ode to the ocean, erupts a cold violence in classic Nakagami style:

A dog comes charging out from the shadow of a telephone pole. A brown, misshapenly fat dog. It slips between our bodies; as it walks away, it is howling and howling as if suffering from hypochondria.

It must have discerned an insecure communication gloomy as the sexual intercourse that is exchanged between you and I (something resembling the passion of love). Well. Beat and kill that dog.[11]

His class status, his anger, his perception of marginalization and discrimination—each contributed to Nakagami's earliest enthusiastic identification with African Americans. Although this identification should not be misunderstood as suggesting that Nakagami was ignorant of the specific differences in the mechanics and histories of oppression against African Americans in the States and the *burakumin* in Japan, Nakagami seems to have consciously sought some general alliance among all oppressed peoples. In a 1982 essay praising the literary works of contemporary African-American women, he used the very particular phrase *hisabetsu buraku* (the modern term for the outcaste slums in Japan) as a generic term for "ghetto": "the various ghettos [*hisabetsu buraku*] that exist throughout the world."[12]

Direct references to jazz punctuate Nakagami's earliest essays and narratives, such as "Takao to Mitsuko" (Takao and Mitsuko, 1966), "Umi e," and the essay on the violent Nagayama, "Hanzaisha Nagayama Norio kara no hōkoku." From "Umi e": "The town was silent and still as death, and the night of hard, glittering jewels sang as though it were song itself (like the festival of grassland nymphs evoked by Coltrane)" (59). By including the names of specific artists or themes of specific songs, Nakagami obviously meant to highlight an emotion, to distill a mood, or to suggest a vibrant, libidinal, pagan abandon. In 1966 he wrote a short, impressionistic piece entitled "JAZZ," in which brief passages follow one another with little linking structure other than personal association:

1. A small, youth hangout in the basement of a building. Young people gathered, poisoned by sleeping pills, stinking of semen, taking sustenance from healthful illusions like those of a Dalí painting.[13] The drumbeat echoed and the trumpet sang like the call of a shrike over the dry trees.

We are dead. We are dead. A tusk offered up to the Pygmy Chieftain, we are dead.

The drums praise the wondrousness of an archaism many billion light years past. When mammoths swaggered the wilderness. Leaned up against the walls; I carved a couple's names. The bass sent blood throbbing through the walls.

2. A swamp there. The crazy rhythm of jazz concealed metaphysical contemplations. A dangling rococo-style lamp.

The piano sang a verse; the young people knew the pathos in the wake of a wretched ejaculation. Cigarette smoke evoked a Venus that had melted into the ocean, floating like teardrops in air. Thelonius Monk's fingertips reducing coke, ashenly, to the present.[14] A Pygmy ceremonial mask evoking Shingū winter. At that time the young people had grown senile. Youth is like a nap in a sunny spot in wintertime. The trumpet rocked emotions, like a shrike singing high up in the dry trees.[15]

Following W. E. B. Du Bois, Baraka wrote, "What is it like to see yourself through the eyes of those who despise you? This is the source of black petit bourgeois self-hatred and defeat, a syndrome or 'double consciousness,' which Du Bois baits with: How to be black and American?"[16] A similar doubleness is characteristic of Nakagami's texts. I do not attribute this similarity to an intentional or even unconscious emulation of the positioning of black narrative or music against mainstream (white) culture within the States. Rather, I read it as an effect of a similarly doubled structure of belonging and alienation that informed Nakagami's experience as a *burakumin* in Japan—How to be both Japanese and *burakumin*? His outcaste protagonists are frequently likened to or associated with dogs, echoing the convention of assigning deceased *burakumin* posthumous titles that incorporated the Chinese characters for dog or pig. The motif of polluted blood is constant and sometimes foregrounded, as it is in *Sennen no yuraku* (A thousand years of pleasure, 1982). The ironic nature of this doubleness is clear in the sudden desire to "beat and kill the dog" as quoted above from "Umi e," in the vacillations between rage directed outward and self-hatred, for example, in his essay on Nagayama, and in his inversions of dominant sociocultural values, often by means of a defiantly different rendering of the literary canon. Regarding jazz, ethnomusicologist Ingrid Monson has said that "Irony and parody in African-American music, it seems, make use of the doubleness of the African-American position in American society by documenting through musical reference."[17] Nakagami's narratives are thick with references to the premodern and modern Japanese literary canon; and as I will show, these references are unmistakably ironic tropings.[18] I am not suggesting and nor do I believe that Nakagami would have asserted that the experiences of *burakumin* and African Americans were the same; there is, for example, the radical difference along the axis of the visual mark of "blackness" for African Americans and the lack of any visual markers differentiating *burakumin* from other Japanese. But Nakagami's perception of kinship with African Americans should not be denied. Nakagami seemed to believe that although the specifics of the experiences of oppression differ, some of the structures of discrimination are endemic.

During a symposium on Nakagami, the writer Okuizumi Hikaru noted that, "Nakagami said something interesting in one of his essays: in comparing narratives [*shōsetsu*] to jazz, he said that the [genre of] *monogatari* is like, in jazz terminology, the chord sequence. In short, there is a [standard] chord progression over which one tries out improvisations."[19] Alongside the political and racial meaning of jazz as resistance, Nakagami considered how jazz positioned itself against mainstream music. Jazz, then, inspired what can be called another signature of Nakagami's prose style: a posture of ironic alternation on existing narrative standards. Nakagami's passion for the structural specifics of how jazz signified (the standard blues chord formation underlying innovative melody and personal improvisation on top of the melody) guided his hand toward a specific sort of textured textual complexity. In his *Inside Jazz*, Leonard Feather wrote, "It has been an increasingly common practice to take some definite chord sequence of a well-known song (usually a standard old favorite) and build a new melody around it."[20] Nakagami's positioning of "original" tales in relation to those of the canon resembles the improvisations on, in Feather's words, "old favorites" in jazz, as he set out to reveal exclusion and discrimination as constitutive elements of "history." As the following two chapters will articulate, when Nakagami cited the canon, it was always in ironic variation. He contorted his source texts through a radical unsettling of conventional literary aesthetics.[21]

The identification of *burakumin* with African Americans in Nakagami's early texts also, predictably, borrowed from a discourse of jazz primitivism. A romanticized racialism rendered African Americans closer to the natural, and therefore privileged, in Nakagami's project to overturn dominant evaluative systems and to somehow free the sexual and social body from its cultural fetters. In "Jyūhassai" (Eighteen, 1966), for example, Pygmy masks adorn the walls of the jazz club where the youth gather; in the previous quote from "JAZZ," the paean to an archaic age when mammoths roamed the wilderness is inspired by the sounds of jazz. There is a tendency to romanticize the primeval and tribal community (perhaps somehow culled from Baraka's *Blues People* or from discussions of the text) in these early works.[22]

In the final analysis, however, Nakagami avoided succumbing to naive romanticism. Nakagami's literary project was never a celebration of premodern precedent; rather, it was a thoroughly postmodern gesture toward a deconstruction of the literary canon's convention of writing "landscape as poetics."[23] An overheavy tendency toward lyricism that weighed down the young Nakagami's first literary texts (as evidenced, for example, by the excessively ornate language of "JAZZ") yielded to, in my opinion, some of the most interesting and innovative writing of the contemporary period. Overt references to jazz abate; instead the texts vibrate with Nakagami's own refrains. The Japanese heartland, its folklore, its histories, and its literary and ideological canon become the central referents for Nakagami's narrative detroping and retroping. The lyrical alternates with the tragic, the violent with the passionate, the awesome with the mundane; throughout his texts, Nakagami's characters move through life surrounded by the inexplicable, posing their unanswerable questions in a relentless void. A breathtaking "orchestration" flows all through his writings, be it the maze of contorted, spidery family relations of *Kareki Nada* (Withered tree beach, 1977), the mercenary complexities and cacophonies of Tokyo's Shinjuku area in *Sanka* (Paean, 1987–89), or the descriptions of the seaside and mountainside panoramas in the Kinki region that alternate throughout his corpus with depictions of human tragedy, violence, confusion, and simply, libidinal drive.[24] Nakagami's narratives are imbued with a somber violence, a pulsing eroticism, and a shocking crudeness, or rawness, that surely also have their roots in modern confessional fiction. As Karatani wrote, Nakagami attempted to link the two textual topographies of what might be called "realism" and "folklore" by shifting the *shishōsetsu* (personal, confessional narrative) itself toward the spatial characteristics of the *monogatari*.[25]

I opened this chapter with a short discussion of Nakagami's clipped sentence style. But just as frequently, Nakagami's terse sentences give way to long, lyrical passages that could be compared to solo improvisation over jazz riffs, passages that in both form and syntax could be said to resemble Kyōka's impressionistic (or, as Shinoda Hajime wrote, "musical") prose more than the realistic writing styles practiced by most of Nakagami's contemporaries.[26] The following is from "Fushi" ("The Immortal," 1980):

Dense clouds roiled up covering the entire scene. The gentle slope of the mountain, which had seemed to melt into the sunlight striking it until just now, the stand of cypresses spreading out beyond it like outstretched arms, and the naked crags in the distance, to the hijiri's eyes like purple flames, all dimmed, as if their colors had been wiped away. For a moment, the hijiri felt pain bearing down on him. Raising his eyes, he spat loudly, and began to mimic the sound of the grass again . . . *jaarajaara jaarajaara* . . . as if he were chanting a holy sutra.[27]

Fortifying the obvious thetic references to Kyōka's *Kōya hijiri* that repeat throughout "The Immortal," occasional passages traced by an imagistic and impressionistic flow of language recall those of Kyōka, albeit touched, even in the passage just quoted, with a note of crudeness—the loud spitting. As Nakagami's version progresses, the meeting between the *hijiri* and a woman in the mountains goes far afield of the eroticism that remained restrained and relatively abstract in Kyōka's narratives, bordering on the pornographic in its explicit detail:

He stripped off the garments he was wearing and stretched his body out beside her. It was enough to do nothing, enough that this woman was there breathing beside him, with her skin of peach blossoms bathed in morning light and her golden down—her red nipples, her navel, which seemed to him the center of this world, the burning shadow of her vagina, and the thicket of hair over it. Not resisting the touch of his lips, the woman opened her legs to the kneeling hijiri and gently stroked his back with her tiny hands. He took the fingers of those hands into his mouth, sucking them one at a time. The woman raised her hips to accept his engorged penis, and pressed her lips over his. He plunged into her, as if by doing so he were arresting the flight of an angel in a feathered mantle, holding her here. (424)

Unlike Kyōka, and more like Enchi, Nakagami *radically* inverts and twists his source texts. Enchi's depictions of sex were blunter than Kyōka's; Nakagami's became hard-core. Like Enchi, Nakagami persistently put into question the categories of the sacred and the profane. For Nakagami, this destabilizing was not limited to the realms of female sexuality and spirituality as it was for Enchi; rather, it involved a widely expanded deconstruction of the binaries that were so important in forming the basis for a modern discourse of discrimination by which people of his class were rendered polluted and bestial, and moreover, that laid the foundations for modern phallic subjectivity.

With maturity and practice, Nakagami was able to tighten his writing, and its excessive symbolism abated, but many of his earliest themes and settings remained integral to his later works. Like repeating chord formations, certain motifs recur: a brother dead of suicide; a derided father; the cries of protagonists into a deathly silence of "who am I?" "help me," and "what does it all mean?"; and certain tropings, such as that of the *roji* (alley, a euphemism for the *buraku* ghettos), the "false" holy man, or "masculinity" itself as sites for multiple inversions.[28]

As the following chapter will articulate in detail, legends and folklore, that is, archaic texts, come to function in Nakagami's texts as a sort of erotic and violent textual unconscious that motivates narrative itself and is further enacted through the experiential body of the protagonists. His acknowledged impossible endeavor to excavate "origin"—and his attendant vision of "transcendental space"—led him toward an attempt to liberate libido from its various inscriptions and to invert dominant discourses on "Japanese tradition and culture" and gender. Because, as the sections on Kyōka and Enchi have shown, in modern Japan "origin"—particularly literary and spiritual origin—was feminized in the formation of the modern Japanese state and the phallicization of the subjects of that state, part of Nakagami's project involved the deconstruction of that feminization. In order to unsettle the feminization of origin, Nakagami turned to a type of phallic (re)troping of archaisms.

The phallic trope that Nakagami employs to deconstruct the canon's feminization of pre-Buddhist Shinto animism is, however, persistently compromised by its own, internal inconsistencies. Many of his protagonists are *burakumin*. *Burakumin*, by virtue of already occupying an abjected position (as nonsubjects) within dominant society, are marked by the same types of viscosities, pollution, and libidinal excesses as is the dangerous woman trope. A repeated reduction of the *burakumin* male body to its "physicality" and phallicism appears to merely mimic dominant social discourses on the bestial nature of *burakumin*. However, as Butler argued in *Gender Trouble*,

> sexuality is always constructed within the terms of discourse and power, where power is partially understood in terms of heterosexual and phallic cultural conventions. . . . If sexuality is culturally constructed within existing power relations, then the postulation of a normative sexuality that is "before," "outside," or "beyond" power is a cultural impossibility and a politically impracticable dream. . . . *To operate within the matrix of power is not the same as to replicate uncritically relations of domination. It offers the possibility of a repetition of the law which is not its consolidation, but its displacement.* . . . (emphasis added).
>
> The replication of heterosexual constructs in non-heterosexual frames brings into relief the utterly constructed status of the so-called heterosexual original. Thus, gay is to straight *not* as copy is to original, but, rather, as copy is to copy. The parodic repetition of "the original" . . . reveals the original to be nothing other than a parody of the *idea* of the natural and the original.[29] (Butler's emphasis)

The last two chapters of this book will argue that the theatrical performances of masculinity by Nakagami's protagonists are a type of parodic repetition of the so-called heterosexual "original" that functions to displace the law rather than to consolidate it. Be it the bisexual Yves of *Sanka* or Hanzō of *Sennen no yuraku*, or the *hijiri* of the *Kumanoshū* (The Kumano tales, 1984), in the vacillating dominances that accompany their social and sexual activities, Nakagami's men inhabit complex sites that commingle what dominant social discourses have defined as "female" positions with "male" positions. Through the narrative incorporation of, for example, sadomasochistic role reversals, anal sex between men, or simply by virtue of their abjected status as outcastes, the hyperbolic phallicism of Nakagami's male protagonists is complicated by varied descents into conventionally feminized positions of submissions and diffusions. Such submissions, since the the phallic subject is "feminized," constitute tears in the fabric of phallic dominance. But as the last two chapters will show, Nakagami goes even further: he undoes the very notion of phallicism itself by positing a penised subject that diffuses, and thus that inhabits abjection, in place of a feminized (non)subject and by writing the male *burakumin* body (impossibly) both "as" the phallus and as "having" the phallus, in the Lacanian sense.[30]

Nakagami topples the dangerous woman from her "unique" site as conduit to desired/abjected premodernity by conflating or replacing her with a "dangerous man." Transferring aspects of feminized abjection to the putative male subject deconstructs the very binaries of modern gendered subjectivity. In the end, what Nakagami offers up for scrutiny is an abjected and diffused, yet penised, subject awash in its own identificatory contradictions, unable to halt a process of significatory implosion, and constituting a polymorphous gender imaginary.

Tracing Origins:
Landscape and Interiority

The celebrated medieval poet Matsuo Bashō is most famous for his accounts of his travels. What appear to be realistic representations of topoi or event in these accounts, on closer examination have been shown to be variously embellished or transformed. As Donald Keene holds, in order to write better poetry, Bashō "changed the order of places visited, or turned rainy days into sunny ones . . . the literal truth was of little interest to him, and he did not hesitate to embroider."[1] Bashō's subordination of realistic description to narrative and poetic concerns exemplifies the foremost conceit of Japanese premodern landscape, in which the requirements of a variety of rigid rhetorical forms dictated the description and appreciation of famous sites previously celebrated in the literary canon. Thus, Karatani has described the premodern landscapes of the classical texts as "a weave of language" which is given signification by poetry.[2] Landscape, as described in medieval travel diaries, shared with the visual arts a transcendental vision of space. Artists and writers sought to transcribe the conceptual place rather than to realistically portray a particular site. According to Karatani, in order for Meiji-period artists to see an actual landscape as the subject of artistic production, "this transcendental vision of space had to be overturned."[3]

This chapter will argue that Nakagami's narratives stand in defiance of the modern, separated, realistic landscape as Karatani has defined it, partly by excavating landscape's oral origins. Karatani has argued that Japanese modern depictions of landscape represented a transformation of subjectivity made possible by new relationships of the self to language and this self-as-subject to the perceptual world as separated object. In premodern Japanese narrative, there is no novelistic "I" commensurate with the modern narrative subject. Realism and "interiority" in modern Japanese literature, writes Karatani, are first established in the context of a defamiliarization process that frees landscape and people from their classical configurations. The Meiji-period *genbun'itchi* movement was one aspect of a changing system of representation that, by continuing a process of subordinating the written language to phonocentrism, "discovered" an inner "voice."[4] For pre-*genbun'itchi* literature, significance lay in the formal categories of style comprising the textual surface, but attenuated by the linguistic quest for simple language to express the inner self, meaning shifted to the hidden interior.[5] As a corollary, the individual is produced as narrating subject. Just as this self must be identified as subject, that which the individual perceives must be delineated as a separated object of observation.[6] Karatani classifies Kunikida Doppo's (1871–1908; hereafter Doppo) "Wasureenu hitobito" ("Unforgettable People," 1898) and "Musashino" ("Musahi Plain," 1898) as the first Japanese texts to reproduce the new discourse on landscape—an innovation made possible by the narrator's alienated stance of observation as a modern subject. By adapting "scientific" principles of observation and description to literary narrative in "Musashino," Doppo relocated the significance of sites from the meanings encoded in the classical canon to the objects of nature itself (that which is actually perceived in the present).[7] This process imparted narrative meaning to what was previously inconsequential narratively, fused with the discovery of the modern self. Moreover, as Karatani has explained, "once a landscape has been established, its origins are repressed from memory. It takes on the appearance of an 'object' which has been there, outside us, from the start."[8] The perception of language as a transparent medium for the expression of an inner voice invents the modern self and the modern landscape and simultaneously represses its own origins.[9]

Resembling that of the classical canon, the landscape of Kumano in Nakagami's work is precisely a weave of language, multilayered with significations and inscribed with narratives and histories that imbue it with transcendental, spiritual import. In the preface to his translation of "The Immortal," Mark Harbison discusses how Kumano has been depicted in the Japanese canon:

Since the age of the *Kojiki*, Kumano has always been an "other" world. In earlier periods, it was shunned as a place of unknown evils, unbound by the laws of the court and the state Buddhism of Nara. The *hijiri* [ascetics] and *bikuni* [nuns], who traced their lineage to the semi-mythical wizard En no Gyōja, were revered as holy men and nuns, but they were also feared and shunned as non-people (*saimin*), wanderers in a sedentary society. . . .

The images associated with Kumano (fire, the Nashi Falls, half-human creatures, crows) can be traced back to the dawn of Japanese history, and readers familiar with the Nō will recognize the structure and rhythm. (414)

Nakagami reclaimed for himself the mystical Kumano mountain range, peopling it with alternating presentations of the sacred and the profane and the spiritual and the beastly and extending the scope of his own *monogatari* into taboo territories of violence, discrimination, incest, and bisexuality. Nakagami's narratives teem with violent, criminal, and passionate larger-than-life antiheroes buffeted about by nonrational impulses, which, in Nakagami's fictional topoi, maintain a deep connection with archaic animism, often epitomized by the figure of the serpent. In Nakagami's Kumano, human bloodshed and animal sacrifices defy both Buddhist doctrines against killing and Shinto defilement prohibitions, excavating an oral lore buried beneath, and predating, Japan's written histories. My use of the term *landscape* in this essay thus designates the weave of legend *inscribed within* a material site and not the physical configurations of the land.

Nakagami's legacy as a child of the *buraku* (outcaste quarters) and of Shingū City in the Kumano foothills near the coast is integral to how he restructures the *monogatari* landscape.[10] With the Edo period came the social and structural relegation of Nakagami's forbearers to the outcaste subclass of "untouchables," including the *eta* (deeply polluted) and *hinin* (nonpeople). There were many outcaste hamlets in and near the Kumano region. Until Edo, written texts remained the property of a small, elite literate aristocracy, and through the Edo period literacy basically bypassed the *burakumin*, who were in general neither spoken of nor able to speak for themselves in text.[11] The literary discourse to which landscape was typically subordinated reproduced a concept of Japan that served the political, aesthetic, and social interests of the literate classes and did not represent Nakagami's "origins." Thus, it stands to reason that Nakagami's rendering of the premodern in defiance of the modern landscape does not result in a replication of the landscapes of the Japanese canon.

Narratives written by Nakagami that are temporally situated in the contemporary period (often called *shishōsetsu* by critics) replace the classic *furusato* (heartland and origin) with the dank, odoriferous, narrow *roji* (alleys) of an underclass unrepresented in the canon.[12] The *roji* becomes

Nakagami's inverted "transcendental space," made up of "a weave of language" imbued with significations and warping the classical production of celebrated literary sites.[13] Some of Nakagami's narratives of the premodern period—these are usually called *monogatari* but should more accurately, I think, be called *setsuwa*-inspired (fable-inspired) tales—reach back beyond the history of a literate Japan to an oral folklore passed down from parent to child in the province of Nakagami's birth.[14] Nakagami seeks out narrative sites antecedent to written text, enfolded within the oral narratives of the Kumano mystics, and suggested in the tales of the prehistoric *marebito* described by Origuchi as sacred and taboo beings who ventured forth from *tokoyo*, the land of the dead and of the gods.[15] Nakagami claims these mystics as his spiritual ancestors. Kumano Prefecture on the Kii Peninsula (encompassing present-day Wakayama and some of Mie), Nakagami's *furusato* (spiritual home), is the matrix of Japanese animism, reshaped by the influx of Buddhism and writing. For Nakagami, Kumano folklore functions as a complex and contradictory conduit to a nonrationalized spiritualism bound to erotic and aggressive drive. The Kumano landscape, the heartland of Shinto animism, invigorates Nakagami's texts with vibrant instinct and pulsing libido, through the medium of legends from the preliterate era. Such legends violate the harmony and closure of written, once-posterior tales (now perceived of as source texts).

This chapter will discuss how landscape functions as the matrix for Nakagami's particularized erotic/oral/aggressive sublime in four short stories. In these works, traces of oral narratives that emanate from the landscape invert and destabilize the dualistic archetype of the Japanese medieval and modern written canon: the feminized serpent demon/deity. The copresence of oral folklore and medieval and contemporaneous narratives lacerates the unity that a modernist reading of Nakagami's texts would seek. Specifically, I will address the following questions: How does Nakagami incorporate previous narrative? How is oral folklore conjoined with unconscious and erotic and aggressive drive? How does the symbol of the snake deconstruct gender binarisms?

Landscape, as "inscribed legends," is the signifier that, above all else, constantly recirculates the archaic within Nakagami's texts and challenges various axioms dominant in later medieval and early modern "pretexts" by unraveling the standardized configurations of the serpent. The following statement by Gonroku, the protagonist of "Ukijima" (Floating island, 1975), can be read as a metaphor for Nakagami's literary project to revitalize oral folklore within the confines of a modern written text.

The swamp called Ukijima no mori [The Floating Island Forest] is dead center to those four Shingū shrines. Directly in front of Ukijima is a whorehouse district. I don't know how long it's been there. The legend of Ukijima is about how Oino is bewitched by a big snake and dragged down into the bowels of the Ukijima swamp, but in Akinari's "Jasei no in" in the *Ugetsu monogatari*, based on this legend, the snake is a woman. But the original snake is a man. It was Oino who was dragged down.[16]

In "Ukijima," Nakagami embeds an ancient, oral story (the Ukijima legend) within a medieval, written tale ("Jasei no in") and inscribes a composite of the two upon the surface of his own narrative. The incompatibility of the variant oral and written versions ruptures textual unity: premodern landscape, saturated with significations, thus functions within the modern (written) text as a mark of difference (the oral) and introduces us to Nakagami's masculinized spiritualism. For the excavated oral origins propel the narrative into a violent arena in which a male protagonist reclaims a position of access to supernatural power that much of the medieval (and modern) canon restricted as a specifically female province.[17] Libidinal drive, symbolized above by both the snake and the proximity of the swamp to the whorehouse, is inseparable from Nakagami's vision of transcendental space.

All four stories under consideration in this chapter rewrite tales of the serpent, culled from oral, performative, and written folklore and other narratives. Two of the four, "Jain" (Snake lust, 1976) and "Ukijima," make overt reference to Ueda Akinari's (1734–1809; hereafter Akinari) "Jasei no in" (Lust of the snake, 1776), the tale of a young man who is bewitched by a snake-demon disguised as an enchanting, lecherous woman.[18] "Fushi" ("The Immortal," 1980) and "Tsuki to fushi" (The moon and the immortal, 1981) clearly invoke Kyōka's *Kōya hijiri* by describing the meeting of a wandering ascetic with a mysterious woman of the mountains, a meeting that brings the immortal *hijiri* in contact with supernatural forces symbolized by snakes and leeches.[19] The source texts by Akinari and Kyōka are, it should be noted, already rewritten versions of antecedent folklore, reworked throughout Japanese narrative history in various genres including *nō*, *monogatari*, and *setsuwa*, but whose origins predate the earliest Japanese written texts.[20] Nakagami's stories are thus stories within stories, increasingly sundered from their immediate and clearly identified pretexts as they chase after the earliest oral folkloric versions. Predecessor Kyōka's *Kōya hijiri* structurally replicates "storytelling" with an identified narrator relating a tale of a tale, and Akinari's "Jasei no in" employs the classical hearsay suffixes *keri* and *kemu* indicating previous oral transmission, while they both echo the written canon in content.[21] In contrast, the structures of Nakagami's texts resemble those of the *shishōsetsu*, with single-perspective narrating subjects merged with the narrators while, as this chapter will show, they radically reshape the narrative events. Nakagami, Kyōka, and Akinari each overtly situate oral legend as the inspiration for their written texts, but they do so differently. In part the different renditions can be read as products of their time periods, Akinari's use of hearsay as a conceit of *setsuwa* transmission, Kyōka's adherence to medieval myth as a conscious resistance to early modernism, with the added and innovative narrative "realism" of the priest's escape (so that the story may logically be passed on) as a construct of the modern, and Nakagami's resistance to closure as a product of the postmodern.[22] Akinari, Kyōka, and Nakagami all sought to revitalize the "womb" of Japanese narrative by employing the erotic body of a serpentine woman associated with ancient animism as conduit to the primordial "origin." The shared desire for origin, however, entices each text to move in a different direction.

Whereas Akinari and Kyōka's protagonists stumble upon the snake-woman, in Nakagami's "Tsuki to fushi," the *hijiri* accesses the preliterate world through intentional pilgrimage to a location where the mundane (written) and the spiritual (oral) interact, guided by an old man's oral tale of the origins of the mountain site's magical empowerment to "somewhere on that mountain bathed by the dead-still sun . . . an entryway to, and the abode of the supernatural" (201). In "The Immortal," there are merely traces of oral narrative issuing forth from the land and a mysterious meeting with a woman of the mountains, filtered through layers of antecedent writings—the *Tales of the Heike* commingled with folklore and myth:

The sound of the brush and the tops of the trees echoed like court music played by noble ladies-in-waiting. As if summoned by the voice of the woman crying inside the mansion, they assembled, pushing through the brush with the same mournful, haunting sound. . . . He turned again to look at the people assembled in the silver moonlight and shuddered. Their outlines were hazy, and they could easily have been mistaken for the grass, or the branches of the trees, now only shadows in the darkness, but if he looked at them more intently, they were monkeys and wild boars. Yet they all had the shapes of human beings, no different from the hijiri himself. Some had human faces but the hands and feet of dogs. Whether they had become this way from being in the mountains for so long, or because the nobles living in the mansion had assembled a horde of yasha and devils, they were all weeping at the words of the woman inside. . . . It was because such things occurred deep in the mountains of Kumano that the hijiri and bikuni who wandered from province to province longed for and worshipped this land. (422)

Archaic serpent legends may be incorporated overtly, as in "Ukijima," in which the premodern tale literally frames the modern one. "Ukijima" is a contemporary tale of lumberjack Gonroku's murder of his prostitute-lover, but it begins with an unspecified narrator relating the ancient Shingū legend of the snake and Oino. The legend is mentioned repeatedly throughout the short story by the narrator, Gonroku, and by the prostitute and reappears to close the tale, thus functioning as both foundation and framework.

Elsewhere, references to old snake stories may be indirect or severed from origin, as in "Jain," which only borrows part of the name and a symbolic rendering of the lustful snake of the medieval version to tell a modern tale of the *buraku*, in which Jun and his girlfriend Kei murder Jun's parents. Flowing through the text as a leitmotiv is a classic medieval association of female eroticism with demonic snakes, evident in Jun's mother's criticism of Kei: "That woman is a snake; a slut [*inran*]" (499).

Oral narrative thus becomes the once-erased "origin" of Nakagami's stories, an origin reconstructed through local legends overlain with layers of written versions (Akinari and Kyōka's tales) and which culminates (is produced) in Nakagami's own renditions. Transcendental space, for example, the *roji* in "Jain," the Kumano mountain range in "Tsuki to fushi" and "The Immortal," and other sites of narrative history, reveal a contradictory multiplicity submerged within the modern text. In Nakagami's work, premodern landscape, whether directly or indirectly cited, operates as a "trace" or signifier under erasure. Jacques Derrida's description of the process that produces the trace is appropriate to this reading, because it is "not only the disappearance of origin . . . it means that the origin did not even disappear, that it was never constituted except reciprocally by a non-origin, the trace, which thus becomes the origin of the origin."[23] Nakagami's written reconstruction of an oral narrative actually produces (originates) the purported origin, while this very production is obscured by its pose of reiterating extant folklore. Moreover, it is the nature of oral narrative that, lacking a material text, it is blatantly subordinated to the circumstances of its retelling: the origin is clearly constituted in the moment of its telling and reception.

The rendering of the primordial landscape (the production of origin) within the modern prose narrative thus gives rise to confounding contradictions that inform Nakagami's texts on a variety of levels. Of course the attempt to write the oral destroys the oral: it is an act of destruction within production. Further complicating the project are the frictions between Nakagami's modern, experimental prose (characterized by his frequent choice of the emphatic sentence endings *ta n da* or *ru n datta*) and the relational, distanced narration (framed as hearsay and passed on by a narrator who is not the protagonist) of the classic *setsuwa* and between the consanguineous thematic layering of legend (exteriority) within self-reflection (interiority). These contradictions complicate the site of writing itself, ultimately reaffirming the primary condition of negated origin.

Embedded legends impart something irrational that is in excess of the written page, mirroring the psychoanalytic configuration of an unconscious surplus to the conscious mind. Antecedent tales inexplicably manipulate the actions of the protagonists, much as the unconscious affects behavior. In "Ukijima," for example, we are not given ample psychological or circumstantial explanations for why Gonroku murders the woman. The narrative present sketchily depicts Gonroku's miserable marriage and his obsession with a prostitute. During intercourse, the prostitute begs him to kill her. He complies. Afterward, remorseful and confused, he cries out for help, and is answered only by the legend, not by insight. The legend structurally replaces psychological interiority for the moment, functioning in place of other information that might divulge, or clarify, character motivation. In "Tsuki to fushi," the embedded tale told to the *hijiri* by an old man, a young man is ambushed by a snake on a night visit to his lover. Although the young man kills the snake, he is tainted by its blood and transformed into a vampire-snake, living a liminal existence in his mountain residence, now a magical site where the spirit and mundane worlds intersect. Having heard the old man's tale, the *hijiri* heads directly toward the abode of the vampire-snake. Here the legend assumes, and so displaces, the modern function of psychological (causal) character motivation.

Nakagami's narratives are thus structurally akin to what Freud described as the "mystic writing pad": a wax slab (the unconscious) covered by a transparent piece of celluloid (the conscious), a prototype Etch-a-sketch® with one important difference from its more modern counterpart—whatever has been transcribed on the celluloid surface is permanently inscribed in scratches upon the wax slab underneath. Although the celluloid (consciousness) is wiped clear by lifting it from the wax, the slab itself (the unconscious) retains the repeated rewritings: "The Pad provides not only a receptive surface that can be used over and over again, like a slate, but also permanent traces of what has been written . . . it solves the problem of combining the two functions by dividing them between two separate but interrelated component parts or systems."[24] For Nakagami, the wax slab (the unconscious) would be comprised of inseparable erotic or aggressive components of drive and a collective myth structure. This "unconscious" pulses through oral folklore as a narrative expression of libidinal and aggressive drives and is revealed as faint scars etched upon the "repressed" component of the mind/text. Nakagami's texts do not seek to rationalize the scratched slab but to celebrate and reveal the existence of the impulse that motivates the production of narrative. The source text of "Jain," "Jasei no in," is invoked by Jun's mother's negative refrain: "That woman [Kei] is lascivious, I tell you, she's a snake" and, like Jun's unanswerable question, "Is she a snake?" (500), alludes to a connection between the murder and something instinctual, erotic, and aggressive. The debate over the (original) gender of the snake of the archaic Ukijima legend likewise evokes a primordial sexuality submerged in Gonroku's present. In "Ukijima," the past echoes through the narrative present in the inexplicable connection between the Oino of legend and the local prostitutes who sing a popular song about Oino "as though it were their own" (70). Shingū folklore (the archaic past) functions as an erotic and violent textual "unconscious," inscribed as traces that affect the conscious (modern) mind (text).

In these tales, Nakagami elects to enter the body of his male narrators and to speak their thoughts, choosing a single, alienated, narrating subject who reflects on the world around him. This narrative stance is an expression of the "interiority" of the modern subject and is, as Karatani has explained, an outgrowth of the changed relationship among "language, the thinking subject and the world of objects."[25] Although each of the four tales is told in the third person, the narrator describes only the inner thoughts and physical experiences of the single male protagonist. Scholar of Japanese literature Edward Fowler has identified this merging of narrator with a single character as the dominant type of modern Japanese narration—that of the now-classic *shishōsetsu*.[26] But unlike the *shishōsetsu*, in Nakagami's narratives, oral and written texts of the classical canon overtly or covertly structurally replace or accompany meditations on the individual self. The narrator of "Jain," tormented by what he has done, cannot understand his own actions and motivations. The rhetorical questions he poses after the murder shift the focus from Nakagami's modern tale to the shadowed source text: "At that moment, in a flash, he felt as though his body had burst into flames. That's how he felt. The woman was naked. Is she a snake, embodying lust, he wondered?" (500). The question propels the text beyond the immediate story into the layered narratives represented by Akinari's "Jasei no in." Similarly, in "Ukijima," Gonroku, having murdered his prostitute-lover, calls out helplessly into the emptiness of her absence, from within the closing frame of the Ukijima legend.

He strangled the woman. No. It was that, his eyes shut, as he ejaculated with a sensation of leaping downward into the woman, he had reflexively strengthened his grip. The woman did not move. He shook her body. She did not move. What has happened? He wondered. Should I follow after the woman's traces?. . . .
   There is the legend of the lust of the snake, according to which woman is the manifestation of the snake . . . [which] originates in distant India, and resembles the *Dōjōji* legend of the *Hokkegenki* and other such tale fiction. The legend of Ukijima originates elsewhere. (88–89)
   He raised his voice and cried out as he looked at the woman. His cry was such that it carried not only through the whorehouse district, but way beyond, audible as far off as the tenements of Ukijima. He was stark naked. He cried, help me. Help me, rubbing the woman's body with his cheek. Help me. (90)

Although these narrator-protagonists possess modern and unknowable selves, the boundaries of their individual selves are compromised by the premodern through such encounters with landscapes scoured with the faded vestiges of oral legend. Past narrative is invigorated by territory, and once encountered is further revived through the erotic, experiential body of the narrator.

The erotic impulses of Nakagami's protagonists, which are inseparable from aggression and merged with the sublime, thus produce a composite erotic/aggressive/spiritual body, which is marked in each of the four texts by the snake archetype. In *Kotodama no ametsuchi*, Nakagami discusses the snake as a recurrent feature of archaic Japanese folklore: "Most likely the so-called Yamato people—we Japanese—were a snakelike [*hebiteki*] culture, you could probably call us snake-people."[27] Following Origuchi, Nakagami states that the ancestors of the Japanese people worshiped and enshrined snakes as deities long before written history.[28]

As discussed in Chapter 9, the importation of Buddhism in Japan was attenuated by the development of a writing system, advancing a process whereby the previously amorphous snake was both named and written, according to Nakagami. Paradoxically, the act of "naming" and "writing" (difference and distinction), while adding meaning simultaneously divested the "snake" of a prior multiplicity (which transcended "naming" and "word") by subordinating it to bounded signification. In Nakagami's narratives the snake remains a product of the archaic landscape and as such embodies a multiplicity that deconstructs the apparent closure of later renditions of the snake.

As the immortals of "The Immortal" and "Tsuki to fushi" draw closer to the landscapes that retain the shadowed traces of archaic memory, the relationship between word and signification weakens and their chants become pure sound, illustrative of the impossibility of capturing the origin in language and the intrinsic distance of the primordial from the semantic: "Raising his eyes, he spat loudly, and began to mimic the sound of the grass again . . . jaarajaara jaarajaara . . . as if he were chanting a holy sutra. . . . He always ended up chanting jaarajaara jaarajaara, like a lewd growling in the throat, instead of the phrases of the sacred sutras" ("The Immortal," 415–16). The *hijiri* of "Tsuki to fushi" will not chant sutras, claiming, "I can read a little, but I have never laid eyes on a sutra" (205). In Kyōka's *Kōya hijiri*, the incantatory power of the words of a *Buddhist* sutra (*dharani*) repels the strange creatures, associated with the demongoddess, that surround the cottage and produce a cacophony of wordless (meaningless) sound.[29]

Unlike the reticent priest of Kyōka's narrative, who fights against and rationalizes bestial impulses or Akinari's bewitched male victim, Nakagami's "immortals" willfully surrender to the instinctual. The closer their affinity to the instinctual, legend, and the spiritual, the more distanced they are from signification. Approaching the oral, the semantic function of the sign weakens, and the attempt to incorporate origin, once again, reveals nothingness. The *hijiri*'s nonsense chants are thereby made reminiscent of archaic Shinto *kotodama* (enunciations endowed with sound-activated spiritual power). *Kotodama*, one of the first forms of Japanese communications with the deities, were words that when spoken summoned the spirits. As I discussed in Chapter 5, it is believed that the sound, not the meaning, of the *kotodama* activated its spiritual power. Kamata Tōji, following Origuchi, describes the connection of Nakagami's claimed spiritual ancestors, the mythic *marebito* who came from the lands of the gods, to *kotodama* as: "*Marebito* were actually *otozurebito* (people bound to sound = visitors). *Marebito* came together with sound. Sound that is first of all the enunciations of the deities, sound that is *uta* [song] and that is *geinō* [performing art]. In other words, the *marebito* voiced *kotodama*."[30] Nakagami's holy/taboo ancestors are thus associated with a phonocentric tradition suppressed in the Japanese adaptation of Chinese characters that split voice from written representation and bound into polarities what was previously plural. Nakagami's incorporation of multiple folkloric and narrative origins collapses the oppositions between them, resulting in significations surplus to word and producing a semantic void.

In Nakagami's texts, the already more-than-dual demon or deity, oral or written serpent is further splintered by gender. It may be alternately male or female, or both—markedly unlike the medieval and early modern texts in which the snake is always female. The snake-woman is overtly present in the antecedent legends and foundational folklore layered within Nakagami's texts: both Kyōka and Akinari follow medieval tradition by gendering the snake female (as does Enchi). Before *Kōya hijiri*'s priest meets the mysterious mountain woman, he must traverse a path infested with snakes, foreshadowing her demonic nature. Upon hearing her voice, he retreats, "expecting a strange creature, white neck scaled like a reptile, to crawl forth, tail dragging" (398).[31] The snake-demon of "Jasei no in" transforms itself into a beautiful woman to bewitch the protagonist. Conversely, the vampire-snake in "Tsuki to fushi" certainly seems to be an index of masculinity:

A single snake came up to the *hijiri*'s feet, which were swollen with clotted blood, and lifted its head as if to speak. . . . "Kill me," the *hijiri* said. As though paying no heed to his words, the snake slithered its long, snaky body up onto his swollen, fevered feet and over his robe, twisted about his upper thigh, encircled the *hijiri*'s body and attached its head to his neck. Because the ascending snake had entwined its tail about his thigh to support itself, the snake looked exactly as though it were the *hijiri*'s extended, long, swollen maleness. (212–13)

Nakagami has argued that the original snake of Kumano legends was male, and that the conceit of the snake-woman was imported along with Buddhism, producing new legends to transform, displace, and/or accompany Japan's existing ones.[32] This ideation is also present in the narrative "Ukijima" when, as quoted earlier, the narrator asserts the maleness of the original Ukijima snake in opposition to later imported Buddhist renditions. The Ukijima legend is a product of the Japanese heartland, Kumano, but the male snake can be located elsewhere as well, in many archaic folk tales from various regions.[33] In the four tales by Nakagami, the process of employing the serpent to overfill or to empty the signifier is thus paralleled by male characters' embrace of the dark continent associated with women. The witches of the Western classics are identified with archaic paganism and therefore threaten Christian order. Similarly, throughout much of Japanese narrative history, women represent the dark forces of nature and the supernatural, metaphorically linked to a Shinto animism rendered as confrontational to a Buddhist "rationalism."[34]

As I discussed in Chapter 9, most historical studies stress the harmonious coexistence of Buddhism and Shinto in premodern Japan. But Japan's adaptation of modes of government that employed Buddhism as a validating ideology also produced narratives that suggest otherwise, narratives indicative of a shifting balance of power. Akin to pre-Christian paganism, primitive Shinto was, of course, not "all female" but became metaphorically linked with femaleness by virtue of its subordination in the Middle Ages to an increasingly malecentric, simultaneously Buddhist state. As Buddhism became associated with bureaucratic, rational male governance, perceived of as superior to shamanic divination (which in turn was increasingly feminized), the metaphoric relationship deepened.[35]

The reforming balance of power between Buddhism and Shinto, and the ideological assignment of gender with the process, affected how the Dōjō tale was refabricated over time. It is worth reiterating that W. Michael Kelsey has documented the ascension of Buddhism over Shinto in the rewriting of earlier serpent stories that appeared in collections such as the *Kojiki*, the *Nihon shoki*, and the *Nihon ryōiki*, in the posterior Dōjō tale of the *Konjaku monogatari shū*.[36] Material object yields to word and symbol, primitive to sophisticated, and Shinto to Buddhism, in an abiding process of rebalancing political power. Subsequent to the importation of Buddhism, and reproducing the historical redistribution of power, in the medieval and modern versions of the Dōjō tales, the snake becomes feminized, and the serpent-demoness has become symbolic of Shinto and threatens (or is ultimately vanquished by) Buddhist order. Many other witches, mediums, and demonesses of the Japanese canon, such as *miko* shamans (women who act as mediums for communications with the spirit realm) or the *yamamba* (women of the mountains who eat men) similarly threaten Buddhist rationalism through their links to ancient Japanese animism. Buddhism took ascendancy in sociopolitical realms, and logocentrism repressed (Japanese) voice and body, producing a synecdochical relationship whereby Chinese characters represented logos and abstraction, while the Shinto shamaness was shifted to the periphery along with voice. Clément has similarly situated the Western witch: "The sorceress, who in the end is able to dream Nature and therefore conceive it, incarnates the reinscription of the traces of paganism that triumphant Christianity repressed."[37] In Japan, the feminization of Shinto was reinforced in the early modern period by folklorists who followed Yanagita and Origuchi.

Such feminized representations inform the embedded variations on the Dōjō tales by Akinari and Kyōka that Nakagami resurrects. A "demon" who transforms men seeking her sexual favors into animals, the mysterious woman of the mountains from *Kōya hijiri*, also has power over the forces of nature: "If she holds her sleeve aloft rain will fall; when she lifts her eyebrows the winds howl. She burns with an innate lust, most fervently for young men" (436). Living deep in the mountains far from any Buddhist temples, the woman's power is nullified by the young priest's Buddhist sutra and strength of Buddhist (moral) character. The demon-snake of "Jasei no in" is first recognized as a demon by an old man affiliated with a Shinto shrine but is only vanquished when the protagonist seeks the help of a highly regarded Buddhist priest.

The phallicization of the snake in "Tsuki to fushi" therefore constitutes a *violence* to the medieval and early modern conceit of the Japanese canon, while it reinvigorates the underlying origins of now-rewritten tales of the snake-deity. As soon as the snake is masculinized in "Tsuki to fushi," the woman who has guided the *hijiri* to the vampire-snake reappears, affirming her deep connection with a now abruptly feminized snake: "Just as one might gingerly separate from a woman at the end of a long caress, the *hijiri* grasped the snake with his hand so sore it hurt to move, and the snake wound its body about his arm. . . . 'Kill it. Please,' the woman . . . spoke, her voice coming from the back of the crowd, 'It is the snake that has cursed me' " (213). Vacillating presentations of the snake as male and female repeat elsewhere, as in "Jain" when Jun's mother repeatedly warns Jun that Kei is a snake (female), while Jun ponders his own prurient (male) culpability. In "Ukijima," too, male protagonist Gonroku claims that men, not women, are the true inheritors of the snake's lust: "It was extremely difficult for him to think of the woman as a snake. Rather, the lust of the snake belonged to him" (90). At the close of "Tsuki to fushi," the *hijiri*'s confrontation with the snake obliterates their mutual boundaries, and the two are collapsed into a composite snake-*hijiri*. "He began to walk, but his hips were unsteady and he fell, and wriggling with pain, this time he slithered through the thick grass like a snake" (214). It should be stressed that Nakagami's problematizing the Dōjō tale's feminization of the serpent accords with a movement toward pre-Buddhist animism. The deconstructed, ambigendered snake and the *hijiri* become an ever more complicated signifier, surplus to the binarisms of human/animal (reptile) and female/male, once again reminiscent of archaic folklore in which animals take on human form, humans are turned into animals, and snakes may be symbolic of both male and female eroticism.[38]

This is the snake of Nakagami's narratives, repeatedly oversignifying and placed simultaneously or alternately in putatively mutually exclusive categories, bringing us not to conclusion but to a state of aporia. In the process, the snake becomes a representation of the erotic divested of gender specificity, undoing the opposition male/female and becoming a symbol of Nakagami's relentless challenge to hierarchized, binary categories. By bringing forth the trace of Shinto animism within the Buddhist body, Nakagami unearths a suppressed historical hegemony and alternates between inverting and reproducing the existing, gendered balance of power. These shifts disintegrate the logic that relegates origin, orality, and animism as women's exclusive domain by locating the male beside the female as an alternate keeper of the animistic flame.

In the tales under discussion here, such reinstatement of masculine animism often precipitates violence, even brutality, in the ensuing struggle between a man and a woman for access to, and dominance within, an alternate, spiritual world, which I have read as evolving from the tensions of Nakagami's mingled modern and medieval narrative and the traces of oral text. Nakagami *intentionally* uses violence, frequently directed against women who represent the Other World, to evoke an animism with the power to lacerate the weave of the works of the canon and to bring forth a complex multiplicity. Violence in Nakagami's texts serves to highlight the traces of instinctual drive that inform the oral pretexts and in turn complicate his written prose. Violence is not, however, simplistically linked to power.

Kyōka's *Kōya hijiri* depicts the woman of the mountains as all powerful, capable of transforming men into beasts at her whim: "This woman's meekness was undergirded with steel, absolute composure smoldered within her frivolity, and conviviality bemasked just how formidable she was, possessed of such poise and potential dispassion that I was convinced of her capacity to dispose of any adversity. No good could arise from inciting such a woman's wrath" (412). Nakagami depicts the dangerous woman in "The Immortal" as possessing tiny, childlike, deformed hands, timidity, and a "weak, pleading voice" (418). Whereas Kyōka's sorceress attempts to seduce the priest, Nakagami's *hijiri* owns the desire and rapes the women. Unlike the women of Kyōka and Akinari's narratives, who offer their bodies to their male victims, in "The Immortal" the wandering *hijiri* appropriates the body of the mysterious woman of the mountains to satisfy his intermingled erotic and spiritual needs. "If she were a flesh-and-blood woman, he could rape her. But if she were an incarnation of Kannon, he could save himself from this existence if he but touched her gentle, infant's hands" (418).

Yet the *hijiri* himself wonders if her superficial weakness in fact conceals a deeper power. "Here deep in the mountains, she could have escaped had she tried, and even as he lifted the cowering woman in his arms, the *hijiri* could not suppress the feeling that he was being deluded" (418). While he is raping the woman, the *hijiri* hears voices and tries to break free from what has become a mutual embrace, but she restrains him with sudden, inconceivable strength. After a night of repeated rape(?) the *hijiri* contemplates murdering the woman with the dawn of a new day. The narrative present dissolves into the *hijiri*'s inner monologue: a memory of killing another woman. When the narrative returns to the present, it is pointedly unclear—has he murdered the mountain woman? He looks back toward the woman's body to discover that: "There was no one there. The *hijiri* thought he had known that from the beginning, too" (428). Violence thus circulates without power being resolutely situated; it merely leaves the memory trace of a disappeared body, or, in the last sentence of "Jain," the soon-to-be incinerated remnants of a home and parents. "He need not have assaulted them. If he loved the woman then he should simply have left home. . . . Tears filled his eyes. . . . He thought they might as well set fire to the house, burning up the two corpses, take a car as far as they could, get on a train, maybe go to Tennōji" (501). Jun ponders his own culpability, wondering if it was not somehow his girlfriend, Kei, who engineered the murder. "Undoubtedly, [she] looked like a snake to the two people whose bodies had been dragged and deposited into the bathroom" (500).

Vacillating and unsettled empowerments inform the other stories as well. The *hijiri* of "Tsuki to fushi" longs for death and begs to be killed but is described as the "man who would not" and "could not" die (198, 205). Doomed to wander and suffer in this world, the *hijiri* cannot cross over into the Other World (symbolized by women in the antecedent texts). In "Ukijima," Gonroku's obsession with the woman is inseparable from her function as conduit: through her body he experiences liminality. "Whenever he was with the prostitute he always felt as though he were at the threshold between living and dying" (82). His prostitute-lover is the source of his connection to the Ukijima legend; by murdering her, Gonroku severs his ties to the snake-deity. Shattered as he holds her lifeless body in his arms, Gonroku yearns to follow her into death, but somehow he cannot.

Although Nakagami's narratives thus often reproduce the premodern source texts' employment of the female body as conduit to the realm of the spirits, the interiorized protagonists remind the reader of their modernity. Their brutality is both modern and archaic, both unleashing the rage of class oppression and challenging Buddhist pacifism and Shinto doctrines on purity through archaic rites of sacrifice. Nakagami inverts the medieval gender-specific power relationship between shamaness and male victim reproduced in Kyōka and Akinari's versions. Each of the protagonists has wrestled, mentally or materially, with the question of the serpent's gender. When Nakagami's protagonists reclaim the power of the snake's lust from the female archetype, they simultaneously deconstruct the conceit of coercion by erotically agentive, dangerous women. Although it cannot be denied that a rhetoric of apparent misogyny often informs Nakagami's works, male protagonists find no peace of mind, no solutions, and no pleasure in their violence, whether directed against other men or against women. Further, as stated previously, their violence does not beget power. Origin wrested from feminization evaporates, or is merely tantalizingly resituated, with the moment of its apparent seizure.

Origin in Nakagami's narratives, be it feminized or masculinized—or bigendered—is negated or obliterated as it is located and revealed to have been constructed by the narrating subject. Repeatedly, the narrative merely collapses upon itself in an avowal of the project's impossibility, for by its violence to the object, the perpetrator suffers. Gonroku cries for help; in "Tsuki to fushi," the *hijiri* begs to be killed but keeps on living; Jun weeps with remorse. "The Immortal" concludes with the disappearance of a woman who already signifies absence. The site of origin (and resistance) is emptied just as the text materially closes. Significance evaporates as the signifier (the woman) vanishes, suggesting that perhaps it (meaning/she) has never really existed.

Reading Nakagami, one is confounded by this profound ambivalence. Through the *hijiri*'s connection to the oral, the inversion of power discourses, the foregrounding of the holy/taboo (conceptual) ancestors of the *burakumin* marked by the ambigendered snake, and the disinterment of a phallocentric animism, Nakagami unsettles the canon's assignment of origin, marginality, and animism as women's exclusive domain—a conceit of medieval Japanese legend uncompromised in Kyōka and Akinari's versions. In Nakagami's works, sites of resistance and conflict are no sooner produced than they are put into question, creating a web of resistances within resistances. But there is further rupture in Nakagami's stories: dissolution of the site of resistance. The Other (the site of resistance) is the oral, which is rendered not-oral by the act of its being written. Thus, the act of inclusion is also the act of destruction.

Landscape, the ultimate polymorphous signifier in Nakagami's texts, ruptures the unified presence and clarity of the story and of language itself and acts as the repository of oral memory and aggressive and libidinal drive, an arena that brings one repeatedly to the expression of aporia. Landscape functions to unlock time and enunciations, filling the pages with question marks. This negation of presence and insistent surplus operates on multiple levels of the text, the inevitable loss of the signifier in the process of attempting to highlight it: the impossible project of writing the oral.

The Body: Deformities, Nasty Blood, and Sexual Violence

This chapter is based on a talk I presented at a symposium on Nakagami held by Meiji Gakuin University in Tokyo in 1996.[1] The day that I first started to consider what to write for the talk, construction workers appeared on the street and began to demolish the house next door. My apartment, littered with Nakagami's narratives, began to shake and sway, as though in response to small-to-moderate earthquake clusters repeating every five minutes or so from eight in the morning until about five in the afternoon. Unsecured objects slid and rattled; I moved breakables to safer spots. I thought that the events were perhaps not unrelated.

As I read Nakagami, I had to move fragile objects to safe places; themes of construction and deconstruction were forcefully reiterated. Literally, because for weeks my street resembled the construction sites so frequently depicted in Nakagami's narratives, teeming with physical laborers driving dump trunks, demolishing the old house next door, and subsequently erecting a new concrete structure. The relentless noise and vibrations also had thematic resonance with Nakagami's texts, which violently reduce to rubble, or else restructure, the *monogatari* and *setsuwa* of the Japanese canon.

The topic of this chapter, as evidenced by the title, is "the body" in Nakagami's narratives. But by "the body" I do not mean the physical body-as-material, but the "enscripted" body. For Nakagami, this enscripted body functioned as yet another site for the reproduction, and attempted dismantling, of dominant contemporary Japanese power discourses.

Of course, in any discussion of a narrative text in which a body appears, that body is enscripted, not material. But that is only the first, most obvious layer of "narrative" that encapsulates the body as written in Nakagami's texts. As I wrote in Chapter 12, landscape in Nakagami's narratives is sundered from any purported direct representation of the geographical configurations of the land per se and derived instead from an attempt to liberate libido—sexual and aggressive drive—through a deconstruction of "landscape as poetics." This chapter begins with a similar gesture in regard to the body. One linkage is concretized in the following selection from "Futakami" (Twin deities, 1985). The protagonist, Yahei, a single male laborer, has been entrusted with the primary care of two relatives who are young children:

Kiwa and Tatsuhiko . . . told Yahei about how they had played all day. He soon feel asleep, having drunken sake, unaware that until they themselves fell asleep, the two patted Yahei's body all over with their little hands, turning it into mountains and oceans, making stars fallen from the skies of the little erections of his nipples.

This juvenile brother and sister made up stories. When it was whispered that there was a tiger, Yahei definitely saw a tiger in his dream; in a broad expanse of space the playing children escaped, battled enemies, killed and were killed. As they made up their stories together in little voices Yahei viewed those very scenes in his dreams. The children were cruel.[2]

Yahei's penis is part of the children's make-believe landscape; they stimulate him until he ejaculates. Maturing from cruel children into strange young adults, Kiwa and Tatsuhiko have polished their art of "narrativizing bodies" to an aesthetic and now overtly sexualized peak. In a tribute to Tanizaki Jun'ichirō (as I discuss further below), the tale climaxes as Kiwa pokes out her brother's eyes so that "real" vision will cease to interfere with the constructed (narrativized) one. The body is here unmistakably subordinated to its function as narrativized poetics, akin to Nakagami's postulation of landscapes as narrativized sites.

For Nakagami, this material body-as-text is nonetheless first and foremost a sexed body. But a sexed body is also no less a "racialized" body, a "classed" body, a "nationalized" body, and a "gendered" body. (Here, as elsewhere, I separate sex and gender: a sexed body refers to the placement within the binary of male/female by virtue of physical attributes, such as type of genitals; and the gendered body refers to the manner in which that sexed body performs itself as a normative or aberrant member of a particular sex). By virtue of these and other discourses that mark the body within a given cultural constellation, the body enjoys (or is denied the pleasure of) degrees of power and domination over others who are differently marked.

The enscription of material physicality in Nakagami's texts is evident in the manner by which his characters also embody the bodies of multiple textual precedents as written in antecedent *monogatari*, *setsuwa*, and oral legend, bearing some similarity to the types of inscriptions that complicate the characters depicted by many of the writers whom Nakagami admired, including Kyōka, Tanizaki, and Enchi.[3] Underlying the contemporary discourses that inscribe bodies with various significations are the ghostly traces of the bodies of the canon. A web of discordant "readings/writings" of the canon obscures the contours of the material or physical bodies that appear in Nakagami's texts. This is precisely how the bodies in "Jūryoku no miyako" (Gravity's capital, 1981) take their plural states:

Exactly as if he had become the nobleman of the rotting bones that the woman said appeared night after night, he laid the woman, clad only in her nightgown, down on her back. She sought to pull down the hem of her nightgown that bared her; he restrained her hand. He spread her thighs wide open, gazing at her vagina glistening red in the firelight, and pressed his lips to her thick thigh, rubbing his cheek against her soft, plump, fleshy leg . . . over and over again he pressed his lips to her tiny feet, dragging his tongue from her instep to the crotch of her toes, and to the arch along her soft, curved heel that was like the one of the naked little princess born in the bamboo pipe. . . . She said, I want you to hurry up. The woman had also said that to the nobleman. She said, do it like the nobleman did it to me; the nobleman whose rotting bones floated out as if melting from beneath his grave in Ise on the other side of the mountain. . . . Yoshiaki envisioned the nobleman. Was he real? Or a fabrication? Had he himself become the mortal body housing the nobleman's spirit? Pondering as he stood on the earthen floor, Yoshiaki stripped off his top, removed his pants, and dropped his shorts.[4]

Typical to Nakagami, conventions of the medieval canon intermingle with violences to their most common gendered precedents: in the above passage from "Jūryoku no miyako," the classic "woman as conduit to the other world" or as *reibai* (medium) whereby she is also transported to a sexual ecstasy (as was standard in Enchi's and Kyōka's renditions) is troubled by an element of inversion in the visitation—it is a man, not a woman, who hails from Ise, the province of the highest Shinto priestess. The source text that inspired Nakagami's inverted version is apparently Origuchi's *Shisha no sho* (Book of the dead, 1939), in which a nobleman returns from the grave to engage in sex with his female lover.[5] In Nakagami's rendition, the nobleman's rotting body transfers its pain to her: he, male, is the source of her female pollution. That the defiled and defiling man comes from Ise reverses the purification function traditionally associated with that site. In addition, since ghostly visitations are more commonly restricted to female-sexed ghosts, here is a phallicization—following Origuchi—of ghosts and ghostly visitations.

Nakagami's afterword also acknowledges "Shunkinshō" by Tanizaki as one source text for *Jūryoku no miyako*'s collection of tales (including "Futakami"), and the referential aspects of his renditions are unmistakable.[6] But there is a gendered swap: in "Shunkinshō," the male lover, Sasuke, blinds himself so he need not gaze at the now-disfigured countenance of his female lover, Shunkin; in "Jūryoku no miyako," Yoshiaki blinds the woman at her request, precisely so that she may no longer perceive a difference between Yoshiaki and the ghostly nobleman. (In "Futakami," as noted above, the sister blinds her brother, but not at his request.) The "tiny" feet shared by the woman of "Jūryoku no miyako" and Shunkin are both a tribute to Tanizaki's infamous foot fetish and simultaneously a reference to the early Heian *monogatari* of the little princess born in a bamboo pipe, *Taketori monogatari*. As I described in Chapter 12, many of Nakagami's short stories retrope tales of the medieval and archaic canon, for example, in his vacillating phallicization of the Dōjō tale. Thus, in Nakagami's texts, "narrativized" discourses take their place among the other (historicized) discourses producing bodies and their significations.[7]

I have also argued that legend and folklore function as a sort of erotic and violent textual unconscious in Nakagami's texts that motivates narrative itself and that is further enacted through the experiential bodies of the protagonists. These experiential bodies show a clear movement toward increasing "nakedness" over time; there is an (impossible) attempt to first locate the body within these multiple inscriptions, be it in the guise of retroping the *monogatari* and oral narrative or by "inventing" the *roji* as a site for exploring (and deconstructing) discursive origins, as the following chapter will elucidate (or in a composite of all three) and once located, to release it as *material* through stoking erotic and aggressive drive.

In his later fictions, Nakagami returned to a more complex reworking of one dominant theme of his earliest fictions, namely, the body as fettered by a web of inscriptions, including those of gender, sex, narrative, discrimination, and power. For Nakagami, this project meant battering whatever inscriptions he encountered to produce the body in its rawest, most gutted, potential form. Thus, the symbolic deformities of earlier texts such as Gen's hand in *Sennen no yuraku*, which is "cloven like the hoof of an animal" (15), the tiny hands of the woman in "The Immortal," and the tiny feet of the woman in "Jūryoku no miyako" become in *Sanka* the scarred anus of the Korean madam, Chonko, the huge, misshapen clitoris of one of Yves's clients, and the "penis as small as a clitoris" of another (6). (Of course the later two "deformities" elide the genital differentiations between male and female, weakening even the assumption that there are two distinct biological sexes.) The pornographic moments that punctuate Nakagami's antecedent fictions are expanded to form almost the entire first half of the long fiction, *Sanka*.

Most of Nakagami's male protagonists are theatrical, hyperbolic performances of masculinity. They are often manual laborers, they are brutal, and they are sexually irresistible. Hanzō, for example, is "so manly that one could smell it even with one's eyes" (*Sennen no yuraku*, 13). They are also consistently bound to pollution, be it as young men of the *roji* or as *hijiri*, the mythic ancestors straddling the binary of sacred/polluted. Nakagami employs the material penis to symbolize the phallus, a gesture that presences loss, genders discrimination and difference, and simultaneously reveals itself to be nothing but an (emptied) signifier. "As" the phallus, the men of the *roji* are, as I will show, the term of lack against which identifications are made possible; simultaneously they are "positionally" feminized, disempowered, and turned into sexually excessive "bodies" (or parts of bodies). Against the more common insistence that lack must be affixed to the absence of the penis, *burakumin* are here made symbolic of a *penised* lack—and thus both possess the phallus (phallus-as-power) and yet paradoxically function *as* the phallus (the phallus-as-lack). This configuration of the *burakumin* body is similar to that of the black male in white racist imaginaries, as Lee Edelman described it:

The black body, as material supplement or signifier, as that which must be possessed in order to validate the dominant subject's putative possession of the phallus, must endure a symbolic inscription corresponding to that of the female body. It must represent, that is, or "be" the "phallus" so the dominant subject can "have" it.

. . .

As viewed through the racist gaze of a culture that privileges straight white men, the African-American male, to return to the literally reductive phrasing I used earlier, must *be* the "part," (i.e., the "tool") that stands for the "hole" (the stripping away, the absence, of "all that constitutes manhood") in order that the white male subject, through his fetishistic deployment of the gaze, can "have" the "part" that the black man, in racist fantasy, both *is* and *lacks*.[8] (Edelman's emphasis)

As both the symbol "phallus" (and therefore as "lack"), and as the possessor of the "phallus" (and thus empowered), as well as the possessor of the material penis, the disenfranchised and polluted masculine heroes— be they *burakumin* or *hijiri*—of Nakagami's texts reverse the dominant power structures by which they are rendered socially powerless: they fuck. They fuck hard. They fuck well. They insist on their masculine dominance through powerful penile thrusts.

"It won't hurt," said Yves, and stroked Akira's sides two times as if to signal the beginning of the sodomy to come. Bracing Akira's hips with his left hand to keep them from collapsing, with his left hand he felt for the hole that when compared with a woman's was virtually nonexistent. He pressed his penis to it, holding it in place with his hand so it would not slip out, and with one stroke thrust it in. It felt only as if his penis had encountered something hard, and not as though he had entered a hole. Akira moaned and started to escape, so Yves just readjusted his grip on Akira's hips to hold him firmly in place with both hands, and kept thrusting. Akira kept whimpering that it hurt. Yves ignored him. (*Sanka*, 52)

It is in the sexual act that the masculine protagonists' power is affirmed. Or is it? "Akiyuki envisioned how his own buttocks, white in the sun from outside, were moving like those of an animal. Lips pressed to the nape of Noriko's neck, he thought he would spurt a beast's semen into her womb" (*Kareki Nada*, 230).

Simultaneous with the erection of the possession of the phallus as the symbolic repository of masculine power (seemingly collusive with dominant phallocentrism) comes forth a series of complications. The most obvious problematics settle the various bodies in overwritten enscriptions; these bodies are not "free," but fettered by gendered, classist, and narrativized significations. Thus, the employment of the penis as phallic symbol cannot be severed from the *burakumin* body to which that penis/phallus is attached. The reduction of the male *burakumin* body to its physicality reiterates a social discourse that links outcastes with animals (evidenced by derogatory terms such as *yotsu*, which means "four," used in reference to the four legs of animals or the posthumous names on gravestones that include the characters for dog or pig.) Such extratextual connotations are further fortified by Nakagami's textual inclusion of such discourses, as in the cloven hooflike hand of *burakumin* Gen in *Sennen no yuraku*. This is a classic configuration of racial othering that is naturalized in the body and its relations to other bodies along the binary axis of nature/culture.[9] The reduction of *burakumin* to their physicality and the linking of outcastes to animals reiterate what Etienne Balibar has termed the "universals" that inform racist discourse, because these ideations have recourse to the question of the difference (or conversely, likeness) between "humanity and animality."[10] When bestiality is phallicized, it also marks the mutual desires and fears between dominant and submissive classes, in a delicious threat emanating from the disenfranchised. Homi Bhabha argued that the psychic mechanisms informing fetishism operate to produce an ambivalent sense of threat and desire in the relationship between colonizer and native;[11] in Nakagami's texts, outcastes endowed with a "fetishized" penis (and thus who are trying to make the phallus of a penis) are presented in an ambivalence of violences and desires. Encounters of the bestial, false *hijiri* with women of the villages or the mountains shift back and forth along an axis of rape and consensual sex; violence drives the desire, and desire drives the violence in a repeating cycle of significatory and power slippages and dominances that spill over into submissions.

Endowing men of the *roji* with "phallic power" embodied in the penis seems at first glance to be little more than a repetition of dominant ways of writing/reading the outcaste body—similar to the manner in which African-American men are thought to "be" the phallus.[12] Yet it must be stressed that the reiteration of phallicism by a *burakumin* is not equivalent to the repetition by a Japanese man enjoying a socially fully empowered status. To rephrase, because they are outcastes, their reactive violence that may frame attempts to reclaim a so-called rightful phallicism (that has been culturally denied them) does not, and cannot, replicate the violence practiced by men in securely dominant cultural positions.

In *Sanka*, the long sequel to *Nichirin no tsubasa*, (The wings of the sun, 1984), two young men who hail from the *roji* have been separated from the old women with whom they had been touring Japan's various famed locations (spatial locations that are collectively symbolic of the modern myth of an ahistorical Japan that also elides the heterogeneous, such as the existence of the *buraku*). "Stranded" in Tokyo the two young men, Tsuyoshi and Tanaka, turn to prostitution and are renamed, respectively, Yves and Ta. That they are renamed, of course, is indicative of their lack of self-determination in their new "careers." The renaming also strips them of their former provincialism. Their new names are short and simple, and they suggest cosmopolitanism and internationalism; Yves evokes France, while Ta cannot be identified as belonging to any particular nation or culture. Both names could just as easily denote a man or a woman, symbolic of their availability to prostitutes of either sex. Focusing its narrative attention on Yves, the first half of *Sanka* consists of relentlessly mechanical and graphic descriptions of his vocational and extravocational sexual encounters with clients and individuals. In Chapter 11, I quoted Butler in regard to the possibility of "parodic" bisexual and homosexual replications of heterosexual constructs, in spite of the fact that sexuality cannot be *transcendental* of culture and power. As I articulate below, though the postulation of the bisexual Yves in *Sanka* most obviously fits Butler's definition of a parodic repetition of the so-called original that functions to displace the law rather than to consolidate it, I hold that a similar displacement accompanies the phallicism of Nakagami's heterosexual protagonists, by virtue of their abjected status as men of the *roji*, their perversions, and the overtones or blatant acts of sadomasochism that mark their sexual encounters. It is in the texts exterior to the canonical ones—most markedly in *Sanka*—that the implosion of gendered significatory terms departs from what might be described as a gentleness and sneakiness, becoming foregrounded and shockingly brutal.[13]

In Nakagami's work, as this chapter will continue to articulate, *burakumin* are presented both "as" the phallus and also as "having it." Inscribed with indices of femaleness, both positional and "naturalized," there is nonetheless a refusal of the position that Edelman identifies as the correlative (feminized) aspect of "being" the phallus, namely, of (coerced) sexual capitulation as penetratee of empowered (in America, whites; in Japan, "pure" Japanese) men. In this manner the shocking assaults on gendered and racial significatory norms are profoundly ambivalent: terms are erected only to be deconstructed by their own internal inconsistencies.

Paralleling the process of canonizing Nakagami's narratives there has been a somewhat tentative posthumous "outing" of Nakagami as "bisexual."[14] Although undoubtedly Nakagami's position as a man who sexually desired other men affected his thinking and his writing about sexuality and gender and surely was a factor as fundamental as his status as *burakumin* in generating his violent attacks on the structure of "difference" itself, it is not his sexual practices per se that entice the reader to have recourse to queer theory in a study of his texts. I say this not only because of the inherent lack of contiguity between the author and the author's narrative productions but also because homosexuality as a signifier in Nakagami's narratives echoes the rhetorical postulation of the *roji* as a site of the abject and of the upheaval of terms of difference. In Edelman's words, homosexuality thus acts as the

unknowability that *is* sexuality as such: its always displaced and displacing relations to categories that include, but also exceed, those of sex, gender, class, nationality, ethnicity, and race. As the figure for the textuality, the rhetoricity, of the sexual, "gay" designates the gap or incoherence that every discourse of "sexuality" or "sexual identity" would master. It constitutes the fissure *in* sexuality out of which sexuality emerges and against which any "sexual identity" would attempt to define itself.[15] (Edelman's emphasis)

In this light, the repeated textual postulation of unstable sexualities that are also aberrant to contemporary Japanese sexual norms functions not only in opposition to compulsory heterosexuality but also to undo the putative stability of all signs of sexed and gendered signification.

Edelman, however, critiqued the author James Baldwin for offering

no imitable social vision of how the phobic resistance to penetration through which the identity of the subject is constructed can be displaced by a receptivity, a non-exclusivity, that would *not* be deconstructive in its undoing of identity as we know it. For Baldwin . . . "invasion" must "destroy" the "hegemony" of constituted identities in a repetitive enactment of the dominant logic that predicates social reality on the ego's aggressively paranoid insistence on its coherence and autonomy.[16]

And indeed, in Nakagami's narratives, too, the contours of "the subject" are thereby placed in jeopardy. A staunch refusal of the passive (feminized, penetrated) position by the phallic *burakumin*, on the one hand, is a reiteration of the conceit that such feminization will effectively diffuse (kill) the phallic subject as such. But on the other hand, following Edelman and others, *burakumin* as a (racial) term designating "Other" would mean that the outcaste is already feminized as being, rather than having, the phallus. Thus, the refusal to be penetrated by Nakagami's outcastes is simultaneously a resistance to the racist fantasy, even while it seems to be a reiteration of the heterosexist one.

In *Sanka*, heterosexualism—as a term dependent on the postulation of homosexualism—(and "sexual norm" in distinction to "perversion") is invaded from within. Unstable or sliding terms of sexual identification are most overt in the depictions of male-male sex in Nakagami's narratives, but they also mark other socioculturally "aberrant" sexual practices by his more staunchly heterosexual (that is, apparently normative) male protagonists or the heterosexual acts performed by male and female characters. To one of his female clients Yves says,

Men's dicks are really fearsome, so let me come first, and then we can pretend, with my soft dick, that I am your lesbian lover. I'll make your vagina smack loudly and wetly. My penis will be in shock, all shriveled up, but I'll come anyway once or twice. We can rest a bit, and although my dick will shriek in protest we can pretend I am a woman with a huge clitoris, a half-erect huge clitoris, I'll stick it in you and just keep it there like that for two hours, or three hours. Lets try it, it's really nasty [*iyarashii*]. (141–42)

This fantasy of Yves is not a replication of more conventional heterosexual male imaginaries of gazing at the spectacle of, or being included in acts of, sex between lesbians. Yves seeks here to "be" a woman, for his penis to "be" a clitoris (linking his phallicism with female "lack"). The sex act he imagines is far more radical in its assault on masculinity than standard sadomasochism in which a woman abuses her male partner, because power positions are not simply reversed. (As E. Ann Kaplan has argued, such reversals maintain the structure of phallocentrism and offer only temporarily inverted rearticulations of dominant power paradigms. For heterosexual women, then, there may be little subversive value in "behaving as the abuser.")[17] But Yves imagines himself to be "like" a woman having sex with another woman. This maneuver, on the one hand, avoids the replication of the *burakumin* "as" phallus and thus as the object of penetration by another man, even as it, on the other hand, *acknowledges* an equivalence of sorts between *burakumin* and woman "as" the phallus.

Acts of sex that are "normative" to a culturally articulated gendered body halt slippages of gendered signs; yet "perversions," as in the passage above, may entice such slippages. The modern desexualization and romanticized, putative purity of children are overturned in the perversion of "Futakami," in which the small orphans are depicted as the sexual aggressors who "seduce" the adult Yahei. But it has been argued that among "perversions," sadomasochism offers a distinctly theatrical environment for laying bare the power discourses that create modern sexuality (and thus, contrary to Kaplan's system, locating subversion in the inversion). Foucault, it is well known, sang the praises of sadomasochism. Leo Bersani wrote that "S/M makes explicit the erotic satisfactions sustaining social structures of dominance and submission."[18] Bersani further postulated that sadomasochism's potential for subversion or displacement of dominant power discourses lies in the reversibility of roles (so that the oppressor may perform, theatrically, the role of the oppressed and vice versa).[19] In *Sennen no yuraku*, there is evidence of such reversal. Shortly after a description of Hanzō tying up his prostitute-lover comes a scene in which the roles are swapped:

He touched and moved the thin red rope that lay uncoiled like a snake at the woman's feet. With that the woman bound Hanzō's hands behind him, commenting on how seductively the red of the slender rope bit into the flesh of his own white arms, Hanzō cried out in intentional imitation of a woman. The woman, as if doling out a cruel chastisement, her face tightened in anger—or was it in excitement— lifted her eyebrows and bit Hanzō's shoulder, leaving distinct teeth marks. (22)

Bersani privileges the masochistic position in sadomasochism for men, arguing that maleness (phallicism) is therein temporarily stripped from the male body, permitting a movement toward *jouissance*, in which the self is threatened with dissolution.

The reversibility of roles in S/M does more than disrupt the assignment of fixed positions of power and powerlessness (as well as the underlying assumptions about the natural links between dominance and particular racial or gendered iden- tities). From that reversibility we may also conclude that perhaps inherent in the very exercise of power is the temptation of its renunciation—as if the excitement of a hyperbolic self-assertion, of an unthwarted mastery over the world, and more precisely, brutalization of the other, were inseparable from an impulse of self- dissolution.[20]

The "space" of dissolution has been traditionally associated with female- ness in modern phallocentric epistemologies.[21] In Japanese literature, most commonly, it is through the female body that men may approach the delight and threat of a *jouissance* of self-dissolution (as, for example, in Tanizaki, Enchi or Kyōka's texts). In Nakagami's narratives, the space of dissolution becomes ambivalently sexed—while the male from the *roji*, as the already (nonconsensual) masochist term of the binary he makes with socially dominant Japanese men, is reconfigured as the sexually dominant *possessor* of the phallus, practicing brutality against the turned-into- penetratee "pure" Japanese man. Unlike the reversibility shown when the men of the *roji* are with women, this sadism is steadfastly irreversible.

As I will continue to illustrate, in the vacillating dominances that ac- company their sexual activities, Nakagami's men of the *roji* inhabit com- plex sites that commingle what dominant social discourses have defined as "female" positions with "male" positions. That their hyperbolic phalli- cism is compromised by varied descents into submission and pollution is a cleavage in the discourse of phallic dominance itself. (Such feminization, however, must be understood as strictly positional and metaphoric and in no way related to a female "essence" or "principle." It is only from the po- sition of dominant phallocentrism that the radical differences between *burakumin* and "woman" are elided in their unified subordinated otherness.) At the same time, the "feminization" of the *burakumin* is halted where it might recast the *burakumin* body as the female term in a binarism with other (dominant) males; instead, there is a violent insistence on reversing the terms of domination, and "Japanese" men are brutally penetrated, and conversely, turned into "the feminized" term.[22]

Much has been made of the "abstract" discourses of ties to bad blood (the conceit of soiled lineage) endemic to Nakagami's corpus. In *Sennen no yuraku*, the paternal Nakamoto blood flows through his progeny, imbuing them with sexual deviation and charm, good looks and a cursed fate. In the Akiyuki saga, it is the paternal blood from Hamamura Ryūzō that appears to compel Akiyuki to repeat the crimes of his father—sexual sins, arson, even murder—against all his efforts to the contrary.

Yet throughout Nakagami's narratives flows a material blood as well. As quoted in Chapter 8, Nakagami praised "bloody" *monogatari* for their superior dramatic quality. The *material* ("nastiest") blood that flows through Nakagami's narratives is often metaphorically or concretely linked to femaleness (and by extension, through the reciprocal discourses on pollution, to the *burakumin* body) as one of the flows perceived as revolting and abjected and, as Grosz has argued, from which semen has been excepted, flows that have been banished from dominant representations of phallic maleness.[23] "Nasty" blood soils the protagonists' pretensions toward dominance and re-marks them as inheritors of oppression and discrimination. Nakagami's protagonists are regularly smeared with blood or with viscosities reminiscent of blood: "Yves twisted the water faucet and water streamed out. He washed the fruit juice that had spilled onto and stained his right thumb and index finger when he split the pomegranate open; the juice that was like the "white pig's" [female client's] menstrual blood (*Sanka*, 129).

In "Futakami," the children's game (in which they turn Yahei's body into a make-believe landscape) progresses quickly past a more "normative" sexual exploration (in which Yahei's penis becomes a toy for them) into sadomasochism. Kiwa tortures her brother, Tatsuhiko, until he bleeds. As a young adult, Tatsuhiko confesses that as a child he had believed it was blood, not semen, that spurted from Yahei's penis (135). Not only do men actually bleed, but here the penis itself is imagined to seep blood. In the *Kii monogatari* (The tale of Kii, 1984), "bleeding genitals stuck to bleeding genitals," when both the man's penis and the woman's vagina bleed together as the couple has sex.[24]

Abetting the connection to feminized positioning through the conceits of dirty blood, blood from the (male) genitals, sadomasochism, and the sadomasochist reversals, the male prostitute of *Sanka* provides a hyperbolic site for ambivalent and vacillating disruptions of gendered categories of dominance and subordination. As wielded by Yves, the penis becomes a "transcendental" emblem of body power. Yet Yves has no control over his sexuality. He is purchased by both men and women, reflective of the vague gender of his name. He is managed by a woman—Chonko, who renames, packages, and sells Yves, all the while asserting her ownership of him and claiming to love him, in alternating refrains. As a prostitute, his job demands phallic performance, his mythic penis endowed with a never-failing potency and vigor. His vocation simultaneously demands that he capitulate all his own desires to fulfill the erotic desires of his clients. Within these inversions lurk other power reversals, be it with rich women who demand to be tied up and urinated on or the wealthy J. who insists on being slashed and abused. Frequently performing as the "sadist" term, Yves is paradoxically in the position of obeying the commands of others in the guise of dominating them. "The 'white pig' wanted to be violated while tied up. Yves at first was at a loss. He stood the 'white pig' in front of the mirror, and began by tying her hands behind her with the rope that she had prepared for that purpose" (124). The client has brought and prepared the rope with which he will bind her. Such power reversals are, of course, "false": Yves's phallic power in those moments is only the exchange value of a commodity purchased by his clients, who are in economic dominance. Yves as "the possessor of the phallus" is thus nonetheless repeatedly placed in a feminized or disempowered position. He simultaneously inhabits both categories of "phallic aggressivity and dominance" and "female passivity and compliance."

In the midst of the repeated theatrical enactments of "phallic power," Yves suffers from a loss of the power to self-determination. He calls himself a "cyborg." Most strikingly, Yves's penis is clearly metaphorized as "the unicorn" (of course, a mythic, stunningly beautiful beast of legend—a nonexistent signifier); Yves is blatantly in possession only of a (phallic) myth. The performativity of his abusive masculine dominance is made clear in the torture of J.: they take a room in a hotel that was, so it is said, rented by Foucault while he was in Japan. When they turn on the lamp, the room is flooded with light "like a stage set" (260).

It is in the context of presenting socially disempowered men who wield their penises as the (emptied) signifiers of "the phallus" that Nakagami also explores the narrative potentials of one of the most "abjected" of sexualities, anal sex between men. Bersani has argued that the "civilized" revulsion at the idea of male-male anal sex stems precisely from the phal-lic-shattering image of a man being penetrated and thereby placed into the feminized position, with the attendant metaphoric linkage with death and self-dissolution. Compare this comment of Bersani's, about cultural images of gay sexuality, with the description from *Sennen no yuraku* that follows it:

A seductive and intolerable image of a grown man legs high in the air, unable to refuse the suicidal ecstasy of being a woman.[25]

Hanzō thrust into the man's asshole. Although he moved as though to avoid the thrust the man had his legs curled and lifted up like a woman's, so Hanzō willfully thrust in and out, pounding the soft wetness [*zubuzubu*] with abandon exactly as he would do it to a woman. (31)

In *Sanka*, Yves boasts of his indifference to types of holes and to the sex of the individual attached to those holes, in a typically phallic assertion of his right to penetrate however, and whatever, he desires. Yves proudly makes no evaluative "distinction" between the sexes of his paying clients: "It didn't matter if it was a young woman, or a 'white pig,' or even if it was a 'black pig' [male client]; [for Yves] pleasure was pleasure" (21). Yves responds when asked if he prefers men to women, "As long as it has a hole I don't care [*ana, arya nan demo ii sa*]" (77). Elided, of course, in this equation of a woman's vagina and a man's anus, are the political and social significations that attend the differing penetrations. In typical Nakagami fashion, moreover, elsewhere in opposition to Yves's assertions that he is thoroughly indifferent not only to the so-called "individual" but also to the sex attached to the (individual's) hole into which he might plunge his penis, Yves admits to a preference for male clients.

Such "perverse" desires would, one might expect, designate Yves as a "homosexual." But Yves is never denoted a homosexual, because in his pairings with men he will not "be" the phallus but only "possess" it. As noted earlier, with other men Yves staunchly refuses to occupy the material, or concretely, feminized position as the masochistic term or even as the penetratee. Yves's occupational feminization aside, his physical masculinity (his mythic phallicism) is never compromised by being the receptor of anal penetration by another penis. The only objects to penetrate his anus are tongues or fingers. *Sanka* repeatedly recirculates a definition of the "homosexual" not by his desire for another man, but by his willingness to be anally penetrated by another man's penis—that is, as repeatedly troped in Nakagami's texts, feminized—in that desire.

The *yakuza* (gangster) Iya acts as a parodic counterbalance to Yves's masculine unyieldingness: an avowed heterosexual, the most cartoonlike macho of all the characters, Iya (implausibly) decides to try the homosexual/female position. When he decides he's had enough, the machismo mannerisms of his speech (how he speaks) resonate discordantly with the content of that comment (what he says): " 'I , the gangster, have definitely been fucked (*yarareta da ze*). I told you I was a virgin girl (*shojo*),' he said. Yves laughed at the ridiculousness of his comment. Iya brandished his fist, 'Hurry and take it out or you're dead' " (99).

Iya's masculine language and threatening posture are made absurd precisely by his simultaneous self-designation as a "virgin girl." Given the terms that appear to designate a "homosexual" elsewhere in *Sanka*, Iya's exploration of the penetrated position does not, curiously, transform him into a "homo." Iya accepts penetration, yet asserts his "masculine authority" to determine the limits of that penetration. Moreover, it seems that it is less sexual acts themselves than a type of *naming* that in *Sanka* transforms a "regular" man into a "homo." Here is an exchange between Yves and a "homosexual" in *Sanka*:

> "Get out faggot [*okama*]."
> "What? Faggot, faggot, what is a faggot?"
> "I said get out." Yves glared at him as though about to hit him.
> "Get out. This sauna is not a place for faggots" (62).

Words anchor slippages by unequivocally determining "Who's the homo?" "He's the homo," and "I'm not a homo." Yves plies his penis as a weapon, as the mythic unicorn, in love and in hate, to penetrate men (and women), but it is always his partner, and never he, who cries out "like a woman" or raises his hips "as a woman would." Thus, Yves is not a "homo." This relentless "girling" (since here homosexuals are likened more often to "girls" than to "mature women") of penetrated males, replicated even in Iya's hyperbolic version, highlights the relation between "word" and "identity." Not sexual behavior, but the voiced designation of the homosexual subject produces the homosexual as such; or more accurately, naming "originates" a sexual (and aberrant) category. The designations of "faggot" and "homo" identify—by feminizing—men as homosexual, by virtue of that feminization. Akira, who at first refuses anal penetration, becomes a "homo" after being raped by Yves; he is transformed into a caricature of a homosexual man (he is girled) through Yves's adamant classification of him as a "homo." The naming is, moreover, inseparable from the violence against him. The *burakumin* Yves inverts the femaling of himself through a brutalization of Akira (and the designer J.); this brutalization is constitutively dependent, however, on their designation as "homos" (which originates in their feminized masochism). To reiterate, notably, even when penetrated, Iya does not become a "homosexual." Here, as Edelman wrote, "language may be a privileged symbol of the symbolic order itself—the counterpart to the phallus through which symbolic identity is articulated—it operates, nonetheless, through the investment of contiguity, the differential arbitrariness of the signifier, with the paradigmatic force of imaginary sameness and presence."[26]

The power of naming in Nakagami's narratives also appears linked to the (Derridean) violence of naming and the discrimination that is constitutive of that naming. It is here the name (language, difference) that produces the gendered subject and produces the forbidden and simultaneously the transgression of the forbidden.[27] As Derrida wrote,

It is because the proper name was never possible except through its functioning within a classification and therefore within a system of differences, within a writing retaining the traces of difference, that the interdict was possible, could come into play, and, when the time came . . . could be transgressed; transgressed, that is to say restored to the obliteration and the non-self-sameness [*non-propriété*] at the origin.[28]

For the masochistic designer J., homosexuality holds the key to a perverse aestheticization of "maleness"; this aestheticization somehow elides the material contours of the phallic subject and restructures it as outside the "law" as an imaginary.

To fuck with a man, and to fuck with a woman, the topographies [*isō*] are different. Not oppositional. Fucking with a man, how should I phrase it, is fucking with something fictitious [*kakū no mono*]. Some people might call the imaginary object a god, or call it beauty, or perhaps call it power. . . . Some people find god in a filthy beggar. The beggar is real but at the moment he becomes the object of sexual love, he is transformed into the far side of the imaginary. . . . The homosexual is not [about] the material [*gutai*]; he is [about] the imaginary [*kakū*], about a concept [*kannen*]. (102–3)

J.'s deeply problematic aestheticization of homosexuality aside, one might relate his concept of homosexuality to the "imaginary" status of the phallus (and the phallus as a fiction) and also to its role as signification or law. Transgression of the interdict, or sex with a man, for J., highlights the phallus as both lack and construct, constituting a simultaneous assault on difference. Yet the aestheticization, much like the "girling" through naming, recaptures difference within its own hierarchized and limiting confines.[29]

I stated earlier in this chapter that Nakagami's texts moved over time toward an increasing "rawness" centered on the sexual body. But the second half of *Sanka* does a sudden turnabout. The narrative shifts from something resembling pornography to *monogatari*, through the impossible, coincidental reappearance of the old women who accompanied Yves (then Tsuyoshi) and Tanaka from the demolished *roji*. Namely, the shift is toward a retrieval of the female term as a discursive dominance that encapsulates narrative itself. (It is a repetition of the conceit of employing a female narration to frame the *monogatari*, as in Oryū no oba's narration of *Sennen no yuraku*.)[30] With the sudden reappearance of the old women, the Yves persona is destabilized, and an "individual" with a personal history (Tsuyoshi) surfaces from its "repressed" site within the cyborg-Yves. Phallus-Yves, as both lack and as the possessor of the phallus, is "reoriginated" as Tsuyoshi by the ascendance of a female term, which renames him with his "original" name and makes him once more a "normal" man (that is, returns him to his supposed "origins"). The retrieval of Tsuyoshi is inseparable from a series of intertwined occurrences: the old women themselves, the Shingū dialect that the women speak, and Chonko's reconceptualization of him in a more standard rendition of committed love relationship. Increasingly violent episodes accompany Chonko's aggressive insistence that Yves love her back; illogically, Yves/Tsuyoshi does so. Frameworks of female agency overlap with webs of feminized narrative tradition and re-enwrap the sliding terms of sex and gender within the "fiction" of an inverted, yet infinitely more stable, *monogatari* as convention. This *monogatari* could be described as transgressed by *shōsetsu* (and thus as repeating in a more overt form one foregrounded theme of the Akiyuki saga—that of the relation of *monogatari* to *shōsetsu*) through its transformation of the tale into a rather mundane love affair between Chonko and Yves/Tusyoshi. Tsuyoshi sheds his "cyborg" identity, even occasionally reverting to Shingū dialect, while his desire for men, which he once claimed had superseded his lust for women, simply fades away into a nonissue. Yves thus resumes his (former) identity as a "regular man, Tsuyoshi"—and gives up his performance as "having" the phallus while "being" it. The sliding terms of sexual aberration are resubsumed within a convention of relative norm. This "regular man" is, however, of outcaste heritage and "in love" with a Korean madam; it is only the more egregiously slippery terms of male prostitution and homosexuality that function here to *stabilize* and relationally to normalize the (less threatening) differences of their (unified) status as "nonsubjects."

The second half of *Sanka*, in which origin is supposedly recaptured and false identities shed, is wrapped in a cloak of mediations no less theatrical than the stage set for Yves's mutilation of J. Transported to Yves's apartment, and observed unknowingly through a mirror, the old women have been transformed into characters who are a curious mixture of Tokyo-savvy, thieving, greedy, and homeless. One might read this mirror image as the opposite of "transparency" and as a reflection of "false" (imaginary) identifications. The mirror is said to "reflect *monogatari* with just the slightest beam of light" (352). The old women are the fictive substance of modern *monogatari*. In the end, "normal" Tsuyoshi and Chonko drive off (one is tempted to say into the sunset) in a grand Hollywood gesture. One set of embodied (fictional) narratives gives way to other embodied (fictional) narratives, equally mediated and distanced from origin or truth. After all, Tsuyoshi and Chonko are headed back to a *roji* that no longer exists. The "female term" is once again nothing more than a "false origin" recirculating a scripted imaginary.

Sanka's return to *monogatari* bares both the fallacy of phallic dominance even as it masquerades it and the contrivance of feminized origin even as it reinstates it—as the terms of the text disavow one another. Fabrications enwrap fabrications; the female agency that frames the narrative is simply one more layer of contrivance. Retreating from the gutted, raw, naked body of drive or impulse and of sexual violence, and from its partnered production as phallic commodity, the text recaptures the violent and transgressive "beast" inside the folds of the conventions of discourse that have produced that very beast-body. The "gutted" body and the "narrativized" one thus melt into each other. In *Sanka*, the enscripted body provides a site for incessant play within codes of power marking sexual or gender categories as well as those of ethnic and racial difference. The gesture toward a denarrativization of bodies collapses on itself in an ultimate disavowal of the feasibility of its own project. The phallus, overtly indexed as myth, is clearly demarcated by a valiant (manly) assertion of its dominance through the constitutive abjection of being penetrated. For Yves, however, the nature of this abjection is that it returns to trouble the purported "seals" of himself as the phallic subject, in the form of viscosities (nasty blood) and desires (for other men or for role reversals). Yves's phallocentrism is most performative in his brutal dominance of "pure" Japanese men for whom, as stated earlier, he will not "be" the phallus. Yet this very phallicism is willfully undermined by the reversals of domination, the surrendering of the penis, and the sharing of the terms of abjection with women. The unrelenting phallocentrism of Nakagami's texts is, finally, yet another deeply ambivalent, socioculturally (modern) fiction.

FOURTEEN

An Ambivalent Masculinist Politics

In 1994, Karatani Kōjin said,

I was surprised when Nakagami died and I took a look inside some bookstores. Even the big Tokyo bookstores had none of Nakagami's major works. Shockingly, it appeared that even the Shingū library had none. I was irritated to think that, this being the situation, then wasn't it materially impossible to read Nakagami? It was then that I considered devoting a special issue to Nakagami in *Hihyō kūkan*. Not immediately, but a level-headed issue to follow one year later.[1]

By now the situation Karatani described has been transformed. The Nakagami *zenshū* (complete collected works) is being published; paperbacks of selected works can be purchased at many small, local bookstores throughout Tokyo as well as at the larger ones.[2] There has clearly been an intentional process of canonization, during which it can be said that Nakagami has been "retrieved" by a handful of Japanese male critics devoted to ensuring that not only would his corpus not disappear from literary history, but that it would become prominent.

There has also been an increase in critical commentary in Japanese on his work in various forms.[3] Yearly symposiums on Nakagami have been sponsored by Kumano University and held in Shingū City. These symposiums have included roundtable discussions attended religiously by Karatani, Asada Akira, and Watanabe Naomi, who each year are joined by a changing roster of other critics, writers, and scholars.[4] In June 1996 Yomota Inuhiko organized and chaired a symposium on Nakagami at Meiji

Gakuin University. Many journals, such as *Yuriika* and *Kokubungaku*, published special sections dedicated to Nakagami in the wake of his passing; an expanded section on Nakagami came out in *Hihyō kūkan* in 1994; *Subaru* greeted the publication of the first volumes of his collected works with a special section in 1995.[5] The momentum has carried over to some degree into English-language studies as well (tempered, no doubt, by the dearth of English-language translations of Nakagami's narratives).[6] A panel on Nakagami was held at the national Association for Asian Studies meeting in 1995 (after a similar proposal was rejected the previous year). Several English-language journals have carried essays on Nakagami.[7]

Most of the critical commentary in Japanese accompanying this canonization has focused on a particular set of texts that can be loosely described as the Akiyuki and the Akiyuki-related series of narratives: "Misaki" (The cape, 1975), *Kareki Nada*, and *Chi no hate shijō no toki* (The end of the earth, the supreme time, 1983) (hereafter *Chi no hate*).[8] The trilogy proper relates the attempt by a young adult *burakumin*, Akiyuki, to come to terms with his irregular paternity and the tragedy of his older brother's death by suicide. Akiyuki's identity struggle drives him to intentional incest with his half sister at the end of *Misaki*, the killing of his half brother, a provoked crime of passion at the end of *Kareki Nada*, and possibly to arson at the end of *Chi no hate*.

Critical acclaim greeted *Sennen no yuraku*, the tale of six young male *burakumin* descendants in the Nakamoto bloodline, framed by a primary narration by the *roji* midwife, Oryū no oba, and its sequel, *Kiseki* (Miracle, 1989). Around this nucleus a set of other, slightly less valorized texts has formed, mostly short stories in which one can identify "Akiyuki variations" such as "Kataku" (Burning house, 1975), or throughout the collection of short tales called *Keshō* (Cosmetics, 1978). (Although strictly speaking, the body of canonical texts are not limited only to Akiyuki stories proper, for simplicity's sake, I will hereafter use "the Akiyuki narratives" to refer to the collective set of texts that include the Akiyuki stories and the related canonical narratives.)

The Akiyuki narratives are without a doubt the best of Nakagami's written texts, according to a set of contemporary Japanese literary standards. The dramas of the Akiyuki narratives are deeply human and larger than the characters themselves; the narratives comment forcefully and passionately on contemporary intellectual, political, historical, narratorial, and philosophic issues. The characters are faithful to themselves. There is pathos, fury, and passion. The prose itself is a masterful mixture of con-

vention and innovation. There are sustained fictional topoi. These particular standards are in general, of course, shared by the American academy.

The narratives that predate the appearance of Akiyuki in any of his
variant manifestations are generally indulgently regarded as immature,
and are therefore critically ignored, while those postdating Akiyuki have.
frequently been disparaged as failed, or lesser, works. For example, critic
and scholar Hasumi Shigehiko blasted Nakagami's last (unfinished) long
fiction, *Izoku* (A different clan, begun in 1991): "If I remember correctly,
the serialization of *Izoku* had already begun when I started writing *Far
distanced from the shōsetsu*. . . . It was because I wanted to make Nakagami stop writing *Izoku* that I was inspired to write *Far distanced from
the shōsetsu* (laughs)."[9] Asada and Karatani agree that *Sanka* reads too
schematically and dramatically, resembling more a dramatic script, or a
screenplay, than a *shōsetsu* proper.[10]

Perusing the body of commentary on Nakagami in Japanese, I began to
wonder why the Akiyuki texts had been singled out for canonical status.
Intriguingly, as Karatani noted in specific reference to the 1995 panel on
Nakagami at the Association for Asian Studies conference in Washington,
D.C., the majority of scholars presenting and writing on Nakagami for
the American academy are women who can be loosely identified as feminists.[11] Even more intriguingly, the limited body of critical writing on Nakagami in English (by both sexes) has often foregrounded texts outside the
Akiyuki narratives, texts that are marginalized in the canonization process in Japan. (Although this is not to say that no attention is paid by the
American academy to the Akiyuki texts.) As recent trends in literary criticism (complemented by similar directions in other fields) have increasingly
stressed, "aestheticism," or judgment based on an evaluation of text having recourse to a putative scale of good and bad or successful or not, are of
course reproductions of sociocultural and political discourses. I recall
Terry Eagleton's discussion of literature as an institution or the historical
problematic of what constitutes "literature": "The value-judgements by
which it [literature] is constituted are historically variable, [and] . . . these
value-judgements themselves have a close relation to social ideologies.
They refer in the end not simply to private taste, but to the assumptions by
which certain social groups exercise and maintain power over others."[12]

There is, then, a surplus of ideologies that underlie the Japanese herald-
ing of the Akiyuki narratives and that provide a framework for discerning
why they offer the most satisfaction to the majority of Nakagami's critically minded Japanese readership. Conversely, a perspectival shift in

agenda informs the feminist engagement of Nakagami in the American academy and the academy's interest in texts extraneous to the Akiyuki narratives. The problem of judging how narrative is evaluated is, of course, an enormous one to which I cannot do justice here. My intention, then, is less to struggle with the problematic of the aesthetic itself than it is to grapple with what constitutes some of the most marked differences between what have been labeled Nakagami's best works and those that have been less enthusiastically received. And the question I mean to address is, What agendas are served in the process? As this essay will articulate, an *ambivalent* masculinist agenda underpins the critical privileging of the Akiyuki narratives. At the same time, in the American academy a contemporary enthusiasm for *overt* assaults on normative gendered and sexual performances—assaults that spill over to affect writing itself—appears to engage feminists' attention and to underlie their interest in the noncanonical narratives.

First, the canonization of the Akiyuki texts, I would suggest, is rooted in the narratorial dominance of "the father" as both a symbolic term, and, quite literally, as paternity. Second, the postulation of the father as "term" has led to it being paired by critics against its expected "other," that is, the mother as "term,"—a move that I understand to be inseparable from the existing naturalization of *monogatari* as an already maternalized and feminized site. Concretely, the very masculine heroes of the Akiyuki narratives are posed as "male and paternal terms" against a naturalized feminization of the *roji*. A more careful reading will, as I articulate below, redescribe the *roji* as a *thoroughly* deconstructive space that unsettles the binaries of gendered terms with the same relentless violence (violence against, and born of, difference) that it does other terms of signification. I will also offer my analysis of how these gendered (and sexed) slippages have been underemphasized in favor of class and ethnic slippages in the dominant critical discourse on Nakagami. (In order to do so, this chapter will reconsider several of the topics of the previous chapter, including the significance of the phallus and violence in Nakagami's narratives.) Disavowing the instability of gender in Nakagami's narratives is also, I believe, an integral element in the critical demarcation between canonical and so-called failed or secondary narratives. One of my intentions, then, is to rethink the question of gender in both the canonical and the noncanonical texts.

I want to stress that I used the word *ambivalent* to modify masculinist when I said above (and in the title to this chapter) that an ambivalent masculinist politics has informed the canonization of Nakagami's work, because *any* celebration of Nakagami's work must accept an assault on gender constructs and indicates a willingness on the part of the reader to undergo a breakdown of conventional gendered discourses and phallic dominance. That being said, as I will show, the Akiyuki narratives proffer the "gentlest" (that is, gentlest to existing phallocentric norms)—or, perhaps, the sneakiest—forays into normative gender and sexual performances.

Like many other modern writers, Nakagami sought to reconfigure *monogatari* within a contemporary literary tradition.[13] Nakagami himself was well aware that this rewriting could only be a mediated gesture toward the origin from a position of (post)modernity. Nakagami did not set out to "recapture" a lost past in a swooning nostalgia; rather, he labored to break apart contemporary myths that shrouded tradition and to reveal their hidden and abjected attributes as precisely those myths' own constitutive Other.

In *Keshō* and *Kumanoshū*, this project took the form of alternating short tales situated in various indeterminate past times with others temporally situated in (most commonly) the *buraku* of contemporary Japan or sites inhabited by individuals denied the status of "subject" (members of subordinate classes). The same nameless protagonist (a variation on Akiyuki) appears time and again in the short stories that comprise *Keshō*—called simply "a big man"—whether the tale is situated in the present time or in the Middle Ages. Thus, Karatani has written that the " 'big man" of the contemporaneous tales is a "certain paradigm of (one type of) *shishōsetsu* hero. However, Nakagami at the same time had to change this 'big man' into a metaphorical 'big man.' "[14] The "metaphorical" version is the figure who appears in the tales of the past, tales that most resemble *setsuwa* or *monogatari*. The dead brother of this "big man," appearing in some of the tales, is called only "Ani" (older brother). He is, writes Karatani, a composite character,

layered over with the people of the distant past who fled to Kumano after losing their battle for power. This is a reiteration of an [actual] event in Japanese history.[15] However, "Ani" is simultaneously nothing more than a despicable character, a drug addict who commits suicide while under the influence. That was a [actual] particular event that Nakagami experienced. "Kare" [the protagonist, called "He"] wonders if he himself is not a repetition of "Ani," and questions that if so, then what does it mean to fortify that repetition? In *Keshō* Nakagami uses illusion to link the general with the specific. In the final analysis, both "Kare" and "Ani" are symbolic structures within which different individuals can be substituted. However, in *Kareki Nada*, they appear with the names of Akiyuki and Ikuo.[16]

Nakagami's reconceptualization of the *monogatari* was actualized not only through juxtaposing a tale of the past against a tale of the present but also within a single (short or long) "realistic" tale, such as, for example, "Jain" or "Ukijima," as I described in Chapter 12, through the displacement and transgression of the modern by the traces of antecedent text (*monogatari*, *setsuwa*, folklore). His shifting of the *monogatari* topoi to the *buraku* through the troping of the *roji* dismantled standard (ahistorical) imaginaries about both the *buraku* and the *monogatari*. As Karatani argued,

Nakagami by no means single-mindedly shuttled about within [the parameters of] *monogatari*. *Monogatari* appears only within a phenomenological reduction [*kangen*], so to speak. Rather, we should be attentive to the fact that Nakagami did not unearth *monogatari* simply as a retrospection [*sokō*] of a historical past, but as a retrospection that occurs within a phenomenological reduction. To rephrase, Nakagami did not deploy it [*monogatari*] as a simple disavowal of the modern, but as a radicalization [*tetteika*] of modern consciousness.[17]

Throughout the Akiyuki series, and the other texts privileged in the critical commentary, is the (development of the) troping of the *roji* as an inverted and destabilized site of history and discrimination. Watanabe postulated: "If we assume that Nakagami contributed a new constituent element to the history of how modern literature has represented the *buraku*, it is the revelation that the *roji* is a site of *monogatari*."[18] Katsuyo Motoyoshi wrote:

To Nakagami, *monogatari* is defined by what he calls *hō*, or *seido* (law/system or institution), and this is nothing other than the hierarchical categories defining Japanese tradition itself. For Nakagami, it is this, even more than modernity, that he cannot take for granted. His provenance, as *burakumin*, precludes him from simply reveling in "Japan the beautiful"; his position in relationship to "tradition" is always identified obliquely, against *hō/seido* and not by them. Thus Nakagami's assertion of his identity as a *monogatari sakka* (writer of *monogatari*) is an impossibility for him, if it is not ironical or mediated. This mediation is found in his fiction in the form of the *roji*.[19]

The *roji* was not a stagnant trope; rather, it was continually reshaped in different texts, yet it functioned repeatedly as a site where opposing terms were collapsed within their mutual interdependencies. The *roji* provided a topos for exploring the role of *sabetsu,* or discrimination, as "history" and in the development of signification itself (although Nakagami undertook this same project in topoi extraneous to the *roji* as well).

Surely, the foregrounding of the *roji* in order to address the previously elided political and social issue of *burakumin* discrimination in modern Japan has contributed to the positive evaluation of the Akiyuki narratives. That Nakagami was the first successful modern Japanese writer to engage the issue of that particular discrimination in narrative text, from an unconcealed subject position as a *burakumin,* also says something about a transformed critical readership that both supported, and commodified, his position.[20] The Akiyuki series (including, of course, *Sennen no yuraku*) most unabashedly writes the postwar *buraku.* It is important to reiterate, however, that the *roji* in Nakagami's texts must be recognized as a *narrative* topos; it is not a mimetic representation of the "real *buraku,*" and there should be no assumption that there exists a transparency, or interchangability, between the two. Thus, the reader should bear in mind that my references to the *roji* and the *buraku* of Nakagami's texts are to this troping and are not meant as commentary on the "actual" *buraku.* Nakagami's *roji* tales are, generally speaking, less about "discrimination" in its manifest sense of acts of domination by an empowered class against a disempowered one than they are about the system, or structure, of difference and discrimination (*sa'i*). (Although there are references to actual discrimination against *burakumin* in his works.) Historical discriminations, for Nakagami, are in part produced in, and by, language. Indicative of a multiplicity similar to that described in the previous chapter, Nakagami's rendering of "difference" is structural, linguistic, and yet historical. "Discrimination" and "difference" function on more than one level, as social violences and as symbolic terms of signification; Nakagami's project catered to a breaking open of the "origins" of difference, as inseparable from the process of signification itself. For Nakagami, this included a dismantling of standard modern notions of gender differences. Although the Akiyuki narratives attend *overtly* to an exploration of identity, class, authority, and difference, they only furtively, or in a manner surplus to the "behavior, actions, and thoughts of characters," assault dominant notions of gender and sexuality. As I hope to show in this chapter, it is in the noncanonical, or secondary narratives, that one finds the boldest probing into the constructivity of gender binarisms.

In *Misaki,* and in *Keshō,* where one can locate Akiyuki prototypes, the "symbolic structure" (as Karatani called it) that is in *Kareki Nada* filled by Akiyuki is without proper name, as are the father and the brother. They are simply "He," "That Man," and "Older Brother"—nameless but simultaneously embodying narratorially dominant, relational terms of identification. Even after proper names have been appended to Akiyuki and Ryūzō, these names, and their "relations," continue to slide and invert: Akiyuki has three names, none of which, he claims, are his; he shifts between referring to his father as "That Man," "Hamamura Ryūzō," and "The King of Fly Shit." Ryūzō calls himself a descendent of Hamamura Magoichi (an actual historical figure linked to the origins of the Kumano *burakumin*).[21] Ryūzō insists on calling Akiyuki "Older Brother" and refers to himself as Akiyuki's "son." Naming here is in vain; it does not halt the rush to self-immolation/dismantling of law and signification. Instead, Nakagami renders *violence* at the origins of (all) classifications and identifications, making them signify something akin to what Derrida has called *différance*. Derrida wrote:

To name, to give names that it will on occasion be forbidden to pronounce, such is the originary violence of language which consists in inscribing within a difference, in classifying, in suspending the vocative absolute. To think the unique *within* the system, to inscribe it there, such is the gesture of the arch-writing: arche-violence, loss of the proper, of absolute proximity, of self-presence, in truth the loss of what has never taken place, of a self-presence which has never been given but only dreamed of and always already split, repeated, incapable of appearing to itself except in its own disappearance.[22]

Throughout Nakagami's corpus, naming cannot be severed from this "originary violence"—the violence of naming and the "difference" inherent in that naming. It is the violence of the Derridean trace—the radically "other" within and the structure of heterogeneity within the sign, the sign that is always both there and not there (that is, under erasure).

In the Akiyuki series, the father is precisely the term of lack and the term by which identity is constructed (the phallus or the law). Though he himself refuses signification by his indifference to "law," he is the constant against which Akiyuki tries in vain to anchor his semblances and dissemblances. The father as phallus-function is, as Carole-Ann Tyler described it, the "nodal point . . . which seeks to totalize meaning so that overdetermined, polysemous signifiers become fixed as part of a structured network of (common) sense about the identities of subjects, objects."[23] But because the father-phallus of the Akiyuki series is simultaneously the abjected (and more commonly feminized) symbol of libidinal excess, disorder, and the instability of signification itself, the term of the father is always dogged by its inverse. This "pluralized" paternal site is, as I argued in Chapter 13, constitutively determined by the status of male *burakumin* as *positionally* feminized.

In *Chi no hate*, the *roji* is demolished and turned into grasslands in the name of capitalist progress (it is slated to be transformed into a shopping center). A clan of people gathers there as squatters. Ryūzō kills himself in front of Akiyuki; the "leader" of the homeless grassland drifters, Yoshi, is shot and killed by his own son, and the grasslands go up in flames, scattering the squatters.[24] It is rumored that the fire was set by Akiyuki, whose whereabouts are, at the end, unknown. This climax, as both Asada and Karatani have argued, is also about the (im)possibility of modern narrative in contemporary Japan. The suicide of the father (who represents "modern patriarchy") near the end of *Chi no hate* is a self-implosion; the internally driven erasure of the modern postulation of origin and the father thus embodies the term of signification and its corollary resistance to or attempt to overcome authority and power.[25] *Chi no hate* is therefore "schematically" postmodern, or as Karatani puts it, posthistorical. Karatani wrote that in *Kareki Nada*, "The subject (*shutai*) is clearly an Oedipal one; thus there is a struggle toward a modern subject, but not only does he [Akiyuki] not kill his father, but in *Chi no hate shijō no toki* the term of the father dies off by itself. It [the narrative] ends as Akiyuki is cast out."[26]

Indeed, Akiyuki's dilemma revolves around the attempt to erase or eradicate definition through the father. The blood bond between them, he fears, will force him to repeat the acts of his father; but he is equally afraid of the consequences of the "term of the mother"—he is terrified that the blood bond between him and his older brother (through the mother) will make him a replication of his older brother. As Karatani points out above, unlike the Oedipal drama paradigm, the Akiyuki series resolves ambivalence toward the father while avoiding patricide. (Although another father—Yoshi—*is* killed by his son.) And I would add that the mother is never figured as a direct source of conflict (as an object of desire and exchange) between father and son. The main problematic of the Akiyuki texts revolves around an overtly disharmonious father/son relationship unmediated by a dynamic third term in the form of the mother. She may "exist," but she virtually does not matter in the drama between Akiyuki and Ryūzō (except through her displaced representation, or more accurately, her "maled" representation through the importance of Akiyuki's brother, Ikuo). Even what might be interpreted as Akiyuki's attempted insertion of the mother into the middle of the conflict between him and his father, through (yet another) displacement onto his half sister (a dubious interpretation to begin with, as I will detail later) has no affect whatsoever on Ryūzō. These canonical works, replete with male-male primacies, detail a fervent, yet nonsexualized (although replete with passionate excess), desire of man for man. Yearning for the father, longing for the brother— these are socially normative patterns of male-male desire and generally untransgressed by any "nasty" (overt) murmurs about homosexuality. Yet this primacy of paternity and patrilineage (nonerotic male-male desire and yearning) in the Akiyuki narratives is at the same time transparently contravened by the internal dissolutions of the very terms of modern paternity (signification and identity).

Paired with the elaboration of the paternal/patrilineal term in the critical corpus and the reading of the *roji* as a space that destabilizes the binarisms of the sacred/profane and that deconstructs law and signification is a postulation of the *roji* as a feminized and maternalized topos. As noted earlier, I read this postulation as inseparable from the critical stabilization of the (intrinsically unstable) term of the father. The feminization of the *roji* is also an example of critical inattention to the constructivity of a metaphoric genderization of discourse. To begin a process of unpacking these assumptions, I'd like to start first with the question of the so-called matrilinearity of the *roji*.[27]

Akiyuki's mother, Fusa, has four children from her first marriage, three daughters and a son. The son, Ikuo, is the older brother who commits suicide. Akiyuki is her fifth child, the product of Fusa's affair with Akiyuki's father, Hamamura Ryūzō. Ryūzō is sent to jail for his involvement in a brawl over gambling; gossip has it that he is also an arsonist who tried to set the *roji* on fire. Fusa remarries, leaving her older children to live on their own, taking only Akiyuki into the new household. Her husband, Takehara Shigezō, adopts Akiyuki.

I have three names, Akiyuki had thought in the past. Actually, it was true. As Fusa's illegitimate child, Akiyuki had been entered into the family registry of her dead husband, Nishimura; when he graduated from middle school, he was entered into the registry of his adoptive father, Shigezō, who regarded Akiyuki as his own child. That man was named Hamamura Ryūzō. Regardless of the fact that, since childhood, Akiyuki had thought that he had no relationship to that man, and that man's children, he felt his body flush whenever he saw him, or heard the name Hamamura. It was strange. They bore a strong likeness of face and of body. Akiyuki knew that he looked more like that man than did any of the other children that man had with the woman he lived with, Yoshie. (49)

Freed from incarceration, Ryūzō seeks out his son, Akiyuki, who is three. But Fusa dismisses his (rather feeble) attempt to claim Akiyuki. The dominant critical insistence on the "matrilinearity" of Nakagami's *roji* seems to be linked to the fact that it is in a sense Akiyuki's mother, and not (any of) his father(s), who determines his "paternity." He nonetheless does not bear his mother's maiden name (which, of course, is her father's name), but those of two of his (nonblood) fathers, in accordance with her change in legal marital status. Still, when compared to more mainstream postwar Japanese family structures, one might call this one "matrilineal." Yet even if one accepts this as matrilineage (and obviously I am rather hesitant to do so), within this framework of "matrilinearity," the Akiyuki series tells the tale of a man coming to terms with his paternity and the suicide death of his older brother. Akiyuki's torment is inseparable from the sliding of paternal and fraternal terms.

More problematic is the "maternalized feminization" of the *roji* topos itself that lurks beside the putative matrilinearity of Nakagami's narratives. Asada refers to the *roji* as "a fundamentally maternalized space" and notes that Akiyuki calls himself "'the illegitimate child that the *roji* was pregnant with, and that the *roji* birthed' "; and that " 'he was not Takehara Akiyuki, nor Hamamura Akiyuki, but Akiyuki of the *roji*.' In short, this could be read as schema in which [Akiyuki] opposes the father while continuing to depend on the *roji*, a space that is like a matrix [*botai*]."[28] I took a second look at the sentences in *Chi no hate* that Asada quotes above. It is imperative to note that the *roji* here appears alongside, or in a class with, *paternal* terms—the names of his fathers. "I am not Takehara, or Nishimura, or even less Hamamura Akiyuki; I am Akiyuki of the *roji* (256)." A sentence a few pages earlier reads, "an illegitimate child has neither father nor mother, nor any siblings at all, thought Akiyuki" (251). Akiyuki's *roji*, as Nakagami tropes it, regardless of the historical actuality, is as much a "father-*roji*" as it is a "mother-*roji*" (it replaces the terms of the father above); or more precisely, the *roji* is a paradigm of the collapsing of identificatory terms *including those of gender*. In it paternity, maternity, even fraternity, are made nonexistent. Akiyuki has no "legitimate" name. There are no absolute terms against which he can identify himself. And the only terms he discovers are inaccurate. Critical insistence

to the contrary, alongside the dissolution of paternal terms is a complementary *refusal*, not erection, of a maternal term. Why then do so many
critics read the *roji* as a fundamentally feminized and maternalized site? I
believe it is due to the tacit acceptance of the pervasive modern myth that
has gendered the *monogatari* as "feminine."

As this study has argued throughout, *monogatari*, as a (metaphorically)
feminized literary genre, is already standardized in the form of a female
narrative stance. As detailed in the section on Enchi, Mizuta has convinc-
ingly argued that in fact *monogatari* became a venue for a phallic agenda
through its inhabitation by male commentary and the male borrowing of
the conceit of a female "voice."

Linked in Nakagami's narratives to a premodern narrative tradition
(whether this is read as a nostalgic recuperation of convention, or as I
read, as a modern deconstruction of convention), and because of its perceived interrelation with the *monogatari*, the *roji* has been called matrilineal (*bokei*), maternal (*bosei*), a matrix (*botai*), and linked to femaleness
(*joseisei*). This maternalized feminization of the *roji* is not attributed to its
positionality as an abjected site but naturalized in a binary schema, borrowing from the modern conceptualization of a feminized premodern discursive tradition. A lack of attention to the constructivity of the linkage of
monogatari with "feminized site" figures the *roji* likewise. For example,
Watanabe wrote that, "One of the paradigms of Nakagami's *roji* that became more and more distinct, is that in every respect, *monogatari*, filled
with the retrogressive flow of the 'sacred and the profane,' and 'Japanese
nature,' have the characteristic of emanating from the female side," and
that for Nakagami, "the *monogatari* invariably emanates from the female. The female body is possessed of a bottomless, pitch-black, dark sexuality that draws in and engulfs men."[29] Although Nakagami himself may
have made statements much to the same effect as Watanabe's comments
above, in the actualization of his fiction, Nakagami assaulted, rather than
reiterated, the conceit naturalizing the *monogatari*, and the *roji*, as "female" terms.

Nakagami's *Sennen no yuraku*'s adoption of a female narrative framework from which to relate its tale is "classical": as a *monogatari*, it employs a female narrative voice, yet the stories told are of six men, quite different from the domestic details of women's daily life that fill page after
page of classic romances like *The Tale of Genji*. On the one hand, as Watanabe has argued, Nakagami's narratives structures are precisely the

framework of the classical *monogatari* transposed to the *buraku*.[30] But on the other hand, the next step that Watanabe does not take is to recognize that this transposition of *monogatari* to the abjected site of the outcaste is complemented by a challenge to the conventions of gender that have already been appended to genre in Japan.[31] Oryū no Oba, as orator, is a conduit through which a "male" *monogatari* flows and by which it claims narrative authority. That her position as orator (narrative authority) is rendered suspect in *Kiseki* (as her tales are then filtered through the untrustworthy medium of an alcoholic old man) shifts the paradigm of the veracity of the "original" (matrix/source) text—*Sennen no yuraku*. Thus, this "feminized" narrative authority is actually disavowed in the sequel. As I noted in the previous chapter, *Sanka*'s female narrative framework reveals itself to be "false." In this sense, Nakagami "guts" the myth of *monogatari*-as-female "voice"; he reveals its phallocentric substructure.

Accordingly, I would redescribe the Akiyuki series as narratives with the (fraudulent) appearance of a female framework (by borrowing the structural contours of the *monogatari* and/or by overturning sexed dominances) within which tales shrouded in an *apparent* masculinist agenda unfold. This apparent phallocentrism is nonetheless relentlessly subjected to a process of its own implosion. That is why I have called the privileging of the Akiyuki narratives an ambivalent masculinist politics. It is a masculinist agenda that ultimately must turn on, and destroy, itself.

The critical insistence on a putatively steadfast matrilinearity, and the unnuanced maternalization of the *roji*, thus posit the mother as "term" in a far less ambiguous manner than do the narratives themselves. The many women—mother, sisters, and aunts—who surround Akiyuki at home impart an atmosphere of femaleness to what is an essentially male story.[32] In the most acclaimed of the three narratives, *Kareki Nada*, Akiyuki's girlfriend appears so peripherally that she is no more than a vehicle for his sexual release, while his half sister, Satoko, with whom he also has sex and who figures far more prominently in Akiyuki's consciousness than his girlfriend does, has little function other than as an intended object of exchange between Akiyuki and his father. Akiyuki engineers a meeting among him, Satoko, and his biological father, so that he may confront his father with the fact that he has had sexual relations with Satoko:

"I slept with Satoko." Akiyuki rephrased it. Even after he spoke the words, other words he wanted to speak were like a whirlpool inside Akiyuki; he thought that he wanted to beg forgiveness. To beg forgiveness, he should humbly scrape the floor with his bowed head. But Akiyuki knew too that a voice in his heart was saying to the man he faced, I have violated you with my penis, which is just like your penis, the one that made me. I will never cease to be your bitter seed for as long as I live. Akiyuki spoke as though he were delirious, "I fucked [*yatta*] Satoko," he said. Akiyuki waited for a moaning cry from the man overcome with suffering. He waited for the man's head to smash and bleed against the wall, and to rip, cut off, and cast away his penis; the penis that had made Akiyuki and Satoko in different stomachs; for the man to put out both eyes, slice off his ears. This was, after all, his father. As his father, he should whip Akiyuki, knock Satoko down.

"It can't be helped. It happens all the time." The man said. He laughed in a low voice. "Don't worry about such things. Even if you two made a baby, even if it were an idiot child, it can't be helped. Although if you have an idiot child, well, it's not easy for the mother." (149)

In the passage above, Akiyuki "fucks" his father, through Satoko, in an act that wields the penis as an agent of rape and power; the violence of his sexual act will both incite his father to castrate himself, and in turn, to beat (and castrate, since the penises are made one) Akiyuki. Throughout the entire imaginary there is a "whirlpool" of confusion over utterance (what to say), over reprisals (what will happen/who will be subjected to violence), and over an essentially homosexual desire. Notably, Satoko is his half sister, but she does not, strictly speaking, represent the mother as term. It is the father whose body she replaces, the father whom Akiyuki wants to fuck (here I mean both meanings of fuck, the penis plied as weapon), a desire for which he wants to be beaten/castrate/be castrated. In the father's rejoinder, the entire imaginary is deflated by his absolute indifference. He rejects Akiyuki's violent, and sexual, gesture toward relation.

Because Nakagami's assault on difference involved a deconstruction of the thoroughly feminized *monogatari* (and the replacement of putatively female spaces with phallic ones), then it logically follows that Nakagami's gesture sometimes appears to be (and sometimes is) misogynist. This is further complicated because Nakagami's resistance takes the form of violent pulverization of convention. Nakagami did not engage in genteel deconstructions along the axis of wordplay; he opted instead for a brutal demolition of tradition and an incessant smashing of putative naturalisms to reveal doctrine, convention, and difference(s) as *constructs* of history. To repeat his own words, quoted in Chapter 11:

Rip apart!
Rip apart the ocean, rip apart the sky, rip apart the boat, rip apart the earth!

· · ·

Why do I write? To fabricate a new Japanese literature? That's shit. To fabricate a new Japanese aesthetic? I would make the lot of those who say such things drink piss. I want to batter and destroy everything.[33]

Especially in the *setsuwa*-inspired short tales in which female characters also function symbolically as vessels for archaisms (in keeping with the culturally metaphoric maternalized-feminization of archaisms as in the antecedent serpent tales and *monogatari*), violence is frequently directed against these female characters. I would like to stress that this violence, which is apparent on both a textual level (as *écriture*, as violence done to language itself) and in depictions of violence by characters in text is, as I described in Chapter 12, inseparable from the attempt to liberate libidinal drive and is entwined with the tensions between modern and medieval textual variants and premodern orality; it is related to the question of the production of origin and is not simplistically linked to power. The two issues, that of the violence of naming and the phallic violence of *burakumin*, are intrinsically related: positional "feminization" and "lack" notwithstanding, the bodies of Nakagami's protagonists are, it must be stressed, *male* bodies with penises. In Nakagami's narratives, in the *roji*, the penis is thus continually situated *within* the more conventionally unnuanced (purely) feminized territories of the *monogatari* and the abject.

It is the critical lack of attention to this positionality of the *burakumin* and the *roji* (within the context of Japan as a modern nation state) that bolsters an appearance of femaleness and a misrepresentation of this femaleness not as positionality, but as bound to "natural" aspects of the female body. If the perspective by which the *roji* is viewed is shifted, to highlight instead the site of abjection as a site shared by women and by *burakumin*, in a mutual configuration as "being the phallus" (that is, the sign of lack) and as the site of foreclosure—the site against which individuation and identification "originates"—then a different reading can be "discovered." Nakagami's *roji* (and the men who hail from it) is beset with gendered ambivalences that rotate on the axis of the *roji*-as-abject, and these ambivalences, rather than naturalizing the *roji* as "female," challenge such feminization with a masculinized relativization.

Violence in Nakagami's texts, by individual against individual, is pervasive. Watanabe wrote that, "within Nakagami's fictional texts, men treat women with a fervent violence, although [this violence] is instigated by the women."[34] Much attention has been given to the violence by men against women in Nakagami's narratives—strangely, in the process, eliding the quantitatively and qualitatively equal depictions of male-male vio-lence. Akiyuki, for example, beats his half brother, Hideo, to death (in a graphically brutal passage); in "Edo" the (false) *hijiri* murders a man; in *Sennen no yuraku*, Miyoshi murders his lover's husband (in collusion with her); the protagonist of "Jyūhassai" is beaten by a gang of other young men. The youth in "Jyūkyūsai no chizu" (The map of a nineteen-year-old, 1973) commits random acts of small terrorisms—his targets are not elected by gender. (This is not to suggest that male battering of men has the same meaning as male battering of women. The different positions of power make the two acts of violence incomparable. Yet in the *roji*, as troped by Nakagami—and arguably, in the "real" *buraku* itself as well— it is important to remember that the terms of power are not standard re-productions of dominant social positions.)

It is perhaps in part the attempt by Japanese critics to exonerate Naka-gami of what looks like misogyny that has contributed to their overem-phasis of a maternalized female "term" in the shape of female dominance and purported aggressivity, matrinilearity, and the framework of female oration in the Akiyuki narratives.[35] A lack of suspicion about the natural-ization of *monogatari* as a feminized site and the maternalized-feminization of the foreclosed as the maternal body, has, I would imagine, deterred crit-ics from emphasizing Nakagami's assault on both these gendered conven-tions. Puzzlingly, in spite of the fact that most commentators do note the bisexual aspects and the slippery nature of sexed terms in Nakagami's nar-ratives, they tend to insist on redelineating the gendered terms that the texts themselves obscured.[36]

When the genderization of those sites remains unproblematized, the "meaning" of the penis/phallus conflation in Nakagami's narratives be-comes even more confusing and confused. Watanabe admits, "Actually, regarding the violence within text, which the text itself discloses on both the level of a bilinear narration and the level of fictionality, I am not sure that one should read this as Nakagami's phallus forcing itself into the text on the level of *écriture*."[37] Hasumi replies by (vaguely) insisting on a clear distinction between "the phallus" and "the penis" and therefore that what is "phallocentric" should theoretically be thoroughly severed from male-on-female violence:

I understand the phallic itself not as a physical violence, but as a conceptual vio-lence. A process of ideation established through recourse to the phallus. Namely, whether it is called *dankonsei*, or phallocentrism, I think that the term refers to that which was most fitting for the systemization of a conceptual device/contrivance, so to speak. This cannot be something discerned on the level of a physical [material] relation. However it seems to me that there was a time when Nakagami equated the two; or perhaps he always did so.[38]

Hasumi laments a shift he perceives in Nakagami's texts, when a material penis replaces other symbols of sociocultural authority, thereby conflating the "penis" as an instrument of power with the "phallus" (symbolic or systematized).[39] Though of course Hasumi is correct in asserting that the penis and the phallus are not the same (and the meaning of "phallus" itself differs according to different theoretical, psychoanalytic, and sociological positions), Nakagami's use of the penis as a signifier of gendered authority need not be, as Hasumi puts it, "a misunderstanding." Although the phallus, since Freud, has increasingly been theoretically "detached" from the material penis, and in Lacan, for example, figured as "lack," in general (nonpsychoanalytic) usage, it is a term for male power as centralized in the symbolic penis—indexed by (having) the penis. (And this is regardless of whether woman is refigured as "being" the phallus as the sign of lack.) And because *burakumin* positionality mirrors that of female positionality, the male *burakumin*, to reiterate, both "is" the phallus and yet "has" a penis.

Moreover, employing rape as a paradigm of the abuse of power—as in Nakagami's narratives—casts the penis as a weapon and discloses the "system" of domination as quintessentially male (sexed) and misogynist. Rape is one endemic (and concrete) form of the expression of male domination in phallocentric systems. Hasumi's comments, unlike most of the critics' discussions of "phallocentrism," which only consider the sexual behavior of the depicted characters, is excessive in the opposite direction, namely, by eliding the (fundamental) relationship between androcentric power, the penis as symbol *and* employed as a material weapon, and phallocentric systems. To reiterate, it also overlooks the pivotal and essential shared positionality of the men of the *roji* with women (in general). In either case, be it the attention only to "acts of sex and violence" or to phallocentrism as a system severed from the male anatomy per se and only beholden to an abstract system of authority, on the whole, the Japanese critics, as Monnet succinctly phrased it, "fail to examine the inscription of violence as structural dynamics in Nakagami's texts, and the fact that the configurations of gender and sexuality in these texts are inscribed in an economy of representation which is itself structured by violence."[40]

To appropriate Edelman's comment on a completely unrelated object text, the rejoinders by the majority of the critics enact a displacement, and not a dismantling, of gender binarisms.[41] Rather, they function to fortify gendered demarcations that, I would suggest, Nakagami's narratives sought to obfuscate. As Monnet wrote, " 'Fushi' fetishises a masculinity which is predicated on and constituted by error and misconstruction: the error of a masculinity which understands, and violently imposes, itself as the norm and end limit of discourse; the misconstruction that conditions other than (fake) dominant masculinity acquiesce in the latter's imposture."[42]

The postulation of a site that is at the same time abject, lack, yet penised (and thus also a nonfeminized topos as the "foreclosed," as I noted above), is most overt in some of Nakagami's earliest texts, ones extraneous to the canonical narratives. Hasumi muses that in these texts Nakagami's rendering of sexuality was transcendental of the bounded sexual body and incorporated an erotic and ecstatic communion with natural phenomenon. The protagonist would, "given water, become soaked with it. Given fire, he [would] flame up with it."[43] This bodily "transcendental" sexuality itself, as well as the (usually feminized) "natural," is "bisexed." In "Umi e," for example, the ocean is retrieved from its mythic Jungian teleology as a symbol of female sexuality and is reconfigured as a composite of male/female sexual elements.

Ocean, there are poets who rhapsodize that deep down you are "mother." But you are not a mother-ocean; you are an ocean of my blood. The ocean that drank down all the words of my brothers, my sisters, my ancestors. (74)

The ocean! That male prostitute, like a degenerate sadist's whore sticky with thick makeup; a rose emitting toxic fragrance in his mouth. (71)

I am looking at the ocean. It is valiant and manly before my eyes. I feel the salty ocean throughout the cells of my body, like my brother's semen, like the fluid from my sister's Bartholin's glands. (76)

I am already about to dissolve. Into the ocean which is my only "Other" [*tasha*]; I seek to assimilate the ocean that is also me. Oh, oh, ooh. I enter the ocean. The origin of sex itself. I enter the ocean, just as the Japanese archipelago was born from sexual intercourse between the deities, just as Venus was born from a cut-off penis in a pearly froth of rising vapors. White, all white, sex is like a white dizziness. My body is hot and flushed. My body mixes with the ocean, a continuity with archaic figures of men swallowed up inside the ocean, trying to assimilate into its deepest recesses. (76)

The above passages describe sex with and ejaculation into the ocean. A standard interpretation of the protagonist's act as purely penetrative = male and the ocean as the "principle" of receptacle = female elides Nakagami's undeniable "male-ing" ("that male prostitute," for example) of the ocean that alternates with a more conventional "female-ing." As refashioned above, the ocean is as masculine as it is feminine, and the narrator both assimilates it into himself and dissolves into it. And all the while, a libidinal brutality attends the diffusion of subjectivity into boundless passion.

Beyond a more standard conceptualization of "bisexuality," which would posit a stable-sexed individual who engages in sexual activities with both sexes as potential partners, the "bi" aspect of most of Nakagami's protagonists is centered on gendered performances, behaviors, and tropes that are themselves indeterminate. Instability frequently takes the form of vacillating empowerments and dominances or empowerments that are deconstructed. In some of Nakagami's earliest texts, this gesture has less to do with issues of an abstract system of authority or power than with naturalized notions of gender and sexuality. Rather than a feminized origin, the ocean is "pure" origin, a topos prior to all difference and one that births all terms in naming. The (castrated) penis (which I *do not* read as a vagina) births, and the spermy, frothy ocean is filled with figures of men. The putatively inviolate, penised body of the protagonist leaks with a sperm that is resituated within the abjected flows—blood fluids—conventionally associated with women.

The ocean, which the protagonist loves and desires, into which he wants to merge and that merges into him, is:

The ocean of the thirty-thousandth embrace, of the condom in the brown dog's mouth, of the bed-wetting urine of someone stoned, of self-deception, of the giddiness of cheap whiskey, of the assholes of men who love men, of the ejaculations of prep-school students, of fleeing soldiers once sent to Vietnam, of the penis soaring above and undulating in the clouds, of a revolution betrayed, of comic tragedy. (72)

Here, the ocean, as repository of the abject (and the objects of abjection, *petit object a*) is *wrested* from its conventional, modern feminization. The *jouissance* sought by the protagonist of "Umi e" is a *nonfemale jouissance*, it is a retrogressive immersion into an erotic, polysexed, nongendered, all-encompassing, abject space prior to difference. Though the Akiyuki narratives veer away from this *jouissance*, and in many of the tales of *hijiri*, to borrow Monnet's words, the "hijiri's awareness of the imposture and fraudulence of his position and existence, his realisation that the abjection inherent in his status and lifestyle is itself a *simulacrum*, as well as the ambivalence constitutive of the historical condition of hijiri, prevent him/the text from celebrating abjection," the protagonist of "Umi e" marches headlong into a *jouissance* that is simultaneously an abjected topos, and refreshingly, shockingly, and stunningly as masculinized as it is feminized.[44] The *burakumin* as penised "subject" is dephallicized through his leakages, excess libido and aggression, lack of self-containment, lack of order, and homoerotic impulse. Leaking viscosities, dissolution, penetration: here these do not point authoritatively to a particular sex. Instead, in the mingle of sperm and vaginal secretions, urine and anuses, sociocultural perversities, the ocean (and the protagonist, who is both intertwined with the ocean and for whom the ocean is simultaneously the only "other" term), becomes a polygendered flow. This is not a simple inversion that turns over the terms of difference, but a true deconstruction that renders both (all) terms invalid. In the young Nakagami's ocean, there are no "sexes," only "sex"; it is a nonsubject (or an amorphous subject) that both ejaculates and diffuses. The declaration of love below is from protagonist to ocean: "I really love you, but my love is exactly like a diffused ray of light striking a tin roof, are you listening? Although I can feel your stiff penis in the palm of my hand, you are frozen like a deep water fish. Why?" (72). This ocean possesses a penis that will not explain (and yet a penis that is not the phallus?); this ocean is a space free of signification, "unseizable" (undefinable, inexplicable) yet from which signification will out. It is overscripted with discriminations, with endless "narratives" from Greek plays to Japanese folklore, from snippets of contemporary banalities to immense and unvocalizable archaisms, and it is replete with violences, both those of recent wars and ancient battles and those of naming and discriminations.

I know the town has swallowed my miserable body secretions; the seaside town impregnates the white amoebae night. The wind blew. Still damp with body flows, the fluids metamorphosed into a sad chill, akin to an encounter with the three hundred and fifth page of the forgotten dictionary named language.
  You try to assimilate into my body. It is impossible. Face-to-face, this advice spasms forth reverberating bitterly with the scripted lines of Oedipus the King. (59)

At the same time, the ocean holds language and the already scripted; and it is scoured with the terms of difference as signified by the father (Oedipal/symbolic). This complex site—the ocean as origin—is still inseparable from discrimination and from terms, specifically the terms that birth the origin itself. It is this impossibility, rather than its more naive aspects, that carry over into Nakagami's later troping of the *roji*. I read the *roji*, and the Kumano landscape itself, oversignified with the traces of narrative and folklore, as sophisticated retropings of the early, narratively "naive" ocean of "Umi e."

Landscape and the *roji* (as one landscape specific to Nakagami's texts) are the sites where naming is always also misnaming and terms of signification dissolve; where violence is endemic and libido races; where materiality intrudes on the symbolic; where there are no logics; where death is everywhere. These topoi are abjected sites filled with a dephallicized, but still genitally male, (non) subject; yet the demarcation of the abject is impossible without "originary" discriminations, and thus it is from these very same topoi that difference/naming originates.

Rather than establishing discrete, binary topoi of a maternal *roji* against a steadfastly paternal father figure, Nakagami's narratives set these gendered terms into mutual slippage. Even more radical is the violence that his texts enact, through a relentless examination of "originary violence" and word-as-difference, against the dominant feminization of the abject, replacing "woman" and her naturalized "lack" with a "penised," yet nonphallic, man.

Afterword

When I contemplated writing a conclusion to this book, I found that I did not wish to summarize the book's contents or to predict the future potential trajectory of the dangerous woman (or dangerous man) trope. Instead, in this brief afterword, I have chosen to take up issues that stem from questions posed by readers of this study in manuscript form. First, why did I choose these three writers in particular? Or, to rephrase the question, what aesthetical judgments informed my choice? As a corollary, I would like to suggest how a study of just three writers, and only a sampling of their texts, can purport to make any meaningful commentary on society or on social imaginaries in general. Second, a few readers seemed puzzled about how I personally regarded the writers—specifically, from a politically feminist vantage point. In part, this question is evidence of the success of my methodological ethics, which have sought to elaborate sites of conflict and not to force closure on terms, images, and discursive slippages in favor of substantiating "theory." In this afterword, however, I want to shift methodologies and to redirect my own argument toward a firmer, political commentary. In a sense, then, if the book has obscured straightforward "political feminism," then this afterword reinserts it, and me, as a materialist-feminist, into its discussion of the trope.

I am well aware of this study's extremely parsimonious choice of primary texts, an outgrowth of the type of close reading I have pursued. Surely it would be irresponsible to hazard an interpretation with a broad scope. But this book appears to have done just that: to have interpreted a smattering of literary imaginaries as implicated in the process of constructing the modern social and psychic Japanese subject. Therefore I want to reiterate that my study is not an attempt to "totalize" the specific portrayals of the dangerous woman that I have analyzed here, but to explore her topos and her attributes, at close range, in a limited number of literary expressions. Although in each literary representation, the dangerous woman takes on different guises and ushers different issues to the fore and background, in the twentieth century she has undoubtedly been an abiding literary topos for the exploration of *jouissance* and the delightfully terrifying dissolution of the modern subject. It would have been possible, given time and other valuable resources, to substantially broaden the list of narrative texts to be explored in this study. Actually, I originally envisioned the book to be on six or seven writers, including Yanagita Kunio, Sakaguchi Ango, Ōba Minako, and Tsushima Yūko, but I kept paring it down as my readings became increasingly close. Of course, even the original list could be greatly expanded, and if I also considered filmic representations, the complexities, variances, and tenacity of the dangerous woman trope could be further documented. But the result would have been either an encyclopedic text incorporating short synopses or an exceedingly long text, and the study would have lost its analytic focus. That focus has been on reading the relationship between specific literary imaginaries and discourses of social abjection, pollution, and othering that made possible the coming-into-being of the Japanese twentieth-century masculine subject in language. (Of course, the dangerous woman is not the only trope, or site of abjection and othering, that functioned as a constitutive other to the formulation of the "normative" subject.)

Out of all the potential candidates, I chose these three writers for several reasons. All three occupy important places in the modern literary canon, but it was less their canonical status per se and more *how* these three writers' narratives had been interpreted in the dominant critical literature that prompted my interest and informed my decision to include them. The significance of the work itself, the putative meaning of its content, and its value as a "work of art" are, of course, produced as much by the critics, publishers, booksellers, and so forth, as by the writer him- or herself.[1] A plurality of cultural beliefs are encoded in every literary text and the secondary literature that explicates it. In the case of each of the three writers, I have sought to identify, historicize, and denaturalize a set of gendered truisms that have dominated the critical literature accompanying their narratives.

Another reason that I chose these writers was simply that Kyōka, Enchi, and Nakagami all tell a good story. This is in part what has earned them the appellation of writers of *monogatari* (more than of *shōsetsu*); moreover, their narratives do not replicate the narcissistic fiction of enclosure, characterized by myopic narrative subjects, that is so characteristic of the most dominant highbrow twentieth-century genre, the *shishōsetsu*. Their narratives are not bound to an exploration of "realism," and the imaginaries that are thus allowed to become hyperbolic in Kyōka, Enchi, and Nakagami's fictions provide, for me, intriguing sites of complexity and conflict, appropriate to my study. And regardless of the limitations of each of the writer's conceptualizations of "woman" for all three, women mattered, women were significant, women were central to their stories. An apparent erotic preference by all three for female fleshiness goes beyond its own aesthetical boundaries: female presence is "fleshed out" in a corpulence that insists itself. (Although for Kyōka, this presence was always also entangled with woman as cipher, in alternations of presence and absence.)

Contrary to one reader's assumption, it is neither with animosity that I have approached Kyōka's renditions of the dangerous woman nor with unmitigated approval that I have read Enchi's, or even Nakagami's. Kyōka was socially concerned with women's status; his sense of justice was outraged by twentieth-century Japanese subordination of women. That his support for women's rights was accompanied by an umbilication of woman, word, and subjectival surplus is symptomatic of his time period and does not negate his (apparently good) intentions. I neither exonerate nor berate Kyōka for being unable to transcend his own history. However, I do object to readings that seek to recuperate him as a producer of a "feminist" language, qua Kristevian poetics; that recuperation of necessity elides the phallocentric *collusion* that resides in his use of language and that for Kyōka was integral to the coming-into-being of the modern phallic subject. In a similar vein, though Enchi clearly endeavored to rethink the dangerous woman as an act of feminist resistance, as my concluding remarks in the chapters on her suggest, she was no more able than Kyōka was to conceive of the trope outside its existing sociocultural, and naturalized, confines. The obvious mutuality drawn in Nakagami's fiction between sociocultural discourses on pollution shared by women and by outcastes in early modern Japan is evidence of Nakagami's conscious attempt to resist both gendered and ethnic prejudice. But unfortunately, his attempt to acknowledge female sexuality and agency collapsed, as I noted in a discussion of his nonfiction critical writings, into a biological determinism. His well-intentioned argument (which is evocative of French feminist critiques of modern phallocentrism) against belittling women's sexuality

by merely regarding the clitoris as a "lesser penis" simultaneously makes
stark the cultural naturalization of women-as-mothers by his troping of
the "womb" as the center of female sexuality.

For all three writers, women are eroticized through word, through language. And their stories, which foreground these women eroticized in language, are often about something *inexpressible* in word, or something surplus to language that, as this book has detailed, in twentieth-century Japan has been naturalized as bound to the woman's maternalized body. These writers' texts were at times as much about language itself, about exploring the possibilities of word, as they were about the stories they told. As I detailed in the chapters on Kyōka, Mishima Yukio lauded his stylistic mastery, calling his texts "monumental," while Kobayashi Hideo wrote that " 'the sentence' is the only god of this writer."[2] To apply Nakagami's words in a different context, these are all narratives that, although to varying degree, themselves engender and destroy language and/or word. The resultant "rush" of language and image that pleases me is not, in these three writers, severed from "history." It is, I think, precisely the interplay of varied but specific historicities that I can "discover" in each of their "play" of words, a coming together of that something "beyond" in the tantalization of word, the shifting displacements of desire, and the social imaginaries that produce the specificities of those images and desires. In these writers it is thus not a "transhistorical" sweep of language toward pleasure as celebrated by Roland Barthes but the complexity of linguistic *jouissance* combined with a rootedness of the text in an historical moment that I have so enjoyed. I have been similarly pleased by non-Japanese authored narratives that share some of these attributes: the crafting of a story in an historicized juncture of erotic word, image, and cultural specificity that also informs the work of American writers such as the late Isaac Bashevis Singer or Toni Morrison.

This pleasure has nonetheless been tempered by my critical readings of the texts. Though my reading has identified Nakagami as the most "antiphallic" of the three writers, as a feminist, I feel it imperative that I also redirect my own argument. First, Nakagami's "radicalism" is as much a product of his generation as Kyōka's "mother-abject" construct and Enchi's limited feminist gesture were (that is, he was no more or less radical to his time than they were to theirs). Moreover, as my last chapter elaborated, the dominant readings of Nakagami's texts "discover" something quite different from what mine does. That I find Nakagami's rendition the most radical does not of necessity promise anything positive for women, either in terms of social imaginaries or political realities. Rather, as the narratives circulate through homosocial Japan, they have overwhelmingly been recuperated by a masculinist agenda. The celebration of "bisexuality" and "boundlessness" in Nakagami's texts has tended, as I have argued, to reinvest his texts within the context of dominant modern Japanese sex/gender politics, thereby obscuring what I have viewed as its most radical aspects.

As I have argued, alongside the critics' and readers' desire for *jouissance*, through a dissolution of their own "boundedness" and reclamation of their own leakages and viscosities, there nonetheless exists, paradoxically, a consolidation of their own phallocentrism in a movement that merely displaces, or reconfigures, the parameters of that phallocentrism without threatening phallocentrism itself. The celebration of Nakagami's radicalism resembles the manner in which "queer theory" has become trendy in Japanese cutting-edge literary and cultural studies journals. In the majority of those journal essays, queer theory has overwhelmingly been severed from its feminist origins.[3] (The term, after all, was coined by Teresa de Lauretis as a category to [temporarily] unite a heterogeneity marking the specifically different, and often antithetical, political and other issues facing gay men, lesbians, and others whose sexual practices fall outside the realm of culturally sanctioned norm.) That recently an editor of such a journal recently eager to publish essays elucidating queer theory saw no role, or necessity, for men to address feminist issues (although in discussion with me appeared to have an epiphany that men, too, can be proactively feminist) is a case in point. For most of these journals, concerned with sales and profit, "feminism" is passé, while the sexier "anything is permitted" trajectory of queer theory (here equated with [gay] male privilege and license) sells. Alongside the intellectual "liberal" sexual-liberation, anything-goes atmosphere is actually a reiteration of phallic privilege and its right to a privacy denied women.

The feminization of Heian literary convention, the (infuriating) naturalization of gendered attributes, particularly maternalism, and the (very one-sided) insistence that Japan as a nation itself was "feminized" by the occupation troops and in general in Western Orientalist imaginaries, continue to bolster an ideological environment hostile to the feminist movement.[4] Feminist scholar Ayako Kano described this epistemic constellation as one in which there is a "metonymic slide from the status of the *abstract term 'Woman' denoting a process of feminization* to the status of *'women' as historical agents*" (Kano's emphasis).[5] Thus, Kyōka becomes the producer of "feminine" language, and in turn, his narratives become quintessentially "Japanese," while Enchi's attempt at subordination is coded by a linkage of women, pollution, and Shinto animism. Strikingly, what Kano has noted as some of the specific terms informing the Japanese intellectual ahistoricization of gender in contemporary discussions (bilineality, matrilineality) also inform those very individuals' discussions of gender in Nakagami's narratives (specifically, Karatani, Asada, Suga, and others to whom I have repeatedly referred in the chapters on Nakagami). Kano writes, "the assumptions of transhistorical femininity . . . [serve] as a defense against the threat of feminism, contributing to the maintenance of the sexist status quo of gender operations within Japan."[6] The valorization of matrilineality and bisexuality in Nakagami's narratives, which collapses together with the naturalization of the twentieth-century gendered split of discursive traditions, frequently functions in much the same way: a persistent misogynist homosociality ensures the continuity of its own political interests.

That being said, there are also signs to the contrary that suggest that the same intellectuals who Kano critiqued are eager to expand the dialogue on Nakagami, and are at least open to feminist criticism, by soliciting and supporting the publication of essays by feminists on Nakagami, even when those essays included harsh criticism of what I have called the "ambivalent masculinist agenda."[7] In addition, Yomota Inuhiko has steadily sought to include the intellectual input of American feminists in various forums on Nakagami, from the first symposium following Nakagami's death onward. That I have already received two inquiries about translating this book into Japanese also suggests that there is an intellectual audience eager to disseminate and to contemplate at least the critique of this feminist. The question remains, nonetheless, of whether the arguments set forth by me and other feminists will help to denaturalize the biological determinism—or, to borrow Kano's phrase, "the metonymic slide" that equates feminization with biological femaleness—that has undergirded the fabrication, and even the subsequent destabilization, of the twentieth-century trope of the dangerous woman.

Reference Matter

Introduction

1. Although I use the words *author* and *writer*, I do not ascribe to the notion of the author as a creator with full authority over his or her text. Not only is the meaning of the text historically and culturally particular, and produced in an interaction between the reader and the material text, but it is further divorced from authorial intent by virtue of the author's and readers' unconscious. Better phrases, but for their unwieldiness in actual usage, might be "author-function" or "writing-subject."

2. After Gayle Rubin and Donna Haraway, I use *ovarian* to replace *seminal*. Thanks to Mark Driscoll for the suggestion.

3. Following Jacques Lacan, I use the word *Symbolic* (capitalized) to refer to the realm of the subject that is differentiated through, and subordinated to, a system of symbols, or signifiers, that accrue significance only in relation to other signifiers. Developmentally, entry into the Symbolic realm is heralded by the emergence of language, taboo (incest prohibition), the repression of desire, and the perception of lack (the phallus). See Lacan, *Four Fundamental Concepts*. In directing critical attention toward the signifying process, Julia Kristeva valorized what she called "the semiotic," which replaces the Imaginary in the Lacanian structure. For Kristeva, entry into the Symbolic realm requires a partial repression of the semiotic (pre-Oedipal, symbiotic, primary process realm), which remains as a sort of pulsational pressure in language. "Poetic language," for Kristeva, is the polyglot language of the novel and tends to subvert the Symbolic (by signaling the plural nature of signification and the contradictions of the unconscious). Regarding Kristeva's "poetic language," see her *Revolution in Poetic Language* and *Desire in Language*.

4. Apparently the German philosophic tradition has a long history of intellectual interaction with East Asian philosophic inquiry. See Graham Parkes's introduction to his translation of May's *Heidegger's Hidden Sources*.

5. Regarding the problematic assumptions inherent in the phrase "Western theory," see Sakai, "Return to the West." On the topic of what he calls "the culturalist scheme of questioning, which tends to reduce philosophical problems raised by Japanese or any foreign intellectuals to the matter of cultural difference" (238), he writes,

> It is very difficult to find the grounds to claim that the fact of one's birth [being born in the "West"] guarantees one's "correct" understanding of Western philosophy. Furthermore, the arbitrariness of the identity "the West" must be thoroughly scrutinized. Of course, the same can be said about "Japan" and "the East". . . . Sometimes "incorrect" comprehension can be caused by the failure on the part of the reader to take into account regional, class, political, historical, and other heterogeneities. But the diversity of those factors cannot be uniformly and exhaustively attributed to national character or nationality. We must be critical of the many sorts of social stereotyping underlying cultural essentialism, which has been increasingly favored in the name of respect for local particularity. (239)

See also May for an "unmasking" of the influence of Eastern thinkers and philosophies on Heidegger.

6. The realm of the Real refers to the material organism and its biological needs, but because these can be approached, or comprehended, only through the veil of language (the Symbolic) or experienced through the Imaginary (developmentally pre-Symbolic imagoes, images), there is no way to explicate, or "know," the Real. It is thus radically excluded, or foreclosed, to the subject, who is produced only in language (the Symbolic).

7. See Sakai's *Voices of the Past*, a brilliant negotiation between supposedly regionally bound subjectivities and between modernity and premodernity.

8. See Derrida, "Structure, Sign, and Play," in *Writing and Difference*, 278–93.

9. See my notes 10 and 11, Introduction.

10. Mitchell, "Introduction I," in Lacan, *Feminine Sexuality*, 17; Rose writes in "Introduction II" to the same text, "Castration means first of all this—that the child's desire for the mother does not refer *to* her but *beyond* her, to an object, the phallus, whose status is first imaginary (the object presumed to satisfy her desire) and then symbolic (recognition that desire cannot be satisfied)" (38; Rose's emphasis).

11. On the phallus, see Lacan, *Écrits* (especially "The Signification of the Phallus," 281–91); Lacan, *Four Fundamental Concepts*; Žižek, *Sublime Object*; Žižek, *For They Know Not*. When I use the word *phallus*, unless otherwise indicated, I mean it in this Lacanian sense. However, I want also to bracket, or question, the Freudian-Lacanian epistemology that sees the foreclosure marked by the phallus-as-lack as transcending culture. I adhere to the position that in spite of the materiality of any given body, it is not only "gendered" but also "sexed" as a *discursive* and *culturally* determined aspect of subjectivity. As Butler writes in *Bodies That Matter*,

> Clearly, the phallus operates in a privileged way in contemporary sexual cultures, but that operation is secured by a linguistic structure or position that is not independent of its perpetual reconstitution. Inasmuch as the phallus signifies, it is also always in the process of being signified and resignified. In

this sense, it is not the incipient moment or origin of a signifying chain, as Lacan would insist, but part of a reiterable signifying practice and, hence, open to resignification: signifying in ways and in places that exceed its proper structural place within the Lacanian symbolic and contest the necessity of that place. . . . If what comes to signify under the sign of the phallus are a number of body parts, discursive performatives, alternative fetishes, to name a few, then the symbolic position of "having" has been dislodged from the penis as its privileged anatomical (or non-anatomical) occasion. The phantasmatic moment in which a part suddenly stands for and produces a sense of the whole or is figured as the center of control, in which a certain kind of "phallic" determination is made by virtue of which meaning appears radically generated, underscores the very plasticity of the phallus, the way in which it exceeds the structural place to which it has been consigned by the Lacanian scheme. (89)

Lacan's insistence that the woman "is the phallus" notwithstanding, I intend that the word *phallus* be associated with a particular epistemological constellation rather than transcending it. It is only in an androcentric system that privileges the penis in relation to the phallus that woman becomes, in Lacan's words, a "symptom of man." For a critique of dominant psychoanalytic phallocentrism, see Butler's *Bodies That Matter*, especially "The Lesbian Phallus and the Morphological Imaginary," 57–91, and "Arguing with the Real," 187–222; see also Butler, "Prohibition, Psychoanalysis, and the Production of the Heterosexual Matrix," and "Subversive Bodily Acts," in *Gender Trouble*, 35–78, 79–141. See Irigaray, *Speculum*, for a feminist critique of Freud.

12. Butler, *Bodies That Matter*, 205.

13. See Kristeva, *Powers of Horror*.

14. See Butler, "Subversive Body Acts," in *Gender Trouble*, especially 79–93.

15. See Felman.

16. Butler, *Bodies That Matter*, 3.

17. Ivy, 85.

18. See Copjec for a compelling argument in favor of giving critical attention to psychological processes in historicist theory.

19. Enchi, *Masks (Onnamen)*, 57.

20. See Freud, *Beyond the Pleasure Principle*. Freud identified the death drive as coexisting alongside the libidinal drive but aimed at the cessation of animation or a return to a preanimate stasis. See also Lacan, *Four Fundamental Concepts*, and Kristeva, *Desire in Language*.

21. See Butler, *Bodies That Matter*, for a brilliant feminist challenge to the phallocentrism of both Freud's and Lacan's rendering of the phallus as a culturally transcendental signifier of foreclosure. See also my notes 10 and 11, Introduction.

22. Kristeva, *Desire in Language*. See also her *Powers of Horror*.

23. Butler, *Gender Trouble*.

24. Melanie Klein postulated that the pre-Oedipal infant believes the mother contains all (good and bad) objects within her body, including the paternal penis. See her *Love, Guilt, and Reparation* and *The Psycho-Analysis of Children*. A good critique of Klein's "materialization" of what is symbolic in Freud's notion of the phallus appears in "Introduction II" by Rose, in her translation of Lacan's *Feminine Sexuality*, 27–57.

25. Newton and Rosenfelt, xxiii.

26. There have been several sophisticated theoretical treatments of the development of modern Japanese subjectivity and literature, such as Fowler; Fujii; and Karatani, *Modern Japanese Literature*. None of these, however, sees gender as a constitutive element of subjectivity but views it rather as an aside, or as somehow separable from the process. In contrast, Yoshimoto essentializes the maternal function in the development of the subject, linked to language through the unfortunate naming of vowels as *boin* ("mother-sound") in Japanese.

27. I use *homosociality* to refer to the social relations between men, which are differentiated from those between women in part by virtue of power differentials. The term does not traditionally include "homosexuality." See Sedgwick. Sedgwick writes, "'Homosocial' is a word occasionally used in history and the social sciences, where it describes social bonds between persons of the same sex; it is a neologism, obviously formed by analogy with 'homosexual,' and just as obviously meant to be distinguished from 'homosexual.' In fact, it is applied to such activities as 'male bonding,' which may, as in our society, be characterized by intense homophobia, fear, and hatred of homosexuality" (1).

28. My understanding of how power functions is similar to that elaborated by Lisa Lowe in her *Critical Terrains*. According to Lowe, power evolves from a "dialogue . . . between Foucault's notion of discourse and the Marxist concept of hegemony, and in particular the notion of hegemony elaborated by Gramsci as the entire social process through which a particular group exercises dominance" (11). As Pierre Bourdieu has shown, however, the field of cultural production (including art and literature) stands in a distinct relation to power, one that may be inverted with regard to economic profit.

29. Butler, *Bodies That Matter*, 194.

30. See, for example, Foucault, *The Order of Things*; *The History of Sexuality*, vol. 1; and *Archaeology of Knowledge*.

31. See, for example, Karatani, "Fūkō to Nihon," 45–56.

32. Henriques et al., 115.

33. *Monogatari* ("tale fiction") literally means something like "told things" and is a vaguely defined genre often posed in opposition to the modern *shōsetsu* (usually translated as "novel"). See Miner et al., *The Princeton Companion*, for a definition of the classical *monogatari*: "Relating of things; narrative [literature]. Tales or prose narratives of various kinds, often including poems. . . .'Monogatari' has two meanings: to relate [kataru] things [mono], and a person [mono] who re-

lates (kataru). History as part of literature and oral recitation are also involved" (290). Modern *monogatari* retains a sense of the orated (the telling of old tales), either the fantastic or the domestic; attention to prose style (sometimes ornate); and lack of narrative verticality (or interiorized depth).

34. Readers interested in biographical data and more conventional literary analyses in English on these three writers are referred to the following sources. On Kyōka, see Keene's chapter 10 in *Dawn to the West*, 202–19; Napier (who also touches on Enchi and Nakagami); and Inouye's forthcoming monograph on Kyōka, *A Similitude of Blossoms*. On Enchi, see Carpenter; Ruch, "Beyond Absolution," which offers both biographical detail and analytic discussion; and Vernon, who compares Enchi's portrayals of women with archetypes of the canon and with depictions by several of her contemporaries. There is not much yet on Nakagami in English. See Napier; Harbison's introductory remarks, which preface his translation of Nakagami's "The Immortal"; and Morris, "Introduction: Towards Nakagami." For a biographical history of Nakagami's life and some synopses of major works, see Rankin.

35. See Freud, "The Uncanny." For an illuminating ethnographic study of the uncanny in modern Japanese folklore, see Ivy, especially 66–140.

36. See Ivy, especially 192–239, for a discussion of the *onnagata*.

37. The term *onnade*, literally, the "woman's hand," originally referred to one of the two Japanese phonetic syllabaries (*hiragana*) that were developed from Chinese characters to represent sound. In the Heian period (794–1185), *hiragana* became metaphorically linked to female discursive production. See Mizuta, *Monogatari to hanmonogatari no fūkei*.

38. Miner et al. distinguish *monogatari* from *setsuwa* by, in part, the fact that *setsuwa* "are usually compilations of anonymous, traditional stories" (290). See also Konishi's *Japanese Literature*, vols. 1 and 2, for archaic to early medieval developments in *setsuwa*, and in contrast to early *monogatari*. Konishi calls the tales of the *Kojiki setsuwa* (1: 160); he regards the *setsuwa* as a historical precursor to fictional *monogatari*. See 2: 308–9.

39. Kyōka by no means conceived and produced the dangerous woman in a vacuum. I recognized her, although admittedly in variant guises, for example, in the literary imaginaries of Akutagawa Ryūnosuke (1892–1927), Sakaguchi Ango (1906–55), and Tanizaki Jun'ichirō (1886–1965). Donald Keene reports that "when Tanizaki completed the first draft of 'The Tattooer,' his first thought was to show it to Izumi Kyōka" (Keene, *Dawn to the West*, 727). In Yanagita Kunio's folkloric studies, her link to motherhood as an institution was made blatant. Mountain witches, he wrote in *Yama no jinsei* (The lives of mountain people, 1941), were once-ordinary women gone mad after childbirth, who had fled the villages for the mountains where they became "feral" (92–93).

40. In "Yamauba no bishō" ("The Smile of a Mountain Witch," 1976) by Ōba Minako (1930–; sometimes written Ohba Minako), the mountain witch (danger-

ous woman) is transformed into every long-suffering, repressed wife and mother. She defies dominant cultural prohibitions against single motherhood and female sexual expression in the more realistic *Yama o hashira onna* (*Woman Running in the Mountains*, 1980) by Tsushima Yūko (b. 1947), referencing, yet defying, Yanagita's "feral mountain women."

41. On the status of Japanese women in the postwar, see Buckley, "Altered States," and Uno, "Death of 'Good Wife, Wise Mother'?" Both essays also have excellent notes for additional readings on the topic, in English and in Japanese. See also Imamura, ed., for essays on postwar changes for women and Buckley, *Broken Silence*, for interviews with ten Japanese feminists. *Broken Silence* also includes a chronology of "significant events in the recent history of Japanese women," which covers the period from Meiji 1 (1868) through 1991.

42. The concept that "woman" is not representable in language has its origins in Lacan and has been a dominant issue in some feminist studies. See Lacan, *Feminine Sexuality*; Kristeva, "Woman Can Never Be Defined"; Irigaray, *This Sex Which Is Not One*. Following Karatani, I use the word *exteriority* to mean "the other" subjective interiority and to describe the noninteriorized narration and characterizations in premodern Japanese texts. See Karatani, "One Spirit." Karatani seems to use the word following Foucault's usage in his *Archaeology of Knowledge*. See Sakai, *Voices of the Past* (11, n. 9), for a concise explication of Foucault's use of the term. I extend the term *exteriority* to include the constitutive outside of, or supplement to, the (specifically gendered) phallic subject.

43. On *kokugaku* (national studies) in English, see Harootunian, *Things Seen and Unseen*; Sakai, *Voices of the Past*; and Motoori. Origuchi Shinobu's postwar etymologies, the Yanagida Kunio "boom" of the 1960s, and ethnographies by Yamaguchi Masao and others are evidence of this trend. See Ivy on Yanagita.

44. The outcaste class has its origins in the Edo-period subclass of "untouchables." In the Edo period, there were four "classes": in descending rank, samurai, peasants, artisans, and merchants. A fifth subclass (composed of the outcastes), which now generally is lumped into one category referred to as *hisabetsu burakumin* (hereafter *burakumin* or outcaste), included at least two categories within it: the *eta* (deeply polluted) and *hinin* (nonpeople). In Edo, outcastes were identified mostly by their occupational ties to labor viewed as impure according to Buddhist and Shinto doctrines (often involving the handling of dead animals and people) and were isolated from society proper in impoverished ghettos (although their exclusive proprietorship over those occupations ensured them a sort of classed monopoly over tanning, butchering, and other necessary services). Many entertainers were classified as *hinin*. Apparently there was greater mobility into and out of the *hinin* category by beggars, criminals, entertainers, tinsmiths, and others. *Eta* had less social mobility, according to contemporary studies. Naramoto Tatsuya writes that in spite of this mobility, *hinin* had lower status than *eta* (21). The class was abolished along with the other four in Meiji, but the stigma attached to descen-

dants lingers. The fact that even today the term *hisabetsu burakumin*, which literally means "people of the quarter who suffer discrimination," is rarely vocalized, and the Edo-period derogatory terms *eta* and *hinin* are taboo, speaks volumes. Although much had already been made in the limited English-language commentary on Nakagami's status as *burakumin* as intrinsic to a reading of his narratives, it was only in the 1990s, after he died at the age of 46, that Japanese critics began to address the issue of his outcaste status in their commentaries and to link the metaphoric troping of the *roji* to actual discrimination suffered by the outcastes. Because the word *roji* by itself simply means "alley," and not necessarily those of the outcaste quarters, the connection was not overt. For information on the outcaste in modern Japan, see Hirota; in English see Hane; De Vos and Wagatsuma, eds.; and Valentine. For a controversial analysis of the origins of the *buraku*, see Ishio; and Karatani's explication, "Hisabetsu buraku no 'kigen.' " For the representation of the *buraku* in modern Japanese literature, see Watanabe's *Nihon kindai bungaku to 'sabetsu'*; and Watanabe's essay, "Sabetsu to ekurichūru." On medieval literary representations of impurity, see Marra's "The Aesthetics of Impurity: A Theatre of Defilement," in *Representations of Power*. See also Marra's "The Buddhist Mythmaking of Defilement" for a discussion of the relationship between pollution myths and female shamans in medieval Japan.

45. See Chapters 13 and 14. I argue that the violence endemic to Nakagami's work, expressed thematically and linguistically, must be understood as it relates to the notion of "difference," or the Derridean notion of a violence that lurks at the origins of (all) classifications and identifications. It is the violence of the Derridean trace—the radically "other" within—and the structure of heterogeneity within the sign, which is always both there and under erasure.

ONE   Speculum

The two epigraphs are from Tanizaki, 67–68, and Tanemura, 128–29, respectively. All translations from Japanese source texts are mine unless otherwise noted.

1. Ikuta, 178.
2. Nakamura Mitsuo, *Modern Japanese Fiction*, 82.
3. Muramatsu, *Izumi Kyōka: shōgai to geijutsu*, 124.
4. Noguchi, "Kyōka no onna," 144.
5. Inouye, *Three Tales*, 148. Inouye gets the story from Muramatsu Sadataka's *Izumi Kyōka* (1966), 38. I found virtually the same sentence on p. 14 of Muramatsu's 1954 *Izumi Kyōka: shōgai to geijutsu*.
6. I am adapting Judith Butler's term *performative* for my own purposes here. In her *Bodies That Matter*, Butler defined gender performativity as "a regularized and constrained repetition of norms. And this repetition is not performed by *a* subject; this repetition is what enables a subject and constitutes the temporal condition for the subject. This iterability implies that 'performance' is not a singular 'act' or event, but a ritualized production . . . under and through the force of prohi-

bition and taboo, with the threat of ostracism and even death controlling and compelling the shape of the production, but not . . . determining it fully in advance" (95; Butler's emphasis). For Butler, it would be the male characters' gendered actions that were truly "performative."

7. Maeda, 138.

8. Inouye, "Water Imagery."

9. Akutagawa, 200; Kawamura, 62; Mishima, "Kaisetsu."

10. See Fujii for a study of literature and the development of the modern Japanese (male) imperial subject.

11. I avoid the use of the terms *homosexual* and *heterosexual* in discussing Edo because they are inappropriate. Until a heterosexual libidinal economy is instituted, same-sex relations are a category within, not perverse to, sexual mores. See Paul Schalow's introduction to his translation of Ihara Saikaku, and Furukawa for more appropriate terms. The absence of reference in my main text to lesbianism reflects the dearth of research on the topic, which in turn reflects the dominance of phallic privilege in Edo same-sex ideologies. See the "Gei ribereshon," *Imago* special issue; some essays include discussions of, and others focus on, lesbianism.

12. See, for example, Schalow's translation of Ihara Saikaku; Mishima, *Way of the Samurai.* For contemporary discussions of gay sexuality, see the special issues "Nanshoku no ryōbun: seisa, rekishi, hyōshō," *Bungaku*; "Gei ribereshon," *Imago*.

13. Sievers, 15–16.

14. In 1873 the Meiji government outlawed and criminalized sodomy. The sodomy ordinance, however, was repealed in 1881. See Furukawa. Although the standard explanation of the establishment of heterosexualism and the repression of homosexuality in Meiji Japan attributes it to an imitation and adoption of Western homophobia, I think the issue is more complicated. Heterosexualism must have resonated in some manner with other Meiji ideological upheavals. J. Keith Vincent sees its origins as inextricable from Meiji *linguistic* reforms and debates (various conversations; Vincent's in-progress doctoral dissertation promises to deal with this in detail). I think it also must be related to changing configurations of "private" and "public"; *covert* homosexual activities are tolerated in modern Japan (thus the issue of power is also important—who is permitted "privacy"). For a large number of men, engaging in same-sex relations does not necessarily mean that those men identify themselves as gay, especially when they also enjoy sexual relations with women. The question of sexuality as intrinsic to identity in modern Japan is a complicated one that begs for in-depth study.

15. Gender ideology within any nation relates to the economic and political system by which that nation functions. I use *ideology* here as defined by Newton and Rosenfelt as "not a set of deliberate distortions imposed on us from above, but a complex and contradictory system of representations (discourse, images, myths) through which we experience ourselves in relation to each other and to the social structures in which we live" (xix). For Japan and other nations, male centrality is inscribed and produced through all the varied social discourses (philoso-

phy, religion, science, politics, and so on) that originate in and reproduce a system of economic and political privilege based on exclusion and inclusion. Moreover, although ideology (including that which produces notions of gender) may operate in economic service to dominant classes, as ideologies circulate the process of reproduction assumes a degree of autonomy from both economic and political functions. See also Henriques et al.

16. Kasahara, "Kyōka ni okeru 'haha naru mono,' " 312.

17. On the abject as eroticized, see Kristeva, *Powers of Horror*. In Chapter 3 I discuss this in greater detail. The reader should be advised that I use quotation marks around the word *perverse* to mean sexual behavior and arousal judged "perverse" according to dominant sociocultural norms; it is not my judgment.

18. See, for example, Yoshimura, *Izumi Kyōka no sekai*; Waki's Jungian analysis, *Gensō no ronri*; and Maeda's interpretation of the serpents of Kyōka's work as symbolic of sexual taboo.

19. I borrow the term *selfsame* from Cixous and Clément.

T W O   Leaky Archetypes

1. Kyōka, *Kōya hijiri*, 417, 418. Hereafter page numbers will follow quotations in parentheses within text. The narrative is almost entirely embedded; the primary narrator relates a tale told him, and opening and closing quotation marks are used somewhat capriciously. Sometimes conversations embedded within the embedded narration are marked with parentheses. I have reproduced punctuation marks as exactly as possible to match the original style of the quoted passages.

2. Inouye, "Water Imagery," 67; Kyōka, "Kechō." Hereafter page numbers from "Kechō" will follow quotations in parentheses within text.

3. *Torioi* were beggars who played the samisen and sang for handouts. *Torioi*, and thus Omachi, belonged to the Edo-period *hinin* subclass of untouchables. It was believed that pollution could be passed from a *hinin* or *eta* through physical touch. See n. 44 of the Introduction for more information and sources on *hisabetsu burakumin* (outcastes).

4. Kyōka, *Yōken kibun*, 644. Hereafter page numbers will follow quotations in parentheses within text.

5. Omachi relates her attempt at purification by sword to the successful self-cleansing of the early Edo Jōdo (Pure Land) Buddhist priest, Yūten. Legend has it that Yūten thrust the sword of the Fire Deity, Fudō Myōo (Sanskrit, *Acala*), down his throat to vomit "bad" blood, which had hindered his memorization of the sutras.

6. The idealization is clearer in the Japanese text, which uses honorifics for Ren's description of his mother. A sample of the Japanese, from the translated passage: "Okkasan no kedakai utsukushii, tanomoshii, ontō na, soshite sukoshi yasete oide no, kami o tabanete shittori shite irassharu kao o mite" (413–14).

7. See Lacan, "Subversion of the Subject and Dialectic of Desire," in *Écrits*. Let

me reiterate that I question the androcentrism that posits a culturally transcendental connection between the penis and the phallus; in other epistemological systems other foreclosures might replace, or displace, the phallus as the transcendental signifier—or any unitary transcendental signifier. See the Introduction, for example.

8. On the *genbun'itchi* movement and Meiji-period debates on narrative, see, for example, Tsubouchi, "Shōsetsu shinzui" (1885–86), and "Shōsetsu sanha" (1890); Futabatei, "Shōsetsu sōron" (1886), "Yo ga genbun'itchi no yurai" (1906), and "Esuperanto no hanashi" (1906).

9. Harootunian, *Things Seen and Unseen*, 411.

10. Ibid., 412.

11. Woman can be both fetishized and yet partial-object. Following Freud, the fetishized object is something (often a body part or an object) that stands in for the "lacking" penis; it transforms the threat of lack into eroticized presence. But of course it is only substitution. See Freud, "Fetishism." Fetishism is not the substitution of a whole or presence for a lack, but always a lack (the substituted object, which stands in for the phallus, that is, lack) replacing a lack.

12. For the imaginary in Yanagita, see, for example, his *Yama no jinsei; Imo no chikara*; and *Mikokō*.

13. Harootunian, *Things Seen and Unseen*, 413. I don't think, however, that Japan has ever "fully assimilated" to the "requirements" of Western epistemology, and I would rephrase this specific statement by Harootunian to foreground Japan's own imperial epistemological requirements.

14. Tanemura, 126.

15. There is a chapter break between the two paragraphs that I have omitted.

16. Kyōka, *Nanchi shinjū*, and "Ehon no haru." Hereafter page numbers from these narratives by Kyōka will follow quotations in parentheses within text. In medieval and early modern Japan, the serpent-deity is steadfastly gendered female. See Chapter 12 for more on these legends. The snake-woman tale has many variants and can be traced back to the earliest Japanese writings. It appears in Ueda Akinari's "Jasei no in." Earlier versions include those in Ogihara and Kōnosu, eds., *Kojiki*, 201–4, English translation by Philippi, 222–23; in Mabuchi et al., eds., *Konjaku monogatari shū*, 487–92, English translation by Ury, *Tales of Times Now Past*, 93–96; in Inoue and Ōsone, eds., *Ōjōden hokkegenki* 217–19; in "Dōjōji" in Keene, *Twenty Plays*, 238–63. For an intriguing discussion of the snake-woman in *nō*, see Susan Klein, "When the Moon Strikes the Bell." Klein argues that the female-body-as-serpent is a phallicized and fetishized body that suppresses the amorphous gender of the serpent. See also Chapter 12, nn. 31 and 33.

17. Muramatsu, *Izumi Kyōka jiten*, 108.

18. On the *yamamba*, see Viswanathan, also Ōba and Mizuta.

19. See Yanagita's *zenshū* (collected works) for recordings of regional folk tales and lore.

20. Yang Guifei was a favored concubine of the Chinese Tang emperor Xuan Zong. Xuan Zong erected a temple, the Huaqing gong, on Li Mountain in north-

west China, Shaanxi Province, which was known for its hot springs. According to the poetic account that was part of the Heian canon, written in Chinese by Bai Juyi, Xuan Zong became enamored of Yang Guifei when he saw her bathing in one of the Li Mountain hot springs. Later he neglected his kingdom because of his obsession with her. An English translation with the title "A Song of Unending Sorrow" appears in Birch, ed.

21. Gunji and Bandō, 9–10.

22. Ibid., 12. A sample of Gunji's rambling contribution to the *taidan* follows. The topic of the first sentence is "a phantasmatic visual perspective [*mugenteki shiten*]":

> I think that in general all Easterners possess that perspective to some degree. For example, a few days ago I saw the Korean movie, *Why Did Dharma Go East?* Although it was only two hours long, it seemed longer—because it was filmed from the perspective of a bird perched on a branch of a tree on a cliff looking down on human activities. Westerners lack that perspective. People over there [*mukō*] can see things only from their own perspective as human beings. Therefore they are not good at looking at things from a different perspective.
>
> Japanese people [*shomin*] can see in several directions simultaneously, as though they had the eyes of dragonflies. This sort of perspective shares nothing with the absolutism stemming from the Westerner's law of conceptualism [*hassōhō*]. In short, that is because this perspective [that of the Japanese] is illogical. Whether by camera or onstage, Japanese can easily shift their perspective to view the human world from the eyes of an "other world" [*ikai*]. *Ukiyo-e* [Edo-period paintings] such as those of Hiroshige [Andō Hiroshige, Edo *ukiyo-e* artist, 1797–1858] often took the perspective of hawks', or kites' bird's-eye views. Through the eyes of those sorts of birds human beings could look down upon the famed pictorial vistas of Edo. It seems that is Japanese people's perception. (12)

23. Tanemura, 133.

24. I appropriate the term coined by Žižek, "the national Thing," as does Ivy, 6.

25. Tayama, 46.

26. Karatani, *Modern Japanese Literature*. See especially his chapters "The Discovery of Landscape" and "The Discovery of Interiority," 11–44, 45–75.

27. Ibid., 69.

28. See Karatani, *Modern Japanese Literature*.

29. See Chapters 4 and 5 for more on narration in Kyōka's texts, which is consistently "deferred" and "transferred" between speaking/narrating subjects.

30. Takahashi, 106.

31. See Nagaike. The comparison is made over and over, especially in more recent studies. See, for example, Nakamura Mitsuo, "Kyōka to Yanagida Kunio," and Kamata.

32. Harootunian, *Things Seen and Unseen*, 417.

33. The use of the Lacanian term *the Real* is mine, not Harootunian's. I do not mean to suggest that Edo notions of the Real were commensurate with those of the twentieth century. In twentieth-century Japan the Real becomes absolutely alienated and unattainable. In Edo, although it perhaps was not definable, it was believed nonetheless to be accessible through "right" word (vocalization). (See Harootunian, *Things Seen and Unseen*; see also my Chapter 5.) I use the word to refer to the structure of *a* foreclosure and not to designate a specific foreclosure. Both Edo nativists and *gesaku* stylists, and both Meiji ethnographers and naturalists, believe that something has been "lost," and a movement follows to recuperate that perceived loss. That which constitutes the realm of loss—a desire for something surplus to the Symbolic, or modes of worded signification (whether that surplus is understood as constitutive of the Symbolic or as temporarily "lost" to it)— is what I mean to designate with my somewhat unorthodox use of the Lacanian term.

34. Harootunian, *Things Seen and Unseen*, 414.

35. See Chapters 4 and 5 for a more detailed analysis of Kyōka's discursive style.

36. Ivy writes, "The figure of the other returns to reinstitute the distinction [between ethnography and literature] now made unstable and tenuous. And this complicity is unthinkable outside the interlinked struggles about literary authority, speech and writing, and the status of representable reality in twentieth-century Japan" (67).

37. Yanagita, *Yama no jinsei*, 92–93; 94. See also his *Imo no chikara* and *Mikokō*.

38. Žižek, *Tarrying with the Negative*, 165.

39. Cixous and Clément, 39.

THREE   Perverse Maternity: Blood from the Breast

The epigraphs are from Kristeva, *Tales of Love*, 76, and Kasahara, "Kyōka ni okeru 'haha naru mono,' " 312.

1. See, for example, Fujimoto; Kasahara, "Kyōka ni okeru 'haha naru mono' "; Waki, "Shisha ga sumu yama—Kyōka no fuamiri romansu"; Yoshimura, "Kyōka/ Jun'ichirō no haha compurekusu"; and Yoshimura, "Kyōka bungaku ni okeru bosei to josei—erosu no botai to shite."

2. See Freud, "Wit and Its Relation to the Unconscious." Jokes, wrote Freud, are formed and understood through primary-process discharge by virtue of their use of analogy, condensation, displacement, symbolism, and metonymy.

3. See Kristeva, *Desire in Language*.

4. See Derrida, *Of Grammatology* and *Writing and Difference*.

5. On *jouissance*, see Kristeva, *Powers of Horror*, especially 9–10; Lacan, "Subversion of the Subject and Dialectic of Desire," in *Écrits*, 292–325. In her *Powers of Horror*, Kristeva writes, "Having provided itself with an *alter ego*, the Other no longer has a grip on the three apices of the triangle where subjective ho-

mogeneity resides; and so, it jettisons the object into an abominable real, inaccessible except through *jouissance*" (9; Kristeva's emphasis); "When I *seek* (myself) *lose* (myself), or experience *jouissance*—then 'I' is heterogeneous. Discomfort, unease, dizziness stemming from an ambiguity that, through the violence of a revolt *against*, demarcates a space out of which signs and objects arise" (10; Kristeva's emphasis).

6. Žižek, *Tarrying with the Negative*, 188.

7. When I say "the transcendental prose of Natsume Sōseki" (1867–1916), I mean that his writing was already "modern" by virtue of the phallic nature of his characters' subjectivities (and thus the system that poses the phallus as transcendental signifier was already in place), and that this is related to the type of narrative issues—modernity, the past, the subject, the father—that so dominate his writings.

8. Žižek, *Tarrying with the Negative*, 202.

9. Kristeva, *Powers of Horror*, 1–2.

10. Butler, *Gender Trouble*, 80.

11. Omachi is also an "outcaste composite." Although, as explained in n. 44 in the Introduction, the categories of *hinin* and *eta* were separated in Edo, in Kyōka's *Yōken kibun* Omachi refers to herself using both appellations interchangeably. See *Yōken kibun*, 678. She warns Seisaburō that he will be tainted by "a *hinin*'s blood, an *eta*'s blood."

12. On the relationship between confession and modernity, see Karatani, *Modern Japanese Literature*, and Foucault, *History of Sexuality*, vol. 1.

13. Karatani, *Modern Japanese Literature*, 77.

14. Ibid., 136–37.

15. See Melanie Klein, "Oedipus Complex," and "Mourning." An ambivalent, eroticized view of the mother is evocative of her presymbolic (pre-Oedipal) image as described by Melanie Klein. Klein wrote that before separation and individuation, the infant believes the mother encompasses all good and bad objects within her body. The maternal dimension not only would encompass both categories of sacred and erotic but also would facilitate their expressions. The infant, holds Klein, creates two imagoes: the ideal, perfect object to satisfy his or her craving for help and security, and the bad, threatening object to punish him or her for aggressive impulses. "To this frightening picture of his mother's 'inside' [which is seen as injured and poisoned and containing the father's penis]—which co-exists with the picture of his mother as a source of all goodness and gratification [centered on the breast]—correspond fears about the inside of his own body. Outstanding among these is the infant's fear of internal attack by a dangerous mother, father or combined parental figure" ("Oedipus Complex," 411). Klein postulates a position called the "depressive position," constituted by "persecution (by 'bad' objects) and the characteristic defenses against it, on the one hand, and a yearning for the loved ('good') object, on the other" ("Mourning," 348), which characterizes infantile defense against perceived loss.

16. *Yōken kibun* is not the only text of Kyōka's in which outcastes appear. The outcaste figures may also be male, such as the beggars of "Hebikui" (1898), and peripheral to the narrative, as is the organ grinder who appears in "Kechō." Women of various marginalities are common major figures, such as the entertainer of *Teriha kyōgen* (1896) or the women in "Ryūtandan" (1896) and in the seven-part saga, "Ichinomaki," "Ninomaki," "Sannomaki," "Shinomaki," "Gonomaki," "Rokunomaki," and "Chikainomaki" (1896–97). For more on marginal characters in Kyōka's work, see Watanabe, *Nihon kindai bungaku to "sabetsu."*

17. Yomota, "Ikai no henyō," 230.

18. Kasahara, "Mori, aruiwa gensō kūkan," 100. Kasahara does not limit the meaning of *forest* (*mori*) to a literal forest but intends that the word refer to phantasmatic topoi in which the sacred and the taboo come together, linked to the archaic meaning of the word.

19. On the breast as original object (predating the penis/phallus as symbol) and as the source of all good, see n. 15, this chapter, on Melanie Klein.

20. Foucault, *History of Sexuality*, 1: 47.

21. In regard to "modern *monogatari* chronicling sexual 'perversion,' " I am thinking of Tanizaki Jun'ichirō, Kawabata Yasunari (1899–1972), Akutagawa Ryūnosuke, for example, as well as the popular fictions by Edogawa Rampo (1894–1965). On hygiene and women, see Narita.

22. Noguchi, "Kyōka no onna," 144; Foucault, *History of Sexuality*, 1: 54.

23. Tanemura, 130.

24. Kristeva, *Powers of Horror*, 3, 54, 55.

25. Grosz, 203. Building on feminist theory by Kristeva in her *Powers of Horror*, Irigaray's *This Sex Which Is Not One*, and Cixous and Clément, as well as on the philosophic work on the body in Deleuze and Guattari, Grosz has argued that femaleness is inscribed with a greater complexity than the notion of female unrepresentability might suggest. In Grosz's words, "It is problematic to see the body as a blank, passive page, a neutral 'medium' or signifier for the inscription of a text. . . . The specific modes of materiality of the 'page'/body must be taken into account: one and the same message, inscribed on a male or a female body, does not always or even usually mean the same thing or result in the same text" (156). Grosz reconfigures the paradigm of female as "lack" into a "lack of self-containment," arguing persuasively that in Western phallocentrism femaleness has been constituted in part through a cultural projection of the (uncontrollable and uncontainable, the abject) bodily secretions and waste products (notably excluding sperm) entirely onto the female body.

F O U R   *Michiyuki* Toward *Jouissance*

1. Almost every essay and monograph in the extensive body of secondary work on Kyōka addresses the two issues of tradition and "style." Although most critics recognize that Kyōka was *different* from his Edo predecessors, many insist

that his prose embodies a purely "Japanese" sentiment culled from premodern aesthetics. Some of these studies will be dealt with directly in this part.

2. Nakanishi, 124, 117.

3. Ibid., 121, 123–24.

4. Karatani, "One Spirit," 619.

5. *Makurakotoba* (pillow-words) are words or phrases that when enunciated or scripted are intended to bring to mind by association other (unenunciated and unscripted) words—often places. Here is a standard definition of *makurakotoba* from Brower and Miner: "A conventional epithet or attribute for a word; it usually occupies a short, 5-syllable line and modifies a word, usually the first, in the next line. Some pillow-words are unclear in meaning; those whose meanings are known function rhetorically to raise the tone and to some degree also function as images" (508).

6. These are three giants of the Japanese premodern canon. Murasaki Shikibu (?–?1014) is the (assumed) author of the celebrated Heian-period *Genji monogatari* (*The Tale of Genji*), English translation by Edward G. Seidensticker; Zeami (or Kanze Motokiyo, ca. 1364–ca. 1443) is credited with having refined *nō* to its highest level in the late fourteenth and early fifteenth centuries; and Matsuo Bashō (1644–94) is perhaps the most highly acclaimed master of Japanese verse. See Miner et al. for an introduction to the literary achievements of all three.

7. Sakai, *Voices of the Past*, 178, 179.

8. Ibid., 181, 183.

9. Konishi, *Japanese Literature*, 2: 99.

10. Noguchi, "Izumi Kyōka kenkyū annai," 393. See my n. 5 (this chapter) on the *makurakotoba*.

11. Donald Keene, *Dawn to the West*, 204.

12. Kobayashi, 219.

13. On Meiji punctuation, see n. 28, this chapter.

14. On Kyōka's movement toward independence from then-dominant literary trends, see Noguchi's "Izumi Kyōka no hito to sakuhin."

15. Kyōka, *Kōya hijiri*, 411. See Muramatsu's n. 26, chapter 16.

16. *Kokinwakashū* (ca. 920). The first of twenty-one official Heian poetry collections compiled by Imperial order. See Earl Miner et al. for an introduction to the anthology.

17. See, for example, Kasahara, *Izumi Kyōka: Bi to erosu no kōzō*, and "Mori, aruiwa gensō kūkan"; Noguchi, "Izumi Kyōka no hito to sakuhin," "Izumi Kyōka kenkyū annai," and "Kyōka no onna"; Watanabe, *Gen'ei no chōki*; and Tanemura, "Suichūka hengen."

18. See, for example, any of the various texts on Kyōka by Muramatsu Sadataka. See also Matsubara; Kojima; Takahashi; and Fujimoto.

19. Takahashi, 106.

20. Yanagita, "Haiku Kyōka kan," 201–3.

21. Itō, 82.

22. Akutagawa, 200. The "genius" is Zeami, credited with having surpassed his father, Kanami, in his contribution to the development of the *nō* theater. See n. 6, this chapter.

23. Tanizaki, 67–68.

24. On Muromachi "multimedia" performative and narrative genres, see Ruch, "Medieval Jongleurs" and "Other Side of Culture."

25. Sakai, *Voices of the Past*, 149, 156.

26. Although discussions of *onnagata* should not reduce *onnagata* performances to Japanese counterparts of American and European drag, Butler's following comment on the "drag ball" of *Paris Is Burning* has some resonance for *onnagata* performance: "We witness and produce the phantasmatic constitution of a subject. . . . [The subject] is constituted in and through the iterability of its performance, a repetition which works at once to legitimate and delegitimate the realness norms by which it is produced" (*Bodies That Matter*, 131). Because *onnagata* in the modern period are more mainstream than they are subversive, they provide, in Butler's words, a "ritualistic release for a heterosexual economy that must constantly police its own boundaries against the invasion of queerness, and . . . this displaced production and resolution of homosexual panic actually fortifies the heterosexual regime in its self-perpetuating task" (*Bodies That Matter*, 126). On the *onnagata*, see Ivy, 212–39.

27. Kyōka, "Tenshu monogatari."

28. Hirata, "Modern Japanese Literature and Punctuation." See Hirata's "Kindai bungaku to pankuchuēshon" and "Kaiwabun to ji no bun." See also Sakai's *Voices of the Past*. That the Japanese language has no counterpart to the past perfect (which delineates narrative textuality in Western modern convention) meant, of course, that Japanese narrative had to use other means for marking indirect narration. Many premodern literary and performative genres used narration in such a manner that the "speaking subject" was ambiguous and/or changeable; in *nō*, for example, the chorus may narrate as an observer, as the protagonist, or as a "multiple" speaking subject. As Edward Fowler has shown, the linguistic disposition against clear narrative distinction has affected modern Japanese narration.

29. Ikuta, 177.

30. See Mishima, "Kaisetsu."

31. The word *itoyū* (literally, "thread-play") may refer either to wispy clouds of late autumn or to (visible) water vapor (heat waves) rising from the warming earth in spring. It is thus evocative of changing seasons and something ephemeral and insubstantial.

32. Mishima, "Kaisetsu," 559–60.

33. Miner, ix.

34. Kyōka, *Kōya hijiri*, 399.

35. Mishima, *Bunshō tokuhon*, 447. The quote is as translated by Ueda Makoto, *Modern Japanese Writers*, 252. What Ueda translated as "the subject"

("hitotsu no mono," and "hitotsu hitotsu no mono") are more literally rendered "a single thing" and "things singularly one after another."

36. See Fowler.

F I V E   Language and Bodies; or, Never Write Words on Sitting Cushions

1. See, for example, Karatani, "Nihon seishin bunseki 1." For a discussion of the Japanese philosopher Watsuji Tetsurō (1889–1960) on subjectivity, see Sakai, "Return to the West." There is no single equivalent in Japanese for all the possible contexts in which the English word *subject* is appropriate. Many different Japanese words translate into the English word *subject*. In his *Voices of the Past*, for example, Sakai differentiates between *shudai* (theme / thematic subject); *shugo* (propositional subject); *shukan* (epistemological subject), and *shutai* (agent of action).

2. Karatani, "Nihon seishin bunseki 1." Some brief comments on the same issue are available in English translation, in the afterword to Katatani's *Modern Japanese Literature*, 187–88. The *shishōsetsu*, as written by Shiga Naoya, effaces rather than expresses narrative interiority. The paradigmatic narrative subject as envisioned by earlier naturalists thus soon shifts away from the "Western" model. See Fowler's chapter on Shiga.

3. As discussed in my Introduction, here, and throughout the book, by the "Real" I am referring to the structure of the Lacanian term, which denotes that which is *foreclosed* to the Symbolic order, but not necessarily to the "content" of that foreclosure. Although the idea of what would constitute the realm of the Real should not be homogenized over the stretch of time between Edo and Meiji, I use the term, albeit with some license.

4. Mishima, *Bunshō tokuhon.*

5. In a short essay, Ann Sherif queries the modern use of these gendered terms but suggests, quite differently from me, that they may be useful critical terms when applied with an awareness of their metaphoric, rather than sexed, meanings.

6. Mishima, *Bunshō tokuhon*, 444, 446–48.

7. Ibid., 422.

8. See Mizuta, "Josei no jikogatari to monogatari." Like Mishima, however, Mizuta seems to employ the binarism of public and private as it exists in the twentieth century in her discussion of Heian. I thank Nagahara Yutaka for drawing my attention to the need to differentiate clearly between modern and premodern notions of public and private. I will take up the issue of the terms *public* and *private* in Chapter 7. Mizuta's use of the word *gender* is sometimes different from mine. Following Judith Butler and other contemporary feminist theorists, I have used the word *gender* to mark the culturally inscribed "performance" of one's "sexed body." See Butler, *Gender Trouble* and *Bodies That Matter*. Mizuta seems to have used it more loosely, as was once common, in relation to both the culturally inscribed gendered performances and sexed bodies.

9. Mizuta, "Josei no jikogatari to monogatari," 66.

10. Ibid., 65–66, 66.

11. Ibid., 66.

12. See Chapter 6, n. 3. There is an annotated English translation of the *Eiga monogatari* by McCullough and McCullough, *A Tale of Flowering Fortunes*. *Eiga monogatari* represents a departure from gendered genre, because it is a supposedly "historical" supplement to the Heian-period fictions, yet is written in Japanese, not Chinese. The McCulloughs attribute this to the female sex of the author; it is possible, of course, that there were other reasons as well for its being written in Japanese, such as degree of "authority" as historical document and its "fictional" flavor.

13. Miller argues that the inclusion of women's "voices" in the Japanese canon is one reason for what she calls "gender-independent co-subjectivity" and "non-logocentrism." Her essay is an example of a critique that both reads premodern female-authored writings as though they were narratives of interiorized subjectivity, or "voice," and reiterates the twentieth-century feminization of polysemy. As all her sources for Japanese texts are in English translation, her essay provokes another question, of the degree of collusion, or coproduction, of these ways of reading Japanese texts within the American academy.

14. Karatani, "Nationalism and *écriture*."

15. Ibid.

16. The *Man'yōshū* was compiled in the late Nara (712–93) or early Heian (794–1186) period.

17. See Sakai, *Voices of the Past*, and Foucault, *The Order of Things*, especially pt. 1 on the premodern epistemological relation between sign and referent.

18. Harootunian, *Things Seen and Unseen*, 127, 136. Hirata, for example, criticized *The Tale of Genji* as depicting degenerate times; Ōhira valorized the *Man'yōshū* above *The Tale of Genji*.

19. See Sherif.

20. Even for Norinaga, *The Tale of Genji* was only one of several archaic texts (including the *Kojiki* and the *Man'yōshū*) that he posed against then-contemporary narratives and poetry that he called vulgar and corrupt and replete with "wrong words" and "false emotions" (Harootunian, *Things Seen and Unseen*, 81, 106–8).

21. Harootunian, *Things Seen and Unseen*, 95.

22. Najita, "On Culture and Technology in Postmodern Japan," and Harootunian, "Visible Discourses/Invisible Ideologies."

23. See Ivy.

24. See Konishi, *Japanese Literature*, 2: 337; see also Noguchi, "Substratum."

25. I am indebted to Karatani Kōjin for pointing out the temporal and historical, constitutively necessary codependence of "female voice," modern subjectivity, and the female emancipation movement. Only after women are freed "as people too" (when humanity is seen to include women in a different organization of like-

ness) from their teleologized premodern subjectivity (by which the category of *man* excludes women) can a movement to address inequities begin.

26. See Sakai, *Voices of the Past*.

27. Karatani, "One Spirit."

28. Miyoshi, *Off Center*, 18.

29. Harootunian, *Things Seen and Unseen*, 73.

30. Sakai, *Voices of the Past*, 91, 92.

31. The Edo subject was "*juzoku*" (subject to; subordinated to). See Harootunian, *Things Seen and Unseen*. On p. 83 he writes that, according to nativist Norinaga,

> Just as the imperial descendants made the august intention of the heavenly deities their own, there could never be a separation between the divine age and the present. The Way always existed in the land and among its people as a condition indistinguishable from the divine creation and the subsequent ordering of things, especially the trust of governance invested in the imperial lineage. . . . Since all humans acquired life from the creation deities, they knew well the deeds [*waza*] that their bodies were supposed to perform. . . . In the imperial age, all people, from high to low, had no trouble in making the "great intention of the emperor" their own.

32. Harootunian, *Things Seen and Unseen*, 74.

33. Shinoda, 39–40.

34. Taneda.

35. See Harootunian, *Things Seen and Unseen*, and Sakai, *Voices of the Past*.

36. As Sakai has eloquently argued, the parodists sought (yet ultimately failed) to challenge dominant discourses on subjectivity and community through the defamiliarization of the classics.

37. See the essays listed in the bibliography by Tsubouchi and Futabatei. In English, see Fowler; Karatani, *Modern Japanese Literature*; and Miyoshi, "The New Language," in his *Accomplices of Silence*, 3–37.

38. See Karatani, *Modern Japanese Literature*.

39. Mishima, "Kaisetsu," 561. *Medium* is written in *katakana*.

40. Konishi, *Japanese Literature*, 1: 207.

41. Kasahara, *Izumi Kyōka*, 5.

42. Harootunian, *Things Seen and Unseen*, 72.

43. Ibid., 71.

44. Noguchi, "Izumi Kyōka no hito to sakuhin," 15–16.

45. Kasahara, *Izumi Kyōka*, 5–6.

46. Žižek, *Tarrying with the Negative*, 189.

47. *Iki* is most well known as the Edo-period "aesthetic," thanks to its "discovery," and thus modern invention, by Kyōka's younger contemporary Kuki Shūzō (1888–1941). See his *Iki no kōzō*; see also Pincus. On Edo-period literature pertaining to the commodification of women, see Griswold; and Ariga, "Dephalli-

cizing Women." Thanks to my student Katharine Anne Farrell for helping me to find the right words to best describe *iki.*

48. Foucault, *History of Sexuality,* 1: 21.

49. Ibid., 1: 152.

50. Ibid., 1: 48.

51. Karatani, *Modern Japanese Literature,* 89.

52. Harootunian, *Things Seen and Unseen,* 417.

SIX   Vengeance

Essays culled from or incorporated into the material on Enchi have been previously published as "Bound by Blood" (also published in Japanese as "Chi no sokubaku"), and "The Fictional Works of Enchi Fumiko."

1. Enchi, *Masks,* 57. Originally published in Japanese as *Onnamen.* Further references are to the translation, and pagination follows quotations parenthetically within text.

2. An English translation of "Nisei no en shūi" is published with the title "Love in Two Lives: The Remnant." See also Bargen's essay "Translation and Reproduction."

3. Enchi, the *Namamiko monogatari,* 289. Further pagination follows quotations parenthetically within text. The subtitle referred to is *Eiga monogatari shūi. Shūi* is often translated as "gleanings." There is an annotated English translation of the *Eiga monogatari* by McCullough and McCullough, *A Tale of Flowering Fortunes.* See n. 12 in Chapter 5. Interestingly, the *Eiga monogatari* was a "history" (i.e., "public" text) that was written by a woman in Japanese, not Chinese. (See McCullough and McCullough, trans., 9–10.) This departure from the conventions of gendered genre (by virtue of authorial sexed difference) surely informed Enchi's choice of the *Eiga monogatari* as a source text in the creation of her *Namamiko monogatari.*

4. Enchi, *Onnazaka.* Translated into English with the title *The Waiting Years.* All quotes are from the English translation, and page numbers follow quotations parenthetically within text.

5. See Karatani, *Modern Japanese Literature,* for an analysis of the "discovery of interiority" in modern Japanese fiction.

6. Ohba, "The Smile of a Mountain Witch," 201. Ōba's name is sometimes, as by the translators of this short story, romanized as Ohba.

7. Etō, 413.

8. One finds such essentialist comments frequently in commentaries on Enchi's work. See, for example, Etō, and Nakagami's section on Enchi in his serialized "Monogatari no keifu." The notion that Enchi's female characters embody an ahistorical "female principle" is also implicit in the common comparisons of her female figures to those of Tanizaki and Kyōka. See, for example, Saeki.

9. She won the Noma Literary Prize in 1957, the Joryū Literature Prize in

1966, the Tanizaki Jun'ichirō Award in 1969, the Distinguished Cultural Achievement Award in 1970, and the Grand Literary Prize of Japan in 1972 and was honored with the highest possible award, the Order of Cultural Merit, presented by the emperor, in 1985. Such honors notwithstanding, in Tokyo in 1995–96 virtually none of her books were available even in the largest bookstores (an exception being her translation of *The Tale of Genji*). Whereas one can still easily obtain Kyōka's or Tanizaki's versions of dangerous women, Enchi's must be sought out at used bookstores. See Ariga, "Literature and the Institution," and "Text Versus Commentary," on how the Japanese education system supports phallocentric (she calls it patriarchal, following Teresa L. Ebert's definition of patriarchy) agendas in the interpretation of literary texts.

SEVEN   (Un)reproductivities: Maternity and Sex

1. Buckley, "Altered States," 347. See also Uno, "Death of 'Good Wife, Wise Mother'?"

2. For historical information and discussions of this epistemic constellation, see, for example, Buckley, "Altered States;" Uno, "Death of 'Good Wife, Wise Mother'?"; Bernstein, ed.; Imamura; and Vogel. Many essays in both the English supplements and the Japanese language issues of *U.S.-Japan Women's Journal / Nichibei josei jānaru* also address this construct.

3. Enchi, "Hebi no koe," 365. Hereafter page numbers follow quotations parenthetically in text.

4. Konishi, *Japanese Literature*, 1: 13.

5. Uno, "Household Division of Labor," 40.

6. Enchi, "Fuyumomi," 383. Hereafter pagination follows quotations parenthetically within text.

7. Irigaray, *This Sex Which Is Not One*, 180.

8. Ibid.

9. Enchi, "Enchantress," 349. References are to the translation, and hereafter page numbers follow quotations parenthetically within text.

10. I am indebted to Mizuta Noriko for this insight into Tomo's deathbed proclamation.

11. As translated and quoted in Niwa, 71, 72.

12. Imai, 52.

13. See Uno, "Household Division of Labor," and on pre-Meiji peasant women, see Walthall.

14. See Pincus, on Kuki Shūzō, for a Meiji / Taisho notion of Edo-period *iki*.

15. See Griswold.

16. Ariga, "Dephallicizing Women," 576.

17. I place quotations around the terms *public* and *private* to highlight their historical variability. As Marx wrote, it is only with the (historical) production of the individual that the terms *public* and *private* take on their modern signification,

and this notion was then naturalized and projected retrospectively into the past. See his *Grundrisse*. Though the Edo period is often called early modern and was a consumer society, the notion of the individual, and thus public and private, was not the same as that of post-Meiji Japan (although women functioned as objects of exchange between men in both Edo and Meiji/Taisho). See also Chapter 5, especially n. 8.

As the following discussion shows, I am also intentionally putting the conventional parameters of "public" and "private" into question here. It is my conviction that in Japan, the gendered (and sexed) aspects of that specific binarism (in the twentieth century) have been, and continue to be, marshaled to antifeminist and antihomosexual ends. Regarding the structure of heterosexualism in modern Japan, see Karatani, "Fūkō to Nihon." Karatani has argued that it is in part the decentralized character of authority in modern Japanese society that diffuses political action (including that which characterizes identity as a homosexual subject in the West); there is no resistance to "theory from without" because there is no "subject" per se to resist. The dissemination of power in Japan closely resembles Foucault's model. In Karatani's words, "In Japan, the center of power [*kenryoku*] is already empty. But that in itself is power; possibly the true essence of power itself" (56). J. Keith Vincent brought this essay of Karatani's to my attention, and I recommend the reader to Vincent's provocative and innovative rethinking of the public/private binarism in relation to coming out and homosexuality in Japan. In his typescript English version, Vincent writes, "Because of this peculiar fit which Foucault's model made with the *dominant* discourses on sex and power in Japan, it has tended to be mobilized here [in Japan] *in opposition* to gay activism, both within the gay community and without" (12; Vincent's emphasis).

18. On the term *homosocial*, see Sedgwick; see also my n. 27 in the Introduction.

19. See Vogel for a study of values and norms among middle-class postwar Japanese families.

20. See Vincent.

21. Butler, *Gender Trouble*, 139.

E I G H T   Scripted Women Bound by Blood: Polluted Flows, Sacred Flows

1. Nakagami, "Monogatari no keifu," 29, no. 5: 148–49.

2. Nakagami, "Monogatari no keifu," 29, no. 6: 131.

3. Grosz, 200. My reading of blood in *Masks* is indebted to this study by Grosz, especially pt. 4, "Sexual Difference." See also my Chapter 3, especially n. 25.

4. Dower, 275–77.

5. Gluck, 78.

6. Medieval practices clearly delineated menstruation and childbirth as differ-

ent types of pollution. My intention is not to describe premodern Buddhist and Shinto pollution beliefs and practices but to sketch in broad outlines how such practices have been perceived generally in the modern period. I am less interested in actual historical events than in an analysis of the gendered metaphoric and ideological significances of modern discourses on the premodern. I also do not mean to suggest that it was only women who were perceived as defiled or polluted. Other defilements, such as contact with dead animals and humans, were believed to pollute both men and women. Readers interested in discussions of premodern pollution ideologies and practices specific to women are referred to Ōsuji and Nishiguchi, eds. Marra's "Buddhist Mythmaking of Defilement" discusses the relationship between pollution myths and female shamans in medieval Japan. On the outcaste in Japan, see above, Introduction, n. 44.

7. Yoshida.

8. As quoted by Yoshida, 68.

9. See Bargen, "Twin Blossoms," for a discussion of the issue of retribution for this interrupted pregnancy.

10. I am indebted to Professor Barbara Ruch for pointing out that Mieko's vision is directly derived from this episode about the Shinto deities, Izanagi and Izanami, in the *Kojiki*, 64–65.

11. The daughter of Fujiwara Kaneie, Senshi (962–1002), was, according to William and Helen McCullough, in 978 the junior consort of Emperor En'yū, the Grand Empress in 986, and the first Imperial Lady in 991. She also birthed Emperor Ichijō. The office of the Kamo Priestess followed the pattern established for the Ise Priestess. See McCullough and McCullough, trans., 1: 386–88, supplementary n. 25.

12. The term *miko* may also refer to a shamaness in general and is not used exclusively for either virgins or young women in service at Shinto shrines. Jean Herbert, for example, uses the word *miko* in reference to "old women" who serve as mediums.

13. See, for example, Saeki.

14. Fujiwara Michinaga (966–1027), Heian court minister, gained political control through skillfully marrying his daughter Shōshi (as the second consort) to Emperor Ichijō. Michinaga is one of the major characters of the *Eiga monogatari*. Empress Teishi, daughter of Fujiwara Michitaka, was the consort of Emperor Ichijō.

15. Butler, *Gender Trouble*, 139.

16. Newton and Rosenfelt, eds., xxii.

17. Ibid., xxiii.

18. See, for example, Yanagita, *Imo no chikara*. Yanagita's influence was apparently widespread, and although he died in 1962, his studies enjoyed a popular revival in the 1960s through the 1970s. Yoneyama quotes Soeda Masataka, a television director, who said in 1974 that he was inspired to make a program on

Yanagita because he saw Yanagita's books at the homes of almost everyone he visited: "professors, literary critics, journalists, artists, and other kinds of professional intellectuals" (30).

19. The quote is from Yanagita, *Imo no chikara*, 25. It appears that the notion of linking archaic Shinto and female shamans was largely a construct of Japan's medieval period and was revitalized in the twentieth century. For example, Yoshie, in her "Kodai no miko to dōjo" and "Tamayoribime sankō," challenges Yanagita's feminization of shamanistic practices. Yoshie argues that many Shinto menstruation prohibitions were a thirteenth-century development, and she documents her assertion that frequently Shinto rituals were carried out along existing gender roles by (historically neglected) mature male-female couples. See also Koschmann et al., eds.; many of the essays debate the historical accuracy of Yanagita's folkloric studies.

20. Herbert, 137.

21. Kitagawa, 33.

22. Yoshida, 58.

23. Ibid., 70, 73.

NINE   Gendered Performances: Masculinizing Buddhism, Feminizing Shinto

1. Kelsey, 18–54.

2. Ibid., 27, 29.

3. Yokota, 27–28.

4. In the early modern period the Meiji government tried to separate the long-intertwined religions and to seek political validation in the newly conceived bureaucracy of "state Shinto" (Kitagawa, 201). The ideological separation of shrine and state Shinto was facilitated by governmental manipulations to maintain separation between church and state while legitimizing the emperor as head of state in the promulgation of the Meiji constitution. See Gluck, 138–43. Yanagita's and Origuchi's folkloric studies, which sought to locate pre-Buddhist indigenous Japanese practices, thus collude with the early-twentieth-century movement to disengage Shinto from Buddhism.

5. Further complicating the issue, as in actual practice, the two belief systems are also syncretistic in *Masks*, where oppositions are posited frequently, only to be deconstructed. Mieko is identified as a shaman, with "a peculiar power to move events in whatever direction she pleases, while she stays motionless" (30), but she is also the daughter of a highly regarded Buddhist priest (37). The traces of Shinto (*suijaku*) inherent in the Buddhist "true body" (*honji*) come to symbolize a feminine tradition suppressed within a dominant phallocentric system. The archetype as written in *Masks* is thus a split or alternate or multiple signifier, producing an ambivalent mythic figure of a variety of resistances and synergisms.

6. Douglas, *Purity and Danger*, 99, 140–42.

7. Ibid., 142.

8. Kitagawa, 25.

9. For example, Mitsuhashi compares Buddhist and Shinto pollution myths in a discussion of the widening social discourses on female pollution in the medieval period. At the same time, some studies undermine any generalizations linking all sects of Buddhism with increased female pollution restrictions. Nakamura Ikuo discusses the radical transformation of medieval Buddhism, highlighting the priest Hōnen's insistence that isolation and restrictions placed on menstruating and postpartum women are Shinto beliefs and are not valid for Buddhists. Hōnen's proclamation can be read as evidence of an early inversion. If early Shinto, as Mitsuhashi and Yoshie in "Tamayoribime sankō" and in "Kodai no miko to dōjo" (see also Chapter 8, n. 19 above) argue, did not restrict women from participating in rituals due to bleeding, and such prohibitions emerged through a specific syncretism of Buddhist and Shinto concepts of impurity and pollution that accompanied a growing bureaucratic malecentrism, then Hōnen's statement is the production of a "rewritten origin."

10. Cixous and Clément, 68, 69.

11. Ibid., 35.

12. Mizuta, "Josei no jikogatari to monogatari," 65–66.

13. See Chapter 5 for a more thorough discussion of Mizuta's argument. See also n. 8 of that chapter on how Mizuta's use of the word *gender* is somewhat different from mine and on the issue of "public" and "private." See also Chapter 7.

14. Mizuta, *Monogatari to hanmonogatari no fūkei*, 32–35.

15. Nakagami and Kamata, 25–30.

16. Ibid., 27, 28.

17. Cixous and Clément, 5.

18. For a discussion of Motoori Norinaga and other Edo-period nativist scholars' inversion of the Chinese writing / Japanese voice binarism, see Sakai, *Voices of the Past*, especially 255, and Harootunian, *Things Seen and Unseen*, on Tokugawa nativism. Harootunian, in his final chapter, "Epilogue," extends his discussion into the modern period to treat Yanagita's and Origuchi's folkloric studies.

19. Mizuta, "Josei no jikogatari to monogatari," 71.

20. See Okada, particularly the chapters on *The Tale of Genji*, for a reading of narration and "resistance."

21. See my comments on the *Eiga monogatari*, a "history" written by a woman in the Heian period, n. 12 of Chapter 5 and n. 3 of Chapter 6.

22. Cixous and Clément, 103–4.

23. See Irigaray, "The 'Mechanics' of Fluids," in *This Sex Which Is Not One*, 106–18.

TEN   Matrix and Metramorphosis

1. Mizuta, *Monogatari to hanmonogatari no fūkei*, 17.

2. Saeki, 212.

3. Mizuta, *Monogatari to hanmonogatari no fūkei*, 47.

4. Carpenter, 343; Takemori.

5. Karatani, *Modern Japanese Literature*, 19–40, 193.

6. Ibid., 45–75.

7. See Chapter 3 for more on Karatani's discussion of modernity and depth.

8. Butler, *Gender Trouble*, 139–40. See Chapter 13 for how I distinguish between *sex* and *gender*.

9. Etō.

10. Ibid., 411.

11. Irigaray, *This Sex Which Is Not One*, 175, 176.

12. This assumption, of course, ignores the many mutual penetrations by members of both sexes in various sex acts involving tongues and fingers, which may penetrate any of the varied orifices of the human (male and female) body. It renders penetration by the penis the only penetration that "matters." See also Chapter 13.

13. Rich, "Compulsory Heterosexuality," 239.

14. Grosz, 201.

15. For example, the Rokujō lady's possession of Genji's wife Aoi in *The Tale of Genji* is described this way in Seidensticker's translation: "It was not Aoi's voice, nor was the manner hers. Extraordinary—and then he knew it was the voice of the Rokujō lady. He was aghast" (168).

16. Namely, her vagina.

17. Lacan, "God and the *Jouissance* of ~~The~~ Woman," and "A Love Letter," in *Feminine Sexuality*, 137–48, 149–61. Such *jouissance*, wrote Lacan, was possible to male mystics, because they too understood a *jouissance* that goes "beyond" (the subject, language).

18. Ettinger, 177.

19. Ibid., 179.

20. Ibid., 198–201.

21. Kristeva, *Desire in Language*, 136, 140–43, 170–73.

22. There is also evidence to contradict this model of female plurality, as Mieko appears to be dominant and to control Harume and Yasuko in spite of Mikame's suggestion that it is Yasuko who controls Mieko. Similarly, in *Saimu*, Sano in the end rejects the plurality and its power. I am suggesting that there is a movement toward a nonhierarchized plurality, which is also contravened by the Symbolic.

ELEVEN   Dangerous Men and All That Jazz

1. Nakagami, "Edo," 88.

2. Nakagami, "Sakka to nikutai," 89.

3. Readers interested in more biographical information may consult Nagashima, "Nakagami Kenji shōden."

4. See Aikura. Baraka (then using the name LeRoi Jones) had written, "Jazz is a music that could not have existed without blues and its various antecedents.

However, jazz should not be thought of as a *successor* to blues, but as a very original music that developed out of, and was concomitant with, blues and moved off into its own path of development" (*Blues People*, 71; Baraka's emphasis).

5. Baraka, "Jazz Criticism," 56–57, 69–70.

6. Given their general acceptance of Baraka's theory of jazz, many Japanese writers seemed to feel it necessary to analyze their passion for jazz by seeking similarity between "being Japanese" and "being black." For some commentators, this took the (somewhat convoluted) form of seeking likeness in a racialized community; Mamiya compares premodern Japanese music with the early blues of black slaves because they both "borrowed instruments from another culture."

7. Yamashita et al., 26.

8. That is, a "day" chosen for the public expression of antiwar sentiment. Interestingly, when I showed this translation to a friend of mine who was active in the student movement of the 1960s in Japan, he suggested that I drop the translation of *saha* into "leftist" since "avant-garde Japanese jazz enthusiasts were, of course, associated with the left in Japan," and translating the word would overstress this association. I leave it in, since "new jazz" (progressive jazz) in the 1960s in the United States was not so clearly linked to political movements or activism.

9. Nakagami, "Jyazu kyōsaha," 243 (originally published in 1983). "Free jazz" is apparently also a reference to Ornette Coleman's recording entitled *Free Jazz*.

10. Nakagami, "Hanzaisha Nagayama Norio kara no hōkoku," 124–25, 127 149. Apparently Nagayama Norio actually worked as a waiter in one of the jazz clubs that Nakagami frequented in Tokyo (personal conversation with Karatani Kōjin, New York City, September 1996).

11. Nakagami, "Umi e," 59. Further pagination follows quotations parenthetically within text.

12. Nakagami, "Toshi shōsetsu," 343.

13. The Japanese reads, "dāru no e no yō" (like a *dāru* picture/painting). Unable to find any definition of *dāru*, I am guessing that it is a mistake and should have been *dari*, for Salvador Dalí. It's a bit of a stretch, but I have no other solutions.

14. The word *coke* is written in *katakana*, *kōku*, and it seems to refer to cocaine being smoked, although crack-cocaine postdates the writing of these passages. Or perhaps it is in reference to the other meaning of *coke* in English—the residue of burned charcoal. I do not think it refers to Coca-cola, which is shortened to *cola* (*kora*), not to *Coke* in Japanese.

15. Nakagami, "JAZZ," 35–36. Further page numbers follow quotations parenthetically within text.

16. Baraka, "Jazz Criticism," 56.

17. Monson, "Doubleness and Jazz Improvisation," 292.

18. On regarding Nakagami's position to convention as ironic, I am indebted to the insights of Katsuyo Motoyoshi, who was the first person to use the word in discussions with me about her (ongoing) work on Nakagami Kenji.

19. Karatani et al., "Nakagami Kenji sankaiki," 245.

20. Feather, 55.

21. I am not insisting, of course, that jazz was the only, or necessarily the primary, influence on Nakagami's narrative style. Nakagami himself said (and wrote) repeatedly that William Faulkner was an important influence. See, for example, his "Fōkunā, hanjō suru Minami," and "Fōkunā shōgeki." The reference to Gabriel García Márquez's *One Hundred Years of Solitude* is evident in the title of Nakagami's *Sennen no yuraku* (A thousand years of pleasure). See Morris, "Gossip and History." Ōe Kenzaburō's writings also apparently influenced Nakagami. Moreover, a different analytic approach could find correlation between some of Nakagami's short, lyrical passages and a distaste for structure that informed the modern *shishōsetsu*, or as culled from modern approaches to the premodern poetic forms of *renga* (linked poetry) and haiku. Nakagami enjoyed verse; he published poems in the late 1960s, mostly in *Sandē jyānaru*, and later occasionally turned his hand to haiku. Readers are referred to, for example, Nakagami and Kamata, and Nakagami and Kadokawa. Repetitions of motifs of the canon and reworkings of classical tales are common to modern Japanese literature, and Nakagami clearly was also influenced by how Kyōka and Enchi, among other writers, reconfigured antecedent text. See, for example, his serialized essays, "Monogatari no keifu" and "Ane no jiyū/ Anākii" and his "Izumi Kyōka: Hito to sakuhin." Nakagami's preference for a single-consciousness narration, however, lies squarely within the Meiji/Taisho–generated *shishōsetsu* style. Concerned about a growing trend toward reading Nakagami's *monogatari* as simply harkening back to premodernity, Karatani admonished commentators on Nakagami's work for misreading the relationship between the two textual spaces—naturalistic and folkloric—that vie in Nakagami's narratives and for focusing only on the *monogatari*, or folkloric aspects, to the neglect of the equally important naturalistic attributes. This myopia, wrote Karatani in his "Kaisetsu: shōsetsu no isō," 260, resulted in a "mediocre critique that resituates Nakagami's relentlessly historicized position within an ahistorical structural theory. That is why I now find it necessary to turn it around, and emphasize instead [the space of] naturalism and the *shishōsetsu* that comprise the other side of the axis." Nakagami's interest in Yanagita's ethnographic studies and his fascination with the search for linguistic "origin" by Origuchi were never "naive." Nakagami takes his place among these predecessors in a historical continuum of a modern gesture toward "reoriginating origin." See his section on Origuchi in *Monogatari no keifu*, reprinted in *Fūkei no mukō e*.

22. Interestingly, though Baraka does not mention Pygmies in his *Blues People*, he briefly notes the "rhythmic sophistication of the . . . Babenzele Pygmies" in his 1990 "Jazz Criticism," 57. In *Blues People*, however, there are comparisons of other native African musical traditions with elements of jazz and blues. For example, after a description of bebop rhythmic innovations, Baraka writes, "There is a perfect analogy here to African music, where over one rhythm, many other rhythms and a rhythmically derived 'melody' are all juxtaposed. One recording of

Belgian Congo music features as its rhythmic foundation and impetus an instrument called the *boyekei*, which is actually a notched palm rib about four feet long which is scraped with a flexible stick to produce a steady rhythmic accompaniment. It is amazing how closely the use of this native African instrument corresponds to the use of the top cymbal in bebop" (195).

23. See Karatani, *Modern Japanese Literature*, on landscape in premodern Japanese literature. I discuss this point in detail in Chapter 12.

24. *Kareki Nada* is a proper name. In the afterword to the *bunko* publication is a photograph of the actual rocky, coastal beach called *Kareki Nada*. Pagination from both *Kareki Nada* and *Sanka* follows quotations parenthetically within text.

25. Karatani, "Kaisetsu: shōsetsu no isō," 260.

26. See Chapter 5 on Shinoda's reading of Kyōka's narratives.

27. Nakagami, "Fushi," translated by Harbison, "The Immortal," 415. All quotations are from the translation, and further pagination follows quotations parenthetically within text.

28. See Chapter 14 for a discussion of the *roji* as trope.

29. Butler, *Gender Trouble*, 30–1.

30. See Chapters 13 and 14 on both being and having the phallus.

T W E L V E   Tracing Origins: Landscape and Interiority

This chapter incorporates some parts of a paper presented at the 1993 annual meeting of the Modern Language Association entitled "The Rape of Tradition: Nakagami Kenji's 'Fushi' and Izumi Kyōka's *Kōya hijiri*." An earlier version of this chapter was published in 1995 in English as "Nakagami Kenji's Mystic Writing Pad; or, Tracing Origins, Tales of the Snake, and the Land as Matrix," and in Japanese as "Nakagami Kenji ron: Fūkei to jendā naratibu no seiji."

1. Keene, *World Within Walls*, 100.

2. Karatani, "One Spirit," 619.

3. Karatani, *Modern Japanese Literature*, 27.

4. Although *genbun'itchi* has usually been translated as "unification of spoken and written language," Karatani argues that it is more accurately described as the development of a new system of writing that sought the subordination of the written to the spoken. See the chapter "The Discovery of Interiority" in *Modern Japanese Literature*, 45–75. For edifying discussions of the *genbun'itchi* movement and literature of the Meiji Period, see Karatani's *Modern Japanese Literature*; Miyoshi's "The New Language," in *Accomplices of Silence*, 3–37; and Fowler's "Fictions and Fabrications" and "Language and the Illusion of Presence," in his *Rhetoric of Confession*, 3–27 and 28–42. For a discussion of the antecedent eighteenth-century nativist movement and its relation to phonocentrism and discursive practices, see Sakai, *Voices of the Past*, 241–79.

5. This shift can be understood also as a perspectival configuration (discovery

of depth) of the modern period. See Karatani, "On The Power to Construct," in *Modern Japanese Literature*, especially 137.

6. Karatani, *Modern Japanese Literature*, 45–75, 19–40, 193.

7. Ibid., 22–23, 65–67.

8. Ibid., 36.

9. Ibid., 67.

10. See the Introduction, especially n. 44, for information on the outcaste in Japan.

11. Literacy rates increased dramatically in the Edo period but remained low among peasants (especially women) and outcastes well into Meiji. See Dore, also Hane. Regarding the *burakumin* specifically, see Wagatsuma, "Non-Political Approaches: The Influences of Religion and Education," and De Vos and Wagatsuma, "Minority Status and Attitudes Towards Authority," both in De Vos and Wagatsuma, eds., 88–109, 258–72.

12. *Furusato* literally means one's place of birth but also has the deeper meaning of a "spiritual home"—the place from which one spiritually and materially originates and to which one eventually returns, if only to be buried. Separation from this spiritual home is broadly believed to produce conditions of yearning, and descriptions of such separation became a frequent venue for depicting romantic nostalgia in modern Japanese narrative.

13. See Chapter 14 for a discussion of the *roji* as a narrative trope.

14. See the Introduction, nn. 33 and 38, on the classical *monogatari* and *setsuwa* genres. It is actually Nakagami's long, present-day narratives that are most evocative of the *monogatari*, but *monogatari* written, as Karatani put it, within the context of *shōsetsu*. See Karatani, "Kaisetsu: shōsetsu no isō." I deal with the issue of *monogatari* versus *shōsetsu* as descriptive terms for Nakagami's narratives in Chapter 14.

15. Origuchi, 5. Paraphrased by Kamata, in Nakagami and Kamata, 256–57. Origuchi Shinobu (1887–1953) was a pioneer scholar who studied ancient Japan through modern folklore. For more insight into Origuchi's influence on Nakagami, see Nakagami's section on Origuchi in his *Monogatari no keifu*; Nakagami's and Kadokawa's rambling discussions of Origuchi, among other things, in Nakagami and Kadokawa. Nakagami apparently saw a structural parallel between the dualistic taboo/sacred status of the *marebito* and the later Kumano mystics (*Haiku no jidai,* 257). On Origuchi, see also Harootunian, *Things Seen and Unseen*, "Epilogue," especially 423–30; Fujii, "Epilogue," in *Complicit Fictions*, 222–56, on Origuchi, narration, and modernity.

16. Nakagami, "Ukijima," in *Keshō*, 70. The stories collected into *Keshō* were written between 1974 and 1976. Ukijima is a proper name and refers to a swampy area on the outskirts of Shingū that seems to float. At the actual site, tourists can obtain a pamphlet that offers a written synopsis of this Ukijima legend. All further quotations from and references to "Ukijima" are to the 1978 hard-cover version,

and pagination follows quotations parenthetically within text. In the 1993 paperback (*bunko*) version, the very last paragraph of the tale (as published in the hardcover version) has been deleted.

17. See Chapter 9.

18. Ueda's "Jasei no in" is translated into English with the title "Bewitched," by Hamada, in *Tales of Moonlight and Rain*. All quotations from "Jasei no in" are from Hamada's translation. Ueda Akinari was a highly celebrated writer, poet, and scholar of the Edo period. For a general introduction to his work, see Keene, *World Within Walls*, 371–95. Pagination from Nakagami's "Jain" follows quotations parenthetically within text.

19. Pagination from "Tsuki to fushi" follows quotations parenthetically within text. Nakagami confessed to a deep passion for Kyōka's work (personal conversation, Shingū City, Japan, February 7, 1990). See also Nakagami's "Izumi Kyōka: Hito to sakuhin," and Nakagami and Kamata, 15–21, for his comments on Kyōka.

20. See Chapter 2, n. 16 for antecedent narratives on the snake-woman/snake-deity archetypes/tropes.

21. *Keri* indicates reporting of a past event not directly experienced by the narrator, while *kemu* indicates past conjecture but may also signify hearsay.

22. I am indebted to Hosea Hirata for the observation that the priest's survival gives the transmission of the tale a modern "realism."

23. Derrida, *Of Grammatology*, xviii.

24. Freud, "Mystic Writing Pad," 179.

25. Karatani, "One Spirit," 619.   26. Fowler, 3–42.

27. Nakagami and Kamata, 47.   28. Ibid., 27–28.

29. It is important to note that the opposition here between Buddhism and Japanese animism is primarily a metaphoric one. The sutra intoned by the priest is a *dharani*, or mystic incantation. Although it is a Buddhist prayer, like *kotodama* it is empowered through enunciation. Compare the description of the otherworldly creatures in Nakagami's "The Immortal" with the scene from *Kōya hijiri*, 426, which elicits the *dharani* (quoted in English in Chapter 5).

30. Nakagami and Kamata, 256. Origuchi's reconstruction postulates two different ways to write the word *otozure* of *otozurebito* (people of *otozure*) in Chinese characters. One uses the traditional single character for *visitor*, while the other is written with a compound character meaning "accompanying sound" (*oto* and *tsure*). Origuchi believed that the word held both significations. See Origuchi, 11–12, and Nakagami and Kamata, especially 256–57. See Chapter 5 for a discussion of *kotodama* in relation to Kyōka's texts.

31. The woman associated with snakes appears not only in *Kōya hijiri*, *Nanchi shinjū*, and "Ehon no haru," but in many other of Kyōka's narratives. In English translation see "One Day in Spring" ("Shunchū and Shunchū gokoku," 1906), in Inouye, *Three Tales*, 31–106.

32. Nakagami and Kamata, 27–28.

33. For example, there is the "*Miwasan densetsu*," in the *Kojiki*, 186–87 (Philippi, 203–4), in which a deity takes the form of a snake to impregnate a woman. A later variant of the tale appears in Nakada, ed., *Nihon ryōiki*, 248–50. Several similar tales appear in the *Konjaku monogatari shū*, discussed by Kelsey, 31–35.

34. See the section on Enchi, especially Chapter 9. On Western counterparts, see Cixous and Clément, 63–132. To quote Cixous: "Either woman is passive or she does not exist. What is left of her is unthinkable, unthought" (64); "Philosophy is constructed on the premise of woman's abasement. Subordination of the feminine to the masculine order" (65); "Shut out of his system's space, she is the repressed that ensures the system's functioning" (67). See also Kristeva, "Woman Can Never Be Defined," her *Desire in Language*, and Irigaray, *This Sex Which Is Not One*.

35. I have discussed this point in each part; see Chapters 5, 8, and 9. The ascension of Buddhist and Confucian ideologies functioned to divest women of a previously powerful influence on governance. Political purpose lies hidden within the developing teleology of such binarisms as public/private and Chinese/Japanese, which rendered gender within their epistemological system of opposites. Narratives produced then conceptualize women as Other, associated with the supernatural, the "other" world, and the abject. As a *burakumin*, Nakagami's appropriation of the feminized "dark continent" was surely also informed by the reciprocal discourses on female and *eta / hinin* pollution.

36. See Kelsey. In Chapter 9 I discussed the historical shift whereby Shinto became increasingly subordinated to Buddhism.

37. Cixous and Clément, 5.

38. In English, see Mayer's translation of *Nihon mukashibanashi meii*, *The Yanagita Kunio Guide to the Japanese Folk Tale*, for examples of folklore in which animals take on human form and human beings turn into animals.

THIRTEEN   The Body: Deformities, Nasty Blood, and Sexual Violence

An earlier version of this chapter was published in Japanese as "Nakagami Kenji no shintai." It was subsequently published in a revised and expanded form as "Nakagami Kenji ni okeru shintai."

1. See Yomota et al.

2. Nakagami, "Futakami," 126. Further pagination follows quotations parenthetically within text.

3. For Nakagami's thoughts on Izumi Kyōka, see, for example, his "Izumi Kyōka: Hito to sakuhin"; on Enchi Fumiko, see his "Monogatari no keifu" and "Ane no jiyū."

4. Nakagami, "Jūryoku no miyako," 20–21. Further pagination follows quotations parenthetically within text.

5. See Monnet, "Ghostly Women 2" for more on the relation between Origuchi's text and Nakagami's.

6. Nakagami, "Atogaki," in *Jūryoku no miyako*, 163.

7. The blindings in "Jūryoku no miyako" are about privileging the aesthetic vision over a naturalist one; Nakagami, however, resistuates the aesthetic in a historicized matrix. As I will discuss in the following chapter, the *roji* provided a topos for exploring the role of *sabetsu*, or discrimination, as "history" and the relationship of *sabetsu* to the development of signification itself. Nakagami undertook this same project in topoi extraneous to the *roji* as well. Nakagami clearly understood the aesthetic to be a product of other conterminous discourses and saw it as inseparable from power constellations. See, for example, his *Sennen no yuraku*, a text that inverts dominant sociocultural evaluative systems, and thus problematizes (historicizes and particularizes) the question of aesthetics. See also Karatani, "Kaisetsu: shōsetsu no isō," 260, for a critique of the tendency to stress the folkloric space over the naturalist one in Nakagami's narratives, as I quoted in the Introduction.

8. Edelman, "The Part for the (W)hole," in his *Homographesis*, 47, 53.

9. See Goldberg. For a discussion of how women have been seen as analogous to "lower races," see Stepan.

10. See Balibar.

11. See Bhabha, "The Other Question," and "Of Mimicry and Man."

12. See Chapter 14.

13. See Chapter 14 for a discussion of the canonization of Nakagami's narratives.

14. See, for example, Hasumi et al.

15. Edelman, xv.

16. Edelman, "The Part for the W(hole)," in his *Homographesis*, 73–74.

17. See Kaplan, "Is the Gaze Male?" in her *Women and Film*, 23–35.

18. Bersani, *Homos*, 97.

19. Ibid., 77–112.

20. Ibid., 96.

21. See Bersani, "Is the Rectum a Grave?"; Irigaray, *Speculum*, and *This Sex Which Is Not One*.

22. This also puts into question the phallocentric positing of penetration by the penis as the only penetration that "matters." See Chapter 10, n. 12.

23. See Grosz.

24. Protagonist Michiko bites Ryōichi's penis, making it bleed; it is her first sexual experience and she is menstruating. See 344–46.

25. Bersani, "Is the Rectum a Grave?," 212.

26. Edelman, "Part for the W(hole)," in his *Homographesis*, 71–72.

27. See Chapter 14 for a more detailed discussion of the relationship between naming and discrimination in Nakagami's narratives.

28. Derrida, *Of Grammatology*, 109. See also Chapter 14 for further discussion of this point.

29. See Karatani, "Fūkō to Nihon," for a critique of the aestheticization of homosexuality in modern Japan. Japanese aestheticization of (male) homosexuality colludes with the depoliticization of homosexuality.

30. See also Chapter 14. The conceit that postulates that *monogatari* must be narrated in a "female voice" should be confused neither with actual female discursive productions nor with a naturalized notion of putative "female" aspects. *Sennen no yuraku*'s female orator is a repetition of the convention by which a *monogatari* authored by a biological male attains narrative authority by adopting a female narrative voice. Thus, it is a feminized "term" and not linked, except metaphorically and positionally, with "femaleness." On the historical process of metaphoricization of female voice in the premodern *monogatari*, and its affect on the modern *monogatari*, see Mizuta, "Josei no jikogatari to monogatari"; and for a more thorough treatment, her *Monogatari to hanmonogatari no fūkei*. See this book's chapters on Enchi regarding the issue in relationship to modern *monogatari*. See also Chapter 14 for further discussion of how Nakagami's narratives unsettled, rather than reproduced, the conceit of *monogatari* as feminized discourse.

FOURTEEN   An Ambivalent Masculinist Politics

1. Hasumi et al., 18–19.

2. Apparently Nakagami did not allow his books to be published in paperback while he was alive.

3. Nakagami's untimely death at the age of 46 from kidney cancer has hastened the process of canonizing his work. Some critics heralded him as one of the most important postwar novelists. Asada Akira argued against the tendency to see Nakagami only as a writer of the "periphery," and the writer Shimada Masahiko posthumously dubbed Nakagami "the last novelist [*saigo no sakka*]." According to an earlier essay by Ogasawara Kenji, the influence of Kumano folklore on Nakagami's work made Nakagami a pioneering author who helped pave the way toward a literary rejuvenation in the postwar period. See Suga Hidemi for a discussion of Nakagami's posthumous significance as a "symbol" for the literary coteries, 238–54. A collection including essays on Nakagami by Karatani, *Sakaguchi Ango to Nakagami Kenji*, won the Itō Sei prize in June 1996. Watanabe Naomi has published *Nakagami Kenji ron*, and Yomota Inuhiko has published a revised and expanded edition of *Kishu to tensei Nakagami Kenji*.

4. Transcriptions of the roundtable discussions have been published as follows: Karatani et al., "Sennen no bungaku"; Karatani et al., "Nakagami Kenji sankaiki"; Karatani et al., "Koyūmei to 'roji' no ba o megutte"; Karatani et al., "Hatenaki tekusuto o megutte."

5. Yomota et al. The *Yuriika* special section was in 25, no. 3 (1993).

6. To date the only English-language translation of Nakagami's texts is Harbi-

son's "The Immortal." Nakagami is, however, widely translated into French, and it is said that several English-language translations are presently in progress.

7. In 1996 the journal *Japan Forum* published several essays on Nakagami. Specifically, the essays were: Morris, "Introduction," and "Gossip and History"; Dodd; and Monnet, "Ghostly Women 1." Part 2 of Monnet's study appeared in the following issue of *Japan Forum*. Monnet's essay is also published in two installments in Japanese in *Hihyō kūkan*; three essays of mine on Nakagami have been published in Japanese. See the first note of Chapter 12 and the first note of Chapter 13.

8. Pagination from these narratives follows quotations parenthetically within text. "Misaki" won the Akutagawa Literary Award in 1976.

9. Hasumi et al., 20.

10. Ibid., 22.

11. Karatani, "Nakagami Kenji to feminizumu."

12. Eagleton, 16. See also Bourdieu on the interrelations among social ideologies, power, and literature.

13. Nakagami also wrote critical essays. Particularly pertinent to this study are his essays revitalizing the "taboo" *monogatari* as genre and positing the word as a modern critical term. See his *Monogatari no keifu* and also Miura, "Monogatari no yukue," 265–81.

14. Karatani, "Kaisetsu: shōsetsu no isō," 261–62.

15. Here Karatani appears to refer to the *ochiudo* legends of the Genpei wars ("the distant past"), which celebrate the historical flight into the provinces by a small group of Heike warriors after losing in battle to the Taira clan. There are many narrative versions of this popular legend. Nakagami layers these legends with others from the Kumano region, such as the legends of the crow or the feather-mantled female deity. In the Akiyuki trilogy proper, Nakagami overtly adds another layer, based on the Ikkō ikki rebellion. Akiyuki's father, Ryūzō, claims to be a descendant of the Hamamura clan, who fled to Kumano after being defeated by Oda Nobunaga during early Japanese unification in the sixteen century and afterward had the hereditary status of outcastes. On the Ikkō ikki rebellion in relation to the modern origins of the outcaste, see Ishio, and Karatani, "Hisabetsu buraku no 'kigen.'"

16. Karatani, "Sa'i no sanbutsu," in *Sakaguchi Ango to Nakagami Kenji*, 184.

17. Karatani, "Kaisetsu: shōsetsu no isō," 263.

18. Hasumi et al., 32.

19. Motoyoshi, 1.

20. Although Nakagami did not hide his heritage, many of his readers nonetheless were unaware of his outcaste lineage for some time. See the Introduction, n. 44.

21. The leader of the Ikkō ikki rebellion.

22. Derrida, *Of Grammatology*, 112.

23. Tyler, 228.

24. Yoshi believes that the people of the *roji*, himself included, are the descendants of the Mongolian warlord Ghenghis Khan, and he tries to spearhead a movement among the squatters to return to the grasslands of their ancestors in Mongolia. Kleeman interprets the pan-Asiatic imaginaries in the Akiyuki trilogy as a type of diasporic narrative.

25. See Karatani, "Kaisetsu," in *Chi no hate*, 605–16; Asada, 12.

26. Karatani et al., "Nakagami Kenji sankaiki," 258.

27. Though taking issue with the notion that the *roji* is an ahistorically matrilineal space (matrilineal since ancient times), Karatani nonetheless also reads the *roji* as matrilineal (much as many have characterized African-American ghettos) due to the specifics of (early) modern Japanese discrimination. See Karatani "Kaisetsu," in *Chi no hate*, especially 614–15. See also his comment on matrilinearity in African-American ghetto communities, in Hasumi et al., 36. Karatani's statement may be accurate in regard to the actual circumstances of the *buraku*, but I think that Nakagami undid the conceit of a maternalized and matrilineal *roji* even as he seemed to so trope it.

28. Asada, 11, 10. Asada glosses the Chinese characters *botai* (which also literally means "womb") with the *katakana* pronunciation of the English word *matrix*.

29. Watanabe, "Sabetsu to ekurichūru," 63; Hasumi et al., 32.

30. See Hasumi et al., and Watanabe, *Nakagami Kenji ron*.

31. Although Nakagami clearly sought to configure gender differently from dominant paradigms, his essays also reveal a sort of biological determinism linked to sex, much in keeping with conterminous ideologies. For example, in his fourth installment to the Enchi Fumiko section of his *Monogatari no keifu*, though he laments a reductive configuration of female sexuality as possessing a "smaller penis," he goes on to insist that there is a "female principle" for female sexuality that is rooted in the "womb." He links the embrace by women of their own sexuality as women (and not as lesser men) to a "textual anarchy" in modern *monogatari* by these women. See Nakagami, "Monogatari no keifu 4," 136–39.

32. Akiyuki is surrounded by women: his mother, Fusa, his three older sisters, his aunts, and nieces. (Although in the most-lauded text of the trilogy proper, *Kareki Nada*, the women are least dominant.) Undoubtedly, Nakagami's female protagonists replicate none of the more standard female textual roles, such as the commodified sex object of male heterosexual erotic and pornographic texts; the silenced, acquiescent, waiting-to-be-violated bride-to-be; the self-sacrificing mother of idealized portraiture, or the complaining wife and mother of another stereotype; or the raging and repressed dangerous women as penned by Enchi Fumiko or Ōba Minako. Neither does Nakagami eroticize the women of the *buraku* as "beauties" (*bijin*), a fictional conceit quite common to post-Meiji narrative and, of course, true of Kyōka. (See Watanabe, *Nihon kindai bungaku to sabetsu*, "Sabetsu

to ekurichūru," and *Nakagami Kenji ron*.) Conversely, the male Nakamoto (*burakumin*) descendants of *Sennen no yuraku*, and Tusyoshi-Yves of *Nichirin no tsubasa* and *Sanka* are all strikingly handsome. Nakagami's range of female characters favor sometimes young, and sometimes not, unwed and remarried mothers, working women, single women, old women, and prostitutes. (Although the prostitute is common enough to Japanese literature, by "normalizing" and historicizing her, Nakagami's renditions in the Akiyuki series bait the more conventional method of using the prostitute to exploit the conflation of ambivalent desire and abjection.) For example, from *Kareki Nada*, "[Akiyuki's stepfather] Shigezō's father died young and there were six growing children with voracious appetites to be fed by one woman's hand alone; when hardship piled on top of hardship, and there was neither food to eat, nor firewood for heat, the eldest daughter, Yuki, who was just about fifteen, was sold to a whorehouse in Ise. They survived for a while on that money. They didn't die of starvation. It was just before the war started that Yuki was brought back" (23). These women are neither passive nor "dangerous"; they are in many ways figured equal to their male counterparts. The omnipresence of the mother, the sisters, and the aunts in the *roji* is underscored by the critics who read, and are struck by, this "difference." What is most different about these women, however, often can be attributed to class: these are, simply, poor women. The portrayal of poor women as the backbone to communities in which "normative" male dominance has been contravened by their lack of socioeconomic status has become one standard by which the disenfranchised are written. The poverty of the ghetto is shown to "democratize" this particular difference, which would be hierarchized in, or shown to invert the power terms of, more mainstream circumstances. This "democratization" is, of course, an imaginary. There were clear hierarchies within the historical *buraku*; women known to be prostitutes might be variously ostracized and denied the use of communal facilities used by others in the quarter.

33. Nakagami, "Hanzaisha Nagayama Norio kara no hōkoku," 127, 149.

34. Hasumi et al., 32.

35. About the problem of violence against women in Nakagami's texts, Asada said, "First, there has been a misinterpretation by feminists that I am afraid will spread alongside the increasing translations [and availability] of Nakagami's narratives in Europe and America. Namely, to define Nakagami as a offensive writer who merely wrote premodernistic *monogatari* in which masculine heroes, who exude a glorified violence, violate women. Certainly, looked at from that vantage point, men just abuse women, and there are scenes in which female personalities are completely unexpressed. But I think that a careful consideration [will show that] the problem of gender in Nakagami Kenji['s narratives] is more complex [than that]" (Karatani et al., "Nakagami Kenji sankaiki," 255).

36. See, for example, Karatani et al., "Nakagami Kenji o megutte." The participants of the roundtable agree that the term *sōsei* is more appropriate to de-

scribe sexuality in Nakagami's narratives than *ryōsei*. *Ryōsei* denotes both sides of two opposing sides (both sides of a binarism); *sōsei* means encompassing all sides. The difference is like that between bipartisan and nonpartisan. For lack of a better word in English, I translate *sōsei* as *pansexual*. Karatani holds that in Nakagami's narratives, sexuality is truly "pansexual" (*sōsei*) and differentiated from a hierarchized binary because neither term is privileged (Karatani et al., "Nakagami Kenji o megutte," 28). I want to stress Nakagami's *deliberate* deconstruction of the modern encoding of the natural, animism, and *monogatari* with gender specificity. Thus, it is not only the female body but any-body that potentially serves as conduit to a primordial site of spiritual, erotic, and violent ecstasy.

37. Hasumi et al., 32.
38. Ibid., 33.
39. Ibid., 31–32.
40. Monnet, "Ghostly Women 1," 15.
41. See Edelman, "Redeeming the Phallus," in his *Homographesis*, 24–41.
42. Monnet, "Ghostly Women 1," 22.
43. Karatani et al., "Nakagami Kenji o megutte," 31.
44. Monnet, "Ghostly Women 1," 22.

Afterword

1. See Bourdieu.
2. Mishima, "Kaisetsu," 559–60; Kobayashi, 219.
3. Although essays by and interviews with J. Keith Vincent, which are also eagerly sought by many of these journals, have regularly drawn attention to feminist concerns as well. See, for example, the interview with Vincent and Kawaguchi by Tasaki Hideaki, "Gei sutadi no kanōsei."
4. As Kano points out, the focus on how Japan has been "feminized" also obscures the role of Japan as oppressor (i.e., masculine and aggressive) during the twentieth century. And I would add that it also obscures Japan's contemporary economic dominance of Asia. Although it would be too long an aside to detail my opposition here, I also want to note that though I think Kano makes several other excellent points in her essay, I find Ueno's notion of "reverse Orientalism," and Kano's application of this notion, problematic. I would also argue that Karatani's remark that Japanese "bilineality" is ideological rather than concretely institutional is more complex than it appears to be in Kano's critique. For example, the fact that in the Edo period Motoori Norinaga lamented the "feminization" of the Japanese canon, and in the mid-twentieth century Mishima Yukio categorized all Japanese literature along gendered demarcations, suggests that there was and is indeed a recurrent ideological, or epistemic, structural genderization of narrative in Japan. Moreover, it is a gendering that does not directly reproduce the organization of power in authoritarian or institutional structures. Again, I refer the reader to Mizuta's rethinking of this structure along the lines of "metaphoric gender."

5. Kano, 24.

6. Ibid., 25.

7. Specifically, it was at Karatani's urging that one essay of mine on Nakagami was published in *Subaru*, and Asada solicited a second from me for publication in their journal, *Hihyō kūkan*. *Hihyō kūkan* also published Monnet's two-part essay, which includes some strong criticism of Asada's and others' comments on gender and violence in Nakagami's texts.

Aikura, Hisato. "Jyazu no naka no daisan sekai: jyazu no hyōgen kōzō aruiwa kasseika riron." *Chūō kōron* 84, no. 1 (January 1969): 406–15.

Akutagawa Ryūnosuke. "*Kyōka zenshū* ni tsuite." In Kyōka *ronshūsei*, ed. Tanizawa Eiichi and Watanabe Ikko, 199–200. Tokyo: Rippu shobō, 1983.

Ariga, Chieko M. "Dephallicizing Women in *Ryūkyō shinshi*: A Critique of Gender Ideology in Japanese Literature." *Journal of Asian Studies* 51, no. 3 (August 1992): 565–86.

———. "Literature and the Institution: Erasure of Women in Schools' *Kokugo*." *U.S.-Japan Women's Journal, English Supplement* 9 (December 1995): 7–28.

———. "Text Versus Commentary: Struggles over the Cultural Meanings of 'Woman.'" In *The Woman's Hand: Gender and Theory in Japanese Women's Writing*, ed. Paul G. Schalow and Janet A. Walker, 352–81. Stanford, Calif.: Stanford University Press, 1996.

Asada Akira. "Nakagami Kenji o saidōnyū suru." *Hihyō kūkan* 12 (1994): 6–16.

Balibar, Etienne. "Paradoxes of Universality." In *Anatomy of Racism*, ed. David Theo Goldberg, 283–94. Minneapolis: University of Minnesota Press, 1990.

Baraka, Amiri (LeRoi Jones). *Blues People*. New York: William Morrow, 1963.

———. "Jazz Criticism and Its Effect on the Art Form." In *New Perspectives on Jazz*, ed. David N. Baker, 55–70. Washington, D.C.: Smithsonian Institution Press, 1990.

Bargen, Doris G. "Translation and Reproduction in Enchi Fumiko's 'A Bond for Two Lifetimes—Gleanings.'" In *The Woman's Hand: Gender and Theory in Japanese Women's Writing*, ed. Paul G. Schalow and Janet A. Walker, 165–204. Stanford, Calif.: Stanford University Press, 1996.

———. "Twin Blossoms on a Single Branch: The Cycle of Retribution in *Onnamen*." *Monumenta Nipponica* 46, no. 2 (1991): 147–71.

Bernstein, Gail Lee, ed. *Recreating Japanese Women, 1600–1945*. Berkeley and Los Angeles: University of California Press, 1991.

Bersani, Leo. *Homos*. Cambridge, Mass.: Harvard University Press, 1995.

———. "Is the Rectum a Grave?" In *AIDS: Cultural Analysis/Cutural Activism*, ed. Douglas Crimp, 197–222. Cambridge, Mass.: MIT Press, 1988.

Bhabha, Homi. *The Location of Culture*. New York: Routledge, 1994.

Birch, Cyril, ed. *Anthology of Chinese Literature*. New York: Grove Press, 1965.

Bourdieu, Pierre. *The Field of Cultural Production: Essays on Art and Literature.* Ed. Randal Johnson. New York: Columbia University Press, 1993.

Brower, Robert, and Earl Miner. *Japanese Court Poetry.* Stanford, Calif.: Stanford University Press, 1961.

Buckley, Sandra. "Altered States: The Body Politics of 'Being-Woman.'" In *Postwar Japan as History*, ed. Andrew Gordon, 347–72. Berkeley and Los Angeles: University of California Press, 1993.

———. *Broken Silence: Voices of Japanese Feminism.* Berkeley and Los Angeles: University of California Press, 1997.

Butler, Judith. *Bodies That Matter: On The Discursive Limits of "Sex."* New York: Routledge, 1993.

———. *Gender Trouble: Feminism and the Subversion of Identity.* New York: Routledge, 1990.

Carpenter, Juliet Winters. "Enchi Fumiko: 'A Writer of Tales.'" *Japan Quarterly* 37, no. 3 (1990): 343–55.

Chow, Rey. *Writing Diaspora: Tactics of Intervention in Contemporary Cultural Studies.* Bloomington: Indiana University Press, 1993.

Cixous, Hélène, and Catherine Clément. *The Newly Born Woman.* Trans. Betsy Wing. Minneapolis: Minnesota University Press, 1986.

Copjec, Joan. *Read My Desire: Lacan Against the Historicists.* Cambridge, Mass.: MIT Press, 1994.

Cornyetz, Nina. "Bound by Blood: Female Pollution, Divinity, and Community in Enchi Fumiko's *Masks*." *U.S.-Japan Women's Journal, English Supplement* 9 (December 1995): 29–58. Translated into Japanese as "Chi no sokubaku: Enchi Fumiko no *Onnamen* ni okeru onna no fujō, shinsei, soshite rentai." *Nichibei josei jānaru* 22 (August 1997): 94–119.

———. "The Fictional Works of Enchi Fumiko." In *Great Works of the Eastern World*, ed. Ian P. McGreal, 392–96. New York: HarperCollins Publishers, 1996.

———. "Nakagami Kenji's Mystic Writing Pad; Or, Tracing Origins, Tales of the Snake, and the Land as Matrix." *Positions* 3, no. 1 (Spring 1995): 224–54. Adapted and translated into Japanese as "Nakagami Kenji ron: Fūkei to jendā naratibu no seiji." *Subaru* 7 (July 1995): 47–71.

———. "Nakagami Kenji ni okeru nikutai." *Hihyō kūkan* 2, no. 14 (1997): 247–65.

———. "Nakagami Kenji no shintai: yogoreta chi, kison, seiki kison." *Gengo bunka* 14, no. 3 (1997): 181–89.

———. "The Rape of Tradition: Nakagami Kenji's 'Fushi' and Izumi Kyōka's *Kōya hijiri*." Paper presented at the annual meeting of the Modern Language Association of America, Toronto, Canada, December 1993.

Deleuze, Gilles, and Félix Guattari. *A Thousand Plateaus: Capitalism and Schizophrenia.* Trans. Brian Massumi. Minneapolis: Minnesota University Press, 1987.

Derrida, Jacques. *Of Grammatology.* Trans. Gayatri Chakravorty Spivak. Baltimore: John Hopkins University Press, 1974.

———. *Writing and Difference.* Trans. Alan Bass. Chicago: University of Chicago Press, 1978.

De Vos, George, and H. Wagatsuma, eds. *Japan's Invisible Race.* Berkeley and Los Angeles: University of California Press, 1967.

Dodd, Stephen. "Japan's Private Parts: Place as Metaphor in Nakagami Kenji's Works." *Japan Forum* 8, no. 1 (1996): 3–11.

Dore, Ronald P. *Education in Tokugawa Japan.* Berkeley and Los Angeles: University of California Press, 1965.

Douglas, Mary. *Purity and Danger: An Analysis of Concepts of Pollution and Taboo.* New York: Praeger, 1966.

Dower, John. *War Without Mercy: Race and Power in the Pacific War.* New York: Pantheon, 1986.

Eagleton, Terry. *Literary Theory: An Introduction.* Minneapolis: University of Minnesota Press, 1983.

Edelman, Lee. *Homographesis: Essays in Gay Literary and Cultural Theory.* New York: Routledge, 1994.

Enchi Fumiko. "Fuyumomi." In *Enchi Fumiko shū*, 383–93. Shinchō Nihon bungaku, vol. 37. Tokyo: Shinchōsha, 1971.

———. "Hebi no koe." In *Saimu / Yūkon*, 352–85. Shinchō gendai bungaku, vol. 19. Tokyo: Shinchōsha, 1979.

———. "Namamiko monogatari." In *Enchi Fumiko shū*, 287–382. Shinchō Nihon bungaku, vol. 37. Tokyo: Shinchōsha, 1971.

———. "Nisei no en shūi." In *Saimu / Yūkon*, 231–44. Shinchō gendai bungaku, vol. 19. Tokyo: Shinchōsha, 1979. Translated as "Love in Two Lives: The Remnant." In *Japanese Women Writers: Twentieth Century Short Fiction*, ed. Noriko Mizuta Lippit and Kyoko Iriye Selden, 97–111. Armonk, N.Y.: M. E. Sharpe, 1991.

———. *Onnamen.* In *Sakaguchi Ango, Funahashi Seiichi, Takami Jun, Enchi Fumiko*, 848–916. Shōwa bungaku zenshū, vol. 12. Tokyo: Shōgakukan, 1987. Trans. Juliet Winter Carpenters as *Masks.* New York: Random House, 1983.

———. *Onnazaka.* In *Sakaguchi Ango, Funahashi Seiichi, Takami Jun, Enchi Fumiko*, 765–847. Shōwa bungaku zenshū, vol. 12. Tokyo: Shōgakukan, 1987. Trans. John Bester as *The Waiting Years.* Tokyo: Kodansha International, 1971.

———. *Saimu.* In *Saimu / Yūkon*, 5–213. Shinchō gendai bungaku, vol. 19. Tokyo: Shinchōsha, 1979.

———. "Yō." In *Saimu / Yūkon*, 214–30. Shinchō gendai bungaku, vol. 19. Tokyo: Shinchōsha, 1979. Trans. John Bester as "Enchantress." *Japan Quarterly* 5, no. 3 (1958): 339–59.

Etō Jun. "Kaisetsu." In *Enchi Fumiko shū*, 408–19. Shinchō Nihon bungaku, vol. 37. Tokyo: Shinchōsha, 1971.

Ettinger, Bracha Lichtenberg. "Matrix and Metramorphosis." *Differences* 4, no. 3 (Fall 1992): 176–208.

Eyal, Ben-Ari, Brian Moeran, and James Valentine, eds. *Unwrapping Japan*. Manchester, England: Manchester University Press, 1990.

Feather, Leonard. *Inside Jazz*. New York: Da Capo, 1949. Originally published as *Inside Be-Bop*.

Felman, Shoshana. "Turning the Screw of Interpretation." In *Literature and Psychoanalysis: The Question of Reading: Otherwise*, ed. Shoshana Felman, 94–207. Baltimore: John Hopkins University Press, 1977.

Foucault, Michel. *Archaeology of Knowledge*. Trans. Alan M. Sheridan. New York: Pantheon, 1972.

———. *The History of Sexuality*. Vol. 1, *An Introduction*. Trans. Robert Hurley. New York: Vintage, 1990.

———. *The Order of Things: An Archaeology of the Human Sciences*. New York: Vintage Books, 1970.

Fowler, Edward. *The Rhetoric of Confession: Shishōsetsu in Early Twentieth Century Japanese Fiction*. Berkeley and Los Angeles: University of California Press, 1988.

Freud, Sigmund. *Beyond the Pleasure Principle*. International Psycho-Analytic Library, vol. 4. Trans. C. J. M. Hubback. London: Hogarth Press, 1922.

———. "Fetishism." In *Collected Papers*. Vol. 5, ed. James Strachey, 198–204. New York: Basic Books, 1959.

———. "A Note Upon the Mystic Writing Pad." In *Collected Papers*. Vol. 5, ed. James Strachey, 175–80. New York: Basic Books, 1959.

———. "The Uncanny." In *Collected Papers*. Vol. 4, ed. Ernest Jones, M.D., 368–407. New York: Basic Books, 1959.

———. "Wit and Its Relation to the Unconscious." In *The Basic Writings of Sigmund Freud*, trans. and ed. A. A. Brill, 633–803. New York: Random House, 1938.

Fujii, James A. *Complicit Fictions: The Subject in the Modern Japanese Prose Narrative*. Berkeley and Los Angeles: University of California Press, 1993.

Fujimoto Akira. "Botai no roman: Kyōka bungaku ni okeru sekai." In *Izumi Kyōka*, 75–93. Nihon bungaku kenkyū shiryō sōsho, ed. Tōgō Katsumi, vol. 48. Tokyo: Yūseidō, 1980.

Furukawa Makoto. "The Changing Nature of Sexuality: The Three Codes Framing Homosexuality in Modern Japan." *U.S.-Japan Women's Journal, English Supplement* 7 (1994): 98–127.

Futabatei Shimei. "Shōsetsu sōron." In *Tsubouchi Shōyō/ Futabatei Shimei shū*, 416–18. Nihon gendai bungaku zenshū, vol. 4. Tokyo: Kōdansha, 1962.

———. "Yo ga genbun'itchi no yurai." In *Tsubouchi Shōyō/ Futabatei Shimei shū*, 418–19. Nihon gendai bungaku zenshū, vol. 4. Tokyo: Kōdansha, 1962.

———. "Esuperanto no hanashi." In *Tsubouchi Shōyō/ Futabatei Shimei shū*, 421–23. Nihon gendai bungaku zenshū, vol. 4. Tokyo: Kōdansha, 1962.

Gluck, Carol. *Japan's Modern Myths*. Princeton, N.J.: Princeton University Press, 1985.

"Gei ribereshon." *Imago tokushū* 6, no. 12 (November 1995).

Goldberg, David Theo. "The Social Formation of Racist Discourse." In *Anatomy of Racism*, ed. David Theo Goldberg, 295–318. Minneapolis: University of Minnesota Press, 1990.

Gordon, Andrew, ed. *Postwar Japan as History*. Berkeley and Los Angeles: University of California Press, 1993.

Griswold, Susan. "Sexuality, Textuality, and the Definition of the 'Feminine' in Late Eighteenth-Century Japan." *U.S.-Japan Women's Journal, English Supplement* 9 (December 1995): 59–76.

Grosz, Elizabeth. *Volatile Bodies: Toward a Corporeal Feminism*. Bloomington: Indiana University Press, 1994.

Gunji Masakatsu and Bandō Tamasaburō. "Kyōka geki o megutte." Taidan (dialogue). *Izumi Kyōka: gensōsō bungakushi, Kokubungaku* 36, no. 9 (August 1991): 6–25.

Hane, Mikiso. *Peasants, Rebels and Outcastes: The Underside of Modern Japan*. New York: Pantheon Books, 1982.

Harootunian, Harry. *Things Seen and Unseen: Discourse and Ideology in Tokugawa Nativism*. Chicago: University of Chicago Press, 1988.

———. "Visible Discourses/Invisible Ideologies." *South Atlantic Quarterly* 87, no. 3 (Summer 1988): 445–74.

Hasumi Shigehiko, Watanabe Naomi, Asada Akira, and Karatani Kōjin. Zadankai (roundtable discussion). "Nakagami Kenji o megutte: sōkeisei to ekurichūru." *Hihyō kūkan* 12 (1994): 18–45.

Henriques, Julian, Wendy Hollway, Couze Venn, Valerie Walkerdine, and Cathy Urwin. *Changing the Subject: Psychology, Social Regulation and Subjectivity*. New York: Methuen, 1984.

Herbert, Jean. *Shinto: At the Fountainhead of Japan*. New York: Stein and Day, 1967.

Hirata Yumi. "Kaiwabun to ji no bun: bungaku tekusuto ni okeru hyōgen to hyōki." *Jinbun gakuhō* 59 (February 1986): 37–52.

———. "Kindai bungaku to pankuchueshon: Meiji shoki sakkatachi no kugiri fugō o megutte." In *Jyūkyū seiki Nihon no jōhō to shakai hendō*, ed. Yoshida Mitsukuni, 527–42. Tokyo: Tōkyō Daigaku jinbun kagaku kenkyūsho, 1985.

———. "Modern Japanese Literature and Punctuation: The Use of Punctuation Marks by Early Meiji Authors." Paper presented at the Meiji Studies Conference, Boston, May 6–8, 1994.

Hirota Masaki. *Sabetsu no shosō*. Nihon kindai shisō, vol. 2. Tokyo: Iwanami shoten, 1990.

Ihara Saikaku. *The Great Mirror of Male Love*. Trans. Paul Gordon Schalow. Stanford, Calif.: Stanford University Press, 1990.

Iijima Yoshiharu. *Kamado gami to kawaya gami*. Tokyo: Jinbun shoin, 1986.

Ikuta Chōkō. "Izumi Kyōka shi no shōsetsu o ronzu." In Kyōka *ronshūsei*, ed. Tanizawa Eiichi and Watanabe Ikko, 168–80. Tokyo: Rippu shobō, 1983.

Imai Yasuko. "The Emergence of the Japanese *Shufu*: Why a *Shufu* Is More Than a Housewife." *U.S.-Japan Women's Journal, English Supplement* 6 (March 1994): 44–65.

Imamura, Anne E., ed. *Re-Imaging Japanese Women*. Berkeley and Los Angeles: University of California Press, 1996.

Inoue Mitsusada and Ōsone Shōsuke, eds. *Ōjōden hokkegenki*. Nihon shisō taikei, vol. 7. Tokyo: Iwanami shoten, 1974.

Inouye, Charles. *A Similitude of Blossoms: A Critical Biography of Izumi Kyōka, Japanese Novelist and Playwright*. Cambridge, Mass.: Harvard University Press, forthcoming.

———. *Three Tales of Mystery and Imagination: Japanese Gothic by Izumi Kyōka*. Kanazawa, Japan: Izumi Kyōka sakuhin honyaku shūppankai, 1992.

———. "Water Imagery in the Work of Izumi Kyōka." *Monumenta Nipponica* 46, no. 1 (1991): 43–68.

Irigaray, Luce. *This Sex Which Is Not One*. Trans. Catherine Porter. Ithaca, N.Y.: Cornell University Press, 1985.

———. *Sexes and Genealogies*. Trans. Gillian C. Gill. New York: Columbia University Press, 1993.

———. *Speculum of the Other Woman*. Trans. Gillian C. Gill. Ithaca, N.Y.: Cornell University Press, 1985.

Ishio Yoshihisa. *Ikkō ikki to buraku: hisabetsu buraku no kigen*. Tokyo: San'ichi shobō, 1983.

Itō Sei. "Izumi Kyōka." In *Izumi Kyōka*, 76–82. Bungei tokuhon, vol. 37. Tokyo: Kawade shobō shinsha, 1981.

Ivy, Marilyn. *Discourses of the Vanishing: Modernity, Phantasm, Japan*. Chicago: Chicago University Press, 1995.

Izumi Kyōka. "Ai to konin." In *Izumi Kyōka zenshū* 28: 241–45. Tokyo: Iwanami shoten, 1940.

———. "Ehon no haru." In *Izumi Kyōka gensōdan* 4: 12–50. Tokyo: Iwanami shobō shinsha, 1995.

———. "Gekashitsu." In *Izumi Kyōka zenshū* 2: 2–28. Tokyo: Iwanami shoten, 1942.

———. "Hebikui." In *Izumi Kyōka zenshū* 4: 107–13. Tokyo: Iwanami shoten, 1942.

———. "Ichinomaki," "Ninomaki," "Sannomaki," "Shinomaki," "Gonomaki," "Rokunomaki," and "Chikainomaki." In *Kyōka zenshū* 2: 87–202. Tokyo: Shunyōdō, 1926.

———. "Itoyū." In *Kyōka gensōdan* 4: 12–50. Tokyo: Kawade shobō shinsha, 1995.

———. "Kechō." In *Kyōka zenshū* 2: 409–35. Tokyo: Shunyōdō, 1926.

———. *Kōya hijiri*. In *Izumi Kyōka shū*, 378–437. Nihon kindai bungaku taikei, ed. Muramatsu Sadataka, vol. 7. Tokyo: Kadokawa shoten, 1970.

———. *Nanchi shinjū*. In *Izumi Kyōka zenshū* 14: 359–448. Tokyo: Iwanami shoten, 1942.

———. *Onna keizu*. In *Izumi Kyōka zenshū* 10: 335–749. Tokyo: Iwanami shoten, 1942.

———. "Ryūtandan." In *Izumi Kyōka zenshū* 3: 1–33. Tokyo: Iwanami shoten, 1941.

———. "Tenshu monogatari." In *Kyōka gensōdan* 5: 12–71. Tokyo: Kawade shobō shinsha, 1995.

———. *Teriha kyōgen*. In *Kyōka zenshū* 2: 223–307. Tokyo: Shunyōdō, 1926.

———. *Yōken kibun*. In *Kyōka zenshū* 11: 629–82. Tokyo: Shunyōdō, 1926.

Kamata Tōji. "Okina/warabe: kannon, kodomo, rōjin." *Izumi Kyōka, gensōsō bungakushi, Kokubungaku* 36, no. 9 (August 1991): 49–53.

Kano, Ayako. "Japanese Theater and Imperialism: Romance and Resistance." *U.S.-Japan Women's Journal, English Supplement* 12 (January 1997): 17–47.

Kaplan, E. Ann. *Women and Film*. New York: Methuen, 1983.

Karatani, Kōjin. "Fūkō to Nihon." In *Misheru Fūkō no seiki*, ed. Hasumi Shigehiko and Watanabe Moriaki, 45–56. Tokyo: Chikuma shobō, 1993.

———. "Hisabetsu buraku no 'kigen.' " *Hihyō kūkan* 12 (1994): 46–54.

———. "Kaisetsu." In Nakagami Kenji, *Chi no hate shijo no toki*, 605–16. Tokyo: Shinchō bunko, 1983.

———. "Kaisetsu: shōsetsu no isō." In Nakagami Kenji, *Keshō*, 256–67. Tokyo: Kōdansha bungei bunko, 1993.

———. Keynote address. Presented at "The Politics of Exclusion in Modern Japanese Literature and Culture," symposium, Boston, March 25, 1994.

———. "Nakagami Kenji to feminizumu." *Subaru* 7 (July 1995): 72–73.

———. "Nationalism and *écriture*." Paper presented at "Globalization and Culture" conference, Duke University, Durham, North Carolina, November 1994.

———. "Nihon seishin bunseki 1." *Hihyō kūkan* 4 (1992): 271–82.

———. "One Spirit, Two Nineteenth Centuries." *South Atlantic Quarterly* 87, no. 3 (Summer 1988): 615–28.

———. *Origins of Modern Japanese Literature*. Trans. Brett de Bary. Durham, N.C.: Duke University Press, 1993.

———. *Sakaguchi Ango to Nakagami Kenji*. Tokyo: Ōta Shuppan, 1996.

Karatani Kōjin, Asada Akira, Yomota Inuhiko, Watanabe Naomi, Shimada Masahiko, Matsuura Rieko, Itō Seikō, Okuizumi Hikaru, Suga Hidemi, Takasawa Hidetsugu, Jacques Levy. Zadankai (roundtable discussion). "Hatenaki tekusuto o megutte." *Subaru* 12 (December 1996): 114–46.

Karatani Kōjin, Asada Akira, Watanabe Naomi, Itō Seikō, Okuizumi Hikaru, Norizuki Rintarō, and Nina Cornyetz. Zadankai (roundtable discussion). "Koyūmei to 'roji' no ba o megutte." *Subaru* 10 (October 1995): 112–42.

Karatani Kōjin, Watanabe Naomi, Asada Akira, and Okuizumi Hikaru. Zadankai (roundtable discussion). "Nakagami Kenji sankaiki: Sa'i / Sabetsu, soshite monogatari no seisei." *Subaru* 10 (October 1994): 240–71.

Karatani Kōjin, Yomota Inuhiko, Watanabe Naomi, Suga Hidemi, and Eve Zimmerman. Zadankai (roundtable discussion). "Sennen no bungaku: Nakagami Kenji to Kumano." *Bungakkai* 7 (July 1993): 138–68.

Kasahara, Nobuo. *Izumi Kyōka: Bi to erosu no kōzō*. Tokyo: Shibundō, 1976.

———. "Kyōka ni okeru 'haha naru mono.'" In *Izumi Kyōka*, 311–19. Kanshō Nihon gendai bungaku, vol. 3. Tokyo: Kadokawa shoten, 1982.

———. "Mori, aruiwa gensō kūkan." In *Izumi Kyōka*, 94–137. Bungei tokuhon, vol. 37. Tokyo: Kawade shobo shinsha, 1981.

Kawamura, Jirō. "Dōshisareta kūkan." In *Izumi Kyōka*, 54–65. Bungei tokuhon, vol. 37. Tokyo: Kawade shobo shinsha, 1981.

Keene, Donald. *Dawn to the West: Japanese Literature in the Modern Era*. New York: Holt, Rinehart and Winston, 1984.

———. *Twenty Plays of the Noh Theater*. New York: Columbia University Press, 1970.

———. *World Within Walls: Japanese Literature of the Pre-Modern Era, 1600–1867*. New York: Grove Press, 1976.

Kelsey, W. Michael. *Konjaku Monogatari Shū*. Boston: Twayne, 1982.

Kitagawa, Joseph. *Religion in Japanese History*. New York: Columbia University Press, 1966.

Kleeman, Faye. "The Ends of the Earth: Ethnic Identity and the Asiatic Vision of Nakagami Kenji." Paper presented at "Nakagami Kenji to gengo bunka," Meiji Gakuin Daigaku gengo bunka kenkyūsho shimpojiumu, Tokyo, Japan, August 1996. Published in Japanese as "Nakagami bungaku ni miru esunishitii to shōsetsu no ekkyōsei." *Gengo bunka* 14, no. 3 (1997): 175–82.

Klein, Melanie. "Mourning and Its Relation to Manic-Depressive States." In *The Writings of Melanie Klein*. Vol. 1, *Love, Guilt, Reparation and Other Works, 1921–1945*, ed. Roger Money-Kyrle, 344–69. New York: Free Press, 1975.

———. "The Oedipus Complex in the Light of Early Anxieties." In *The Writings of Melanie Klein*. Vol. 1, *Love, Guilt, Reparation and Other Works, 1921–1945*, ed. Roger Money-Kyrle, 370–419. New York: Free Press, 1975.

———. *The Writings of Melanie Klein*. Vol. 2, *The Psycho-Analysis of Children*, ed. Roger Money-Kyrle. New York: Macmillan, 1975.

Klein, Susan Blakely. "When the Moon Strikes the Bell: Desire and Enlightenment in the Noh Play Dōjōji." *Journal of Japanese Studies* 17, no. 2 (Summer 1991): 291–322.

Kobayashi Hideo. "Kyōka no shi sono hoka." In *Kyōka ronshūsei*, ed. Tanizawa Eiichi and Watanabe Ikko, 217–23. Tokyo: Rippu shobō, 1983.

Kojima Nobuo. "Kami o yobu sugata." In *Izumi Kyōka*, 20–35. Bungei tokuhon, vol. 37. Tokyo: Kawade shobo shinsha, 1981.

Konishi, Jin'ichi. *A History of Japanese Literature*. Vol. 1, *The Archaic and An-cient Ages*, ed. Aileen Gatten and Nicholas Teele. Trans. Earl Miner. Princeton, N.J.: Princeton University Press, 1984.

———. *A History of Japanese Literature*. Vol. 2, *The Early Middle Ages*, ed. Earl Miner. Trans. Aileen Gatten. Princeton. N.J.: Princeton University Press, 1986.

Koschmann, J. Victor, Oiwa Keibo, and Yamashita Shinji, eds. *International Per-spectives on Yanagita Kunio and Japanese Folkloric Studies*. Cornell University East Asia Papers, no. 37. Ithaca, N.Y.: Cornell University Press, 1985.

Kristeva, Julia. *Desire in Language: A Semiotic Approach to Literature and Art*, ed. Thomas Gora, Alice Jardine, and Leon S. Roudiez. Trans. Leon S. Roudiez. New York: Columbia University Press, 1980.

———. *The Powers of Horror: An Essay on Abjection*. Trans. Leon S. Roudiez. New York: Columbia University Press, 1982.

———. *Revolution in Poetic Language*. Trans. Margaret Waller. New York: Co-lumbia University Press, 1984.

———. *Tales of Love*. Trans. Leon S. Roudiez. New York: Columbia University Press, 1987.

———. "Woman Can Never Be Defined." In *New French Feminisms*, ed. Elaine Marks and Isabelle de Courtivron, 137–41. New York: Schocken Books, 1981.

Kuki Shūzō. "Iki no kōzō." In *Kuki Shūzō zenshū* 1: 1–85. Tokyo: Iwanami shoten, 1981.

Lacan, Jacques. *Écrits: A Selection*. Trans. Alan Sheridan. New York: W. W. Nor-ton, 1977.

———. *Feminine Sexuality: Jacques Lacan and the École Freudienne*. Trans. Jacqueline Rose. New York: W. W. Norton, 1982.

———. *The Four Fundamental Concepts of Psychoanalysis*. Trans. Alan Sheri-dan. New York: W. W. Norton, 1978.

Lebra, Takie S. "Fractionated Motherhood: Status and Gender Among the Japan-ese Elite." *U.S.-Japan Women's Journal, English Supplement* 4 (February 1993): 3–25.

Lowe, Lisa. *Critical Terrains: French and British Orientalisms*. Ithaca, N.Y.: Cor-nell University Press, 1991.

Mabuchi K., Kunisaki H., and Konno T., eds. *Konjaku monogatari shū*, 1. Nihon koten bungaku zenshū, vol. 21. Tokyo: Shōgakukan, 1971.

Maeda Ai. "Izumi Kyōka *Kōya hijiri*: Tabibito no monogatari." In *Izumi Kyōka*, 137–40. Nihon bungaku kenkyū shiryō sōsho, vol. 48. Tokyo: Yūseidō, 1980.

Mamiya Yoshio. "Modan jyazu nōto." *Ongaku geijutsu* 8 (1968): 6–11.

Marra, Michele. "The Buddhist Mythmaking of Defilement: Sacred Courtesans in Medieval Japan." *Journal of Asian Studies* 52, no. 1 (February 1993): 49–65.

———. *Representations of Power: The Literary Politics of Medieval Japan*. Hon-olulu: University of Hawaii Press, 1993.

Marren, Christine. " 'Poison Woman' Takahashi Oden and the Spectacle of Female Deviance in Early Meiji." *U.S.-Japan Women's Journal, English Supplement* 9 (December 1995): 93–110.

Marx, Karl. *Grundrisse: Foundations of the Critique of Political Economy*. New York: Vintage, 1973.

Matsubara Jun'ichi. "Kyōka bungaku to minkan denshō to." In *Izumi Kyōka*, 291–310. Kanshō Nihon gendai bungaku. vol. 3. Tokyo: Kadokawa shoten, 1982.

May, Reinhard. *Heidegger's Hidden Sources: East Asian Influences on His Work*. Trans. Graham Parkes. New York: Routledge, 1996.

McCullough, William H., and Helen Craig McCullough, trans. *Eiga monogatari. A Tale of Flowering Fortunes: Annals of Japanese Aristocratic Life in the Heian Period*. 2 vols. Stanford, Calif.: Stanford University Press, 1980.

Miller, Mara. "Canons and the Challenge of Gender: Women's Voices in the Japanese Canon." *Monist: An International Journal of General Philosophic Inquiry* 76, no. 4 (October 1993): 477–93.

Miner, Earl. *Japanese Linked Poetry*. Princeton, N.J.: Princeton University Press, 1979.

Miner, Earl, Hiroko Odagiri, and Robert E. Morrell. *The Princeton Companion to Classical Japanese Literature*. Princeton, N.J.: Princeton University Press, 1985.

Mishima Yukio. "Bunshō tokuhon." In *Mishima Yukio zenshū* 28: 414–564. Tokyo: Shinchōsha, 1975.

———. "Kaisetsu (Nihon no bungaku 4: Ozaki Kōyō/ Izumi Kyōka)." In *Mishima Yukio zenshū* 33: 553–67. Tokyo: Shinchōsha, 1976.

———. *The Way of the Samurai: Yukio Mishima on* Hagakure *in Modern Life*. Trans. Kathryn Sparling. New York: Basic Books, 1977.

Mitsuhashi Tadashi. "Nihon no 'kegare' to nyonin kinsei." Paper presented at "Kenkyūkai: Nihon no josei to bukkyō," summer seminar, Tokyo, August 1993.

Miura Masashi. "Monogatari no yukue." In *Merankorii no suiha*, 265–81. Tokyo: Fukutake shoten, 1984.

Miyoshi, Masao. *Accomplices of Silence: The Modern Japanese Novel*. Berkeley and Los Angeles: University of California Press, 1974.

———. *Off Center: Power and Culture Relations Between Japan and the United States*. Convergences: Inventories of the Present, ed. Edward W. Said. Cambridge, Mass.: Harvard University Press, 1991.

Mizuta Noriko. "Josei no jikogatari to monogatari." *Hihyō kūkan* 4 (1992): 64–79.

———. *Monogatari to hanmonogatari no fūkei: bungaku to josei no sōzōryoku*. Tokyo: Tahata shoten, 1993.

Monnet, Livia. "Ghostly Women, Displaced Femininities, and Male Family Romances: Violence, Gender and Sexuality in Two Texts by Nakagami Kenji." *Japan Forum* 8, no. 1 (1996): 13–34 and 8, no. 2 (1996): 221–40. Translated into Japanese as "Yūreiteki na onnatachi, okigaerareta joseisei, soshite dansei kazoku shōsetsu." *Hihyō kūkan* 2, no. 10 (1996): 156–79 and 2, no. 11 (1996): 167–86.

Monson, Ingrid. "Doubleness and Jazz Improvisation: Irony, Parody, and Ethnomusicology." *Critical Inquiry* 20, no. 2 (Winter 1994): 283–313.

Mori Ōgai. *Vita Sexualis*. Tokyo: Charles E. Tuttle, 1972.

Morris, Mark. "Gossip and History: Nakagami, Faulkner, García Márquez." *Japan Forum* 8, no. 1 (1996): 35–50.

———. "Introduction: Towards Nakagami." *Japan Forum* 8, no. 1 (1996): 1–2.

Motoori Norinaga. *Kojiki-den, Book 1*. Trans. Ann Wehmeyer. Cornell East Asia Series, no. 87. Ithaca, N.Y.: East Asia Program, Cornell University, 1997.

Motoyoshi, Katsuyo. "Reading the Roji in Nakagami's Narratives." Unpublished abstract, Columbia University, 1994.

Muramatsu Sadataka. *Izumi Kyōka*. Tokyo: Bunsendō, 1966.

———. *Izumi Kyōka jiten*. Tokyo: Yūseidō, 1982.

———. *Izumi Kyōka: shōgai to geijutsu*. Tokyo: Kawade bunko, 1954.

Murasaki Shikibu. *The Tale of Genji*. Trans. Edward Seidensticker. New York: Alfred A. Knopf, 1976.

Muta Kazue. "Images of the Family in Meiji Periodicals: The Paradox Underlying the Emergence of the 'Home.'" *U.S.-Japan Women's Journal, English Supplement* 7 (December 1994): 53–71.

Nagaike Kenji. "Kaisetsu." In *Yanagita Kunio zenshū* 4: 507–35. Tokyo: Chikuma bunko, 1989.

Nagashima Kiyoshi. "Nakagami Kenji shōden: idō suru kajō na ba to shite no Nakagami Kenji." *Yuriika* 25, no. 3 (March 1993): 140–50.

Najita Tetsuo. "On Culture and Technology in Postmodern Japan." *South Atlantic Quarterly* 87, no. 3 (Summer 1988): 401–18.

Nakada N., ed. *Nihon ryōiki*. Nihon koten bungaku zenshū, vol. 6. Tokyo: Shōgakukan, 1975.

Nakagami Kenji. "Ane no jiyū/Anākii: Enchi Fumiko *Hanakui uba*." *Waseda bungaku* 6, no. 10 (October 1974): 71–74.

———. *Chi no hate shijō no toki*. Tokyo: Shinchō bunko, 1983.

———. "Edo." In *Keshō*, 77–93. Tokyo: Kōdansha bungei bunko, 1993.

———. "Fōkunā, hanjō suru minami." In *Jidai ga owari, jidai ga hajimaru*, 443–53. Tokyo: Fukutake shoten, 1988.

———. "Fōkunā shōgeki." In *Jidai ga owari, jidai ga hajimaru*, 454–64. Tokyo: Fukutake shoten, 1988.

———. "Fūkei no mukō e." In *Fūkei no mukō e*, 9–62. Tokyo: Fuyukisha, 1990.

———. "Fushi." In *Kumanoshū*, 7–27. Tokyo: Kōdansha bungei bunko, 1993.

———. "Futakami." In *Jūryoku no miyako*, 123–41. Tokyo: Shinchō bunko, 1988.

———. "Hanzaisha Nagayama Norio kara no hōkoku." In *Tori no yō ni kemono no yō ni*, 124–53. Tokyo: Kōdansha, 1994.

———. "The Immortal." In *The Shōwa Anthology*, vol. 2, ed. Van C. Gessel and

Tomone Matsumoto, 412–28. Trans. Mark Harbison. New York: Kodansha International, 1985.

———. "Izumi Kyōka: Hito to sakuhin." In *Shōwa bungaku zenshū* 2: 960–66. Tokyo: Shōgakukan,1988.

———. "Jain." In *Nakagami Kenji zentanpen shōsetsu*, 487–501. Tokyo: Kawade shobō shinsha, 1976.

———. "JAZZ." In *Nakagami Kenji zenshū* 1: 33–39. Tokyo: Shūeisha, 1995.

———. "Jūryoku no miyako." In *Jūryoku no miyako*, 7–31. Tokyo: Shinchō bunko, 1988.

———. *Jūryoku no miyako.* Tokyo: Shinchō bunko, 1988.

———. "Jyazu kyōsaha." In *Fūkei no mukō e*, 241–44. Toyko: Fuyukisha, 1990.

———. "Jyūhassai." In *Nakagami Kenji zenshū* 1: 7–32. Tokyo: Shūeisha, 1995.

———. "Jyūkyūsai no chizu." In *Nakagami Kenji zenshū* 1: 371–414. Tokyo: Shūeisha, 1995.

———. *Kareki Nada.* Tokyo: Kawade bunko, 1980.

———. *Keshō.* Tokyo: Kōdansha, 1978. Reprint, Tokyo: Kōdansha bungei bunko, 1993.

———. *Kii monogatari.* In *Nakagami Kenji zenshū* 4: 313–567. Tokyo: Shūeisha, 1995.

———. *Kumanoshū.* Tokyo: Kōdansha bungei bunko, 1992.

———. "Misaki." In *Misaki*, 171–267. Tokyo: Bunshun bunko, 1995.

———. "Monogatari no keifu / hachinin no sakka: Enchi Fumiko 1–6." *Kokubungaku kaishaku to kyōzai no kenkyū* 29, no. 5 (April 1984): 148–50; 29, no. 6 (May 1984): 130–34; 29, no. 7 (June 1984): 130–31; 29, no. 11 (September 1984): 136–39; 29, no. 14 (November 1984): 138–40; 29, no. 15 (December 1984): 136–38.

———. "Sakka to nikutai." In *Tori no yō ni kemono no yō ni*, 89–97. Tokyo: Kōdansha bungei bunko, 1994.

———. *Sanka.* Tokyo: Bungei bunko, 1990.

———. *Sennen no yuraku.* Tokyo: Kawade bunko, 1992.

———. "Takao to Mitsuko." In *Nakagami Kenji zenshū* 1: 41–52. Tokyo: Shūeisha, 1995.

———. "Toshi shōsetsu no minamoto o tsuku an'yu to shite no sogai ya sabetsu: Toni Morisun cho *Aoi me ga hoshii*; shohyō." In *Jidai ga owari, jidai ga hajimaru*, 342–45. Tokyo: Fukutake shoten, 1988.

———. "Tsuki to fushi." In *Kumanoshū*, 197–215. Tokyo: Kōdansha bungei bunko, 1993.

———. "Ukijima." In *Keshō*, 67–90. Tokyo: Kōdansha, 1978. Reprinted and revised in *Keshō.* 57–76. Tokyo: Kōdansha bungei bunko, 1993.

———. "Umi e." In *Nakagami Kenji zenshū* 1: 53–78. Tokyo: Shūeisha, 1995.

Nakagami Kenji and Kadokawa Haruki. *Haiku no jidai.* Tokyo: Kadokawa shoten, 1993.

Nakagami Kenji and Kamata Tōji. *Kotodama no ametsuchi.* Tokyo: Shufu no tomo sha, 1993.

"Nakagami Kenji tokushū." *Yuriika* 25, no. 3 (March 1993).

Nakamura Ikuo. "Shinbutsu kankeiron saikō—'imi' no henyō to jisshakai no seikaku." Paper presented at "Kenkyūkai: Nihon no josei to bukkyō," summer seminar, Tokyo, August 1993.

Nakamura Mitsuo. "Kyōka to Yanagida Kunio: Kyōka no hokkai minzokugaku." *Bungaku* 51, no. 6 (1983): 41–48.

———. *Modern Japanese Fiction, 1868–1926.* Tokyo: Kokusai bunka shinkōkai, 1968.

Nakanishi Susumu. "The Spatial Nature of Japanese Myth." In *Principles of Classical Japanese Literature,* ed. Earl Miner, 106–29. Princeton, N.J.: Princeton University Press, 1985.

"Nanshoku no ryōbun: seisa, rekishi, hyōsho." *Bungaku tokushū* 6, no. 1 (Winter 1995).

Napier, Susan J. *The Fantastic in Modern Japanese Literature: The Subversion of Modernity.* Nissan Institute/Routledge Japanese Studies Series, ed. J. A. A. Stockwin. New York: Routledge, 1996.

Naramoto Tatsuya. *Buraku mondai.* Kyoto: Chōbunsha, 1955.

Narita Ryūichi. "Women and Views of Women Within the Changing Hygiene Conditions of Late Nineteenth- and Early Twentieth-Century Japan." *U.S.-Japan Women's Journal, English Supplement* 8 (1995): 64–86.

Newton, Judith, and Deborah Rosenfelt, eds. *Feminist Criticism and Social Change: Sex, Class and Race in Literature and Culture.* New York: Methuen, 1985.

Niwa Akiko. "The Formation of the Myth of Motherhood in Japan." *U.S.-Japan Women's Journal, English Supplement* 4 (February 1993): 70–82.

Noguchi Takehiko. "Izumi Kyōka kenkyū annai." In *Izumi Kyōka,* 387–401. Kanshō Nihon gendai bungaku, vol. 3. Tokyo: Kadokawa shoten, 1982.

———. "Izumi Kyōka no hito to sakuhin." In *Izumi Kyōka,* 5–43. Kanshō Nihon gendai bungaku, vol. 3. Tokyo: Kadokawa shoten, 1982.

———. "Kyōka no onna." In *Izumi Kyōka,* 138–46. Bungei tokuhon, vol. 37. Tokyo: Kawade shobō shinsha, 1981.

———. "The Substratum Constituting Monogatari: Prose Structure and Narrative in the *Genji Monogatari.*" In *Principles of Classical Japanese Literature,* ed. Earl Miner, 130–50. Princeton, N.J.: Princeton University Press, 1985.

Ōba [Ohba] Minako. "The Smile of a Mountain Witch." In *Japanese Women Writers: Twentieth Century Short Fiction,* ed. Noriko Mizuta Lippit and Kyoko Iriye Selden, 194–206. Armonk, N.Y.: M. E. Sharpe, 1991.

Ōba Minako and Mizuta Noriko. *"Yamamba" no iru fūkei.* Tokyo: Tahata shōten, 1995.

Ogasawara Kenji. "Hippii kara marebito e." In *Kōza Shōwa bungaku shi.* Vol. 5, *Kaitai to henyō,* 62–63. Tokyo: Yūseidō, 1985.

Ogihara A. and Kōnosu H., eds. *Kojiki, Jōdai kayō*. Nihon koten bungaku zenshū, vol. 1. Tokyo: Shōgakukan, 1973.

Okada, H. Richard. *Figures of Resistance: Language, Poetry and Narrating in* The Tale of Genji *and Other Mid-Heian Texts*. Durham, N.C.: Duke University Press, 1991.

Origuchi Shinobu. *Origuchi Shinobu zenshū 1*. Tokyo: Chūkō bunko, 1975.

Ōsuji Kazuo and Nishiguchi Junko, eds. *Josei to bukkyō*. Vol. 4, *Miko to joshin*. Tokyo: Heibonsha, 1989.

Philippi, Donald L., trans. *Kojiki*. Tokyo: University of Tokyo Press, 1968.

Pincus, Leslie. *Authenticating Culture in Imperial Japan: Kuki Shūzō and the Rise of National Aesthetics*. Berkeley and Los Angeles: University of California Press, 1996.

Rankin, Andrew. "Nakagami Kenji—Against the Grain." *Japan Quarterly* 44, no. 2 (April–June 1997): 43–54.

Rich, Adrienne. "Compulsory Heterosexuality and Lesbian Experience." In *The Lesbian and Gay Studies Reader*, ed. Henry Abelove, Michèle Aina Barale, and David M. Halperin, 227–54. New York: Routledge, 1993.

Ruch, Barbara. "Beyond Absolution: Enchi Fumiko's *The Waiting Years* and *Masks*." In *Masterworks of Asian Literature in Comparative Perspective*, ed. Barbara Stoler Miller, 439–56. Armonk, N.Y.: M. E. Sharpe, 1994.

———. "Medieval Jongleurs and the Making of a National Literature." In *Japan in the Muromachi Age*, ed. John W. Hall and Toyoda Takeshi, 279–309. Berkeley and Los Angeles: University of California Press, 1977.

———. "The Other Side of Culture in Medieval Japan." In *The Cambridge History of Japan: Medieval Japan*. Cambridge: Cambridge University Press, 1990.

Saeki Shōichi. "Genkei no saisei: Nihon no 'watakushi' o motomete, 8." *Bungei* 11, no. 9 (September 1972): 204–14.

Sakai, Naoki. "Modernity and Its Critique: The Problem of Universalism and Particularism." *South Atlantic Quarterly* 87, no. 3 (Summer 1988): 475–504.

———. "Return to the West/Return to the East: Watsuji Tetsuro's Anthropology and Discussions of Authenticity." In *Japan in the World*, ed. Masao Miyoshi and H. D. Harootunian, 237–70. Durham, N.C.: Duke University Press, 1993.

———. *Voices of the Past: The Status of Language in Eighteenth-Century Japanese Discourse*. Ithaca, N.Y.: Cornell University Press, 1991.

Sedgwick, Eve Kosofsky. *Between Men: English Literature and Male Homosocial Desire*. New York: Columbia University Press, 1985.

Sherif, Ann. "Salvation from a Barren Paternity: The Concept of Masculinity and Kōda Rohan's Writings." *Review of Japanese Culture and Society* 6 (December 1994): 24–30.

Shimada Masahiko. "Nakagami Kenji: Saigo no sakka." *Shūkan asahi* (August 28, 1992), 34–36.

Shinoda Hajime. "Izumi Kyōka no ichi." In *Izumi Kyōka*, 36–53. Bungei tokuhon, vol. 37. Tokyo: Kawade shobō shinsha, 1981.

Sievers, Sharon L. *Flowers in Salt: The Beginnings of Feminist Consciousness in Modern Japan*. Stanford, Calif.: Stanford University Press, 1983.

Stepan, Nancy Leys. "Race and Gender: The Role of Analogy in Science." In *Anatomy of Racism*, ed. David Theo Goldberg, 38–57. Minneapolis: University of Minnesota Press, 1990.

Suga Hidemi. *Bungaku jihyō to iu mōdo*. Tokyo: Shūeisha, 1993.

Takahashi Yoshitaka. "Kyōka bungaku no tokushoku." In *Izumi Kyōka*, 106–8. Bungei tokuhon, vol 37. Tokyo: Kawade shobō shinsha, 1981.

Takemori Takao. "Enchi Fumiko: hito to sakuhin." In *Sakaguchi Ango, Funahashi Seiichi, Takami Jun, Enchi Fumiko*, 1046–52. Shōwa bungaku zenshū, vol. 12. Tokyo: Shōgakukan, 1987.

Taneda Wakako. " 'Sanjyakukaku' ron: irinkusu no kōkei." *Kokubungaku* 36, no. 9 (August 1991): 90–96.

Tanemura Suehiro. "Suichūka hengen." In *Izumi Kyōka*, 124–33. Bungei tokuhon, vol. 37. Tokyo: Kawade shobō shinsha, 1981.

Tanizaki Jun'ichirō. "Junsui ni 'Nihonteki' na Kyōka sekai." In *Izumi Kyōka*, 67–68. Bungei tokuhon, vol. 37. Tokyo: Kawade shobō shinsha, 1981.

Tayama Katai. "Futon." In *Tayama Katai*, 42–72. Nihon bungaku zenshū, vol. 12. Tokyo: Shūeisha, 1972.

Tsubouchi Shōyō. "Shōsetsu sanha." In *Tsubouchi Shōyō/ Futabatei Shimei shū*, 205–10. Nihon gendai bungaku zenshū, vol. 4. Tokyo: Kōdansha, 1962.

———. "Shōsetsu shinzui." In *Tsubouchi Shōyō / Futabatei Shimei shū*, 140–205. Nihon gendai bungaku zenshū, vol. 4. Tokyo: Kōdansha, 1962.

Tsushima Yūko. *Woman Running in the Mountains*. Trans. Geraldine Harcourt. New York: Pantheon Books, 1991.

Tyler, Carole-Anne. "Passing: Narcissism, Identity, and Difference." *Differences* 6:2, 3 (Summer–Fall 1994): 212–48.

Ueda Akinari. "Bewitched." In *Tales of Moonlight and Rain*, trans. Hamada Kengi, 20–52. Tokyo: Tokyo University Press, 1971.

———. "Jasei no in." In *Ugetsu monogatari*, 411–41. Nihon koten bungaku zenshū, vol. 48. Tokyo: Shōgakukan, 1973.

Ueda Makoto. *Modern Japanese Writers*. Stanford, Calif.: Stanford University Press, 1976.

Uno, Kathleen S. "The Death of 'Good Wife, Wise Mother'?" In *Postwar Japan as History*, ed. Andrew Gordon, 293–322. Berkeley and Los Angeles: University of California Press, 1993.

———. "The Household Division of Labor." In *Recreating Japanese Women, 1600–1945*, ed. Gail Lee Bernstein, 17–41. Berkeley and Los Angeles: University of California Press, 1991.

Ury, Marilyn, trans. *Tales of Times Now Past*. Berkeley and Los Angeles: University of California Press, 1979.

Valentine, James. "On the Borderlines: The Significance of Marginality in Japanese Society." In *Unwrapping Japan*, ed. Eyal Ben-Ari, Brian Moeran, and

James Valentine, 36–57. Manchester, England: Manchester University Press, 1990.

Vernon, Victoria. "Between Osan and Koharu: The Representation of Women in The Works of Hayashi Fumiko and Enchi Fumiko." In *Daughters of the Moon: Wish, Will, and Social Constraint in Fiction by Modern Japanese Women*, 137–69. Berkeley: University of California, Institute of East Asian Studies, 1988.

Vincent, J. Keith. "Idō suru riron: teki wa Fūkō?" In Keith Vincent, Kawaguchi Kazuya, and Kazama Takashi. *Gei sutadizu*, 69–71. Tokyo: Seidosha, 1997.

Vincent, J. Keith, and Kawaguchi Kazuya. Interview by Tasaki Hideaki. "Gei sutadi no kanōsei." *Imago* 6, no. 12 (November 1995): 22–42.

Viswanathan, Meera. "In Pursuit of the *Yamamba*: The Question of Female Resistance." In *The Woman's Hand: Gender and Theory in Japanese Women's Writing*, ed. Paul G. Schalow and Janet A. Walker, 239–61. Stanford, Calif.: Stanford University Press, 1996.

Vogel, Ezra F. *Japan's New Middle Class: The Salary Man and His Family in a Tokyo Suburb*. 2d ed. Berkeley and Los Angeles: University of California Press, 1963.

Waki Akiko. *Gensō no ronri: Izumi Kyōka no sekai*. Tokyo: Kōdansha gendai shinsho, 1974.

———. "Shisha ga sumu yama—Kyōka no fuamiri romansu." *Bungaku* 51, no. 6 (1983): 128–31.

Walthall, Anne. "The Life Cycle of Farm Women in Tokugawa Japan." In *Recreating Japanese Women, 1600–1945*, ed. Gail Lee Bernstein, 42–70. Berkeley and Los Angeles: University of California Press, 1991.

Watanabe Naomi. *Gen'ei no chōki: Izumi Kyōka ron*. Tokyo: Kokubunsha, 1983.

———. *Nakagami Kenji ron: Itoshisa ni tsuite*. Tokyo: Kawade shobō shinsha, 1996.

———. *Nihon kindai bungaku to "sabetsu."* Tokyo: Ōta shuppan, 1994.

———. "Sabetsu to ekurichūru." *Hihyō kūkan* 12 (1994): 56–68.

Yamashita Yōsuke, Adachi Motohiko, Terayama Shūji, Aburai Shōichi. "Wareware ni totte jyazu to wa nani ka?" *Ongaku geijutsu* 8 (1986): 26–31.

Yanagita Kunio. "Haiku Kyōka kan." In *Kyōka ronshūsei*, ed. Tanizawa Eiichi and Watanabe Ikko, 201–3. Tokyo: Rippu shobō, 1983.

———. *Imo no chikara*. In *Yanagita Kunio zenshū* 11: 7–304. Tokyo: Chikuma bunko, 1990.

———. *Mikokō*. In *Yanagita Kunio zenshū* 11: 305–415. Tokyo: Chikuma bunko, 1990.

———. *Tōno mongatari*. In *Yanagita Kunio zenshū* 4: 7–72. Tokyo: Chikuma bunko, 1989.

———. *Yama no jinsei*. In *Yanagita Kunio zenshū* 4: 77–254. Tokyo: Chikuma bunko, 1989.

———. *The Yanagita Kunio Guide to the Japanese Folk Tale*. Trans. Fanny Hagin Mayer. Bloomington: Indiana University Press, 1986.

Yokota, Gerry. "The Nō Drama of Japan: Formation of a Canon." Ph.D. diss., Princeton University, 1992.

Yomota Inuhiko. "Ikai no henyō: gensō shōsetsu wa doko e itta ka?" *Shinchō* 82, no. 3 (1985): 224–53.

———. *Kishu to tensei Nakagami Kenji*. Rev. and expanded ed. Tokyo: Shinchō-sha, 1996.

Yomota Inuhiko, Faye Kleeman, Nina Cornyetz, Jacques Levy. Zadankai (round-table discussion). "Nakagami Kenji to gengo bunka." Meiji Gakuin Daigaku gengo bunka kenkyūsho shimpojiumu. Tokyo, Japan, June 1996. Transcript of roundtable published in *Gengo bunka* 14, no. 3 (1997): 196–207.

Yoneyama Toshinao. "Yanagita and His Work." In *International Perspectives on Yanagita Kunio and Japanese Folkloric Studies*, ed. J. Victor Koschmann, Oiwa Keibo, and Yamashita Shinji, 29–52. Cornell University East Asia Papers, no. 37. Ithaca, N.Y., 1985.

Yoshida Teigo. "The Feminine in Japanese Folk Religion: Polluted or Divine?" In *Unwrapping Japan*, ed. Eyal Ben-Ari, Brian Moeran, and James Valentine, 58–77. Manchester, England: Manchester University Press, 1990.

Yoshie Akiko. "Kodai no miko to dōjo: Ise Jingū 'monoimi' kō." Paper presented at "Kenkyūkai: Nihon no josei to bukkyō," summer seminar, Tokyo, August 1993.

———. "Tamayoribime sankō: *Imo no chikara* hihan." In *Josei to bukkyō*. Vol. 4, *Miko to joshin*, ed. Ōsuji Kazuo and Nishiguchi Junko, 51–90. Tokyo: Heibon-sha, 1989.

Yoshimoto Tadaaki. *Bokeiron*. Tokyo: Gakushū kenkyūsha, 1995.

Yoshimura Hirotō. *Izumi Kyōka no sekai: gensō no byōri*. Tokyo: Bokuya shup-pan, 1983.

———. "Kyōka bungaku ni okeru bosei to josei—erosu no botai to shite." *Izumi Kyōka, Kokubungaku kaishaku to kanshō* 7 (1981): 100–104.

———. "Kyōka / Jun'ichirō no haha compurekusu." *Kokubungaku kaishaku to kanshō* 6 (1973): 45–52.

Žižek, Slavoj. *For They Know Not What They Do*. London: Verso, 1991.

———. *Tarrying with the Negative: Kant, Hegel, and the Critique of Ideology*. Durham, N.C.: Duke University Press, 1993.

———. *The Sublime Object of Ideology*. London: Verso, 1989.

In this index an "f" after a number indicates a separate reference on the next page, and an "ff" indicates separate references on the next two pages. A continuous discussion over two or more pages is indicated by a span of page numbers, e.g., "57–59." *Passim* is used for a cluster of references in close but not consecutive sequence.

LIBRARY OF CONGRESS CATALOGING-IN-PUBLICATION DATA

Cornyetz, Nina.

Dangerous women, deadly words : phallic fantasy and modernity in three Japanese writers / Nina Cornyetz.

p.   cm.

ISBN 0-8047-3212-4 (cloth)

1. Japanese literature—20th century—History and criticism.   2. Sex in literature.   3. Feminism and literature.   4. Izumi, Kyōka, 1873–1939. 5. Enchi, Fumiko, 1905–   .   6. Nakagami, Kenji, 1946–   .   I. Title.

PL726.67.S5C67   1999

895.6'093538—dc21   98-30575

CIP

Rev.

♾ This book is printed on acid-free, recycled paper.

Original printing 1999

Last figure below indicatess year of this printing:

08 07 06 05 04 03 02 01 00 99